Archibald Monteath

Black River, by Joseph Kidd. Courtesy National Library of Jamaica.

Archibald Monteath

Igbo, Jamaican, Moravian

Maureen Warner-Lewis

University of the West Indies Press

Jamaica • Barbados • Trinidad and Tobago

University of the West Indies Press
7A Gibraltar Hall Road   Mona
Kingston 7   Jamaica
www.uwipress.com

11 10 09 08 07   5 4 3 2 1

CATALOGUING IN PUBLICATION DATA

Warner-Lewis, Maureen.
Archibald Monteath: Igbo, Jamaican, Moravian / Maureen Warner-Lewis.

p. cm.

Includes bibliographical references.

ISBN: 978-976-640-197-9

1. Monteath, Archibald. 2. Slaves – Jamaica. 3. Moravian Church – Jamaica –
History. 4. Igbo (African people) – Jamaica. 5. Jamaica – History. 1. Title.

F1886.W38 2007   927.9204

Cover illustration: Igbo fabric design, Odinani Museum, Nigeria, and Kep Estate,
St Elizabeth, Jamaica. Artist: Errol Stennett

Book and cover design by Robert Harris.
Set in Adobe Garamond 11/14.5 x 24
Printed in the United States of America.

To Rupert

Contents

Illustrations

Maps

Figures

Acknowledgements

In a project that has taken a decade and a half to accomplish, there are many persons and institutions to be cited for their assistance. In the 1970s my husband, Professor Rupert Lewis, drew my attention to the story of Archibald Monteath, and our family friend Reverend Dr Horace Russell of the Eastern Baptist Theological Seminary at Wynnewood, Pennsylvania, facilitated my contact with Reverend Otto Dreydoppel of the Moravian Theological Seminary at Bethlehem, Pennsylvania, and his wife Susan Dreydoppel. She, as executive director of the Moravian Historical Society, secured for me in 1992 a copy of the *Transactions of the Moravian Historical Society* containing the Joseph Kummer text of the Archibald Monteath autobiography. Reverend Robert Windolph, as associate dean of students at Moravian College, Bethlehem, Pennsylvania, made gratuitous accommodation available at the college during my first research foray there in 1993. This visit allowed my meeting with Vernon Nelson, archivist at the Moravian Archives in Bethlehem, who was helpful then and in subsequent years. Vernon Nelson also put me in contact with Dr Paul Peucker, curator of the Moravian Archives at Herrnhut in Germany, who made available copies of the narrative versions in the archives' holdings and, like Vernon Nelson, gave permission for re-publication of these texts. In 2002 I again visited the Moravian Archives in Bethlehem and the Reeves Library at Moravian College, where the librarian Bonnie Jean Falla proved of particular assistance.

In 2002 I personally conducted research on Scots migrants to the Caribbean at the Glasgow University Library and was grateful for the help and guidance of Moira Rankin, senior archivist at the Glasgow University Archives and Business Records Centre. Sunita Crawford, a school friend from Trinidad, made excellent arrangements for me in Edinburgh where I consulted the Scottish Record Office and the nearby National Register House. My fortuitous meeting with Hazel Anderson, team leader of the Scottish Wills segment of the Scottish Documents project, was to prove useful in gleaning details about the Monteath family. In 1993 I had established contact with Michael Moss, archivist at the University of Glasgow, and through him, with Alice Stewart, an independent research assistant, who did important spadework on my behalf.

During the early years of this inquiry, I was fortunate to have the research assistance at various times of Rupert Lewis, Deon McCalla, Kathleen Monteith, Carolyn Allen and Claudette Anderson in helping to mine the records of the Jamaica Archives in Spanish Town. My daughter, Yewande Lewis, was thorough in her newspaper searches at the West Indian Reference Library at the University of the West Indies, Mona, for information regarding the Scots Monteath merchants in Hanover parish.

In 1994, with contacts in Nigeria suggested first by Professor Chukwudum Uche of the Department of Sociology and Social Work at the University of the West Indies, and then by Professsor Angulu Onwuejeogwu of the Department of Anthropology of the University of Benin, I was able to undertake my first trip to the eastern part of Nigeria in an effort to understand the cultural background of Archibald Monteath. At the new University of Awka, Professor Azubike Uzoka, Dr C.C. Agbodike, Dr Nwamefor and Dr Anyagbugbu were most informative and hospitable. They facilitated my visit to the town of Nri, my attendance at a *mmanwu* masquerade festival, my tour of the Odinani Museum under the guidance of the curator, Ben Akunne, and my reception at his palace by the Eze of Nri, Eze Obidegwu Onyesoh. In general, my return to Nigeria met with warm hospitality from my personal friends, the chiefs Ebenezer and Doreen Ojurongbe of Ibadan, both now departed, and from Professor David Olatunbosun Oke and family at Akure.

A five-month fellowship in 1998 at the Humanities Research Centre of the Australian National University on the recommendations of Professor Barry Higman and Professor James Walvin provided the first opportunity to concentrate on secondary source research and analysis. This concerned the economic history of eighteenth- and nineteenth-century Scotland and the Chesapeake, and the British East India Company aspects of the Scots Monteath finances. Apart from the university's main library, I received useful research material from the reference library of the Australian Defence Force Academy in Canberra.

In Jamaica, my sporadic bursts of research work over the decade of investigation have been greatly assisted by the professionalism and consideration shown by Hortense Taylor and other officers at the Island Record Office of the Registrar General's Department at Twickenham Park and by the staff at the Jamaica Archives in Spanish Town. The latter location houses the Moravian Archives, the Parish Registers of the Anglican Church, and various documents relating to plantation society and economy. I also thank the librarians at the University of the West Indies Main Library for providing consistent support and facilitating inter-library loans and Internet searches when necessary; and commend Eppie Edwards and the librarians at the National Library of Jamaica for their cooperation and diligence with regard to their map, art, print and manuscript collections. David Boxer of Jamaica's National Gallery provided helpful specifics regarding the Duperly prints.

The more one connected with the people and places thrown up for one's attention by the Monteath narrative, the more one felt the need to acquaint oneself with the topography of the Westmoreland–St Elizabeth hinterland and the families that have emerged from the nexus of estates there. I am grateful for the practical help, hospitality and information given by Joyce Buchanan of Lenox, Westmoreland, and by her brother at Black River, Kenneth Monteith, and his wife, Marjorie, during my visits to the Black River and Newmarket areas in 1995 and again in 2004. A cousin of these Monteiths, Edna Lawrence, had also been generous with her knowledge of family history on my visit to Montego Bay in 1994. Acquaintance with the local history and traditions of the Moravian Church was possible through the assistance of Lucinda Peart and Grace Peart, and of Reverend Levi Watson, pastor at Carmel church in 1995, while the Moravian Church elders, Garth Smith and Travis Spence, gave authoritative tours of the Huntly and Maidstone districts in Manchester, and of Bethabara, Manchester, respectively. Reverend Nigel Powell of the Zorn Moravian Church in Christiana, Manchester, readily made available a fine image of Jacob Zorn. In 2004 Irma Watson of Black River showed us through the Petersville and Robbin's River region. My photographs and illustrations have then been enhanced by the dedicated technical expertise of Joseph Bell and Robert Harris.

All through this endeavour, I have tried to scour widely through the records in the event that tendentious issues could throw light on mainstream concerns. While I have not been able to answer all the questions that have occurred to me, I trust that I have been faithful to the materials I unearthed and have done justice to the memories of the lives recalled here.

Notes on Spelling Variations

Readers will observe the occurrence of divergent spellings of personal and place names across the various texts and documents quoted in this book. These discrepancies reflect the indeterminate spelling practices in written English in earlier centuries. The expansion of print since its fifteenth-century inception in the West together with the gradual spread of education resulted in the standardization of certain spellings that then gained ascendancy over others which still continued to be used, both officially and unofficially, in individual writing styles.

Abbreviations

l. or £	pound, a unit of currency, here either sterling (English) or Jamaican
f.	folio
IRO	Island Record Office, Registrar General's Department, Twickenham Park, Jamaica
JA	Jamaica Archives, Spanish Town, Jamaica
MA	Moravian Archives at the Jamaica Archives
MAB	Moravian Archives, Bethlehem, Pennsylvania
MLA	Mitchell Library Archives, Glasgow
Ms.	Manuscript
NAS	National Archives of Scotland, the revised named for the Scottish Record Office
NLJ	National Library of Jamaica
OPR	Old Parochial Registers of the Church of Scotland
PA	*Periodical Accounts Relating to the Missions of the Church of the United Brethren*
PRO	Public Record Office, Kew, England (now the National Archives)
SRO	Scottish Record Office, Edinburgh
WIRL	West Indian Reference Library, Main Library, University of the West Indies, Mona, Jamaica

History of the Autobiographical Texts

THE LIFE STORY OF ANIASO, later Archibald John Monteath, is one of the few Caribbean slave narratives to have so far been recovered. It encapsulates the experience that converted an Igbo boy from West Africa into a slave on estates along the St Elizabeth/Westmoreland parish borders on the Caribbean island of Jamaica. His enslavement lasted apparently from the very first years of the nineteenth century until he purchased his freedom in 1837, the year before the general emancipation of slaves in most British colonies.[1] Monteath's death in 1864 meant that his life extended into the period that saw the parcelling off and liquidation of many plantations and the establishment of a free peasant citizenry on previous estates and on estate peripheries.

It was the Federal Writers' Project, established in the 1930s by the United States president, Franklin Delano Roosevelt, as a means of providing employment to artists during the Depression, that was responsible for the wealth of narratives collected from ex-slaves in North America. However, lacking any such single-minded initiative in the scattered territories of the Caribbean, the experiences and emotions of millions of our forebears have been lost. Some aspects of their lives are recoverable through historical documentation, particularly in cases where they ran afoul of the law, but also through mention in the writings of their owners and European visitors to the islands. The diaries of planters and overseers revealed aspects of slaves' lives;[2] European visitors and residents commented on slave life and conditions;[3] some missionaries wrote vignettes of slave converts;[4] and fiction writers recreated the world in which the slaves lived.[5]

In the case of Archibald Monteath, it is clear that his force of personality and his particular dedication to the cause of Christianity endeared him to the missionaries with whom he came into contact. There were many other Christian converts whose commitment made the missionaries' arduous work of conversion in far-flung territories seem worth the struggle.[6] But the intensity and extent of Archibald's service to the Christian faith came at a time that was particularly meaningful to the "toilers in the vineyard". The Moravian mission was the first Christian ministry to attempt in Jamaica the conversion of the African and African-descended enslaved population.

The Moravian Brethren had emerged out of the Reformation in fifteenth-century Bohemia and Moravia, regions of the present-day Czech Republic. Under Catholic persecution they had withdrawn from Czech territory to found an egalitarian settlement on the lands of the Lutheran Count Nicholas Ludwig von Zinzendorf in Saxony where they consolidated their theological positions and organizational structures. While Germany remained the Brethren's headquarters, by the early decades of the eighteenth century the Moravians had begun their missions overseas and in December 1754 three of their missionaries arrived in Jamaica from England at the instigation of two northern English absentee owners, the brothers William Foster and Joseph Foster-Barham, who had inherited several estates in the west of the island.

By the late 1820s the Moravians found in the committed Archibald John Monteath an individual who was not only a local assistant to the European missionaries and their few overseas staff, but who by the 1830s was prepared to work full time in the church's ministry. Furthermore, his evangelical zeal was enhanced by his learning to read and write – rare commodities in a local population with minimal literacy skills. Indeed, it is highly likely that the Moravian establishment was instrumental in helping to secure his release from bondage. However, because he bought his manumission in 1837, just a year before general slave emancipation in 1838 in the British colonies, the official notation of his release came too late to be of archival relevance, since it took months, even years, before official records from the parishes were entered in centralized records in Spanish Town. As such we lack official evidence of his manumission. In any event, Monteath had already decided, before his release on 1 June 1837, that on his attaining free status, he would devote his career to full-time proselytization. Thus, by October 1837 the American Jacob Zorn, who was superintendent of the Moravian mission in Jamaica, was canvassing overseas contributions to finance a salary for Archibald Monteath. He wrote to a colleague in Bristol, England:

Another project, by which, I am convinced, those contributing to it would be directly furthering the glory of our Saviour and the salvation of souls, is the following: – An African, named Archibald Monteith, who has learned to read the Scriptures, and is not only well acquainted with them, but possesses a peculiar tact in applying them to the hearts of his countrymen, especially native Africans, has lately, by the help of some kind friends, obtained his full liberty. Gladly would he spend *all* this time in the service of the Lord; visiting from house to house, addressing small companies of an evening, praying with the sick, etc; but he must maintain himself and family. For the sum of 12 *l. sterling per annum,* this "mass of zeal and experience", as our late Brother Collis termed him, might be secured. This is worthy of the consideration of all those who have at heart the salvation of immortal souls; and I should think, hardly needs much pressing on those who love the Negro race.[7] (italics his)

The magazine's editor then added that the appeal had netted "a liberal subscription, by friends in Bristol and its neighbourhood", amounting to £35 10s.

In the 1850s, by the time Monteath had dedicated a decade and a half to full-time ministry, the Moravian missionary establishment in Jamaica clearly felt it necessary to memorialize his outstanding contribution. In 1865 a former resident missionary at New Carmel church recalled with deep appreciation:

As Helper in the congregation of which he was a member, he was unweariedly active, a most valuable assistance to the resident missionary; nor did he confine his labours to one spot, but wherever there was need of help, he was ready to work, and the appearance of his portly figure, mounted on his pony, was hailed with joy by old and young.[8]

The editor went on to describe his physique twenty-five years earlier, in the 1840s: he was "a tall, stately man with very black skin and thick, wooly hair, genuine flat African facial features, but a very attractive, friendly expression of those features".[9] The editor also attributed his kindly appearance to the "preferential treatment" that he had received in his youth as a house-servant; this may in part have accounted for "his pleasant appearance and his cheerful, clever personality",[10] but that would be to romanticize his condition, unreasonably imagining that no fear, no punishment, abuse, or false witness compromised his teenage years. Rather his attitude could have been part of his genetic heritage; it may also have stemmed from the positive outlook on life that he developed and his own determination to succeed and grasp opportunities to improve himself; it may also have come through the sense of authority to which he knew he had been born and reinforced through the calmness induced by his submission to a divine will.

The editor went on to elaborate his character reference: "He is a worthy

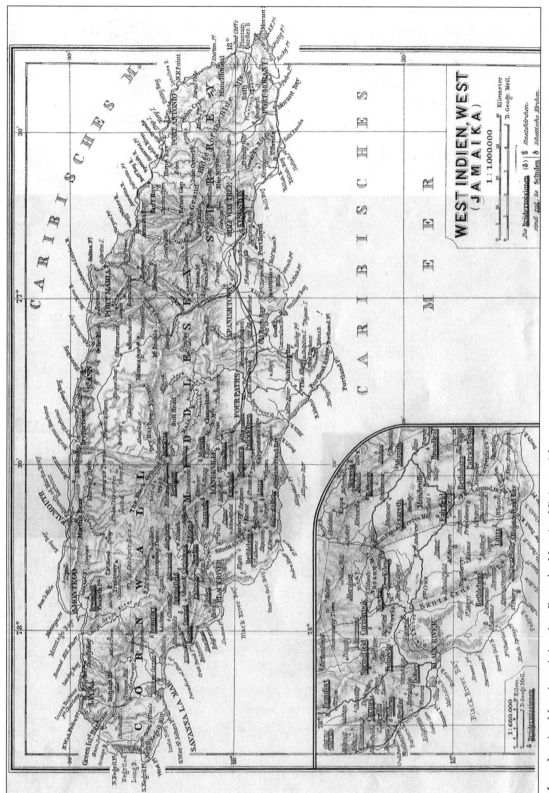

Map 1 Jamaica: Moravian mission sites. From the *Moravian Missionary Atlas*.

man, who has done much good by his ministry in the Gospel, being our first national assistant, and not labouring for one congregation alone, but visiting in all."[11] The reiteration of comparable praise abounds. Joseph Kummer, who helped formulate Monteath's semi-autobiography, himself confessed: "I considered him a *remarkable* man. An eminent subject of *divine grace*; very humble; full of confidence in the Lord Jesus; believing with all his heart the glorious gospel, and delighting to make it known to his fellowmen. I was always much impressed by listening to his prayers & addresses" (italics his).[12]

The 1865 editor of the *Periodical Accounts* described these sermons as "forcible"; in addition, they were "characterized by great originality and depth of thought, as well as by great earnestness of manner, manifestly flowing from a heart full of love to the Saviour and his Brethren".[13] By 1855 an overview of the mission's progress paid tribute to "many of the old and worthy members" of the mission congregations among whom "the most eminent for his truly Christian character, spiritual experience, and varied usefulness, is the well-known Br. Archy Monteith, of New-Carmel congregation, who for many years past has been a true apostle among his countrymen".[14] The visiting American Quaker missionaries Joseph Sturge and Thomas Harvey testified that, on their visit to Hutchinson Mure Scott's Hopeton Estate in 1837, "Archibald Monteith was named to them as an eminent christian character, though an African negro and still a bondsman, and as one whose labours for the conversion of others were often greatly blessed". On Harvey's return to the district in 1866 after Monteath's death, his life was spoken of as one of "memorable usefulness".[15]

The Memorial Tradition

Given his high repute among the Jamaica-based Moravian hierarchy, a project was devised to memorialize him in writing. And rather than producing a condensed third-person manuscript, it was thought appropriate to give the subject's eloquence full rein by recording his thoughts and narratives in first-person format. It is not documented whether the American, Brother Joseph Kummer, and the German, Sister Hermine Louise Geissler, *née* Haneman, were specifically instructed to carry out the task and whether they were counselled on the methodology to be used. However, it is evident that they expended considerable time and effort in listening, transcribing, formulating, translating and composing Monteath's recollections. As such, their texts are at once both biographical and autobiographical. When concerning myself more with the recorders' composition of the narrative, I refer to their work as "biography"; when relating more to Archibald's own telling of his life story, the term "autobiography" is applied.

Part of the rationale for this memorial project lay, no doubt, in the plan to treat Archibald's funeral, whenever it came, with special honour. The only report on that event, which did not take place until 1864, was made by Brother Abraham Lichtenthaeler, then the resident missionary at New Carmel, who spoke in limited terms, gauging the quality of the event by the social approval from whites which Monteath enjoyed: "On the day after his death his body was conveyed to its last resting-place, many whites from the neighbourhood, some of them belonging to the higher classes of society, following in the procession, and thus showing in a pleasing manner the love and respect which our late Brother had enjoyed."[16] However, the distinction of his funeral was conveyed not only by the attendance of white landowners – who turned up at the funerals of the black elite, such as well-considered slave drivers[17] – but also by the quality of the stone slab acquired for Archibald's grave and the elaborate preparation of the biography itself. The thick, plain, black graphite slab that still marks Archibald Monteath's grave in the Carmel churchyard occupies the row parallel to that with graves memorialized with similarly styled slabs where the nineteenth-century overseas missionaries were laid to rest. The biography, for its part, constituted the memoir that must have been read in whole or in part at the funeral service. In some measure it fits the format of the spiritual autobiography or *lebenslauf* that members of the Moravian Church in Europe and the United States were encouraged to compose. This spiritual memoir was retained by the hierarchy of the congregation to which the member belonged and was retrieved and read out at the member's burial service. One of the officiating elders provided an addendum to the autobiography by recounting the spiritual condition of the deceased in the closing months of life, describing the deathbed scene and finally "crown[ing] the departed with the beauty of a glorious passing to the Savior".[18] A stanza or two from an appropriate hymn or from the deceased's favourite sacred song added a literary touch to encapsulate the mood or spiritual philosophy of the departed. This practice followed the advice of Count Zinzendorf, who became one of the major figures in the organization of the Moravian Brotherhood, that hymns were "the best method for bringing God's truths into the heart and to preserve them there".[19]

The memorial began with the subject's date and place of birth, mother's and father's identity, religious affiliation and attitude to religion. The subject then provided a character self-portrait by way of "conversations . . . or stories about habits or peculiarities".[20] In the mid-eighteenth century "biographies reflected lives structured around a person's growing relationship" with the Saviour since all other aspects of earthly life were subordinate. But by the early nineteenth century "[a] person's development was structured around his or her usefulness to family and society".[21] In the course of this autobiography the individual spoke of his or her previous religious experience, his or her "awakening" to Christ, acceptance into the church, first communion, struggles of faith, moral and physical trials, marriage and profession, grief at a personal loss and premonition of death. This religious and literary tradition necessitated conciseness, precision, self-examination and critique, together with meditative depth.

For these cultural, psychological and technical reasons, the project to prepare a fitting memoir for Archibald required one or more mediators. For although Archibald could write, the prelude to one of the biographical texts noted that he could not write fluently.[22] One might modify "fluently" to imply "extensively", that is, "to sustain in writing a topic with fluency, in the manner of a discourse or composition". The prelude's comment is a shorthand way of accounting for what today might, to some extent, be called "functional" literacy, that is, the use of reading or writing to accomplish certain utilitarian tasks. In contrast, self-generated writing is bred of long-cultivated cultural habits of private thought, introspection and analysis, in addition to practised manual manipulation and the personal will and discipline to make time to perform these activities. To produce an extended piece of literature such as an autobiography requires therefore a greater familiarity with literacy than the making of notes and jottings: it means devoting the self to protracted activities such as shaping of letters, adherence to spelling rules, and sequential topic organization. A telling comment regarding the narrative made in the introduction to "Experiences of a Former Slave in Jamaica" notes that "[i]t would be easy to re-word this story into a novel, according to the modern fashion, in which our readers are accustomed to learn only the simple, reliable, historical truth".[23] What is intriguing about this comment is that the strong, almost epic, narrative outlines of Monteath's life story were recognized – its quality to engage the attention and its deployment of climactic episodes. Admittedly in the 1860s the novel was still a new (novel) art form for some European audiences and it was still perceived, as its eighteenth-century precursor had been, as a means of relaying, as the introduction concludes, "simple, reliable, historical truth" rather than as the imaginative exercise or outlet into which it later evolved.

Having prepared the life story, the missionaries withheld publication for a decade. But the 1863 slave emancipation in Suriname, where the Moravians also had a vigorous mission, freed the Moravians from their former restraint that had prevented open condemnation of the slave institution, and the *Periodical Accounts,* which collected extracts of reports and diaries from mission stations worldwide, now carried features on "the conditions of slavery in the distant colonies". This must have excited some degree of interest in

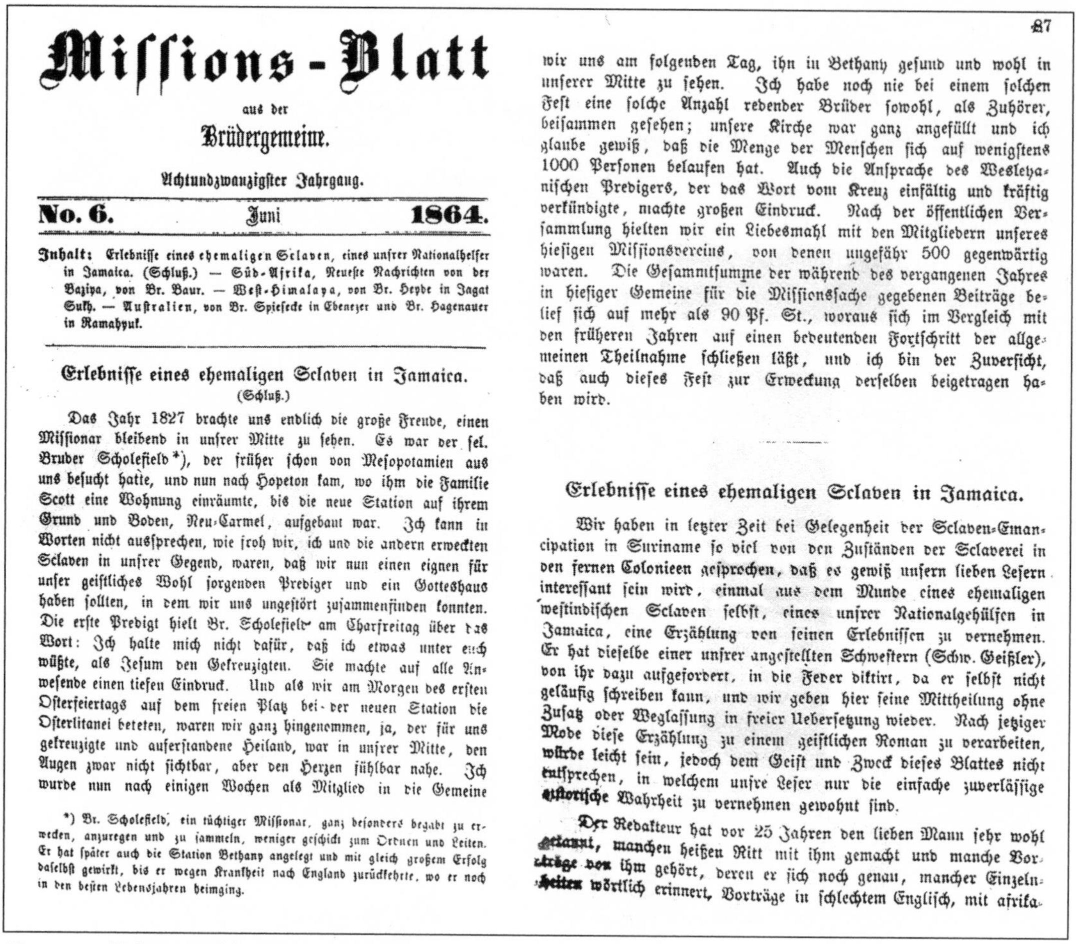

Missions-Blatt

aus der
Brüdergemeine.

Achtundzwanzigster Jahrgang.

No. 6.   Juni   1864.

Inhalt: Erlebnisse eines ehemaligen Sclaven, eines unsrer Nationalhelfer in Jamaica. (Schluß.) — Süd-Afrika, Neueste Nachrichten von der Baziya, von Br. Baur. — West-Himalaya, von Br. Heyde in Jagat Suth. — Australien, von Br. Spieseke in Ebenezer und Br. Hagenauer in Ramahyut.

Erlebnisse eines ehemaligen Sclaven in Jamaica.
(Schluß.)

Das Jahr 1827 brachte uns endlich die große Freude, einen Missionar bleibend in unsrer Mitte zu sehen. Es war der sel. Bruder Scholefield*), der früher schon von Mesopotamien aus uns besucht hatte, und nun nach Hopeton kam, wo ihm die Familie Scott eine Wohnung einräumte, bis die neue Station auf ihrem Grund und Boden, Neu-Carmel, aufgebaut war. Ich kann in Worten nicht aussprechen, wie froh wir, ich und die andern erweckten Sclaven in unsrer Gegend, waren, daß wir nun einen eignen für unser geistliches Wohl sorgenden Prediger und ein Gotteshaus haben sollten, in dem wir uns ungestört zusammenfinden konnten. Die erste Predigt hielt Br. Scholefield am Charfreitag über das Wort: Ich halte mich nicht dafür, daß ich etwas unter euch wüßte, als Jesum den Gekreuzigten. Sie machte auf alle Anwesende einen tiefen Eindruck. Und als wir am Morgen des ersten Osterfeiertags auf dem freien Platz bei der neuen Station die Osterlitanei beteten, waren wir ganz hingenommen, ja, der für uns gekreuzigte und auferstandene Heiland, war in unsrer Mitte, den Augen zwar nicht sichtbar, aber den Herzen fühlbar nahe. Ich wurde nun nach einigen Wochen als Mitglied in die Gemeine

*) Br. Scholefield, ein tüchtiger Missionar, ganz besonders begabt zu erwecken, anzuregen und zu sammeln, weniger geschickt zum Ordnen und Leiten. Er hat später auch die Station Bethany angelegt und mit gleich großem Erfolg daselbst gewirkt, bis er wegen Krankheit nach England zurückkehrte, wo er noch in den besten Lebensjahren heimging.

wir uns am folgenden Tag, ihn in Bethany gesund und wohl in unserer Mitte zu sehen. Ich habe noch nie bei einem solchen Fest eine solche Anzahl redender Brüder sowohl, als Zuhörer, beisammen gesehen; unsere Kirche war ganz angefüllt und ich glaube gewiß, daß die Menge der Menschen sich auf wenigstens 1000 Personen belaufen hat. Auch die Ansprache des Weslehanischen Predigers, der das Wort vom Kreuz einfältig und kräftig verkündigte, machte großen Eindruck. Nach der öffentlichen Versammlung hielten wir ein Liebesmahl mit den Mitgliedern unseres hiesigen Missionsvereins, von denen ungefähr 500 gegenwärtig waren. Die Gesammtsumme der während des vergangenen Jahres in hiesiger Gemeine für die Missionssache gegebenen Beiträge belief sich auf mehr als 90 Pf. St., woraus sich im Vergleich mit den früheren Jahren auf einen bedeutenden Fortschritt der allgemeinen Theilnahme schließen läßt, und ich bin der Zuversicht, daß auch dieses Fest zur Erweckung derselben beigetragen haben wird.

Erlebnisse eines ehemaligen Sclaven in Jamaica.

Wir haben in letzter Zeit bei Gelegenheit der Sclaven-Emancipation in Suriname so viel von den Zuständen der Sclaverei in den fernen Colonieen gesprochen, daß es gewiß unsern lieben Lesern interessant sein wird, einmal aus dem Munde eines ehemaligen westindischen Sclaven selbst, eines unsrer Nationalgehülfen in Jamaica, eine Erzählung von seinen Erlebnissen zu vernehmen. Er hat dieselbe einer unsrer angestellten Schwestern (Schw. Geißler), von ihr dazu aufgefordert, in die Feder diktirt, da er selbst nicht geläufig schreiben kann, und wir geben hier seine Mittheilung ohne Zusatz oder Weglassung in freier Uebersetzung wieder. Nach jetziger Mode diese Erzählung zu einem geistlichen Roman zu verarbeiten, würde leicht sein, jedoch dem Geist und Zweck dieses Blattes nicht entsprechen, in welchem unsre Leser nur die einfache zuverlässige historische Wahrheit zu vernehmen gewohnt sind.

Der Redakteur hat vor 25 Jahren den lieben Mann sehr wohl gekannt, manchen heißen Ritt mit ihm gemacht und manche Vorträge von ihm gehört, deren er sich noch genau, mancher Einzelheiten wörtlich erinnert, Vorträge in schlechtem Englisch, mit afrika-

Figure 1.1 Title page of the *Missions-Blatt* text

their readership and it was now thought that it would be a timely follow-up for their readers "to hear the experiences of a former West Indian slave, one of our national assistants in Jamaica, in his own words".[24] But since Monteath was still alive, the editor of the first printed biography refrained from naming the subject and requested the Moravians in England, where the English translation from the German texts was done, "not to record the story of this dear man in public, current newsletter". This was because they felt that the sin of pride would damage the moral fibre of Monteath, should he see himself "become an object of public conversation". Rather than recognize that narcissism and self-importance were common responses to the glare of publicity, even more so in the case of persons who had hitherto been ignored and demeaned, the temptation was regarded as the especial pitfall of black people. So the authoritative editor opined that "[e]veryone who is acquainted with the characteristic disposition of the Negro will find this concern justified. Such a religious man should not be led astray in this way. Of this we are convinced, and we also wanted to spare him the temptation."[25]

Publications of the Autobiography

So without identifying him by name, Monteath's autobiography was first published in German in the Moravian religious periodical *Missions-Blatt* or Mission Newsletter, number 5 of May and June 1864 as "Erlebnisse eines ehemaligen Sclaven in Jamaica" (Experiences of a former slave in Jamaica).[26] Then immediately following his death the very next month, the second variant took the form of a translation into English of "Erlebnisse", issued in volume 25 of *Periodical Accounts Relating to the Missions of the Church of the United Brethren* published in September and December 1865 as a "Memoir of Br. Archibald Monteith" in pages 433–41 and 481–85. It concludes (484–85) with an account by Brother Abraham Lichtenthaeler of the final months of Monteath's life. The third publication, called the "Autobiographical Sketch of Archibald Monteith", formed Appendix C in Thomas Harvey and William Brewin's *Jamaica in 1866: A Narrative of a Tour through the Island* (1867). This was in fact a reproduction of the "Memoir" of *Periodical Accounts.* In 1898 the fourth version appeared when the Moravian Brethren published at Herrnhut in Germany a fifteen-page German-language brochure on Archibald, in predominantly third-person reportage, as Mission Lesson no. 21. It was entitled "Missionsstunden aus der Brüdergemeine, Archibald Monteith". Such memoirs advertised, promoted and validated the church's worldwide missions in "heathen" lands and thus helped elicit moral and financial support for these tasks. As a "mission lesson" it stimulated meditation and group discussion among candidates for church membership, new converts and seasoned adherents, showing them diverse paths toward salvation and underlining the physical and spiritual international brotherhood of which each church member had become a part. For example, an early handwritten journal, *Die Gemeinnachrichten,* included samples of "the most 'edifying' biographies from Moravian settlements around the world", just as the later *Periodical Accounts* would do. As a means of instilling in adherents the Moravian way of life, then, "the biographies idealized the lives of their subjects".[27] The fifth publication appeared as late as 1966 and was based on a manuscript, dated 1853, that fills all but one page of an 8¾-inch by 6¾-inch exercise book. The manuscript was written by Reverend Joseph Horsfield Kummer (1820–97) and it lay forgotten for roughly one hundred years in the Moravian Archives in Bethlehem, Pennsylvania until it was unearthed by Vernon H. Nelson, the archivist in Bethlehem. Nelson published it in an issue of the *Transactions of the Moravian Historical Society* under the title

Als Manuskript gedruckt.

Missionsstunden

aus der Brüdergemeine.

Nr. 21.

Archibald Monteith.

Neu Carmel ist eine unserer Missionsstationen auf Jamaika. Entstanden ist es vor ungefähr 70 Jahren, als die Sklaverei auf dieser westindischen Insel ihr Ende noch nicht gefunden hatte. Zwar sollte den armen Schwarzen die Befreiungsstunde auch hier bald schlagen. Aber noch seufzten sie unter ihrem harten Joch. Allein das Evangelium von der freien Gnade Gottes in Christo Jesu, und von der herrlichen Freiheit der Kinder Gottes, die unter jedem Druck, selbst unter dem der Sklaverei erworben und behauptet werden kann, hatte auch hier bereits festen Fuß gefaßt und fand gerade bei den Sklaven offenes Ohr.

Einer unter ihnen, welcher in ganz besonderer Weise dafür empfänglich war, war Archibald Monteith. Wenn im Folgenden von ihm die Rede sein soll, so verdient er es, einmal in Erinnerung gebracht zu werden; denn in das Amt eines Nationalhelfers eingesetzt um die Zeit, als Neu Carmel entstand, hat er sich eine lange Reihe von Jahren hindurch um das Gedeihen des Missionswerkes auf diesem Platz und seiner Umgebung ganz erhebliche Verdienste erworben und unter seinen schwarzen Brüdern und Schwestern in großem Segen gestanden. Leider müssen wir es uns versagen,

Figure 1.2 Title page of the *Missionsstunden* text

"Archibald John Monteith: Native Helper and Assistant in the Jamaica Mission at New Carmel". As the product of a part-ecclesiastic, part-academic organization, this version was footnoted for exegetical clarifications. Although it was the last to have come to light, the manuscript's dating makes it the earliest extant version of the autobiography. In 1990 Angelo Costanzo introduced this text to a literary readership by republishing it with less footnoting in the journal *Callaloo*.

Even before the availability of Nelson's edition, the Monteath story was already part of the sanctioned history of Moravian overseas missions. Augustus Thompson's *Moravian Missions: Twelve Lectures* (1882) discusses Archibald's contribution on pages 98–99; and a description of Archibald Monteath written by Bishop Augustus Westphal appeared on page 165 of *The Breaking of the Dawn, or, Moravian Work in Jamaica, 1754–1904* by Walter Hark and Augustus Westphal (1904). The *Periodical Accounts* story was again heavily sourced for the 1920 Bachelor of Divinity thesis submitted by Walser H. Allen to the Moravian College and Theological Seminary, Bethlehem, Pennsylvania. A brief recognition of Monteath's historic role occurs on page 208 of J.E. Hutton's *A History of Moravian Missions*, volume 2, *The Builders* (1923) in its first chapter entitled "Jamaica; or West Indies – Western Province, 1805–1914"; and a brief appreciation ends the first part of S.U. Hastings and B.L. MacLeavy's *Seedtime and Harvest: A Brief History of the Moravian Church in Jamaica, 1754–1979* (1979).

Product of Narration, Dictation and Translation

The three most extensive texts of this autobiography deserve some comparative discussion. The editor of the 1864 *Missions-Blatt* in which the "Erlebnisse" was published indicated that Monteath had "dictated [his experiences] to one of our sisters (Sister Geissler), at her request".[28] When the memoir appeared in 1865 the same explanation was offered by the editor of *Periodical Accounts*: "The following narrative was dictated by the subject of the memoir to Sister Geissler, the wife of the Missionary at Carmel." The fact, however, that a manuscript edition of Monteath's life story accounts in similar fashion for its genesis teasingly complicates the textual history of the Archibald Monteath biography, as it indicates a collaborative project by two amanuenses. In a prefatory endorsement of the narrative, Kummer reveals that in Archibald's capacity as church helper he often visited the mission station while Kummer was serving at New Carmel "during 1853 and part of 1854". Those visits were the basis of Kummer's "many interesting and edifying conversations with him. He gave me at various times this account, or fragments of account of his life."[29] The same assertion in the prefaces of both the Geissler and Kummer texts therefore indicates that the missionary amanuenses were both recipients of Monteath's confidences, even if we are unsure as to whether they were always both present at the same time to hear his recollections. Indeed, they may not have always interviewed him together and it is possible that the narrating/transcribing sessions may have been both formal and informal. By formal I refer to a process in which dictation and notation were simultaneous; while informal conversations could have yielded material that the collectors would have reconstructed post hoc facto. In the case of the former methodology, the subject would have been aware that his words were being taken down; in the latter, he might well have had no idea that his words were being purposefully stored for subsequent mnemonic retrieval by his listeners. One is confident that both methods may well have come into play, since there is external evidence that Archibald was in the habit of regaling his principals with accounts of incidents in his life. That evidence emerges from 1861 remarks by a touring missionary how "Near the school [at Rosehall], in a good two-storied house, lives the venerable assistant, Br. Archy Monteith. He placed refreshments before us, and then accompanied us down the mountain, nearly to New-Carmel. On the way, he related much concerning his past life and labours."[30] The editor of *Periodical Accounts,* volume 25, probably Joseph Roemer, also testified similarly in the preface to the "Erlebnisse".

> The editor knew the dear man very well 25 years ago. He made many a hot ride with him, and heard many of his lectures, many details of which he can still remember word for word. They were lectures in poor English with African accents, but original, thorough, full of examples from experience, full of fire, and of love as well as gravity. He [the editor] also heard many of the life experiences of this dear man from his own mouth and can guarantee that these corroborate exactly with what is told here.[31]

No doubt Archibald had another stock of stories for his friends, but his stories for the missionaries appropriately touched on his role and experiences in the furtherance of the religious endeavour.

The language issue that the editor raised deserves some attention, if only because the text has moved, at the overt level, between two European languages, German and English.[32] All the same, we need to consider first and foremost the conversion of Archibald's speech into these two languages. His own language in the 1850s would have been Jamaican Creole English, judging from the evidence of multiple replications of this language in written form.[33] Either Geissler reinterpreted all Archibald's discourse directly into German formulations, or Kummer converted it directly into Standard English, or, what was more likely, some episodes were reconstructed into either language depending on which of the transcribing conduits was conversant with a particular narrative segment. If Kummer was comfortable with German, which is possible, given his German ancestry and the language culture of the church, a fair portion of the preliminary drafting might well have been in that language. This would mean that his English-language text was a translation, in whole or in part, from German. But this particular issue is hypothetical. He may equally have converted Archibald's Jamaican Creole English statements into what he considered Standard English equivalents.

In whatever language(s) they initially used to reduce Monteath's episodes and ruminations to writing, it would seem that Kummer and Geissler collaborated in identifying those topics that would compose the entire narrative; they may even have worked on shaping separate sections. However they went about it, the conversation fragments of which Kummer spoke had already been combined and subjected to drafting and editing processes by the time Kummer produced his manuscript in 1853, which in a subscript locates the text at "New Carmel, Jamaica" together with its date of completion. It represents a finished work with little sign of deletions. Furthermore, the collaboration was very close, as both the German "Experiences" and Kummer's text, in terms of content, structure and style, are parallel documents. One major affective difference lies in the omission in "Experiences" of a concluding summarizing hymn stanza – a set requirement for a funerary testimonial. The two versions of the memoir, those in the *Periodical Accounts* and in Harvey and Brewin, carry the stanza and it occurs in Kummer's version as well.

> The Saviour's blood and righteousness,
> My beauty is, my glorious dress;
> Therein array'd I need not fear
> When in God's presence I appear.

One may surmise that "Experiences", printed while Archibald was still alive, did not include this signifier of a post-mortem tribute; however, this signature of life's ending and summation of life's endeavour had already been chosen in 1853 when Kummer had completed his script.

Once Kummer and Geissler had agreed on content and sequencing, Geissler evidently produced a formal German translation that could fulfil a number of church objectives. In the nineteenth century German was the language of the church's headquarters and its original publications. However, no sooner did the church deem it politic to publish a slave narrative, as indicated earlier, than Archibald passed away, and the English-language version of the church's international journal, the *Periodical Accounts,* considered it appropriate to reissue the German "Erlebnisse" in an English

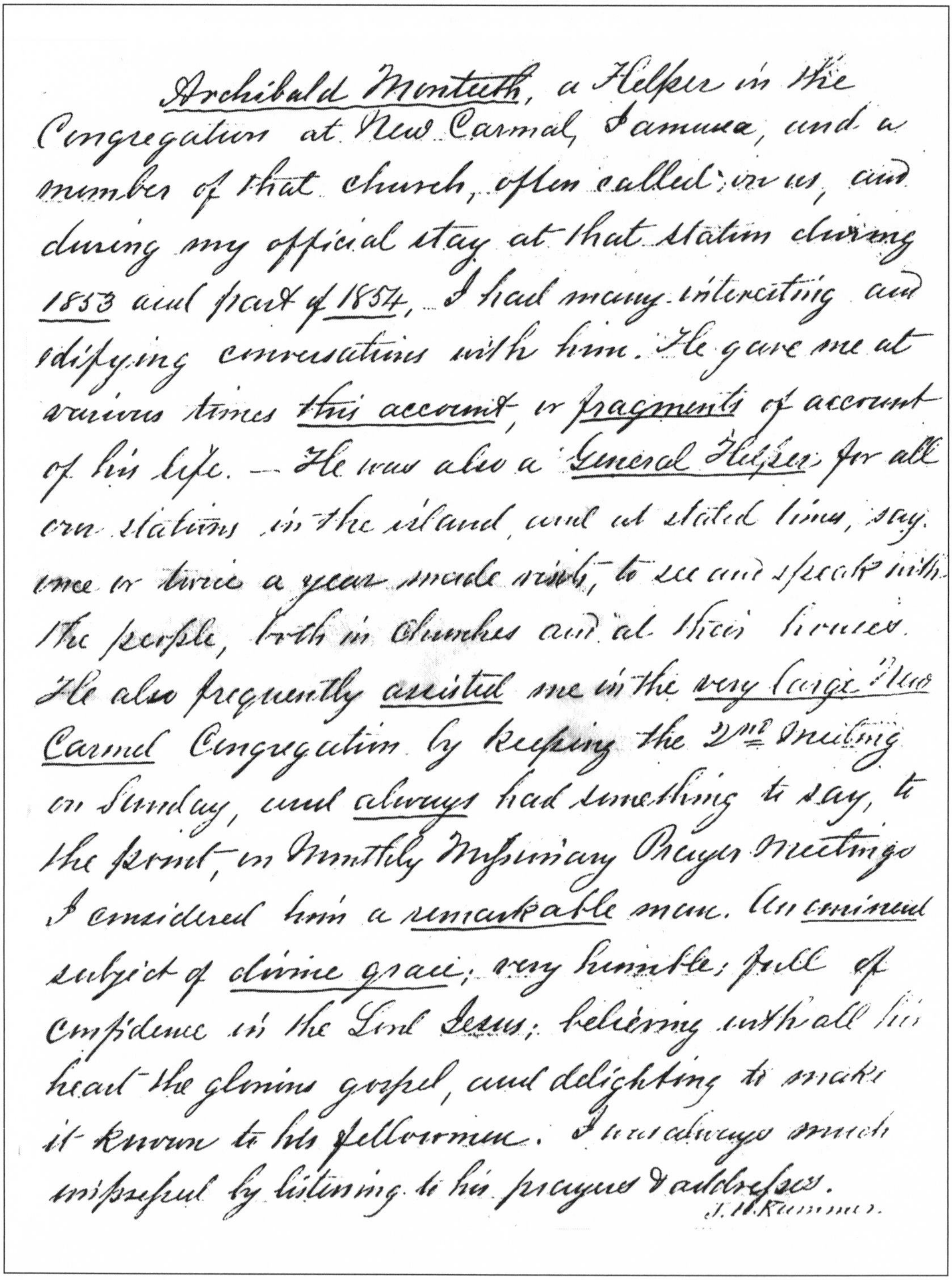

Archibald Monteith, a Helper in the Congregation at New Carmel, Jamaica, and a member of that church, often called on us, and during my official stay at that station during 1853 and part of 1854, I had many interesting and edifying conversations with him. He gave me at various times this account, or fragments of account of his life. — He was also a General Helper for all our stations in the island, and at stated times, say once or twice a year made visits, to see and speak with the people, both in Churches and at their houses. He also frequently assisted me in the very large New Carmel Congregation by keeping the 2nd Meeting on Sunday, and always had something to say, to the point, in Monthly Missionary Prayer Meetings. I considered him a remarkable man. An eminent subject of divine grace; very humble; full of confidence in the Lord Jesus; believing with all his heart the glorious gospel, and delighting to make it known to his fellowmen. I was always much impressed by listening to his prayers & addresses.

J. H. Kummer.

Figure 1.3 The first page of Kummer's manuscript.

version, this time with the concluding hymn of the memoir format. This emergency precipitated a need that was filled not by the already extant English version, that of Joseph Kummer, but by a new translation. How do we account for this? We have no evidence to date that Kummer's version was available in Germany, or England, for that matter, where *Periodical Accounts* was published. When he left Jamaica he obviously took the manuscript back to the United States with him. Why? Had he penned another copy that he left in Jamaica? After his tour of duty at New Carmel, he served for several years in Brooklyn, New York, Lancaster and Philadelphia, so he was not out of reach.[34] It is therefore not clear why his version was inaccessible to his New Carmel successors who needed an English-language version in readiness for Archibald's eventual passing, and why it was likewise not accessible to the English-language *Periodical Accounts* editor who, it would seem, had to rely on the funeral tribute. One may hazard a conjecture here. It concerns the culture of writing that had been developed and nurtured within the Kummer family. That they indulged in copious letter writing is evidenced by the material in the Kummer Collection at the Kemerer Museum of Decorative Arts in Bethlehem, Pennsylvania, and the Horsfield-Kummer Family Collection at the New York Public Library. Moreover, the contents of Box 8 in the Kummer Collection at the Moravian Archives in Bethlehem, catalogued as "Various Biographies", give evidence that Joseph's father, John Gottlob Kummer, and Joseph himself made a practice of collecting and soliciting life stories and memorials. Perhaps there was more of the documentalist and historian in this practice than the efficient church functionary. This penchant may have accounted for Kummer taking the biography back with him to the United States to add to his personal archives. If so, there may have been an understanding between Kummer and Geissler that her version, not his, would be the church's property and therefore serve the church's needs when the time came for its release.

Style and Organization of the Full-Length Biographies

As a translation from Jamaican Creole English to German to English, it is not surprising that the memoir conveys less emotional immediacy between narrative voice and subject/topic than occurs with the Kummer text. Despite the casualness of expression in some of the memoir's turns of phrase, and the occasionally sophisticated vocabulary of Kummer's text, Kummer's expository style is more discursive, to the point of indulging the parenthetical, and is more concrete and specific in its references. A few passages of illustration follow:

Of four children I was the only son, and therefore my father's pet; he always liked to have me near him, and even when he went out to work he would take me along with him. The same fruits of the earth are cultivated there as here in Jamaica.[35]

As an only Son I was the favorite of my father with whom I generally labored in the field and provision ground, the yield of which is very much the same as here in Jamaica; yams, potatoes, Indian Corn etc. etc.[36]

We called it "Chukudama," *i.e.* Thunderer, and appealed to it for aid in case of illness. We fancied that death was the total termination of man's existence in any form, knowing nothing concerning the future.[37]

[Tschuku-damma] makes the thunder and lightning etc. etc. We only prayed to him when we were sick, so that he should speedily make us well. Did we recover and get well again, then there was an end to prayer. When death came, then every thing ceased to be, at least so we thought, and as is customary among the heathen, we did not trouble ourselves about futurity.[38]

Despite this difference, however, both the Kummer text and the memoir gain energy from the inclusion of first-person episodes and conversations, which recapture the story's rehearsal to an audience familiar with the speaking subject. Indeed, it is precisely the quality of a heard voice and the projection of a bold and lively personality that distinguish "Experiences" and the two versions of the memoir from the condensed third-person reportage of Mission Lesson 21. Yet stylistically the memoir is less attractive because it is at second remove from the Kummer-written original, the memoir being a competent translation into English from the German "Erlebnisse". An additional stylistic factor concerns the German "Erlebnisse" itself which, as its 2002 translator recognized, contained several long, convoluted sentences that made for a certain turgidity and weightiness, and that, for a sensitive translation, needed to be fragmented in order to give speech liveliness and move along the narrative. This apart, the Kummer and Geissler-based texts capture Archibald's story-telling zest and his wordiness, even apart from his possession of bold convictions. His delight in narrating his life's events becomes evident: he was clearly proud of himself – his family heritage, his accomplishments, his spiritual journey and resolute faith.

Structurally, whereas the paragraph breaks in the "Erlebnisse" and the memoir are consistent, there is sometimes a difference in segmentation between these and Kummer's text. There are also differences in the flow of ideas: whereas in Kummer the paragraph about the facial cicatrization ends with the disgrace of flinching under the ordeal, in the 1864, 1865 and 1867 texts Archibald's aristocratic maternal lineage occupies that position in the narrative order. Other minor variations in paragraph sequence are also evident: in the "Erlebnisse" and the memoir Archibald's decision to refrain from field labour on Sundays precedes his admission of antagonisms between himself and his master, while the order is the reverse in Kummer. The "Experiences" and Kummer both mention Archibald's fathering of a daughter outside of marriage, an issue dropped from the more doctrinaire Mission Lesson and the post-funerary "Memoir" (1867). In the latter case, it might have been thought to have been insensitive to the daughter in question, who was in attendance at the funeral. The concluding devices in the various versions are inconsequential in their variation. Both Kummer's text and the "Erlebnisse", having been scripted in the 1850s, end with Archibald's confessions of spiritual humility and thankfulness to God for his personal freedom and liberty for other ex-slaves. He then goes on to recall his family in Africa and attempts to emotionally and spiritually reconcile their paganism with his achieved spiritual wealth in Christianity. He concludes with encouragement to his offspring and community in Jamaica to walk the Christian road. Both the 1865 and 1867 memoirs are extended by a postscript under the name of Brother Lichtenthaeler, minister at New Carmel, which narrates the closing months of Archibald's life and his attitudes of initial resistance to his illness, followed by patient resignation to his condition.

The versions also betray slight differences of detail: Kummer says that after the first day of being kidnapped, Archibald and his captor walked for several days, while the other texts say that they walked for another day; Kummer specifies that the young Igbo initiate was fed with a piece of yam or corn cake, while in other texts no reference is made to food being eaten during the process and "Experiences" speaks non-specifically about his being given something to eat; where Kummer's text highlights the role of Mrs Cooper in Archibald's moral guidance, it is Mr Cooper in the others; Kummer speaks about the ridicule faced when Archibald and Rebecca got married, without specifying the ethnicity of their tormentors, but the other texts mention that it was whites who broke into laughter; "Experiences" attributes the land for the New Carmel church to the Scott family, a detail omitted in Kummer and the memoir; Kummer attributes Archibald's healing from arthritis to a coloured man whereas the other texts refer to this anonymous agent as black;[39] and Kummer includes the story of Archibald's influencing a man to marry rather than cohabit, while this fragment is omitted in the other two. In "Experiences" and the memoir, Archibald gains spiritual insights from dialogues with Mr Cooper, while Kummer's text says they were with Mr Coke. A glaring error in the print versions is the attribution of emancipation to April 1838 rather than August 1838; and there are discrepancies regarding the date of Archibald's death. In the memoirs this is put as 5 July 1864, while the List of Persons Departed at New Carmel for 1864, as well as Archibald's gravestone, put his date of death as 3 July.[40] The discrepancy is perhaps an indication that 5 July was really the date of burial.

Research Responses

Without a doubt, publication of Kummer's manuscript has breathed new life into the Monteath saga. It not only allows for a more textured understanding of the composition and editorial processes involved in production of a slave narrative, but also lends further insights into Monteath's life story and personality. It certainly encouraged Angelo Costanzo to rehabilitate it in the literary journal *Callaloo* (1990) with an accompanying article that places the autobiography in the traditions and purposes of the slave narrative genre, comparing the literary style of Kummer's version to that of the 1865 *Periodical Accounts* narrative. In resurrecting this testimony, Costanzo noted that it had been "long-neglected and unappreciated", whereas it was "an honest, moving account related by an intelligent, skillful storyteller who perceptively understood the tragic effects of slavery upon all men and women".[41]

It is therefore somewhat strange that Monteath's autobiography has not achieved more salience in the mind of the Caribbean public and among local and overseas academic circles, since it has been available in print since 1864 and was reissued in several versions, some of which are reproduced here as appendixes. Perhaps it is because previous publication arenas have largely been church-related, added to which the piety of the narrator's sentiments are likely to be distasteful to some, even contemptible; as such, it has remained confined to a limited religious niche. More pertinent to the matter of its relegation is the fact that this biography was not intended for the anti-slavery agenda, does not therefore fit the conventions of anti-slavery discourses and does not satisfy the post-1970s unidimensional lionization of the slave as resister, runaway, or rebel. There is no harrowing account of physical and psychological brutality here, there is no carte blanche verbal attack on slave owners, no frontal denunciation of their moral turpitude, though there is critique of both the white slave owners and administrative personnel for their sexual abuses of female slaves and general encouragement of hedonistic attitudes among the slave cohorts. Worse still, Monteath portrays himself as loyal to the interests of his owners during the December 1831–January 1832 slave uprising in western Jamaica and speaks appreciatively of several whites with whom he came into contact and who helped him in significant ways. But sensitive reading of his narrative reveals an individual with tremendous self-confidence, even in his relationships with Europeans, and there is little doubt that the emotional high point of his story is his determination to buy his way out of slavery, even at a time when the wheels of gradual slave emancipation were slowly grinding to effect momentous change. Indeed, the 1831–32 uprising played a crucial role in further bringing the slave system into disrepute and demonstrating the unmanageability of such a regime. But as this book sets out to demonstrate, Archibald Monteath's story, painstakingly mined, reveals useful nuances about the varied experiences of Caribbean slavery and the subsequent evolution of a peasant society.

The refocus on African ancestry spurred by the Black Power movement of the late 1960s and the 1970s, and the possibility of tracing genealogical African-Caribbean connections demonstrated by Alex Haley's book *Roots* and its subsequent television series prompted at least one Jamaican researcher's interest in the Monteath story. John Aarons, then senior librarian at the Institute of Jamaica, today the National Library of Jamaica, was moved to research "The Story of Aneaso, the Son of Durl and Dirinejah" using the supportive resources of the Jamaica Archives. That article, published in the *Jamaican Historical Society Bulletin* (1977), attempted to coordinate dates, place names and personal identities with data in official documents. This article attracted the attention of Vera MacLeavy, Honorary Archivist of the Moravian Church in Jamaica, who apprised Aarons of Kummer's version as reproduced in the *Transactions of the Moravian Historical Society* in Pennsylvania (1966). This new information allowed Aarons to produce a sequel article entitled "The Story of Archibald Monteith" in *Jamaican Historical Society Bulletin* (1978).

Scope of the Present Project

My own attachment to the narrative was spurred by an interest in genealogy. My husband, Rupert Lewis, a descendant of Edward Monteath, a member of the New Carmel congregation, had in the 1970s drawn my attention to the Harvey and Brewin version. He, like other Monteith family members today, suspected that Archibald Monteath may have had some connection with his maternal family history. Already, the possibility of this connection had been publicly signalled by Ernest John Monteith of Kilmarnock, a claim of blood kinship reproduced in Hastings and MacLeavy's *Seedtime and Harvest*, page 156, and alluded to in Aarons's "The Story of Archibald Monteith". Ernest Monteith had also prepared a document of family history that began with Archibald – a manuscript that was discovered after his passing in 1975 by one of his daughters, Joyce Buchanan. Ernest's niece, Edna Lawrence, had also drafted a typescript account of the Monteith family, citing Archibald as its progenitor. The resuscitation of Archibald's story and its iconic use by the Kilmarnock and Paynestown Monteiths is recounted in Angelo Costanzo's "A

Figure 1.4 New Carmel Moravian church, *c.* 1900. From Hark and Westphal, *The Breaking of the Dawn.*

Living Slave Narrative" (2003). These claims have been influenced as much by the co-residence at Rosehall Estate of Archibald and Edward and David Monteath as by the accessibility of today's Moravian community to the printed sources of Archibald's contribution to Moravian religious life.[42]

I began concerted work on Archibald Monteath in the early 1990s. My researches concentrated on two lines of St Elizabeth/Westmoreland Monteiths, those of Edward and David Monteith who were born during slavery, apparently at Kep, the same estate on which Archibald Monteath was first resident. Although it was clear that Edward and David were brothers (documentary evidence records their mother, an African whose slave name was Jeany), it was not, however, possible to establish who fathered them because this information was not supplied in the Slave Returns and we have no records whatever of the administrative, work, or private papers regarding Kep and Dumbarton/Rosehall estates where Archibald, Edward, and David Monteath were employed. Jeany herself drops out of the documentary record, apparently because she did not become a Christian, at least a Moravian, or she became one after the church records ceased to indicate slave name as well as Christian name. All said, it has not been possible, therefore, to establish any biological connection linking Edward and David to Archibald. Just as tellingly, Archibald was in his mid-twenties when Edward and David were in their pubescent years.

Since it proved impossible to establish a blood link between Edward and David to Archibald, I was therefore obliged to redirect the research along lines that had been initiated by John Aarons. In other words, to attempt a social and historical contextualization of the narrative, an exegesis of its events and an identification and amplification of the characters whose lives and actions impacted those of Monteath himself. Years into the project, I was to feel a correspondence between my research agenda and the account of Gary Collison's painstaking recovery of the life story and personhood of a New England runaway slave. "I found to my dismay that I was merely dredging for facts. It was tedious work, and I was seldom rewarded by the discovery of even the tiniest morsel of information directly connected to Shadrach Minkins. . . . There was simply not enough material for a conventional biography." But inspired by Monteath's original driving narrative and my curiosity about the personalities I was encountering, urged on by my interest in societal forms and their evolution, and, like Collison, having a background in literature – these all fed into a feeling for character and setting, which allowed me to connect a "vast collection of disconnected facts" about individuals and events.[43] Correspondingly, having finished my manuscript, I discovered a work with a related subject and methodology to mine. This was Jon Sensbach's *Rebecca's Revival* (2005), which uses the life of an enslaved then manumitted mulatto woman to trace the inception of Protestantism during the early eighteenth century among the slave population on the island of St Thomas in the then Danish West Indies, now the Virgin Islands. In parallel with my present work, Sensbach's primary data are sourced from the spiritual testimonies, diaries, letters and reports of Moravian missionaries on St Thomas.

Probing and following up the motivations and actions of individuals in the Monteath story meant that the writer developed an intimacy with them over time, so that I grew to feel, like the narrators of Toni Morrison's *Beloved* and Erna Brodber's *Louisana,* that I was ridden by duppies – ancestral spirits – in my endeavour to unveil their lives and resurrect their presence among us. And what if they did not want the veil to be lifted? This conflict laid on me the charge to be as accurate and as respectful as could be achieved in the recreation of their lives.

Apart from Archibald himself, the focus of my attention was also seized by the family history and socio-economic motivations of Monteath's first owner, John Monteath of Glasgow, Scotland (circa 1770–1815); the work and perspectives of the Moravian missionaries; profiles of the enslaved community, their attitudes and social networks, and their attempts to establish family and village life after slavery had been abolished. Monteath's autobiography becomes therefore a matrix from which to reconstruct the pen-keeping and agricultural plantation and post-plantation societies in southwestern Jamaica as experienced by slaves, slave owners and missionaries in the late eighteenth century and into the sixth decade of the nineteenth. As such, it should furnish a companion social documentary, although from a contrasting socio-economic and ethical perspective, to Douglas Hall's *In Miserable Slavery* (1989), an edited selection of diary entries made between 1750 and 1786 by Thomas Thistlewood, the slave owner of a property immediately west of the Monteath narrative setting and in a period just prior to the Monteath narrative's beginning. More recently, in 2004, Trevor Burnard published an analytic study of this same subject, entitled *Mastery, Tyranny, and Desire: Thomas Thistlewood and His Slaves in the Anglo-Jamaican World.*

As social history, Monteath's life story offers a paradigm of the processes by which a child conditioned towards high sociopolitical status eventually achieved in adulthood, though enslaved and exiled, leadership roles in new and hostile economic environments. Analysis of this type of slave story thus allows a re-reading of the possible impact of slavery on individuals through an examination of the role of ancestral mores and memory in shaping the goals and demeanour of slaves and their descendants.

The role of Christian missions is intimately implicated in the westernization of Africans. The involvement of literacy in this process, together with the external and interiorized changes in ethnic and cultural identity among sectors of Jamaica-based society are issues crucial to the psychology and social formation of classes in colonial territories. The bases of later social differentiation in a colonial society are already evident in, though not determined by, the differences between life in crowded huts on large sugar estates served by hundreds of slaves as against estates with smaller slave cohorts, just as it is between slaves who were able to amass earnings and those who were destitute during their servitude. In order to flesh out and contextualize Monteath's data, and to analyse tendentious issues of class formation and class attitudes, as well as black–white religious, sexual and social relationships, one has had to have recourse to external sources, both primary and secondary, of a social, demographic, religious and economic nature, as well as to oral interview data and mail discussion.

This study may well be called "The Life and Times of Archibald John Monteath", and there may be an argument for ending the analysis in 1864 when Archibald died. But I have found it helpful to extend my concerns to events and conditions up to 1870, in order to glean, from the western side of Jamaica, the harsh ecological and economic conditions that helped to fuel the urgency of the folk in the eastern parish of St Thomas whose rioting in 1865 led to as savage a response from the authorities as the uprising of 1831–32 started in the western parish of St James. The years immediately following Archibald's passing also witnessed the demise of his wife and several of his associates. This microstudy of the life and times of a significant individual allows us to traverse from life in one West African society to life in the plantation and pen-keeping socio-economic constructs of the Caribbean and to sharpen our understanding of the minutiae of human relations during a seminal period of our history and social formation.

2

Aniaso

Ethnic Identity

ARCHIBALD MONTEATH INITIATES HIS narrative by stating his personal name as Aniaso, spelled Aneaso in the texts. Four of the five extended accounts of Aniaso's life begin with lineage information, memories of some of the beliefs and customs in Igboland and an outline of his capture and enslavement. These are all very significant data even if they are somewhat compromised by the difficulty of Igbo words being rendered in German and English spellings, the constraints of the memoir format and Aniaso's memory deficiencies after an approximately fifty-year separation from his origins.

Ibo, or Ebo, now preferably spelled Igbo, is the collective name given to a large number of human settlements with high population density in present-day southeastern Nigeria. Perhaps because the term "Igbo" was used by indigenes and because local usage became reinforced by the conventions of ethnic naming and ethnic consolidation established by Europeans,[1] our subject, Aniaso, identified himself ethnically as Igbo, giving no further indication of the district or village from which he came. The Igbo-speaking area lies to the east of the River Niger and inland from the Bight of Biafra. The Igbo heartland, that is, the location of its oldest settlements and securest self-conscious Igbo identity, lies in the Awka–Orlu–Okigwe triangle of north central Igboland. The Anang, Ibibio, Ijaw and Ogoni peoples occupy the coastal strip along the Bight, but in-migrations, out-migrations, and trade interactions over centuries between these peoples and the hinterland Igbo-speaking communities have led to uncertainties, both within the pertinent geographical area and in the West Atlantic, as to the ethnic and even linguistic identity of various communities in and around the Igbo-speaking collectivity.[2] Since the eighth century, Igbo have also migrated westwards across the Niger, interacting there with the Edo or Bini peoples of Benin.[3] The lack of cohesion among the Igbo-speaking peoples seems to be traceable to the non-development throughout their linguistic area of centralized rulership with its attendant administrative and ritual networks. This segmentation and stateless structure has characterized their civic organization with the exception of three institutions: the ritual authority of the Nri priesthood beyond the town of Nri itself, dating from the tenth century;[4] the trade and religious networks established by the Aro peoples and spread throughout the southern Igbo-speaking region from the late seventeenth century till the late nineteenth;[5] and the culture of kingship among the western Igbo under the influence of the Benin kingdom as of the eighteenth century.

While there existed and still exists a problematic with regard to which geographical groups self-identify as Igbo, the term itself has been used for centuries as an ethnonym within West Africa. Its first written occurrence dates from the early years of the 1600s,[6] and there is ample evidence of its use by Europeans. Dating from about the ninth century, it also occurs among Igbo-speaking and Yoruba-speaking communities as well.[7]

The Homeland: Its Physical Characteristics

Aniaso came from the region of the *uwa* or world called *igbo* or "hinterland; forested area". Thus the ethnonym "Igbo" most likely means "people of the forested interior".[8] Here the land grew crops "very much the same as here in Jamaica; yams, potatoes, Indian Corn".[9] Of these, yams were the prize crop of men,[10] while women tended vegetables, white maize and cocoyam or *ede*, a small tuber used as the carbohydrate base of a meal but also useful in thickening soups and sauces.[11] It is significant that Aniaso did not mention cassava, a root crop introduced by the Portuguese from South America to the Biafran coast in the late sixteenth century, and which grows well in less fertile soil and "with less labour and skill" than is required for successful yam cultivation.[12] Perhaps it had not yet reached inland to Aniaso's people, but even if it had, it was clearly not a staple or a prestige food, for it "was never ritualized by the Nri. Cassava was an effective substitute for yam as a means of subsistence, but it was not an effective substitute for wealth."[13] Communities held annual yam festivals and titles and chieftaincies were named in reverence to yam. Aniaso also mentions "leaning on a Kenepp tree",[14] though the 1865 version indicates he "lay down under a large tree".[15] However, the kenep does not grow in Igboland. Kenep is the Arawak name

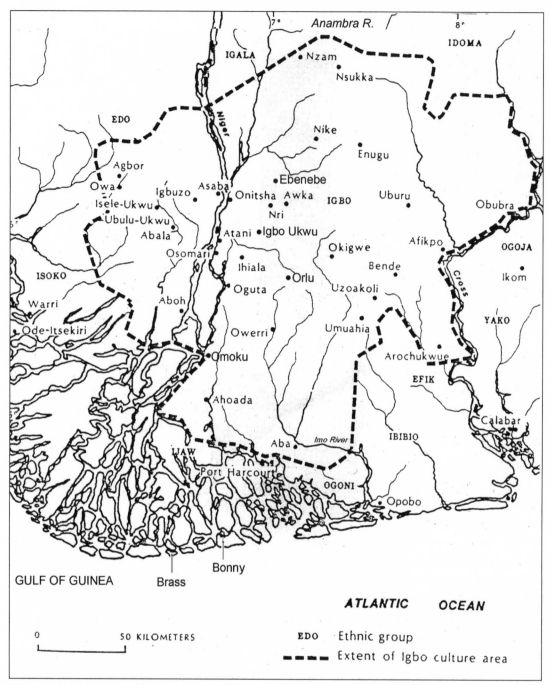

Map 2 Igboland. Miers and Roberts, *The End of Slavery in Africa.*

for a South American tree, *Melicoccus bijugatus (Sapindaceae)*, known in several islands of the eastern Caribbean as "kinep"/"kenep", "kenepa" or "canop", in Trinidad as "chenette", and in Jamaica as "guinep". The fruit, borne in bunches on a tall, shady tree, is small and round "with a tough, green skin and a single hard seed covered by scanty, slippery, pleasant-tasting, salmon-coloured flesh".[16] The fruit most like this in Igbo country would be the *utu*, which bears a fruit with a pinkish shell on the outside while the inside is pulpy and the seed within brownish. This is clearly a case where the narrator arrived at a correspondence rather than an identical correlate.[17]

Family Names

The subject's personal name is spelled "Aneaso" in the 1853 Kummer version,[18] though in *Periodical Accounts* (1865) and in Harvey and Brewin (1867), it is printed as "Ancass", which may have resulted from a misreading of the handwriting in the original German. *Anaso*, meaning "as Earth forbids", is a common name in the Awka–Nri area,[19] while *Anyaaso*, "outrage, eyesore", is a name specifically associated with the Ihiala area.[20] These two names are not far removed from the most likely form – *Aniaso*, "what the land forbids/detests", that is, *nso*, "that which is to be avoided or that which if done, said or seen defiles the doer".[21] The Earth forbids sacrilege or outrage and the principal ideology of Nri culture was opposition to ritual and religious "abomination". The name is therefore a moral exhortation that the child should avoid what Ani, Earth, prohibits, and the highly religious direction which Aniaso assumed as his life's calling should be understood as his approach to realizing the injunction declared by his given name. At the same time, the name could also be *Aniazor*, "Earth saves". The Earth is not only a physical entity but also carries a powerful spiritual force in traditional Igbo religious understanding, as it is believed to regulate individual and therefore societal behaviour. Earth is a female *alusi* or supernatural force to whom the following actions are anathema: incest, murder, stealing and poisoning. Other meanings associated with Ani include names such as *Anazo*, an abbreviation of *anazo ba*, "let Ana prosper/save". *Ani* is the variant word for Earth in the Awka–Nri and Enugu regions; it is *Aana* in Ihiala and *Ala* in Abia, Ebonyi and Imo of northeast Igboland. Other possible interpretations of the name include *Anaaso*, a common name meaning "(when) we fear/respect", as in the phrase *anaaso Chukwu*, "it is God that we fear, (not you)",[22] while with a different tonal contour[23] *anaaso* can mean "when we are happy", identifying a child born during a major festival.[24]

In the Kummer version there is a dash where Aniaso's father's name should go, which implies either some uncertainty on Aniaso's part or a memory lapse that remained unfilled. On the other hand, Aniaso's father's name is rendered as "Durl" in the initial German version and in the 1865 and 1867 translations. But "Durl" carries a non-Igbo phonological sequence of the consonants r and l, so the word is a misrepresentation of the original. But it may have been that a blot of ink in the earlier manuscript had coalesced the final u into an l. Or perhaps the difficulty of deciphering [r] from [l] in many African pronunciations may have confused the amanuensis whose rl spelling must have signalled some wavering on the writer's part as regards choice between the two liquid consonants, while a throaty colouring of back [l] or flapped [r] and the [u] following must have caused the final vowel to have been heard as elided. Thus this name may have been *Dulu,* "lead, be in the forefront". However, every Igbo speaker recognizes this word to have been *Duru.* In Imo–Owerri, a more southerly region than that from which Aniaso came, *Duru* is itself a male title substituting for the titled status of *ozo.*[25] One ascended to the *ozo* title by way of other intermediate titles, since that title marks the highest rank accorded Igbo males, except among the eastern Igbo settlements around the Cross River that are matrilineal. In Ihiala, which is within the zone from which Aniaso originated, *Duru* is a princely proper name, but it is also used as a title there. When used as a title, the bearer would be greeted in the following manner: his fan of animal hide, an insignia of his high position, would be touched three times by another titled man's fan, then the two would verbally greet each other and then they would each call the other's title name, the latter a procedure that would be repeated several times.[26] *Duru* also obtains as a proper name in the Isuama (Okigwe–Orlu–Owerri) area, east and southeast of the Awka–Nri area. All said, Aniaso's father appears from his name, whether as title or personal name, to have been an individual of importance and to have come from an elite family. Given the royal associations of the name or title *Duru,* Aniaso's father was a man of worth, though obviously he did not command the same status as his father-in-law.

In all versions, Aniaso's mother's name is given as Dirinejah. If, as in German orthography, the letter j represents [y], as in "yam", then the name could have been *Derenneya,* "stay for mother; give mother company",[27] suggesting that this child was born after the loss of others and was particularly precious. A similar meaning emerges in the abridged name *Dili* meaning "stay with us".[28] But if j is interpreted as indicating [j], as in "judge", the name may have been *Diriji,* "the wife who was married with income realized from yam", because *Diji* was among the yam titles taken by individuals who owned large land acreages and were able to grow in one season either thousands of yams or many varieties of the crop. It is also possible that her father's attribution was *Dinri,* that is, "Nri's lord or husband", to reflect not only his

Figure 2.1 Entrance to chief's compound. From Basden, *Among the Ibos of Nigeria.*

town of origin, Nri, but also his prominence. In which case, *Nne Dinri,* "mother of Dinri" would signify that the daughter was understood to be a reincarnation of Dinri's mother, just as *Nne Diji* would indicate that the daughter was the reincarnated mother of Diji. Or was the name in question a shortened form of *Oyiridiyah,* "she who bears a striking resemblance to her own husband"? Such a name would have been a pet name or alias.[29] But the name offers other possibilities, including *Dirinije* from the phrase *Kodirinije* from *ka o di(ri) n'ije,* "let it be in the journey; let matters be settled by the journey; let us suspend judgment until a journey has been made". Or it could be a shortened form of a longer name such as *Egodirinije,* "money is in the journey", that is, "there is wealth to be garnered from travel".[30] Yet again, as *Irejina* it would have meant "tongue holds the key to peace/harmony".

Aniaso recalled that his maternal grandfather "was a prince, and the daughter was named after the father".[31] In a patrilineal society a woman was unlikely to have been accorded the name of her father, unless he was particularly great. Such distinction would, in the Nri area, have been accorded to a highly productive farmer, a high-ranking member of the *ozo* society, or a chief priest of a cult, such as the Earth cult. A chief priest, who necessarily holds the *ozo* title and who may be the eldest of his lineage, together with carrying responsibility for the observances due to one or more *alusi,* would be a man of "tremendous political and ritual power and authority".[32] Dirineja's father was clearly a man of very high rank. Was he particularly dedicated to the Earth cult and was Aniaso's name a reflection of an inherited family association?

Nri Socioreligious Foundations

Further helpful information in the initial segment of Aniaso's life story concerns the practice of tattooing the forehead, an honour reserved for "young people, of distinguished parents".[33] This locates Aniaso within the Nri culture area of northern Igboland. The term *Nri* is not only the name of a town, but is also the nomenclature of the highest ritual-political title there, and the designation applied to the subjects of the *Eze Nri* or holder of that office. Further afield, it applied to the lineages on either side of the Niger River settled by migrants from Nri town, such as those located within Awka, Ihiala, Nnewi, Nsukka, Orlu and Udi. *Nri* is also applied to towns founded by the descendants of the first Nri town located south of the Anambra River, the Nri culture having arisen "in the valley of the upper Anambra and diffused southwards by migration".[34] Nri exerted ritual power over its sphere of influence in Igboland. Its ideology rested on pacifism and, since the shedding of blood was anathema, it controlled no army. Rather, its elite males were credited with sacro-political functions such as cleansing persons, places and things from *nso* and *alu* offences, that is, crimes, taboos and "abominations"; negotiating peace between communities; the encoding and dissolution of sacred and secular laws; the ordination of ritual and political officials; the coronation of chiefs; the conferment of the *ozo* title and its symbol of office, the *ofo* staff, which "linked the community with the departed members of the lineage and their ancestral lands";[35] the founding, dissolution and removal of shrines and markets; and promotion of general fertility, especially yam growth.[36] The *ozo*-titled men were furthermore a political elite who were involved in civic and religious deliberations and decision-making, and who carried out administrative and executive functions on behalf of the polity. Few men achieved the heights of the *ozo* title,

> which guaranteed its holder a seat in the governing council of his town and entitled him to certain portions of livestock slaughtered in his lineage and portions of all fees paid by new initiates into the title association. Most importantly, the title exempted its holder from all manual labor. His red cap, decorated with eagle feathers, and his staff of office, or *otonsi*, were immediately recognized anywhere he went. He was greeted with the salutation, "*igwe*" (His Highness).[37]

As titled men, they enjoyed diplomatic immunity in their travels between villages, their external symbols of authority being the *otonsi*, a spear of peace, and their *alo*, a thin staff of wood "symbolizing the power that the lineage received from *Chukwu* during the time of its creation".[38] Nri males both migrated to and were invited to become residents of various villages. "Such an invitation and its acceptance were sealed by a ritual oath between the leaders of the settlement and any Nri man who represented Eze Nri [ruler of Nri]." Such representatives "were the eyes and ears of Eze Nri, who manipulated many aspects of the internal and external affairs of these settlements through them and through visiting Nri".[39] Nri priests not only travelled on ritual business but also took the opportunity to engage in trade, selling elephant tusks, hides, beads, iron spearheads and bronze objects.[40]

However, the maintenance of an Nri political hegemony was limited by a number of factors. Among these were: insufficient manpower to service the client settlements; the distances between the settlements, especially given the slowness and hazards of ambulatory communication via forest paths; the encroachment of militaristic and mercantile ideologies spread by the Aro subgroup of Igbo to the south; and the demographic and political destabiliz-ation wrought by slave-raiders from the river areas as well as by the Aro.[41]

The Significance of *Ichi*

Aniaso was entitled to undergo the *ichi* initiation rite because, he recalled, his mother "was the daughter of a great chieftain".[42] His main claim to aristocracy clearly derived from his maternal line.

The process of inscribing the *ichi* marks is as follows: warm water is first poured on the areas of the body to be scarified in order to minimize the flow of blood. A very sharp razor, apparently at one time a piece of snail shell called *nmanka,* is used to slit the skin. Parallel longitudinal or horizontal slivers of skin were removed, but the design differed from place to place. In towns like Egbu, Oguta and Owa, marks were made around the mouth and neck. At Ebenebe, the skin was slit horizontally on the forehead and accumulated over the eyebrows in a manner similar to that described by Equiano;[43] and interestingly, Aniaso alludes to this design when he described the skin as being "so loosened from the head, that after the healing has taken place the skin hangs over the eyes for a considerable space".[44] In Udi, the entire face was scarified; only the forehead was marked at the neighbouring towns of Ogidi and Umudioka, the latter being famous for its smithing, woodcarving, and *ichi*-carving, all related arts. In fact, the striated effect of *ichi* clearly constitutes an ancient design in the Nri culture since it is to be observed on human forms and other objects in bronze and pottery excavated at Igbo-Ukwu in the Nri area and carbon-dated to AD 850. Late-fifteenth-century objects excavated at the Nri-related town of Ezira also bear *ichi* marks.[45]

After the skin carving had been done, a liquid known as *mmesi* was applied as a sterilizer, while potassium, *nnu akanwu,* and charcoal or soot were smeared over the wounds as antiseptics. About two days later leaves of plants such as the *nsoopia, utubele, okpokolo* and the *olodu* lily were applied to the wounds to prevent festering and removed about a week later.[46] After the *ichi* had healed, the *nwa ichi,* "sons/children of *ichi*", would be brought into the marketplace to dance wearing *ebu,* bells of dried seeds, and were given gifts. The process took about a month.

Aniaso knew that he was to have undergone the tattooing ritual and looked forward to it even though "the operation is very painful and the loss of blood so great". His views are in line with the traditional perception of *igbu ichi* or *ichi* marks as " 'an emblem of endurance', among the Igbo. . . . Anyone who was to engage in any serious undertaking had to show his capability for endurance, his ability to meet the vicissitudes of life by, first of all, undergoing the excruciating pains which *ichi* entailed."[47] For this reason,

> the suffering subject, for the sake of his honour must not make the slightest noise, or give any token of feeling. After some time, when the wounds have been healed, and the lad comes for the first time into company, there is great rejoicing and festivity. He is highly honoured; receives many presents, and can obtain any rich woman whom he desires, for his wife.[48]

It is of interest that Olaudah Equiano who had published his *Interesting Narrative* in 1789 also mentioned this ritual of young manhood. In the part of Igboland from which both Equiano and Aniaso came, this facial scarification was called *ichi* and was a necessary prelude to the taking of the highly regarded *ozo* title in adulthood. Of this leadership system Equiano had this to say:

> My father was one of those elders or chiefs . . . styled Embrenché, a term . . . importing the highest distinction, and signifying . . . a *mark* of grandeur. . . . Those Embrenché or chief men decided disputes and punished crimes, for which purpose they always assembled together.[49]

The Igbo word for "men bearing *ichi* marks", which Equiano tried to represent by the spelling "embrenché", was *mgburichi,* in currently accepted orthography. The applicant for such a title needed to be "free from any social stigma – he should neither be an outcast, *osu,* nor a slave, *ohu*; he should hail from a responsible family and should not be morally depraved".[50] The cost of paying the surgical artists or *nneni* was also substantial enough to debar poor persons from engaging in this ritual. In some communities wives were also expected to receive *ichi* like their

Figure 2.2 Nri elder with *ichi* marks, 1994.

husbands. Select other women also took *ichi,* for instance, the first daughter born to an *eze,* "ruler", after his ascension to the throne, and women who were earmarked for very high office.

Because one's status in the community hinged on this ordeal, Aniaso indicated that to fail meant either to die from loss of blood or to deserve derision for the rest of one's life. He described the half-hour to hour-long ceremony as being performed in the open air in the midst of a large circle of onlookers. "When several youths of good family attained the age of early manhood, great festivities took place. A plot of ground was cleared, levelled and covered with mats, and a hole dug to receive the blood."[51] Then when the operation was finished, "the wounds were rubbed with powder and salt, and to the one tattooed was given a piece of yam or corn cake".[52] Aniaso's enthusiasm with regard to taking *ichi* marks is an index of how keenly he was aware of his social standing in his home community; he recognized that he was born into leadership and that, on both his mother's and father's sides, he was marked as a person of honour and prestige. As he grew older, he found the means to embody and enact this family and community responsibility, and although he did not make the overt connections in his autobiography, as reported, the significances he attached to the ordeal as a badge of honour help account for his mentioning it at all, especially as it was not a culturally acceptable practice to his European listeners and was not, on the surface, an aspect of his spiritual journey. However, the fact that he devoted some time to this subject in his reminiscences obliges us to attend to the meaning of this ceremony within the terms of his natal society.

Captivity

As we are aware even today, children become easy prey for adults who seek to exploit their gullibility, their trust and their thirst for novelty. Aniaso knew no reason to distrust a young man who was recognized as a visitor to his family's compound, apparently in quest of marriage with one of Aniaso's sisters. This young man invited Aniaso to accompany him to a large marketplace; he was able to describe it so vividly that the little boy was enticed to leave his father's compound without having had the time or the thought to say that he was going on an outing.

Rather than proceeding directly to the sea, it would appear that the destination of Aniaso's kidnapper was the inland lake at Oguta. From the inland town or village in the Nri culture zone to which Aniaso belonged, there was more than one route by which Aniaso and his kidnapper might have reached Oguta on his way to the Bight of Biafra. According to Kummer's account, it took a little over one day for them to walk to the

Figure 2.3 *Tenth-century pot excavated at Igbo-Ukwu and bearing* ichi *striations.*

waterfront, though the 1865 account makes it longer: "We walked all that day . . . and our journey continued all the next day."[53] Either way, by calibrating on the basis of this general timeline, elders at Nri town in 1994 suggested to me that Aniaso's point of departure was one of the villages in the Nri area. From there the kidnapper led him to Ihiala, then Amorka and then to Oguta. Another route may have taken him from Umudioka, say, to Ihiala, a distance of 40 miles, which would have occupied one day's journey of twelve hours. Then they would have passed through Uli, on to Egbu and then reached Oguta – this second segment of the journey requiring about six hours' walking. But he may also have been taken to Onitsha, the large market town on the banks of the Niger, via either Nnewi or Ozobo or Oba. Ihiala, for instance, is less than a day's walk from Nnewi and the whole journey from Ihiala to Onitsha would have taken one and a half days.

Initially, one might speculate that his captor was not in regular slaving business – in that case he would have linked up with other captives and a posse of captors on his way to Oguta. On the other hand, he may have been a small-time operator garnering one person at a time and gradually building up capital. That this may not have been his first outing of this type or certainly that he was part of a network of trading allies is suggested by the fact that he knew where he could find hosts with whom to overnight. So he may have been secretly recruited by the Aro traders who specialized in securing captives for the slave trade. But he was known and apparently trusted in Aniaso's village, so he may have had an alibi for his periodic disappearances, such as trade in metal or agricultural goods, because he would have needed to account for his absence from his village at the same time that the disappearance of the boy had taken place. One assumes that by the rules of exogamous marriage in Igboland, he belonged, not to Aniaso's village, but to a neighbouring settlement. Some present-day Igbo commentators think that the captor may not have returned to his neighbourhood. But perhaps abductions were frequent enough not to draw particular suspicion in his direction, and if we take into account the capture of Equiano in that general vicinity some forty years previously, in the 1750s, then perhaps the incidence of kidnapping was sufficiently frequent and yet, on the other hand, haphazard. In any case, the fact that "persons who met us often asked the man what he was going to do with the boy he had with him, whether he was intending to sell him",[54] infers that minors in the company of persons for some reason not recognized as parents attracted the suspicion that they were innocent victims of abduction, and that this was a common enough occurrence. For instance, an English sea captain who traded out of the Benin and Biafran coasts between 1786 and 1800 took note of the large quantity of Igbo shipped across the Atlantic in the late eighteenth century.[55] In fact, slave trading out of the Niger Delta had become a vigorous business since the seventeenth century, and while the riverside chiefs and would-be chiefs attended to the sale and transporting of unfortunates down the great waterway and its many tributaries, hinterland peoples were drawn in as suppliers for the trade. Thus Aniaso himself must have been one of the many victims of the infiltration of the Aro subgroup into the Igbo heartland during the eighteenth century. That heartland lay in close proximity to the densely populated Awka–Nri region. Aniaso's entrapment was an instance of the insidious corrosion of Nri idealism by the Aro mercantilist *raison d'être*. Such kidnappings were an ancilliary mode to the militaristic raiding that they launched against village settlements. By these strategies of overt and covert aggression, they furthered their trading enterprises, foremost among which was that of slave supplying to the Atlantic trade.[56] The Aro handled some 70 per cent of the captives of the Biafran slave trade, while more than 85 per cent of all the Aro captives resulted from "the efforts and exploitations of individual Aro scattered in permanent settlements".[57]

Whatever the case, Aniaso's kidnapper might have resorted to little-used paths, where possible, to avoid detection. But to have kidnapped the only son of a family was a dastardly act. As his father's heir, Aniaso's abduction rendered the family not only bereft of one of its younger generation, but also bereft of a future lineage head. Furthermore, the implications for Aniaso's mother were not only emotional but status-related as well, for the boy's removal is likely to have increased the possibility of his father taking another wife in order to improve the chances of male succession. In this connection, one wonders whether this act was not political and intended to belittle the family: there may have been some jealousy or inter-clan rivalry between the captor's family and Aniaso's parentage, some intrigue of which the little boy was unaware.

Or was the kidnapping an act of revenge or a subterfuge by which the criminal sought to realize some capital? Was there a connection between the kidnapping and the fact that the captor was a suitor for the hand of one of Aniaso's sisters, or appeared to be a suitor, given the 1865 interpretation that he was "a young man" who "began to pay us frequent visits, under pretence of wishing to marry one of my sisters, but in reality, doubtless, with a view

Figure 2.4 A nineteenth-century river crossing, southern Nigeria. From *Church Missionary Intelligencer* 10 (1859).

to getting possession of me, a growing, healthy boy"?[58] This must have been an explanation that issued from discussions Aniaso doubtless had on countless occasions with his countryfolk in exile in Jamaica. Given the family's high social standing, the dowry for the young girl would have been high, if the young man were seriously inclined. Did this suitor therefore seek to make himself worthy of this alliance by accessing some quick money? Or was the realization of a dowry his intention at all? Or was it the accumulation of capital for some other purpose? The fact that he mentioned to inquiring persons that his captive was "a great man's son"[59] may have been his way of ratcheting up the price he hoped to get. Or perhaps he had gleaned that his bid for Duru's daughter was likely to have been unsuccessful and he was avenging his resentment in this way. And was Aniaso deliberately removed before the visible sign of his aristocracy was indelibly stamped on his face, alerting all who saw him to the oddness of his displacement along forest paths and thus hastening his rescue? And might it have been considered an advantage to sell him without such marks, since these were not prized by the Europeans? In any case, the possession of *ichi* marks could make for disruptive behaviour on the part of Igbo captive cohorts on board ship, as reported by Captain Adams, because the Africans, even after reaching the West Atlantic,[60] retained attitudes of respect and deference toward persons of honour in their home societies. Feelings of outrage at the dishonouring of nobles obviously unsettled the rank and file on board ship.[61] Perhaps word had gone out to the kidnappers that *mgburichi* were therefore not favoured by ship captains. Furthermore, if Aniaso's tattooing was imminent, his kidnapper may have reckoned that the month it would have taken to allow Aniaso to go through the ceremony and recuperate from his wounds would have made him miss the sale, if he had information that the boats were ready to be loaded.

Trade Routes

For Aniaso, one of the most striking aspects of his dislocation was the impact on his psyche of the change in physical environment. Hitherto his consciousness had been shaped by the topography of town or village clearings with their interconnected dirt paths and surrounded at their margins by tropical rainforest. His journey from that comfort zone brought the shock of vistas of expansive waterways and heaving market crowds. This marked his passage from the world of *igbo* to the world of *olu* or *oru,* that is, water territory. He recalled, for instance, that at the waterside marketplace "I saw a great many things I had never seen before, and which greatly astonished me; but most of all was I pleased with the great water, the ocean . . . I was filled with astonishment to see the boats floating on the water, and most of all to see the great water itself."[62] The 1865 account reads:

> What most of all attracted my attention and filled me with intense awe and admiration was the wide expanse of the ocean, to which there seemed no bounds at all; its smooth surface was dotted here and there with numerous boats belonging to some vessels, riding at anchor at a small distance from the shore. Overwhelmed with the impression caused by this magnificent sight, I lay down under a large tree, and gazed on the scene with indescribable delight.[63]

This first "great water" that Aniaso would have encountered was very likely the lake at Oguta whose waters spread as far as eye could see. It was, and yet was not, strictly speaking, as the 1864 and 1865 texts say, "a trading-place on the coast".[64] It was not on the sea coast of the Bight of Biafra. Rather, Oguta Lake is fed by the River Ulasi or Orashi, also called Engenni, and Oguta stands on the estuary of the Ulasi and the mighty Niger River pouring from the savannah lands of northwestern West Africa. The lake therefore provided a deep-draught port where European vessels discharged their goods and refilled. It was one of the interconnected market towns on the Orashi or Engenni River linking towns such as Idu, Kregeni, and Omoku to delta ports like Bonny and New Calabar.[65] As such, Oguta attracted sellers of slaves, palm oil and oil-palm kernels who were paid with guns, gunpowder, flint, salt, soap, snuff, cowries and manufactured cloth.

As of the sixteenth century provisioning was "a significant economic activity" that accompanied the trade in slaves from hinterland regions to the coast downriver along the Niger; it was a lucrative "trade in yams, palm oil, maize, and other foodstuffs normally taken by European ships' captains for the sustenance of crews and slaves when ships were anchored on the coast and during the middle passage".[66] For instance, a teenage sailor on a slave ship between 1800 and 1804 described the meal regime for the slaves:

> Every morning, at eight o'clock, they are all brought on deck, when, to every six of them is set down a wooden dish containing a sufficient quantity of boiled rice, beans, or Indian corn, as the case may be, mixed with palm oil ... with which they season all their victuals, – besides two gills of fresh water each. At four in the afternoon, they get a similar mess, and go below.[67]

Among the preparations for the voyage out of Africa, he also mentions the ship's loading up of "as much fresh water, fire-wood, sheep, goats, young pigs, and poultry for the use of the cabin and sick slaves, as we had stowage for".[68]

In addition to supplying the overseas market, large trading posts all along the Niger serviced the local inland trade in goods such as "gunpowder, flints, yams, beads . . . iron bars . . . knives, rice, goats, fowls, calabashes, mats, country beads, horses and ivory . . . kola nuts, guns . . . cottons, rum, looking-glasses, palm oil, dogs . . . livestock [and] red wood".[69] Transportation of slaves, livestock and agricultural goods was carried out by chiefs and merchants who owned fleets of large war and trading canoes, and who employed their relatives, sons-in-law and eunuchs to conduct this long-distance river trade on their behalf. Such boats could carry as many as seventy people at a time; and if large quantities of goods were being moved, the boats travelled in flotillas of several hundreds, accompanied by well-armed canoes to protect them against water-pirates.[70]

In one version of his tale, Aniaso mentions the "busy turmoil and abundant show of attractive articles of merchandise" that "had at first quite a bewildering effect on me", so much so that the country bumpkin needed "much persuasion" to be induced "to mix with the crowd, and gaze on the wonderful objects exposed to view".[71] Amid this novelty Aniaso would have been boarded onto a small boat that ferried cargo to the large ships. The ships then sailed down the Niger and through the Niger Delta, exiting into the Bight of Biafra in the Gulf of Guinea at either Elem Kalabari (New Calabar) or Bonny. Given the fact that Bonny lies to the east of New Calabar and therefore further away from the westerly direction that the boat would eventually take, it seems quite possible that Aniaso's vessel may have called at New Calabar before putting out to sea. This is very plausible because the Orashi/Engenni River flows through Oguta Lake and then joins the New

Figure 2.5 A creek in the Niger Delta. From Allen, *Picturesque Views on the River Niger.*

Calabar River on which New Calabar stands, the river itself being a north–south tributary of the Niger. The Orashi/Engenni River was one of the main routes that allowed New Calabar to dominate important commercial networks within its hinterland.[72] Oguta itself, together with Abo, Aro, Onitsha and Osomari were "the most outstanding examples" of "initially non-Igbo societies" that absorbed many migrant Igbo and some of their cultural hallmarks.[73] Aniaso had been caught in the web of Aro trading contacts feeding captives into the Atlantic supply routes.

A Child Enslaved

While we remain unsure of the captor's motive or motives, Aniaso's account certainly furnishes much evidence of his own naivety. Such evidence suggests that he was both visibly and mentally a child when he was enslaved. Not only does he appear to know only superficially his society's customs and beliefs, but the manner of his abduction reveals the trusting nature of a child towards a familiar, who easily lured him from home by promises of a treat for his eyes. He did not therefore realize that he was being abducted, never tried to abscond from his "companion and guide", did not question the length of his journey through the forests, overheard suggestive conversations about enslavement yet his curiosity about these allusions does not appear to have concretized into real fear or suspicion. He was merely "struck by the circumstance" of inquiries about the likelihood of his being sold.[74] The 1853 account expresses this with greater immediacy, for it is only when he is physically seized to be put aboard a boat that scepticism yielded to certainty: "Now I immediately knew that I would be made a slave, for I remembered that during the whole day I had frequently heard, when my guide was asked; – 'What are you going to do with boy; Sell him?['] say in reply; 'Oh no; he is a great man's son!'" To crown his guilelessness, he was simpleton enough to send parting regrets to his father by the same person who had so heartlessly deceived him in the first place:

> The man who had brought me from home and sold me to the traders looked on unmoved as I was hurried to the water's edge, and I could only implore him to take a last message to my dear father, letting him know what had become of me.[75]

"Experiences" lingers on the scenario of betrayal:

> Then a strange man came up to me and said: Come, my boy, come into my boat and try to pilot it on the water. I drew back and answered: No, that I won't do! However, in that same second the man grabbed me with his strong hand and I was carried by force in to the boat. Now it was clear that I had been betrayed by my guide and had been sold as a slave; my guide stood calmly on the shore and watched while I was carried away. I rushed to call to him to ask him at least to greet my father and tell him what had become of me. I screamed and cried, as did the other poor blacks whom I saw in the boat, some already bound and some arriving after me in chains.[76]

Kummer's account abbreviates the event: "[w]hen the right man came along, he sold me, and I could do nothing but call to him; 'tell my father where I am, and salute him'".[77] The sending of greetings to absent relatives or associates was the normal and appropriate behaviour expected in contexts of parting. Of course, for his abductor to have delivered such a message would have amounted to an admission of guilt in the terrible affair. On the other hand, one observes that by the time, almost fifty years later, when Aniaso recounted these events pains were taken either by himself or his amanuenses to conceal the deceiver's name, which surely Aniaso must have known, given his familiarity with that individual.

Aniaso's childlike behaviour at that turning point in his life is reinforced when he speaks of the ease with which he fell asleep:

> When the boat put off for the ship I was so exhausted with crying, that the gentle rocking motion lulled me into a sound sleep, from which I awoke to find that we were being lifted into the vessel.[78]

Kummer records: "I was frightened and wept a little, but soon comforted myself, because I was fond of sailing in the boat. The other slaves screamed loud, and would neither eat nor drink. I however soon fell asleep."[79] Just as his understanding of his abduction was shallow, so was his consciousness of the separations that he was undergoing in those moments. In like childishness too was the rapidity with which his attention was distracted by novelty:

> When I awoke I saw a large ship before me. I was not a little astonished to see such a beautiful house floating on the water; and when I was put on board nothing surprised me more, than to see the Captain with white face and hands, and with shining black feet without toes; (he wore boots).[80]

Much later, probably months after, on arrival at port in Jamaica, his truculent behaviour and the reluctant but placatory response of the captain are reminiscent of an adult's reaction to a child's tantrums:

> We lay in the harbour about six weeks; as yet I had never got on shore, which I wished very much to see. I then said to the Captain; "Let me go on shore!" he answered, "No you shall remain with me and be my servant!" I answered, "No! That I do not wish, I want to go on shore, if you will not let me go, I will jump overboard." In the afternoon the Captain consented.[81]

Given the childlike behaviour of Aniaso as evidenced in his account of his kidnapping and sale at the Igbo waterside, my own estimate of his age at that time is nine or ten. In other words, my supposition is that Aniaso had been born around 1792. He himself supposes that he was about ten or twelve years old when he was seized.[82] Both his biography and his tombstone, however, read that he was born in Africa in 1799. Such a date seems to me unlikely. It would mean that he would have arrived in Jamaica around 1808, so that he would only have known John Monteath who bought him and who died in 1815 for about six or seven years. This conflicts somewhat with the timeline of his story. Another investigator too detects that in this matter, "Archibald's chronology cannot be reconciled".[83] And even earlier, Thomas Harvey had made a footnoted revision to the 1799 date, suggesting rather that it "evidently ought to be 1789",[84] clearly in realization that the nature, length and quantity of events which occupy the subject's childhood dictate the allowance of a longer period for their realization; Harvey thus calculated Archibald was about ten years older than the apparently accepted hypothesis.

Aniaso reports that he and about eleven other boys travelled across the Atlantic in the captain's cabin and were allowed freedom to play and move about. This fact alone suggests that he was so young that he was considered as non-threatening. This aspect of slave ship protocol is mentioned in the fragment of the biography of Florence Hall, also an Igbo. She attempts to account for her youthfulness at the time of her capture in her home village by referring to herself as "still unclothed". As a pre-menstruating girl, she would have worn no cloth, perhaps only a string of beads on her hips, whereas as a pubescent young woman from her waist to below her pubes would have been covered with a *jigida* made of rows of coloured beads. Continuing her reference to their clothing practices, she complained: "The white people . . . stripped us of all our beads, and shells, and while the naked children were permitted to walk about the ship, the men & women were chained and kept in darkness below."[85]

Like Akeiso or Florence Hall, Aniaso was pre-adolescent. Their youthfulness confirms a "striking feature" of the slave trade in the last quarter of the eighteenth century and continuing into the nineteenth: it was not only that "more females, in particular more women, left Bonny and New Calabar than left Old Calabar", but also that "among males [there was] the move to more boys".[86] The voyage would have lasted anywhere between seventy-eight days, as was the case with the *Fredensborg*,[87] to three months.

Having reached the ship's destination, the captain seemed to have had no intention of letting him land in Jamaica. When Aniaso's curiosity got the better of him however, he harassed the captain to let him go ashore. In any case, being a child of *igbo* and terra firma, he must have felt quite uncomfortable about prolonging his stay on the unstable element of water. But might it also have been that Aniaso's young shipmates were among the last to be sold off and that he felt afraid of being abandoned by his new friends? Whatever the emotional dynamics of the situation, we are given the impression that, wearied by the boy's insistence, the captain ceded to his wishes. However, another possibility is that, unknown to him, Aniaso had

Figure 2.6 A slave market in Zanzibar, East Africa, 1872. From Davidson, *Africa: History of a Continent*.

become the private acquisition of the ship's captain, which is why the captain insisted that Aniaso should stay with him and be his servant. But he may have wished to retain him for disposal in England, following the custom whereby "captains of slaving vessels often sold their black servants to wealthy families when they embarked again for Africa". During the eighteenth century, the English elite flaunted black servants as an "index of rank" and "[s]mall black boys occupied a special position as exotic ornaments. They were the favourite attendants of the great ladies and courtesans of the period."[88] Indeed, it was generally the case that some of the ship's crew acquired goods and persons during their African stay which they used for private sale in other ports.[89] Furthermore, "up to 20 per cent of slaves on any shipment were sold by slave captains and crews as part of their commission for making the voyage from Africa".[90]

3

Toby of the
Monteaths

THE AUTOBIOGRAPHIES SAY LITTLE about the details of Aniaso's career under slavery and the nature of his work regimes. The outlines of his working life are sketchy, but some of the accounts in his narrative bear elaboration by bringing external evidence to bear on the almost non-existent internal references to his working life. In the initial section of the chapter, we consider some of the events in his Jamaican estate experience and the timeline he sets up for them. While some of these events are not easy to verify in their point of detail, the general thrust of his biography points to as trustworthy a narrator as an individual's perspective can be.

Jamaica, Bound

Aniaso says that the ship which brought him to Jamaica dropped anchor at Kingston, the island's commercial capital. So far it has not been possible to locate the date of his arrival in Jamaica: there is no documentation concerning John Monteath's purchase of a batch of about twelve slaves. Aniaso gives this as the number of slaves purchased by a factor on behalf of John Monteath from the same shipment, a purchase effected during the sixth week of the ship's presence in Jamaican waters. One has also investigated whether John Monteath received a deed of gift of a dozen or so slaves, but again there is no evidence of this in the records. What may, however, be pertinent in explaining this lack of evidence is that cash or vendue sales of slaves were not recorded, further to which, sales made privately, rather than between shipping companies and merchant companies, are difficult to locate.[1] Captain Ferentz of the Danish ship *Fredensborg,* which anchored on 9 July 1768 at St Croix, helpfully reports on the occurrence of these transactions that left no paper trail: "yesterday all the slaves have been sold privately, though it is unknown to me at what price, to whom and in what way. At the last meeting of the [ship's] Council it was decided, if possible, to sell all the slaves privately, in order to receive cash payment and thus free us from risk", that is, the risk of exposure to purchasers with spurious or unreliable credit notes.[2] It is clear that the cohort of approximately a dozen enslaved persons that included Aniaso was sold very late in the ship's stay in harbour, which suggests that their prices were depreciating. This was to the advantage of the buyer and what is more, he was purchasing in bulk – a further inference of good market strategy. Such a purchase would have been attractive to an investor who was just starting to build up his labour force.

Aniaso claims that the boat remained for six weeks in harbour before he was put ashore. One may question the accuracy of this timeline, since one would wonder how and why a child would calculate the length of a stay with such a level of precision, unless he had asked an adult to do the computation. One doubts whether he did put such a question, and who such an adult would have been. However, it does emerge that slave ships stayed several weeks in harbour before they set sail once more, since both the off-loading and on-loading processes lasted several weeks.[3] When the sale of slaves required a stay of some three months, their price by this time could be some £10 less than what was being asked at the start.[4] However, in the second half of the eighteenth century sale prices in the western end of the island were higher than those being asked in Kingston, since "[d]emand was probably higher in the booming new settlements of western and northern Jamaica than in the older and slower growing areas of central and south-eastern Jamaica".[5] Wealthier merchants either got first pick, in terms of quality, of the slave offerings for sale or entered well after the first purchasers and bought up a larger quantity at discounted rates, while smaller buyers got the leftovers from these heavier purchases.

Another doubt may concern whether Aniaso indeed landed at Kingston, since nearer ports in the west were available by the 1790s, at Lucea, Montego Bay and Savanna-la-Mar. Indeed, by 1801 there were Customs at Kingston, Lucea, Montego Bay, Port Antonio and Savanna-la-Mar[6] and by 1808 there were inspectors of new Negroes stationed also at Falmouth, formerly Martha Brae-Point, in the parish of Trelawny.[7] However, it was still the practice for rural-based estate owners to acquire some of their slaves from Kingston. Kingston had been the sole port of entry into Jamaica between 1702 and 1758, but Montego Bay, Port Antonio and Savanna-la-Mar became operational ports after 1758, as did Lucea after 1766.[8] All the same, when one understands

Figure 3.1 Falmouth. Lithograph from photo by Adolphe Duperly, *c.*1845. Courtesy National Library of Jamaica.

that Monteath had merchant uncles at Green Island in Hanover parish in the west, and that they had close links with shipping interests, the probability that Aniaso landed at a northwestern port cannot be discounted. For instance, on Monday 23 December 1776, Captain Fraser of the *Alexander* had for sale at Lucea 325 "choice Eboe" from Calabar,[9] and the following day was the turn of Captain Robert Boyd to display at Montego Bay 473 "choice Eboe" from Bonny.[10] Again, on 18 October 1783, 294 "choice Ebos" were for sale,[11] while a few months later, 590 "choice Africans: Ashantee-Coromantee" were up for the buying.[12] What is more, in the small white world of western Jamaica, the merchant Monteaths would have been close with John Ingram, treasurer for the St James Assembly in 1790 and who was the principal in J. Ingram & Co. which owned ships such as *African Queen, Elizabeth* and *Susannah.* While Ingram & Co.'s *Favourite* brought pitchpine and timber, and others brought flour and rice, their *Philip Stevens* headed back to Liverpool after landing 226 "choice, young, Windward Coast Negroes from Cape Mount".[13]

As to the date when John Monteath acquired Aniaso, one could hazard a guess that this could have taken place around 1802, the period in which Monteath was consolidating his landholdings and residence at Kep Estate on the St Elizabeth/Westmoreland border, and also at the time when he set up house for, and probably also with, Nancy and their three children to date. His first acquisition of slaves in the available records indicates his purchase in May 1800 of a male named Ned from a Hanover-based planter. This was just prior to his buying in mid-August the same year what appears to be his first piece of land, 114 acres. Not surprisingly for someone about to set up his own farming and livestock enterprise, Monteath must have wanted a strong and mature hand, given Ned's handsome purchase price of £125. Monteath's largest recorded cohort of slave purchases comes two years later, in October 1802, when he buys out fifty-two slaves forfeited by James Downie in mortgage default. Downie had been an overseer on Forrest Estate in 1797[14] and had apparently followed the path of proceeding from overseer to slave owner to landowner, but like so many others before and after him, he had fallen into debt. For Downie's slaves, Monteath laid out £4,275 in immediate payment to Thomas William Hardin, deputy marshal for Westmoreland, St Elizabeth and Hanover.[15] So it is possible that around 1802 Monteath needed house servants as well as field hands for his new enterprise and may have been willing to lay out some money for some less expensive young slaves such as Aniaso.

However, as indicated above, it has not been possible to locate a record of John Monteath's purchase of a batch of labourers that might have included Aniaso. The nearest possibility, with regard to numbers, is his purchase of "8 negroes and other slaves" from William Channer of St Elizabeth for £810 on 1 February 1810. But their names are given as Fortune, Parthenea, Blackwall, Hall, Rose, Darcy, Phillis and Emma. No Toby is there, unless Monteath changed a name Channer had already given. Nevertheless, 1810 seems an unlikely date by which he would have acquired Aniaso, as it would mean that the boy would have known Monteath for only five years before Monteath's passing. It would be difficult to square all the events of Aniaso's early estate life with such a short period of time.

Aniaso narrates that his batch of shipmates stayed for eight days at the factor's yard before someone came to fetch them for Mr Monteath. Perhaps this was an aspect of the slave market within the island whereby the initial purchaser bought in bulk and then retailed his stock to secondary buyers.[16] The journey from Kingston, presumably, to Kep may have been either overland or by boat putting in to coastal harbours, but Aniaso says nothing about the length of time it took to travel from the southeastern sector of the island where Kingston lay to John Monteath's southwestern location, nor does he indicate the means by which the journey was made. Having arrived at Kep, Monteath's estate (cited as Krepp in "Experiences"), they were allowed a week's rest. Probably this was a further week in which they were fed, fattened and brought up to strength. Aniaso then indicates that the estate

Figure 3.2 Slave sale, Cuba. From Ortiz, *Los negros esclavos*.

manager, either the attorney but more probably the overseer, took him as his house servant, and that before a year was out, John Monteath made him a house servant at his own home.

As a houseboy, he would have done "odd jobs and errands, helped with the cleaning of plate, harness, and guns, and the grooming of horses".[17] The latter task would have been especially important on a livestock farm such as Kep. He may "also have waited upon the master and his friends when they went out shooting for duck or baldpate pigeon, or into town in the coach-and-four".[18] Given the number of young children in the household of John and Nancy Monteath, Aniaso is also likely to have helped in entertaining the children, including "drawing the cart and horse of '*young massa*' or '*little missas*'".[19] As he says, "we jumped, and danced and romped, and did pretty much as we pleased".[20] In fact, he considered that during this period, "I was treated well there and was loved as the playmate of [the master's] children".[21] He may also have occasionally been deployed on field tasks with the so-called small gang, "employed in carrying grass to the horse-stable in little bundles two or three times a day, and wild vine to the hog-stye in the morning, at noon, and again in the evening".[22]

A Family Heirloom

On being purchased by John Monteath, Aniaso was given the name Toby. We are not told at what stage Toby was moved from domestic duties to full outdoor work. But on growing into his teens, he would likely have joined the "second gang", who did work such as "hoeing the weeds from the grass, clearing corn pieces, shelling corn, etc.". And well before John Monteath died in 1815, he must have already belonged to the "great gang", "consisting of the ablest people" who undertook "the chipping of logwood, making and mending of fences, planting of corn, provisions" and other such physical activity.[23] Without being specific, Archibald refers to the period before he assumed a supervisory role as the time during which he had been "a common field worker".[24]

During the period in which John Monteath was his owner, Archibald recounts that Monteath went to Britain for three years. This was after Archibald had worked for him for eight years. This could have been around 1810. But these dates have been difficult to verify since there are no shipping manifests for the period, and in any case there is no solid reason to lay infallible store by Archibald's three- and eight-year periodizations. Even so, one might wish to query the likelihood of an estate owner absenting himself from his fledgling business for two or three years. Yet if one considers the dates of mortgages devised with relatives and friends in Scotland, and assumes that these agreements, if not drawn up in Glasgow, had been agreed on in Glasgow, then one might deduce that he must have returned to his native country several times between 1800 and 1815. One such deed, the loan from his brother's estate, was contracted in January 1801, another was made in August 1804, and by August 1806 he had co-opted the monies of several Glasgow merchants and manufacturers to purchase further land in the vicinity of Kep. Yet if one seeks consolidated periods of time when he could have been away, we notice that there are gaps in his regiment service between 1801 and 1803, and during 1805–6. Indeed, 1800 was the last year of his service as overseer at Mexico, and he reappears in 1802 as overseer at Font Hill and Hampstead, which suggests that he may in fact have gone back to Scotland in 1801. There is also a noticeable gap in the crop accounts for Font Hill and Hampstead for 1804, and we know that he arranged a mortgage with his sister, Agnes, in August 1804. So he may have been abroad prior to and during the negotiation of this loan. There is a further gap in the crop accounts for Font Hill and Hampstead for 1806, which may suggest the absence of an overseer and/or bookkeeper; and although John Monteath was also attorney for Forest and Grandvale during this time, there might have been some allowance for him to have spent some months away from his supervisory position around 1805. So another absence of several months may thus have fallen between 1805 and 1806, a period during which he engaged a Glasgow consortium in his Jamaica project and during which there is no evidence of other legal contracts being made by him in Jamaica. It is also probable that he took his son James with him to Scotland some time around 1808, since his 1809 will indicates the boy's absence from Jamaica. While it was not unknown for parents to send their children to school in the "Mother Country", having entrusted them to friends travelling by boat, it might have been more likely that Monteath would have wanted to personally introduce his coloured male heir to his friends and family before leaving him there on his own. Archibald's narrative probably consolidates these absences of his master, speaking of them as one absence of three years. Archibald then declares that "not long after" Monteath's return to Jamaica he died. This would suggest that Monteath travelled to Britain between his first major health scare in 1809 and his death in Jamaica in January 1815. He would have had to have been in Jamaica nine months before the birth of his son, John Wilson Monteath, but as we only know the year and not the month of his birth, we cannot date with precision his presence in Jamaica during 1810 and 1811.

Archibald relates that during Monteath's absence, he and other children were sent to stay at Savanna-la-Mar in Westmoreland, "to attend school", he says, in Kummer's version. Here he does not specify whether those other children were slaves as well; but in "Experiences" he speaks of accompanying the master's children "as their servant" and he continues that "we were also supposed to attend church and school". Indeed, Toby had been taken along both as a house servant and as a play companion for Nancy's children – his roles no doubt also at Kep. In fact, the purpose for the removal to Savanna-la-Mar was very likely connected to tutoring of the master's children. Toby would have audited their classes by default merely because he might have been in the vicinity of the classes, not that the teaching was intended for him at all. But he felt in retrospect that "the opportunity [for learning] was offered to me as well". However, he admits that "I had no interest in that . . . I didn't want to hear anything about learning, and during church services I ran around outside in front of the church and enjoyed myself, as the children of the master usually did as well."[25]

One is free to speculate that, as a seaport, Savanna-la-Mar afforded more reliable educational facilities than the Monteath children could access in the rural environment of Kep. John Monteath would have needed to hire a private tutor to educate his children at Kep, whereas a British clergyman, teacher, bookkeeper, or a nanny or nurse may have been resident at Savanna-la-Mar and willing to undertake classes for one or more groups of planters' children. In addition, we may recall that Nancy's mother, together with Nancy's eldest son and daughter were baptized at the Savanna-la-Mar home of a Sarah Wilson in 1817. Nancy's mother, Jannet Ramsay Ford, had herself been born in the environs of Savanna-la-Mar. It is therefore likely that Nancy and her children relocated to Savanna-la-Mar for a period of time to afford the children a better, more concentrated and consistent education than would have been available in the country. Nancy was illiterate and so was not in a

Figure 3.3 Savanna-la-Mar, by Joseph Kidd. Courtesy National Library of Jamaica.

position to coach the children. And if John Monteath intended to introduce his elder son to his family in Scotland he would have had to possess some modicum of formal knowledge and technical skills such as reading, writing and mathematics. It is therefore likely that the Savanna-la-Mar stay must have pre-dated James Monteath's journey to Britain some time before 1809.

The fact that in 1804 John Monteath served as attorney to neighbouring Westmoreland parish estates helps us to make some sense of his assertion in his January 1809 will that he owned a bedstead at the Forest Estate. The estates in question were Grandvale owned by John Cunningham and Forest Estate owned by David Fyffe. Monteath continued as attorney for Forest between 1805 and 1807, and in 1808 he acted as attorney to the trustees of the will of David Fyffe, deceased. Reference to his bedstead at Forest implies that he had lodgings there, especially given that Fyffe had been an absentee landlord since at least the start of the 1780s.[26] His estate house was therefore probably available for Monteath's use. Another likelihood concerns the fact that, in November 1808, in the name of Nancy Monteath, John Monteath purchased a 6-acre property, Whitehouse, immediately south of Grandvale, bounded to the west by the sea and to the northeast by a creek. At the time of this purchase Toby would already have been about sixteen, and too old to have still been serving as a playmate for John's children; it therefore seems that the Savanna-la-Mar stay took place before 1808.

Just before John Monteath's death in 1815, Toby became the property of John's mistress, Nancy Monteath. Toby had not only been bequeathed by John Monteath to his consort, Nancy, in a codicil to his will dated 9 May 1810, together with Judy, Juliet, Beatrice and Richard, but he had been deeded to Nancy by reason of an indenture drawn up on 15 May 1814, several months before John died. The relevant section ceded to Nancy "the following eleven Negroes slaves named Jack Richard Toby Dennis John Jeany Bella Beatrice Rose Juliet Peggy Ann".[27] So even before John Monteath's death, Toby had passed into Nancy Monteath's ownership, which is why his name is not in the 1817 or 1820 Returns of Slaves for Kep. He is, however, listed in the Returns of Rosehall slaves owned by Nancy Monteath. One assumes that Nancy lived with John at Kep, so no physical relocation was effected by John's deeding of Toby to Nancy.

At some point in his ownership by Nancy Monteath, probably after the passing of John Monteath in 1815 and prior to the initial sale arrangement for Kep in 1816, Nancy must have had lodgings built on the neighbouring property of Rosehall. By the time Kep was finally sold in 1819 she would have had time to consolidate a residence and outhouses there. But it appears that Rosehall was in a sense part of the Dumbarton property, or vice versa. Dumbarton, we are told on the St Elizabeth map 805, was the previous name of "Rosehill". Rosehall was the name by which Nancy Monteath's property is recorded in the crop accounts and on St Elizabeth map 965.[28] The name Rose may have indicated a historical link with prior landowners in the vicinity, such as John and Matthew Rose.[29] Yet there may be some link between this name and the name of property owned by the Monteaths in Scotland, given that John's brother, James, is referred to in a nineteenth-century text as "James Monteath Douglas, Esq. of Rosehall and Stonebyres".[30] Its name may therefore have been another instance of the transfer of a Scottish place name to the Jamaican landscape, part of an overall intent to name lands in Jamaica for family property in Scotland. For example, out of the 320-acre parcel of land "in the confine of the parish of Westmoreland . . . known by the name of Kilmarnock",[31] which she had acquired in February 1813, Ann Monteath [Nancy] sold several parcels of land to ex-slaves in the 1830s, including a 14-acre piece to "Archebald John Monteath".[32] And speaking in the 1850s, Archibald refers to having bought his "dwelling place in Rose Hall where I still live with my wife and daughter".[33] In addition, the document of sale in 1832 to Robert Smith "a free black boy" specifies the land under consideration as "30 acres of land part of Rose Hall Plantation".[34] So there was a correspondence, or at least some partial overlap, between Rosehall, Dumbarton and Kilmarnock. It therefore appears that both Rosehall and Dumbarton occupied land of which Kilmarnock was a part, and that Rosehall was a plantation, perhaps for coffee, while Dumbarton must have been the name given to the pen that adjoined it. "Plantation" was, apparently, a term indicating lands "on which are cultivated coffee, pimento, ginger, cotton, arrow-root, and other minor products".[35]

After Monteath's passing in January 1815, Archibald understood himself as belonging to Monteath's son, James. However, Archibald was mistaken on two counts: with regard to the identity of his legal owner, and with regard to the legal owner of the property on which he eventually worked, Dumbarton. As the property of Nancy, then, Toby belonged to the Rosehall cohort of slaves, but was effectively made "head manager" for the adjacent property of Dumbarton, which he understood to be James Monteath's "large property". He might well have thought so, since it is clear that James was his mother's man of business. Not only does his presence figure strongly in the few comments that Archibald makes about his working life and his relationship with his employers, but we also know that James signed documents on Nancy's behalf. James witnessed her mark on land sale documents and also witnessed to the survey diagrams. While for the first Returns of Slaves in 1817, Nancy Monteath's data are signed by her X mark, it appears that in 1820 and 1823 she does sign, but in 1826, already twenty-eight years old, James signs. His younger brother, A.J. Monteith, signs in 1829 when he was twenty-two; and for the last register, in 1832, James Monteith again signs. But, in point of fact, Dumbarton was bought by Ann Monteath from John Monteath's sole executor, Taylor Cathcart, for Jamaican £500 on 28 March 1821. It covered 431 acres.[36] What James acquired for himself was the 200 acre parcel "known by the name of Upland"; that was on 1 January 1825. To acquire this, he paid £400 to the executor, Taylor Cathcart.[37] This parcel, surveyed in February 1823, lay immediately north of the "Dunbarton Settlements". Newspaper advertisements in 1816 for the sale of John Monteath's properties described Upland as a "run of Woodland adjoining Dumbarton, of two hundred and forty acres". So it is quite likely that the adjacency of Dumbarton and the Upland as well as the joint management of the two properties by James blurred the distinction between them. This meant that Archibald perhaps moved residence and work activity between Rosehall, Dumbarton and the Upland with relative ease, concentrating his work regime increasingly on Dumbarton/the Upland as of 1825.

"Head manager" may be understood as "headman" or "head driver", a position of intermediary between the master and his labourers, and which, in a relatively small livestock establishment such as Dumbarton, could substitute for "overseer". The charging of a slave with this responsibility of supervising the labour force had the effect of saving overhead costs. It was a handy device in situations where there were found to be black men capable of leadership and responsibility, for it emerges that drunkenness was the scourge of many white overseers; as such, employment turnover could be high, which led to a restive workforce, on top of which owners had difficulty finding cash with which to pay white employees. "Jamaica was short of working capital, and planters operated in an interlocking web of credit and debt in which cash changed hands infrequently."[38] So the engagement of black overseers was a situation that was not altogether unusual, for "many plantations in Jamaica were practically managed by black men". This aspect of plantation management is confirmed by Augustus Hardin Beaumont, "a Jamaican plantation overseer who testified before the House of Commons Select Committee on Apprenticeship in 1836". Among his statements was one in which he claimed to "have known estates managed for weeks together entirely by the blacks, and very well managed".[39] A contemporary proprietor delineated the work assignments on a pen, such as Kep:

> A certain portion of [the enslaved] belong to the horse-stable, whose duty it is, under the head groom, to bring in the horses for sale in the morning, rub and clean them well down, and go through the various gradations of breaking to the saddle and draft. At the usual periods the horses are fed, watered, and turned into the pastures. These grooms also clean the stable, repair the tackling, twist new ropes, and clean the break and harness; another division belong to the breeding cattle department. All this is under the charge of a trusty and skilful negro, called the *head penn-keeper,* who has several assistants, and a vast number of boys, who scour the pastures, on some old mare or hack, and bring in all stray animals. In the penn-keeper's duty, all milking, dress and curing, breaking of steers to the cart, &c. is included; and it is the province of the head penn-keeper to report to the overseer all increase or decrease of stock, gaps in fences, intrusions from neighbouring cattle, &c.[40]

This hierarchical administrative arrangement made the employee chosen to be driver or head driver an agent of the white authority structure who was in control of all or sections of the estate's enslaved workforce. "There is a *driver* to each gang, and a *driveress* to the small one. The *head driver* is the man responsible for all. To him the overseer looks for the orders being carried into effect."[41] These were positions of privilege, but they could be abrogated if for any reason the master felt that the driver's loyalty to the superstructure was open to question. However, a head driver of many years' experience was "highly respected by all the negroes, his influence among them [being] very great".[42] Another asset that such a person could possess was loyalty. In the case of Archibald, his loyalty had been tested in the 1831–32 upheavals in western Jamaica. These events had clearly demonstrated the trustworthiness of Archibald John Monteath to his owners.

This momentous time is recalled by Archibald in the following way: "one morning Mr Monteeth told me that the slaves around Montego Bay . . . were revolting, and setting fire to properties, in order to become free. I could hardly believe it, but alas! it was too true." During this time, he asserted, as many as fifty militia men stationed themselves on Sundays at New Carmel church, expecting trouble. As such, "[m]any negroes allowed themselves to be frightened from coming to Church, yet, as regards the most of them, so great was their hunger to hear the word of God, that the fear of man, and the red coated soldiers could not keep them away from Church".[43]

Indeed, the 1831–32 rebellion proved a stormy and trying time. Already in 1823, eight years earlier, there had been an incipient revolt in Hanover. At the trial in July 1824 at the Slave Court in Lucea, Hanover, six slaves belonging to John Malcolm were tried for "a rebellious conspiracy and Rebellion" and were condemned to hang at the mill yard of Argyle Estate.[44] The missionary, Lewis Stobwasser, referred to it in a report dated 2 March 1824, briefly noting that "[a]bout Christmas, we were alarmed by various rumours of a spirit of disaffection and rebellion prevailing among the negroes, and here and there some disturbances took place, but by God's mercy, they were quelled, and we spent Christmas very quietly".[45] But the insurrection was not to be circumvented in 1831–32. Several missionaries wrote reports about their experiences of the period, experiences that indicate their fear as free white people among an enslaved majority and their role as churchmen solicitous for the well-being of their black flock, yet nervous about the perception of their links with the blacks among European officials and citizens like themselves. The initial rumblings took the following forms: "Ten days before Christmas, slight disturbances took place in St. James's; but, though this gave some alarm, they were generally thought of no consequence."[46] But the rebellion then continued with arson:

Figure 3.4 A driver. Engraving by Kemble, *Century Magazine* 1887. From Ortiz, *Los negros esclavos.*

> The first property fired was Kensington, situated in the highest part of the mountain ridge, which bounds the parish of St. James's on the south and east. Within half an hour after this conflagration, on the evening of the 27th of December, Windsor Castle, distant about 8 or 9 miles from the former, was also in a blaze. On the second night, seven large fires were seen in the higher parts of the parish; and on the third night, 14 were burning in a most fearful manner.[47]

"Retirement estate . . . adjoining our place" was torched on the afternoon of 29 December. Brother Light was moved to lament that "a most terrific fire presented itself before our sorrowful eyes".[48] By 2 January a large estate, Belfield, was ablaze, as well as "another lovely property, called The Ramble". Indeed, "a number of delightful habitations, settlements of very respectable people" were all in ruin. Among these were Williamsfield, Worcester and Round-Hill – their masters' residences, overseers' and bookkeepers' houses, boiling houses, storehouses and mills. The rioting affected not only the parishes of St James and Hanover, but spilled over into the northern part of Westmoreland and St Elizabeth. There, the estates of Pisgah and Ipswich, "about 7 miles from Spring Vale, had been already burned by the rebels" on the last day of 1831, and "Y.S. estate was threatened".[49] Prior to this, two nights before, Richmond Hill, Darliston and Enfield in St Elizabeth had been set on fire, while by the new year, in the mountains between St Elizabeth and Manchester, at Mile Gully, and in places like Pepper, Northampton, Goshen and Long Hill, the enslaved people had gone on strike.[50] In the long term, property damage, which included physical installations and enslaved persons killed and deported, amounted to more than £1,154,589.[51]

In general, white families fled from inland areas to the sea ports of Montego Bay, Falmouth, Lucea and Black River Bay, on the ready to board ship or be rescued by frigates sent out by the governor in Spanish Town. The local militias were called out for duty. These comprised white and coloured males, as well as free blacks. In Archibald's vicinity, some of the free blacks and coloureds were servants of the missionaries, so that with their males absent, "many of the free people of colour, whose husbands and sons were among the militia, came to us [at the mission station] for shelter, so that we had more than 40 females on the place, including the teachers and some children from the schools at Woodlands and the Cruse".[52] The mission stations served therefore as hubs of community self-protection and control centres for the pacification of the localities. Brother Scholefield, for example, wrote: "My mind was made up not to quit my post, but to remain and do my utmost to encourage the people to attend to their duty."[53] The mechanisms of control operated in the following way: "Several owners of slaves sent their head-people to get advice, and some came of their own accord, all of whom we admonished to be faithful to their masters. Many of them were much alarmed, but they promised to defend their masters' property to the last, and on no account to join the rebels."[54] This strategy led him to claim that

> where we had influence over the majority of the Negroes, the properties were not burnt, even in the Darliston Mountains, and the neighbouring district. Several of our people were nearly losing their lives for their faithfulness. . . . [T]he plan of operation with the insurgents was to send one or more of their party to the estates, and that these individuals influenced the ill-disposed negroes to burn their master's property. It was seldom the case that a property was burnt, where the people of the estate refused to join.[55]

It would be safe to infer that Archibald was among those employees who "watched faithfully, day and night, in defence of their master's property; for, although there were not wanting a few, who felt as if they would *dig cane-holes no more,* they were all agreed faithfully to defend what had been entrusted to them, though surrounded by evil-minded people".[56]

Reprisals were taken by whites and free browns who suspected Baptist and Methodist preachers in particular of having incited the blacks to revolt through misrepresentations about their having been granted freedom by the King in England while being denied it by the whites in Jamaica.[57] In the resulting acts of revenge, "chapels were either pulled down or burnt" in St Ann's parish, in the north of the island east of Montego Bay and at Falmouth and Stewart Town in Trelawny parish.[58] Persons of the mission fraternity were attacked or threatened. So much so that the Baptist

> Rev. Mr. Burchell and family, have been constrained to leave this island, and have sailed direct for America; he would, in all probability, have lost his life last Wednesday, had not a body of soldiers, with his friends, screened him from the fury of the mob. He had been several weeks in jail. . . . His brethren, Knibb and Gardner, have been arraigned, and are to be tried next Monday. . . . Their spacious chapel at the Bay is . . . a heap of ruins.[59]

Later, following their arrests, the Baptist ministers, Knibb, Whitehorne and Abbot, were granted bail, following which "they have since kept within their own lodgings to avoid needless observation. . . . The Baptist and Methodist chapels are, however, occupied by troops, who sadly injure . . . these fine edifices." Other missionaries, "Mrs. Blyth and Waddell, of the Scottish church, [who] with Mr. and Mrs. Cowie, arrived on the 22nd of December last, took refuge in the town of Falmouth, being in imminent danger; for, though the slaves ha[d] not fired the estates in their neighbourhood, they ha[d] in general refused to work."[60] And later, in August 1832, as one of many sequels to the December/January uprising, riots broke out at Savanna-la-Mar, "during which several houses were pulled down belonging to some brown men called Deleons, who protected the Baptist missionary", Mr Kingdon. In fact, the harassment of the Savanna-la-Mar Baptist community, both men and women, during August and September 1832 makes chilling reading, as detailed by Reverend Henry Bleby.[61] Even the Moravian clergy were threatened, and word was sent to Brother Scholefield, officiating at Archibald's New Carmel church, that he would not live more than a fortnight, and that his mission station would be destroyed.[62] Months after the heat of the rebellion, Zorn, the Moravian superintendent, could still tell his brother in Pennsylvania that "the missionaries are threatened with deportation, which is rather milder than hanging or shooting as was proposed in the rebellion".[63]

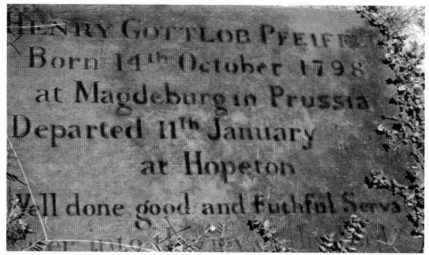

Figure 3.5 Gravestone for Heinrich Gottlob Pfeiffer, Carmel Moravian churchyard.

In fact, the Moravians suffered a severe shock, given their placatory posture towards the plantocracy and its political organs. In January 1832, Brother Pfeiffer of New Eden in Manchester had been arrested and imprisoned at Mandeville, the parish capital. He was put on trial and was only just saved from the gallows by a witness's withdrawal of false testimony against him. The Moravian establishment was so shaken by these events that they resolved to arrange for "a number of letters from respectable friends in the island" to be placed in the newspapers to counter the "calumnies circulated against us missionaries", and "testifying to the good conduct of their negroes under our instruction".[64] "Much odium", they complained, was directed towards their "private speakings", but, as Zorn was to write in his diary entry of 21 July 1832, this aspect of Moravian "Church-discipline" was a method of "acquiring a knowledge of our hearers", a system by which pastors conversed privately at regular intervals with individual members of their congregations; however, it was being maliciously represented by the church's detractors as "a system of espionage", a way of prying into "the concerns of the overseers on the estates".[65]

On 14 April 1832, writing to his brother in Bethlehem, Pennsylvania, and summing up the implications of the uprising, Zorn wrote: "A religious war is spoken of here as not unlikely! The leading Journal boasts of resistance to the Mother Country with 18,000 bayonets, the maximum of our militia force"; this was the threat of secession from Britain on the part of the whites. On the other hand, Zorn predicted that the "religious free people of colour will not take arms against their sovereign", while amid this conflict there was "the temptation to revolt for the slaves".[66]

Indeed, as frightening and life-threatening as the rebellion had proved for the whites, it was "hell and powderhouse" for the enslaved. Six hundred and eighteen were tried in civil (slave) courts and by courts martial, of whom seventy-five were women. The tally of their dead was 307 killed in open rebellion and some 312 executed. Two of these were women.[67] Against this, only fourteen whites had been killed and twelve wounded.[68] This was a terrible price paid by individuals and the collective to protest inhumane treatment and to win the right to liberty.

Although Archibald did not participate in the general struggle for freedom in 1831–32, he was not disinterested in the proposition of free status. As will be outlined in chapter 9, he was seriously investigating the likelihood of securing his own freedom and, no doubt at a later date, the liberty of his wife as well. When general emancipation was announced on 1 August 1834, the sting in the tail was that slavery was proposed to last another six years while the slaves remained still tied to the estates in limbo. Impatient at waiting, Archibald purchased his release from slavery in mid-1837. In the event, the final date of general emancipation was eventually brought forward by two years and so took place on 1 August 1838.

By 1839, already free, Archibald was able to buy land and build a house. Having been employed as of that time as full-time native assistant to the Moravian mission, he must have saved from his salary of £12 per annum as well as selling surplus produce from his agricultural labours to amass the £74 with which he bought the land.[69]

Textual Silences

One of the most salient omissions in Archibald's text relates to the nature of estate work. While he does speak of estates, both his and others', it is with reference to either his supervisory status or his evangelical mission, but not the work schedule his positions carried, or else he touches on his relationship with his masters in general terms, and his relationship with other estate owners in respect of their religious attitudes to his proselytization. And while he speaks of the reactions of other enslaved persons to himself with regard to their moral life, he does not discuss the work and social interrelationships he had with them. Furthermore, we have no information about his work skills: was he a skilled horse trainer, a sensitive herdsman, a green-fingered agriculturalist, an adroit carpenter or a careful sawyer? No inkling of this kind emerges from the narrative material recalled by his amanuenses. But we hear of him building a house for a close friend, which implies that he had some carpentry and perhaps some masonry skills; perhaps too he knew how to chip limestone – so abundant in his area – to shape uneven blocks to construct low walls that marked off fields and properties. We know as well that he rode a pony to go about his business, so he must have had animal grooming and feeding skills in addition to riding prowess. He would have had to manoeuvre his animal up rough paths, for even today, the road to Frazer, his home settlement, from Nightengale Grove and Cool Retreat lower down is uninviting even by automobile.

Indeed, it is only by way of investigation that we come to realize that Kep was a pen, that is, an estate devoted to livestock rearing and breeding. "[O]n it are bred horses, mules, steers (*i.e.* oxen,) and all kinds of stock, and from which the butcher is supplied with fat cattle for the market."[70] In 1816, Kep (also referred to as Kipp Plantation) was estimated to house 49 slaves and 154 livestock; in 1817 (as "Kepp Plantation") 50 slaves and 82 livestock.[71] These figures are somewhat less than the post-mortem inventory of John Monteath's holdings of 12 December 1815, which amounted to 95 slaves, of which 54 were male and 41 female. Livestock tallied at 117 cows, 47 bull calves, 64 cow calves, 4 bulls and 3 young bulls, 41 three-year-old steers, 16 two-year-old steers, 14 two-year-old heifers, 30 "very indifferent" sheep and 4 horses.[72] In addition to the sheep, horses and cattle being reared at Kep, it had also been producing coffee. Even today, in the early twenty-first century, it is evident that the lands of Kep and its surroundings are suitable for multipurpose investment. It lies only at 500 feet and more above sea level, and is characterized by undulating green hillocks, deep limestone gullies covered in wild vegetation and wide grassland. Highland coffee, as it is called to differentiate it from higher-elevation "Blue Mountain" coffee, could be grown on its hillsides; just as cattle, horses and goats would have much space to graze in the valleys and slopes. Wooded areas may have grown much logwood and other types of timber, while its soil today supports much yam, maize, ackee trees, sweet potato and cho-cho (cayote/christophene) vines. But its lower areas were given to prolonged flooding after heavy rains, when the limestone gullies filled with water from underground watercourses, forming impassable and treacherous pools. In the districts between today's Newmarket – which was part of Kep and Moco – and Darliston there are ponds constantly fed from invisible sources even during the longest droughts.

During the time of Spanish occupation, from approximately 1500 to 1655, Jamaica was used largely for ranching purposes. Some sugar cultivation had been started by the Spanish, but not on the large, export-oriented scale it assumed after the English conquest in 1655. Yet even so, by 1782 there were still about 300 pens and by 1832 one-eighth of the island's slave population resided on livestock farms.[73] This was due in large measure to the topography, climatic conditions and savannah ecology of certain sections of the island, and also to the fact that the sugar industry demanded animals for certain

Figure 3.6 A rancher. Engraving by E. Vilardell from an oil painting by Landaluze. From Ortiz, *Los negros esclavos.*

work routines and for milling purposes. "According to some estimates, Jamaica's 710 estates in the late eighteenth century needed between 56,000 and 71,000 oxen alone, not counting mules (or horses) and spayed heifers."[74] The principal role of pens was therefore to produce goods for the domestic market by way of "large and small stock, meat, grass and food provisions". In addition, pens offered the sugar estates manpower services such as jobbing and wainage or cartage. Pen slaves were therefore occupied in daily and annual routines such as tending animals, cleaning and preparing pastures, and planting guinea grass and provisions. "Some worked as watchmen, some did odd jobs and still others were engaged in skilled trades and in the marketing of livestock and other commodities." Skilled workmen were horsebreakers, groomsmen, saddlers, jockeys, spayers, and butchers.[75] Senior points out that each pen had work for one or two saddlers "who repair the damage done by the young colts to the harness".[76] We note, for instance, that one of John Monteath's younger sons became a saddler in Black River, and we know as well that Ernest Monteith, the grandson of one of the Rosehall workers, Edward Monteath, was adept at riding horses.[77] These skills accord well with the pen-keeping traditions of the area. And we know too that Archibald rode a pony, though that was normal enough for peasants of his time. However, having spent so many years in animal husbandry at Kep and the subsequent estates, he must have been very familiar with the care and feeding of animals, and in the riding, training, and general management of them. Food for the owners, administrators and the enslaved themselves was supplied by fishing and catching prawns and, according to the area, pond or sea crabs.[78] More men than women were directly involved in tending and rounding up the cattle; and the same gender preference showed in the tenure of supervisory positions. Female slaves were domestics, field cooks and field hands, nurses, washerwomen and seamstresses. Domestics were usually coloured, that is, mulatto or quadroon, while the smaller the pen the greater concentration of male Africans and conversely, the larger the establishment the more the number of Creoles.[79]

The field labourers were divided into gangs, but these were smaller than on sugar estates, and on very small establishments work could be individualistic. The first gang consisted of the most able-bodied, usually in the fourteen to thirty-five age group; they were hired out to sugar estates while on the pen itself they felled trees for cultivation runs, chipped logwood, which yielded a dye and was an export commodity, mended fences, planted pasturage, and hoed corn and coffee lands. "Logwood was planted in June and November. Live penguin [*Bromelia pinguin*] for fencing . . . from September to December, but general fencing, repair jobs, house construction, branding, weeding and so on were done as the need arose." The second gang comprised the old and adolescents; they cleaned and weeded pastures and corn plots. The third gang, consisting of children and the "weakly", fed the small stock and gathered "hogmeat", that is, weeds used to feed pigs and goats. Newly imported slaves were "given 'light' work in the fields in the process of 'seasoning' ".[80]

As such there was a less regimented lifestyle on pens than on sugar estates and slaves did not have to endure the long night hours required for the manufacture of sugar. For instance, at a conference of Moravian mission heads convened on 27 April 1830, the representative from Irwin Hill near Montego Bay complained about "[t]he hard labor of the negroes during

Figure 3.7 Cane-harvesting. Éditions Phos, Guadeloupe. From Renault, *Bons baisers de la Colonie*.

harvest and their close confinement to work . . . from 4 o clock on Sunday evening till 5 o clock on the following Sunday morning with but little intermission day and night". In the few hours they had to themselves on Sundays they had to tend and reap agricultural crops for themselves lest they "subject themselves to starvation through the week", in a situation where their kitchen grounds were "frequently at a distance of 6 to 10 miles" from their huts.[81] In contrast, hours on coffee estates were more flexible, and from this it followed that workers were better placed to husband their own livestock holdings, which meant greater access to private earnings and to a meat diet.[82] Furthermore, the waggoners "who drove animals to and from estate markets were . . . given small financial incentives or rewards as planters and penkeepers tried to ensure the good treatment of livestock".[83]

It becomes clear then that pen slaves were not exclusively involved in the raising and sale of animals. It was general practice for pens to diversify by producing crops requiring less intensive and continuous labour than sugar. One such crop was coffee, which grows well in certain of the island's highlands and mountain foothills. "In 1774, the number of properties producing coffee for export stood at 150"; by 1792, this increased to 607, and by 1799, it was 686, so that the industry constituted "the second largest after sugar and its derivatives, as far as production and export were concerned", contributing "a little more than 25 per cent of the value of exports between 1805 and 1830. In 1832, some 45,000 slaves, or 14.4 per cent of the total slave population, laboured on coffee plantations in Jamaica."[84] However, in common with other agricultural crops, coffee was subject to the ravages wrought by hurricanes, plant blight, erosion, epidemics and slumps in export prices, factors which in turn led to the transfer out of coffee into sugar cane cultivation.[85] The highland location of coffee estates often correlated with relative isolation, but whether or not this was extreme, it has been observed that many "coffee planters were resident owners, for whom isolation meant both greater interaction with the slaves and greater self-sufficiency of the unit. . . . Coffee units also tended to raise relatively more animals for internal consumption in relation to the size of their labor force, as well as a high proportion of slaves employed as domestics."[86] Crop time lasted between nine weeks and three and a half months, most often after the end of the summer, but even with the increased hours during crop time, the annual average hours of work needed were generally lower than those necessary for sugar production. The important tasks were mainly weeding, pruning and picking the berries. Berries were picked when red and then soaked in large stone or brick basins to soften their cortices to allow for easier pulping to release the seeds, called beans. The berries were then put out to dry on level stone surfaces called "barbeques" in Jamaica, and then "run through a rudimentary mill – activated most often by two mules, sometimes by water or by wind, or more rarely by two or more slaves".[87] This milling broke the outer skin in preparation for the manual pulping in which the skins and spoiled berries were discarded. Wholesome beans were bagged, ready for market and for roasting and crushing. The drivers were usually men; women and children assisted in fertilizing the fields with manure; while those at either generational pole sorted the beans after decortication.

These activities were certainly familiar to the speaking subject, but neither Archibald nor his amanuenses considered them appropriate to their purpose. In addition, boundaries of propriety were erected because certain topics fell outside the restrictions of the narrative of spiritual growth and trial, or they compromised persons alive or those whose memory or reputation it was felt should not be offended, or were persons adjudged to be unimportant to the trajectory of the narrative's intention. Or they were issues that were considered sexually indelicate and likely to offend the readership, or topics that were ideologically controversial and shunned by the Moravian brethren. As such, feeling needed to be restrained except, for the purposes of the conversion narrative, in relation to the expression of spiritual ecstasy. By the reverse, it is instructive to note that when Archibald does fulminate against the oppression of slavery, it is at the point in the story concerned with the Middle Passage journey, and not connected with plantation life in the Caribbean. Here is how he admits the trauma of enslavement:

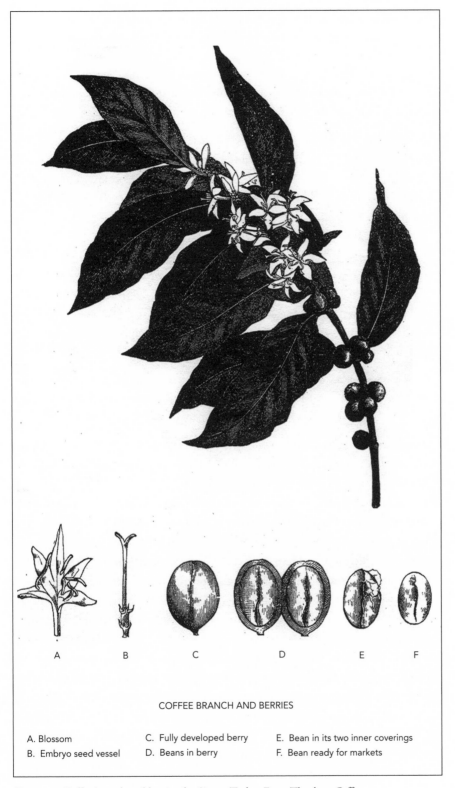

COFFEE BRANCH AND BERRIES

A. Blossom
B. Embryo seed vessel
C. Fully developed berry
D. Beans in berry
E. Bean in its two inner coverings
F. Bean ready for markets

Figure 3.8 Coffee branch and berries, by Simon Taylor. From Thurber, *Coffee*.

[t]he next morning I was horrified to see great numbers of blacks brought up from the hold on deck to be fed with yams and rum. . . . Only the daily recurrence of the dreadful scene with the poor prisoners below filled me with keenest grief; it was most touching to see the wretched figures, and hear the cries pressed from them by acute bodily suffering, or the feeling of separation from husband and children, and all they love in the world.[88]

At this point, the narrative comes very close to an anti-slavery set scene. The canvas is generalized, and the adjectives and phrasing seem *de rigueur*: "dreadful scene", "keenest grief", "wretched figures", "daily recurrence", "poor prisoners", "acute bodily suffering", "cries pressed from them". Archibald's manner of expressing these ideas is very much submerged beneath that of the ghostwriter and/or translator.

Were the story's main motive political, the strongest feelings and most sustained treatment would have been devoted to abhorrence of the abuses of slavery. Even so, the Monteath story amazes by its restrained references to the physical and psychological brutalities of slavery. One almost starts when the visiting absentee landlord stoutly recommends whipping, in answer to a proposition from Archibald:

"If you, dear sir, commanded one of your slaves to do something, and he refused and wanted to do something else, because he referred to what had been the custom on the plantation during your father's time, would you allow him to do it?"

"No", answered the master. "I would have him whipped."[89]

Given this avoidance of the topic of violence, we are left curious as to Archibald's own experiences and feelings as he changed status from domestic pet and gofer to field hand and the difference this brought in his relationships with his owner's family and with others of the enslaved fraternity. Unlike the treatment which the change from childhood to adolescence receives in narratives like those of Frederick Douglass and Mary Prince,[90] the Monteath story offers no such analysis. But we suspect that bitterness on his part and his frictions with John Monteath's son, James, must have been responsible for Archibald's slightly etched complaint against his later "owner", for they had grown up together as playmates, but the mixed-race man increasingly asserted himself as "young master", so that later years would bring tensions between them, especially harsh in the context of former "friends" turned master on one hand while the other remained his slave. As emerges in his analysis of the tortured relationship between Thistlewood and his longest-serving slave, Lincoln, Burnard notes that "intimacy with whites greatly increased the likelihood of punishment".[91] But we are told nothing about the corporal punishments to which Archibald himself must have been subjected, and the insinuation of physical and verbal suffering is not concretized:

He treated me very harshly and strictly and sought opportunities to find fault with my work. When I was not able to work as usual because I was sick, he never missed the chance to add to his invective that all this came from my running to the accursed Paynestown and from the praying. He wouldn't stand this piety in the blacks any longer, and so on.[92]

Furthermore, Archibald says nothing about the punishments he himself, as overseer-driver, must have been involved in dispensing.

Another area of erasure pertains to the narrative's euphemistic and delicately worded mention of sexual abuse and undesirable sexual relations. With regard to the former, Archibald records his campaign against an overseer who had been encouraging sexual laxity:

whereas formerly [the estate manager] had been able to follow the bent of his own vicious inclinations with the young people, without let or hindrance of any kind, now those young people had learnt at church to know the sinfulness of giving way to his seductions, and resisted his attempts, and I had on my visits among them encouraged them in this course to the utmost of my power.[93]

The 1853 version similarly balances disclosure with reticence and generalization, although the sense is slightly different:

At Mount Edgecomb there was a married overseer, who continually sought to draw the young people into sinful ways and doings; and now, they were not any more willing to do such things, for, as they said, "Archie Monteeth had told them, and read to them out of the Bible, that such life is sin, and they would be excluded from the Congregation, if they would not renounce these things."[94]

But his remarks are plain when he points to the contradictions between Christian morality and the sexual conduct of Europeans: "Every day I saw and was a witness to the fact that the white gentlemen, who were Christians and were far above us in education, lived the same way",[95] that is, cohabited with women and had sexual relations with women to whom they were not married.

The finessing of matters considered sexually indelicate, even improper, in addition to avoidance of sharp critiques of individuals and worse still, their naming, were doubtless proprieties observed by Archibald's amanuenses, Geissler and Kummer, and were also a reflection of the genteel tastes of their intended readership. Moreover, the public printed media of the time refrained from unabashed exposure of material that would "bring scandal" to individuals, whether to the speaker or to the reader. The missionaries' testimonial was not intended to have the accusatory purpose and invective tenor of Robert Wedderburn's *The Horrors of Slavery*. The restraint they, and perhaps Monteath himself, applied to condemnation of the slave system was part and parcel of the Moravian approach to matters political, while the story's suppression of labour matters, although inevitably linked to slave abuse, was also intended not to distract attention from the salient issue for the amanuenses, which was Archibald's relationship with God and his dedication to God's service. Both these issues will be elaborated on in chapter 9.

4

Family and Inheritance

John Monteath: Genealogical Profile

JOHN MONTEATH WAS THE eldest of the sons of Walter Monteath I.[1] When he was buried in Jamaica at his Kep Estate on 23 January 1815, the Anglican church recorded his age as "about 44".[2] This suggests that he had been born around 1770. There was indeed a John Monteath who had been baptized on 7 January 1776 at Barony, a parish of Glasgow, to a John Monteath and Margaret Dunbar, though the father's name seems to represent an error, given that subsequent children produced by this union were entered with the father's name as Walter Monteath:[3] Ann, the second child, on 7 September 1777 and Margaret, the fourth, on 30 September 1781.[4] Walter Monteath had married Margaret Dunbar at Barony on 10 March 1775.[5] Only in respect of John and Ann do their children's names coincide with those we know to have been John Monteath's siblings, as there was a George baptized in 1779[6] and Margaret baptized in 1781 whom we cannot connect with John Monteath's family profile. Did they die before adulthood? Thereafter, a Walter Monteath, resident as well at Barony, and a wife named Jean Dougal or McDougall produced James, baptized in 1785, Ann baptized in 1786 and Robert baptized in 1791.[7] Was Jean Dougal the second wife of the same Walter? Perhaps. Yet, we have the incidence of two Anns across the sets (but we know that similar names did occur in families), and no Archibald Douglas in either.[8] Was one of these Anns the sister Nancy, also called Agnes, who had responsibility for a mortgage made to John in 1804? We are even more unsure of the identity of John Monteath's mother. Other than the two women named in the baptismal records in connection with Walter Monteath, we lack corroborating evidence of their family connection, though one of John Monteath's brothers, Captain Walter Monteath, in his will referred to Robert and Campbell Douglas as his maternal uncles. "Uncles" could also have meant "great-uncles".

John's father, Walter, was the eldest of several sons born to Archibald Walter Monteath. Archibald Walter's marriage to Jean Douglas took place at Kippen in Stirlingshire on 18 June 1738.[9] Some documents situate Kippen in Perthshire, which suggests its border location. Jean was one of the five daughters of James Douglas, thirteenth laird of Mains, who died in April 1743. His name had been James Campbell, but on inheriting Blythswood in 1767 from his maternal grandfather, a Douglas, he took the surname Douglas and acquired the coat of arms of Douglas.[10] His first wife was Isobel Corbet of Hardgray. His second wife was Rebecca Wallace, whose will was entered on 10 May 1766. Jean was also called Janet. We are unsure when she was born, but by 1803, according to the will of her brother Robert, she was already deceased. Her eldest sister, Margaret, daughter of Isobel Corbet, married Archibald, first Duke of Douglas, on 1 March 1758,[11] a marriage that did not last long, on account of the duke's death on 21 July 1761, aged sixty-six.[12] But the marriage left Margaret a very wealthy woman. Margaret, Duchess Dowager of Douglas, died on 24 October 1774; her will of 18 August 1773 occupies many folios[13] and gives evidence of an imperious, albeit generous, woman intent on shaping the lives of her relatives and superintending her family inheritance.[14] One could speculate that family members must have in general been careful to accede to her wishes as their fortunes could be made or broken by their attitude towards her. One of the executors to her will was her brother-in-law, Walter Monteath I.

Among Jean Douglas's male siblings was Robert, who became the fifteenth laird of Mains in county Dumbarton, and died in October 1803. He also owned lands called "Casburg and Lurg contiguous to the estates of Mains in the Parish of Kilpatrick".[15] Together with a business partner, Mr Robert Lambert, he ran a prosperous tailoring business at St Martins Lane in Middlesex; and resided at Chelsey (Chelsea) in Surrey. There was also Walter, of whom little is known; and Colin, who went out to Westmoreland, Jamaica, as either a merchant or planter;[16] his wife Margaret made her will on 23 December 1775.[17] And there was Campbell, who worked as factor for Lord Douglas and who may also at one time have owned lands in Jamaica.[18] Another brother was James, who became a merchant in Virginia and who died at Dumfries, Prince William County, Virginia, on 18 November 1766.[19]

Walter Monteath I was the eldest son in a cohort of ten children born to Archibald Walter Monteath and Jean Douglas. Walter seems to have been

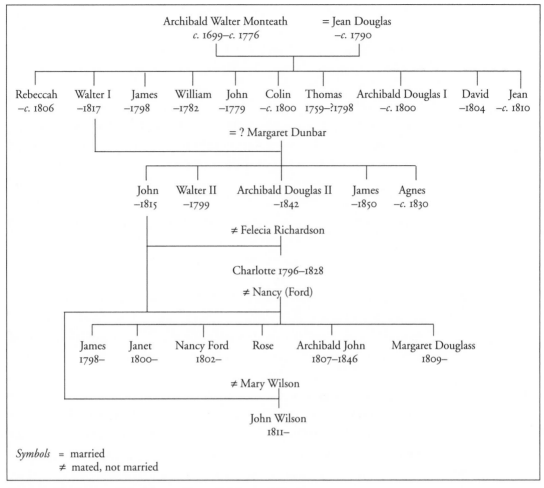

Figure 4.1 Family tree of John Monteath's antecedents and offspring.

born in the late 1730s, and he matriculated in 1753 at the University of Glasgow.[20] On information culled from the will of Dowager Margaret Douglas in 1773, for which Walter was an executor, the sequencing of Walter's siblings indicates that the most senior child was Rebecca, also spelt Rebeccah. Rebeccah seems to have gone out to Jamaica at some time, since her brother John's will on 16 March 1776 refers to her as living there.[21] She had been settled with £100 by Dowager Margaret and died in the early 1800s quite wealthy, as indicated by the legacies she left in a series of settlements made jointly with her younger sister, Jean. These settlement deeds are dated 5 April 1806, 13 September 1808, and 21 January 1819. After generous bequests, the balance of their joint estate amounted on 15 May 1842 to £9,080 10s. 9d.[22] Walter followed Rebeccah, then came James, William, John, Colin, Thomas, Archibald Douglas and David, while Jean brought up the rear.

Five of the males became merchants: Walter, James, William, Thomas and David. John went to sea, becoming fourth mate on the East India merchant ship *Triton*. He appears to have retired to Jamaica, wrote his will probably on a visit to London in 1776, but he died in Jamaica in June 1779.[23] John had received £200 from the Dowager Margaret before she passed away. Colin had also been a recipient of the same amount. He became an ensign in the East India Company's Bengal army in India, where he was stationed when he signed an affidavit on 6 February 1779 in Calcutta.[24] Colin died around 1800. Archibald Douglas Monteath too received the Dowager's £200 inheritance. He appears to have emigrated to St Vincent in 1775,[25] later becoming an ensign in the Forty-ninth Regiment of Foot also stationed in India, where he died, at a date unknown, though his will was registered on 19 December 1804.[26] In his will, undated, but apparently made either in late 1799 or in 1800, Archibald Douglas Monteath I[27] lists among his assets an inheritance of £100 from an "Elizabeth Douglass", widow of Robert Wallace, a Glasgow merchant, which had been inscribed in a codicil to her will dated 27 March 1799. This Elizabeth Douglas was his aunt. She may have been the same person as the widow of Thomas Wallace; in other words, she may have married Robert after Thomas had died.

In the 1770s James, like his brother Archibald Douglas Monteath I, was a merchant with Messrs Turner and Paul operating out of Kingstown, St Vincent,[28] but by the early 1790s he was based at Belfield Estate near Martha Brae in Trelawny, dying in Jamaica on 17 September 1798.[29] Perhaps the harassment of the British by the St Vincent Caribs had made the island inhospitable, and this threat to life and limb may have been responsible for the relocation of these brothers to other imperial outposts. James had been bequeathed £100 by the Dowager, "over and above sums already advanced". William, Thomas, and later David became merchants in western Jamaica between the 1770s and 1790s. The earliest records of William's business activities there date from 1773. He was in Glasgow in 1777, however, when he signed an affidavit on 21 October indicating receipt of his £200 inheritance from Dowager Margaret. David, who died in May 1804, returned to Glasgow where in August 1803 he entered a co-partnership in Monteath Dickson and Company, a rum and wine merchant house.[30] Much earlier he had been bequeathed £200 by the Dowager and it would appear that David had been a minor when on 13 October 1784 he absolved his elder brother, Walter, of further responsibility towards him in respect of the Dowager's provisions. The legal discharge states that David was acting on the advice of his curators, Jean Douglas his mother, and her brother, Colin Douglas of Mains.[31]

The sequence of the children born to Walter Monteath I and his wife or wives is not clear, but we can account for five children. There was the John

Figure 4.2 Castle Douglas at Mains, Lanarkshire. From Hannan, *Famous Scottish Houses.*

of our story who went out to Jamaica to become a landowner. A son named after his father, Walter (referred to here as Walter II, for the sake of clarity), like a brother, Archibald Douglas Monteath II, named after his uncle, entered the British army. This younger Archibald Douglas retired from the British army as a major, returned to Glasgow and died in 1842. There was also James, who became a Glasgow merchant, registered with the Glasgow Burgesses and Guild Brethren on 26 February 1801,[32] and who was also a lawyer, a merchant, later "distributor of stamps in Lanark and Dumbarton", and who died in 1850. A sister named Agnes, also referred to by the pet name for Agnes, Nancy, appears to have been unmarried; she was alive in 1810 when John Monteath included her in his will, and she is named in a codicil to the will that he added before his death in 1815. She is also named in a codicil to a will made by her aunts Rebecca and Jean Monteath on 21 January 1819 which stipulates that she should receive £50 to purchase mourning clothes at their deaths. Agnes was, however, herself deceased by 1850 when her brother James made his will.

It is possible that there were other siblings born of prior unions of either Walter I or his wife or wives. In his will, Walter II names James Maxwell of Dargavel as his brother. "Brother" in Walter II's usage might have meant "brother-in-law", "stepbrother", or "male relative".[33] John Maxwell, sixth laird of Dargavel, had married Margaret, daughter of John Campbell of Succoth, lands that by cross-cousin marriage were linked to the Douglases.

From fairly early in his exposure to the plantation mores of Jamaican society, John succumbed to the permissive sexual lifestyle of the island. As was the prerogative of the white male, he was sexually accessible to women of various ethnicities. Apparently John did not marry, either in Scotland or in Jamaica, but the Jamaican partner with whom he established an apparently residential family bore the Monteath surname, as did his acknowledged children both by this partner as well as by other women outside of that union. In some cases, as occurred here, free women of mixed ethnicity appropriated as their own surname that of their acknowledged male partner. Was this done at the suggestion of the man? Or was it done as an indication of coresidential status? Or was it to signify the longevity of the relationship? Or was it effected when the woman produced a son, particularly a first-born son? The latter appears to have been the case with John's partner, Nancy Monteath, who bore John a son in 1798, apparently early in their relationship which continued until his death in 1815. Another factor operational in this case was the assumption of the surname of one's manumitter from slavery. Depending on attendant circumstances, this could serve as an index of the cementing of a relationship between the person freed and the person who had bought the freedom of the enslaved.

Another issue in naming concerns its reference to ancestral kin. Thus either the mother's original surname or the father's maternal surname could be incorporated into the names given to a child. This practice helped in the identification of John's permanent partner, Nancy Monteath, since one of the children of the union was named Nancy Ford Monteath, which led this investigator to "Ford" as a forebear's surname. Another girl was named Margaret Douglass Monteath but, as has been established in the previous section, Douglass or Douglas was a family name of particular importance in John Monteath's genealogy. The name, Margaret, may have been meant to honour John's paternal great-aunt who had been such a benefactress to his family's fortunes. But then, if Margaret Dunbar was indeed John's mother, then Margaret was being given the name of her grandmother as well.

John's first child, as recognized in the available records, was Charlotte Monteath, born in July 1796 to a black enslaved woman called Felecia Richardson who was owned by Joseph Royal. By 1828 Charlotte had died, being buried on 10 July at Black River.[34] Her burial at Black River suggests that she may not have died as a slave, though she may have been in urban domestic servitude. But perhaps she had bought her freedom or, more likely, someone else had done so on her behalf. Charlotte and her mother's two earlier mulatto sons, Thomas Howard, born 1789, and John Howard, born

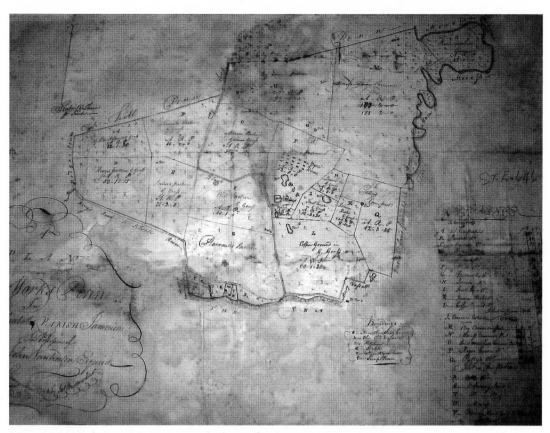

Map 3 Lower Works Pen. Courtesy National Library of Jamaica.

1792, were baptized on 30 March 1800 at the Black River Anglican church in St Elizabeth.[35] Had John taken over Felecia as a sexual partner when he succeeded William Howard as overseer or bookkeeper on some plantation? We will never know how these things transpired. But we do know that in his will of 15 January 1800 William Howard instructed his executors to buy the freedom of his two mulatto sons, Thomas and John, the manumission being eventually effected on 6 January 1804. The manumission document refers to the boys' mother as "Phillis belonging to Lower Works Penn" near Black River Bay in St Elizabeth, while Howard's will also supplies the alias, Philly.[36] The manumission deed indicates that John Griffith, sole surviving executor, paid over Jamaican £100 in each case to compensate Joseph Royal, the owner of the boys, with additional monies so that the St Elizabeth church wardens could ensure "good and sufficient security" for Thomas and John for the rest of their lives at the mandatory £5 per annum.[37]

Two years after Charlotte's arrival, that is, in 1798, a son, named James, was born to John by Nancy Monteath. In 1800 Nancy gave birth to Jane, also called Janet, the personal name of Nancy's mother. Nancy Ford Monteath was born in 1802. Like mother Nancy, little Nancy was called Ann, Nancy being a diminutive form of Ann.[38] James, Jane and Nancy were baptized exactly one month after their mother underwent the ritual on 22 January 1805.[39] The next child Nancy bore for John was called Rose, though no birth date is available in her case. Rose, also called Rosey, was baptized on 22 January 1806, at the same time as Isabella and Ann Ford,[40] her maternal aunts, who were the children of Dr Thomas Ford, Nancy's father. One may note that Dr Ford had two children named Ann or versions of it. As regards Nancy's children, Rose preceded Archibald John, and Margaret Douglass was the last. Archibald John, born on 11 April 1807, was baptized on 18 June 1821 together with Margaret Douglass, who was born on 22 July 1809. Both were identified in the baptismal records as "free quadroons", which they were not (see chapter 6).[41]

Of all Nancy's children, we know most about Archibald John. Having already bought 30 acres of Rosehall land from his mother in 1835, he married by licence Sarah Ramsser on 12 April 1837. But he was a younger son and therefore without the financial backing needed to undertake his own investment in land and slaves. So it appears that he removed to Black River, where he became a storekeeper, probably for the government, and then a saddler. A daughter, Margaret Elizabeth, was born on 17 February 1839 and baptized on 16 June 1839, but was buried on 2 October 1844. By the time a second child was born, named Mary Augusta, on 2 February 1841, Archibald John was no longer the storekeeper at Black River, but had begun his independent trade as a saddler. A son, Christopher James, was born a year later, on 17 February 1842, and another daughter, Valeria Williams Monteath, on 5 June 1844. When Archibald John passed away on 27 July 1846, Sarah was a few months pregnant with another son she named Archibald John after his father, but the infant lived only seven days, having been born on 14 February 1847.[42]

Yet another child of the Scotsman John Monteath was born in 1811. This was John Wilson Monteath, whose mother was Mary Wilson. In the baptismal record, dated 23 January 1831, John is identified as a mulatto, which suggests that his mother was black, although we are now well aware of the inaccuracy of racial classifications in the records.[43] Since John Wilson Monteath's place of abode was given as "Kepp", can we deduce that his mother was employed there, and was one of John Monteath's slaves? Or was she the Mary Wilson owned by Henry Palmer, owner of Greenland Plantation, and who was baptized at Black River on 7 September 1813, estimated to be about twenty-five years old at the time?[44] Or was she related to the Sarah Wilson of Savanna-la-Mar at whose home the Fords and Monteaths were baptized in 1817, an inference being that Mary Wilson could have been a relation or a friend of Nancy's? Or was she the mulatto Mary Wilson manumitted by Alexander Wilson, a mason of Trelawny, on 6 July 1816?[45] We may also wish to consider Mary Wilson, daughter of Hugh Wilson by Sarah Townsend, and baptized on 16 May 1785. We have no idea what colour Sarah Townsend was.

Nancy Monteath was the same person referred to in a codicil to John Monteath's will of 1809 as "Ann Monteath of St. Elizabeth, a free Woman of Colour".[46] She was the daughter of John Monteath's doctor, Dr Thomas Ford of Westmoreland, "Practitioner in Physic and Surgery".[47] In 1800 Dr Ford was the assistant surgeon for the Westmoreland Regiment of Foot.[48] But apart from this, doctors were employed on plantations to carry out daily or weekly inspections of the indisposed workers. In the mid-1790s their pay was 6 shillings a head for attending to slaves, and more was paid for difficult cases.[49]

Ford lived at Belford, an apparently small plantation, and at Darliston Pen, which lay in the vicinity of Lenox Estate owned by Ford's "most respected Friend Hutcheson Scott Esq.", in the words of Ford's will.[50] His residence appears to conform with Senior's remark that "almost every merchant, medical, legal, or other practitioner, has what he calls his 'penn', which is a comfortable, and often handsome establishment . . . a short distance out of town".[51] Ford made his will on 1 July 1826 when he was already 70 and "at an advanced period of life and infirm state of body". He had had four children with Jannet Ramsay, also named Jane Ramsey Ford, the daughter of a liaison between a planter, Charles Ramsey, and Jane Dorrant, "a free sable [black] woman of Westmoreland". Jannet is described as "a free woman of colour" from near Savanna-la-Mar. There are two baptisms reported for Jannet, who apparently had been baptized at Lucea in Hanover parish, but she discovered that her baptism there was not recorded.[52] Perusal of the Hanover Copy Register for the period, though very neatly written up, affords ample evidence that several records of significant rites of passage were not entered or not entered in the correct sequence. As much is admitted on page 148 of the register where there is a note that reads: "Kelly Atkins is a Sambo woman born at Lucea formerly baptised but probably no record of it kept." A similar comment had been made regarding the Black River records for St Elizabeth, with Reverend Thomas Warren acknowledging in writing the deficiencies of their recording.[53] Apparently a victim of this type of oversight, Jannet ensured another baptism, in St Elizabeth this time, at the hands of the Black River Anglican parson on 5 June 1817, when the pastor estimated her to be about twenty-nine years old. This estimate of age appears rather low, given circumstantial evidence. The parson had reckoned that Nancy, Jannet's daughter, was "about 24" when he baptized her in 1805. If this assumption is anywhere accurate, it would mean that Nancy had been born about 1780, and therefore gave birth to James Monteath when she was around eighteen years old. Even if Jannet had given birth to Nancy at fifteen years old, Jannet would have had to be born around 1765 and therefore almost fifty in 1817. The mystery of her age is further compounded by the ascription of sixty-six years to "Jane Ramsay" resident at "Belfour", who was buried at St John's Chapel on 7 July 1846.[54] Such an age would mean that she had been born in 1780. Either Nancy was younger than the pastor read her age in 1805 or Jannet consistently looked younger than her actual age.

Jannet Ramsay's children born to Dr Ford were listed in his will as John Thomas Ford, Sarah, Nancy and Augusta. The last, described as "a free quadroon", was born on 25 August 1820 and baptized on 18 June 1821.[55] John and Sarah were baptized on the same day in 1817 as their mother. The baptism took place at the house of Miss Sarah Wilson in Savanna-la-Mar. If there was not a blood relationship between Jannet Ramsay Ford, Nancy Monteath and Sarah Wilson, then there appears to have been a close friendship. Whatever the case, Sarah Wilson had formerly been a slave on Paradise Pen in Westmoreland, but by 1831 she was already free. She had borne three children for James McGregor: Margaret, Alexander and James.[56] She also had the mulatto Thomas McKenzie with Alexander McKenzie. He had been born on 11 April 1827 and was baptized on 4 April 1828.[57] If indeed Thomas McKenzie was mulatto, then Sarah Wilson was black.

Dr Ford had children by other women as well. There was Thomas Ford, a partial echo of the name given to John Thomas Ford, mothered by Jannet Ramsay. But this Thomas Ford was the child of Elizabeth Ford Stephenson. And there was also Ann Ford and Isabella Ford. Ann was "a child of colour" according to the Anglican baptismal record, a description corroborated by that of "a free person of Colour" according to a deed of gift made to her by her father in 1811.[58] Together with Isabella and a Sarah Ford, "an adult of colour", the three were baptized on 22 January 1806. This leads to the impression that Sarah was the mother of Ann and Isabella, but this is speculative. Isabella had been born at Enfield Pen,[59] which suggests that her mother belonged there. Sarah, Ann and Isabella were subsequently freed by Dr Ford on 3 March 1809,[60] but Sarah Ford was already dead in 1826 when the doctor made his will.

As we have indicated, among the mothers of Dr Ford's children were Jannet Ramsay and Elizabeth Ford Stephenson. He bequeathed to Jannet two male slaves, and to Jannet, together with her four children, 24 acres of land on Darliston Pen together with its house, its household furniture, his gray horse and his portmanteau. To Elizabeth Ford Stephenson and her son, Thomas Ford, he gave two-thirds of his money, 14 acres of Darliston Pen, one male slave, a horse, half his saddlery and half his wearing apparel. To Ann

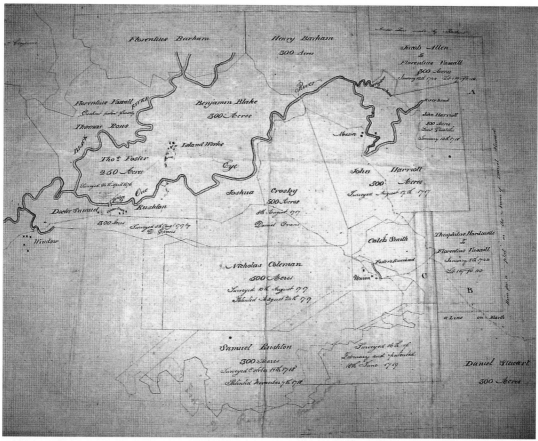

Map 4 John Harriott's Mexico Plantation. Courtesy National Library of Jamaica.

Ford he left one-third of his cash, 15 acres of Darliston, his gold watch, its chain and seal and a silver snuff box. He had already, in 1811, deeded her a female slave and her two children. But there is no mention of Isabella in his will. Was she dead, or had she made a financially profitable alliance? For instance, no specific bequest was left to Nancy (apart from the land she was to share with her mother), since she had established an apparently steady liaison. Then there are two further female Fords, "free quadroons", baptized as Anglicans on 16 October 1821: Margaret, then nine months old, and Eliza who was four years old. Might these have been further children of Elizabeth Ford Stephenson, or did they belong to another unnamed woman? They are not likely to have been the children of the doctor's sons who, being quadroons themselves, would have had to father these children with mulatto women for them to have remained quadroons. But it is useful to remember the terminological inconsistencies with regard to colour categorizations in the official documents.

The doctor's affairs speak to a chaotic kinship situation that he attempted to regularize by the provisions of his will and deed. Further chaos lies in the social and psychological vulnerability of his children, an exposure that becomes clearer when we learn that on 4 January 1802 John Monteath paid for the manumission of "a mulato woman slave named Annie and her three Quadron children named respectively James Janet and Nancy and the future issue offspring and increase". This refers to Nancy and her three eldest children, James, Janet and Nancy the younger. To secure her freedom, Jamaican £440 was paid to Annie's owner, William Harriott of Great Britain, through John Monteath's attorney, John White of St Elizabeth. On 3 March 1802 another £340 was paid to the church wardens for St Elizabeth, Alexander Girdwood and Alexander Rose, as security according to the stipulation of the Legislative Act of 1784 which decreed that £5 per annum for the rest of their lives should be provided to those manumitted as a guarantee against their becoming vagrants or a burden on the state.[61] William Harriott at the time owned the Mexico and Santa Cruz Park estates, both in St Elizabeth. Mexico lay in the western foothills of the Mexico Mountains, part of the Dom Figuerero mountain chain. John had served as overseer at Mexico between 1796 and 1800. By 1802 he was employed as overseer at Fonthill and Hampstead, the latter a neighbouring property to Kep. Both properties were owned by Thomas Smith. It was also in 1802, when John paid for the manumission of Nancy and the three children, that he no doubt settled them at Kep, the property he was consolidating as his base.

John's Assets and Bequests

By 19 January 1809, in the same year that his daughter Margaret Douglass was born, John Monteath felt it incumbent to make a will. This was followed on 9 May 1810 by a codicil. In fact, John's will contains four parts. Part A designates his will made on 19 January 1809, which came to be the will recognized in law; part B, a codicil dated 9 May 1810; part C, another codicil nominating a new executor and bearing the names of the witnesses to the will; and part D, a purported will, undated and reiterating some of the provisions in part A.[62] Another important legal instrument was a deed dated 15 May 1814, making specific provisions for Nancy, now named as Ann Monteath, and five of her children.[63] Since persons tended to make wills in situations of emergency, these legal documents, including the deed, suggest that John experienced several crises of health between 1809 until his death in January 1815.

In the 1809 will he left sterling £500 to "James Monteath a son of mine by the above named Nancy Monteath who is now in England . . . for his use at the disposal of my friends in Scotland". James was only eleven years old at the time, which is why his legacy was to be administered by adults. This instruction regarding the bequest for James is reiterated in 1810, by which time he indicates that James had returned to Jamaica. Perhaps James's Glasgow stay had included attendance at one of the academies to which overseas Scots sent their white and mixed-race children for schooling.[64] John also stipulated that his sister in Glasgow, Nancy Monteath, should receive a legacy of sterling £500 as well. The other provisions in the will were for Jamaican Nancy who was bequeathed "the following Negroes vizt Duke, Billy, Jenny and Bella and failing her to the Surviving Children she has or may have by me". He also left her sterling £500, and "all my wearing apparel to be at her own disposal with a Bedstead of mine now at the Forest [Estate]". His 1810 codicil suggests that he recognized some incompleteness in his 1809 will, which appears to have been rushed. He now made further provisions for Nancy and the children:

> my Executors are hereby empowered to build [a house] on her own Land at Whitehouse the Expences is (*sic.*) Left to themselves. I wish that every arrangement for herself and the family Should be comfortable and till this is done I request that she . . . shall have the use of the House at Kepp with the Store, Small Stock furniture etc. I likewise give her two of my riding horses named Archy and Ball, I likewise leave the said Nancy the following Negroes, Judy, Juliet Beatrice, Richard and Toby and failing her to her Children by me.

The instructions relative to the slaves in question were to be cemented in the deed of 1814. The 1810 codicil also instructed his executors to "sell all my Negroes land, Stock in fact every thing I am possessed of and after my Legacies above mentioned are carried into effect the residue of my fortune is to be remitted to my Brother James Monteath in Glasgow".

The 1809 document names Taylor Cathcart of Westmoreland and Alexander Girdwood of St Elizabeth as his executors.[65] Witnesses were James and Alexander McGregor, and David Walker. Witnesses to the first codicil were Thomas Ford and John Hill. In part C, the second codicil, Alexander McGregor is named as an executor. Witnesses to this codicil were Thomas Ford, A. Rose and Alexander Stewart.

In addition to his bequests, John made a deed, dated 15 June 1814, conveying to Ann Monteath – the same Nancy – and the five junior children, Janet, Ann, Rose, Archibald and Margaret, "the following eleven Negroes slaves named Jack Richard Toby Dennis John Jeany Bella Beatrice Rose Juliet Peggy" together with the issue of the slave women. Nancy was to possess these persons "for and during the term of her natural and no longer and during that period not liable to be levied on or sold under any writ of rendition".[66] On

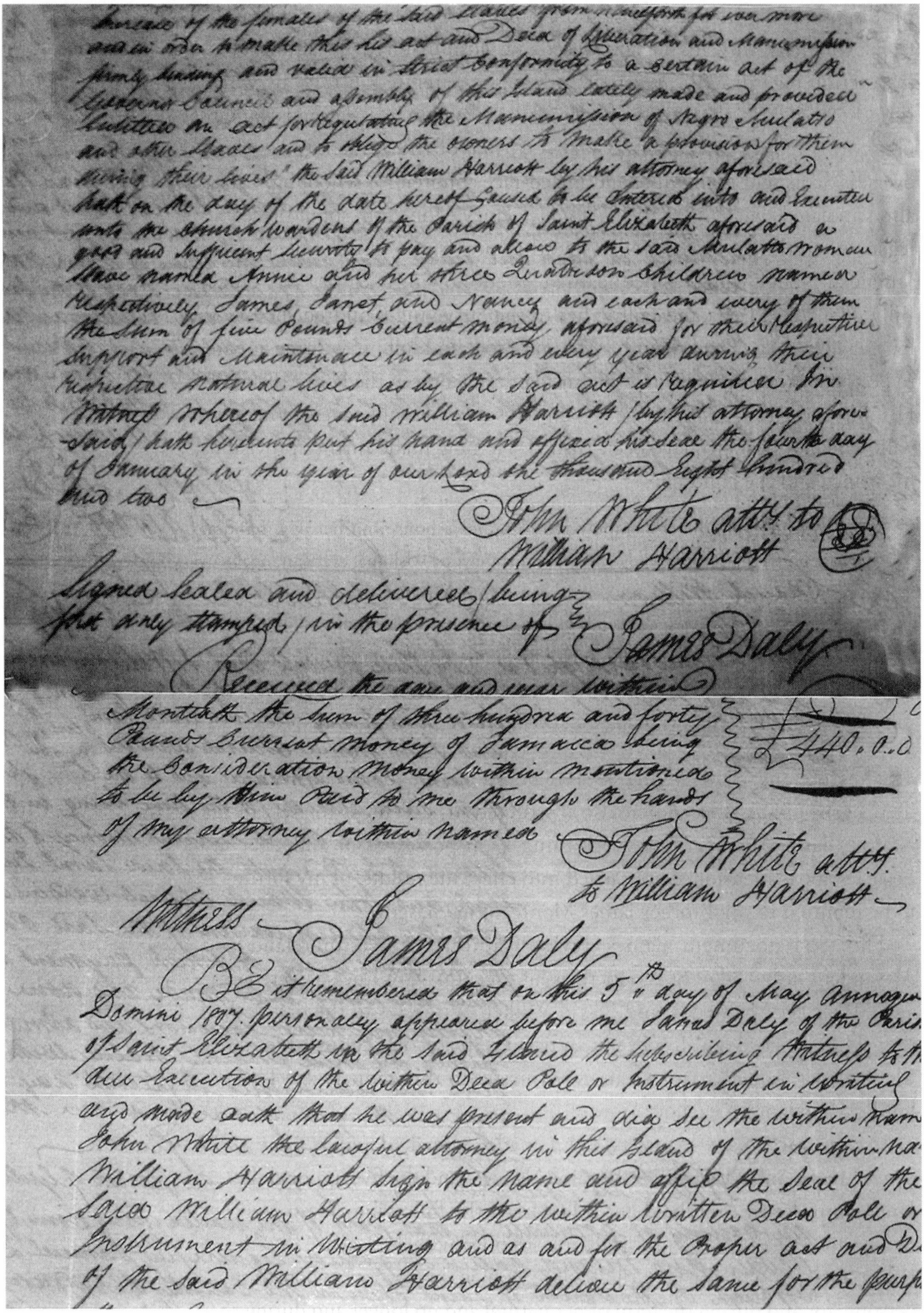

Figure 4.3 Manumission documents concerning Nancy and her first three children, 1802. Courtesy Jamaica Archives.

the death of Ann, "the said Eleven Negro slaves with their issue that may be alive shall be equally divided share and share and share alike amongst my five reputed children". This deed was witnessed by John Alice, and the witness's affidavit witnessed by A. Girdwood. The conveyance of chattel slaves to Nancy prior to his passing seems to have been a measure intended to protect Nancy from financial claims that were deemed likely to have been pursued in the future. And there is evidence that such legal claims were made. In a judgement given in June 1822, Duncan Robertson, executor for Thomas McCracken, was unable to levy on Nancy for the eleven slaves, in respect of unspecified debts, on account of the protection afforded by the 1814 deed.[67]

The various bequests from his estate allow John Monteath to emerge as a caring provider for those he clearly considered as constituting his closest family units. He made provision for his unmarried sister, for his father, for his eldest son, for his "wife" and his children by her, and he had nominated a brother in Glasgow to take control of his financial affairs on that side of the Atlantic. But we also note that his will made no mention of his children who were not Nancy's, for example, Charlotte and John Wilson. Of the latter we hear nothing after his baptism.

In addition to his willed provision of labour units, cash, horses and furniture for Nancy and the younger children, John's connection with Dr David Fyffe as attorney for Forest Pen provided him the leverage to negotiate for the £70 purchase by Nancy on 1 November 1808 of a 6-acre seaside parcel of land at Whitehouse Bay in St Elizabeth. The land being purchased lay north of Grandvale Estate, for which John was also attorney in 1804. These premises must have been intended to serve as the location for a beach cottage or holiday home for the family.

Forest Pen was an extensive property of 1,373 acres, as shown on the St Elizabeth map 565,[68] which includes Whitehouse Bay and wharf. In a codicil to his 1809 will Monteath directed his executors to supervise the erection of a house there for Nancy. However, it would seem that this suggestion was not carried out, since a decade and a half later, on 13 April 1826, Nancy sold this property "situated in the Surinam Quarters[69] in . . . Westmorland . . . northeasterly on the King's Pen Southerly on Whitehouse Wharf northwesterly and southwesterly on the sea". No mention was made in the deed of sale of any structure on the land and its price, at Jamaican £56, further cements the deduction that no sizeable premises had been built on it. It was bought by Jane Moore, a "free person of colour".[70] Seeing that the land, now reckoned at 7 acres, was being sold for less than it was bought, might one suppose that the purchaser may have been a relative? In any case, Bernard Senior has discussed the drastic fall in real estate values between the first two decades of the nineteenth century and the 1830s.[71]

Five years after the Whitehouse purchase, John bought Nancy a 320-acre parcel of land south of his estate Kep. On 1 February 1813, Monteath, as attorney to Thomas Boyd of Glasgow who owned lands in St Elizabeth, arranged for Nancy, referred to in the purchase agreement as Ann Monteath of St Elizabeth, to acquire this parcel of land on the border of Westmoreland known as Kilmarnock. This purchase cost £450 according to the copy of the deed and the receipt, though erroneously £250 is the sum indicated in the body of the title.[72] This property appears to have become part of what was Rosehall or Rose Hall, and was also sometimes referred to as Rose Hill.[73] Rosehall is also the property's name as entered in the returns printed in the Jamaica Almanacs. An adjoining property of hills and gullies and valleys called Dumbarton or Dunbarton, containing 431 acres, was acquired by Nancy (we may ask: for herself? or for James?) in 1821 after John's passing. Dumbarton, recorded variously in the Monteath biography as "Dunbarken",[74] and Dumbasten,[75] was the larger property for which Archibald became a driver after fulfilling duties for several years at Rosehall. Yet a query remains. Rosehall or Dumbarton was estimated at an acreage of 431, and Ann or Nancy had already purchased Kilmarnock land in 1813, an acreage of 320. What then became of the Kilmarnock land, since her combined acreage should have amounted to 751? Had Kilmarnock been forfeited because of debts? Is there a connection between this inference and the complaint by Archibald that James Monteath, Nancy's son, had during the 1820s piled up such debts that creditors were likely to have snatched up the Monteath slave property to retrieve their loans and advances?

By the 1830s Nancy began to reduce her Rosehall acreage. On 17 October 1832 she disposed of 30 acres to Robert Smith, described in the title as "a free black boy", for the sum of £150. This Robert Smith must be the same person who in the 1832 Returns of Slaves is noted as manumitted from Rosehall. The rather dismissive language used to identify him in the title deed is suggestive of the minimal courtesies accorded the free black person in a society in which slavery was still the major economic system. Some years later, on 16 May 1835, when he was twenty-eight, her younger son, Archibald John Monteath spent Jamaican £120 to acquire from his mother 30 acres of Rosehall "bounded east by Woodlands, south by lands belonging to John Bowen Wells Esq. and Robert Smith, and on all other parts by Rose Hall".[76] In 1839 several parcels were sold. The first, on 1 January was to "Archebald John Monteath", our subject, who bought 14 acres for £74; and it would appear that it is he, rather than Nancy's son by the same name, who acquired a further eighteen perches for £15 on 10 April the same year. The latter piece was bordered on its northeast by "land intended to be conveyed to Thomas and Mary Brown", and southerly on "Rose Hill land". In both documents "Archebald John

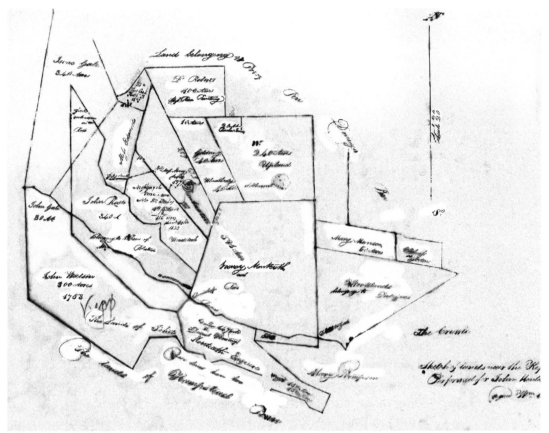

Map 5 At centre, Nancy Monteath's Rosehall; at bottom, Kep. Courtesy National Library of Jamaica.

Monteath" is identified as "planter".[77] By 1839 slavery had been abolished and new terms of reference were now considered politically correct. Robert Beckford, likewise "planter", acquired 7 acres on 2 January for £35.[78] Then on 9 January the title for Thomas and Mary Brown was in fact drawn up, indicating that they were purchasing 12 acres for £64. The couple were described as "agriculturalists".[79] By 14 May 1839 Ann Monteath sold 6 acres to the "planter" Thomas Vassal for Jamaican £32.[80] Three years before, it may have been the same Thomas Vassall who bought more cheaply from Robert Nisbett, a planter of Westmoreland, 11 acres for Jamaican £38 10s. That land was bounded on the west by Woodlands Plantation, southerly by Robert Grahame and northerly by Cheriot Hill. Vassal, described in that document of sale as a "free Black man" of St Elizabeth,[81] may also have been the same who married Isabella Salmon, like himself from Woodlands, on 24 September 1926.[82] The sales effected by Nancy Monteath meant that in the decade of the 1830s, 99 acres of Rosehall's 320 acres had been sold off. There was also a commensurate depletion of animal stock. Between 1818 and 1824 Nancy owned in the region of twenty-five to twenty-eight slaves, while her livestock ranged between fifty-two and seventy-four. By 1832, however, there was a dramatic decrease in stock to one, while her slave cohort remained at thirty.[83] This suggests that she must have been making an income off hiring out her workers, either to her son or to other people's enterprises.

The Disposal of John Monteath's Assets

John Monteath's will was probated on 9 September 1815,[84] a few months after his passing. The "Inventory and Appraisements of all and Singular the goods and Chattels Rights and Credits which were of the Estate of John Monteath late of the parish of Saint Elizabeth Esq. deceased" showed his worth as of 12 December 1815 to be Jamaican £15,531, a tidy sum to have amassed in a relatively short time. This moderately strong financial position had been achieved within a decade of property acquisition, based apparently on a prior decade of savings, and capitalized from family loans and partnership arrangements in Glasgow. His male slaves were valued at £6,375; the female at £6,575; livestock, which included cattle, horses, and thirty "indifferent" sheep were appraised at £4,458; and household furniture and stores at £468.[85] Returns in the years immediately preceding his passing and up to 1817 illustrate the type of business that brought in John's earnings. In 1814, sixteen steers had been sold at £32 each, amounting to £520; thirteen cows and their young at £22 10s. each, totalling £292 10s.; and seven heifers at £20 each for £140 altogether. The total value was £1,229 5s. Then in the year of his death, 1815, between 24 January and 31 December, coffee amounting to nine tierces, 6,750 pounds at 80s. a tierce and valued at £276 15s. had been consigned to Walter Monteath on the ship *Marian*. And from 31 December 1815 to 31 December 1816 just half the previous year's coffee, this time weighing four tierces at 75s. a tierce, and 2,996 pounds at 15s. per pound amounting to £115 7s. was sent to Glasgow by the *Ann Grant*. Camp Savannah Estate bought a hundred tierces of coffee for £4 each. According to the crop accounts, "Kipp Plantation" this year, 1816, was home to 49 slaves and 154 livestock. By the following year, 1817, "Kepp Plantation" carried just as many slaves as the previous year – 50 slaves, but only 82 livestock.[86] That the properties were being wound down is additionally reflected in the fact that sixteen labourers had been hired out to assist with planting at Spring Garden Estate at £32 10s. each, totalling £520; "Negro labour" had been hired out to Middlesex Pen for £128 18s. 1½d. and to Thomas Pond for £33 8s. 1½d. Livestock sales included a small 282-pound cow for £14 2s.; fifteen heifers had been bought by Mount Edgecombe Penn for £18 each, earning £270; while Dr Alexander Rose, owner of Mount Lebanon Estate,[87] had purchased a prime bull for £60;

and James Daly had acquired 296 head of cattle for £2,800. The total income this year amounted to £4,054 3s. 5d.

But it took several years to wind up Monteath's business. Throughout January 1816 the *Cornwall Chronicle* 45, nos. 1, 2 and 3, and their supplements, carried the advertisement:

> In Saint Elizabeth's, the following properties of the late John Monteath, Esquire: Kepp and Dumbarton Pens consisting of about eleven hundred acres of land partly in guinea grass, common pasture, provision grounds and woodland, with ninety prime negroes, among whom are some valuable tradesmen, and three hundred head of horned cattle. On Kepp there is an excellent dwelling House with offices, in good repair. The new line of communication between the parishes of St. James and St. Elizabeth, goes through part of these properties. A run of Woodland adjoining Dumbarton, of two hundred and forty acres. Flower-Hill Wharf, with house and store.

One may note the exaggeration regarding the acreage of land being sold. Kep covered 410 acres, while Dumbarton contained 431. Of further interest is the fact that the last item in the advertisement had not been included in the inventory, at least not explicitly so, and how it was eventually disposed of is not clear. But the possession of private wharf facilities in St Elizabeth indicates that John had arrived, or saw prospect of arriving, at enough success in his businesses to have established an independent wharfage for his goods and was also in a position to have leased his facilities to others. He had, in fact, secured this wharf on 1 May 1809 when he paid William Pight, a St Elizabeth planter and his wife Ann £200 for 10 acres of land bounded by the Kings Road on one side and the Black River and its morass on another, land known as Flower Hill Barquideen.[88] Flower Hill lay in the vicinity of Middle Quarters in Westmoreland.

According to several indentures drawn up in the years following his death, the settling of John Monteath's assets became mired in "controversies and disputes". This was because John had made several codicils to his first will of 1809, one of which, written in 1810, appointed Alexander McGregor as an executor, which went counter to the propriety of said Alexander McGregor having served as witness to his original will. Furthermore, John's part D codicil, which purported to be a will, bore no date, and thus had not been "executed as by law is required so as to pass real Estate and slaves", since John "did not revoke the herein before in part recited will as to the real Estate whereof the said John Monteath died seized and possessed". This meant that the bequest of horses and furniture to Nancy was void. However, for the most part, the provisions of this purported will replicated in large measure the bequests he had already indicated in the first will of 1809. It was almost as if he had forgotten that he had made the 1809 will, or that he or another person had mislaid it. Was he absent-minded, or careless, or too ill at times, perhaps sedated, to know clearly what he was doing?

For reasons to which we are not privy, John did not reinstate Taylor Cathcart as an executor when he made what was intended as a second will. Was his omission an oversight? Or did he mean to retain Cathcart and Girdwood and only add a third? Cathcart was the son of James Cathcart of Pitcairly, Fife, in Scotland, and had been educated at Glasgow University in 1793.[89] Monteath, Cathcart and Alexander Girdwood had known each other for some time and had served as joint executors for the will of Alexander Stewart the younger of Port Perthshire, Scotland, which had been settled in 1814. Cathcart was named together with Alexander Girdwood in John's first will, but in the undated will Cathcart was omitted in favour of Alexander Girdwood and now Alexander McGregor. Ironically, both Alexander Girdwood and Alexander McGregor died before John's assets were disposed of, McGregor passing, aged forty-two, at Dunstassnage in Westmoreland, in December of 1822.[90]

In any case, by virtue of the fact that John did not revoke the first will of 1809, Cathcart legally remained the sole surviving executor, and it was Cathcart who seems to have had the bulk of the unsavoury mess to sort out. One of the most salient difficulties surfaced in events related to the sale of Kep – both its lands and its slaves. It would appear that during the first year after his passing, John's father, Walter, and John's brother, Archibald Douglas Monteath,[91] negotiated a sale agreement regarding these assets with Peter Campbell the younger of Upper Montague Street in Marylebone in Middlesex for a sum slightly above Jamaican £11,000[92] for John's slaves, and Jamaican £4,170 for Kep itself. This arrangement was devised on 10 September 1816. But the preamble to the mortgage agreement eventually drawn up in 1819 indicates that Campbell (very likely a relative of the Monteaths) did not in fact pay according to the schedules arrived at, so that by 15 April 1818 a tripartite deed between Peter Campbell, Archibald Douglas Monteath and Taylor Cathcart settled that Campbell should pay Monteath sterling £1,000 to be released from the previous contract and should also reconvey Kep and its slaves to John Monteath's estate.[93] This then cleared the way for a quadripartite mortgage agreement on 12 March 1819 devised among Archibald Douglas Monteath, acting through his attorney George William Hamilton at Spanish Town, Taylor Cathcart, George Kirlew of Westmoreland and George Marcy of Westmoreland for the sale of these assets to George Marcy. Kep and its slaves were to be acquired for Jamaican £15,000, starting with a deposit of sterling £3,271 8s. 6d. 3f., which amounted to Jamaican £5,000, and with four subsequent payments of Jamaican £2,500 with interest over a ten-year period. The uncertainties, "controversies and disputes" over this legal settlement account for the fact that in the Returns of Slaves for 1817 a total of 103 people – 56 males and 47 females – with names and numerical quantity matching those in John Monteath's inventory after death, are entered by Robert Blair "as overseer in possession", while Peter Campbell is identified as their owner.[94] Three years later, a list of 101 males and 71 females, again largely recognizable as those named in John Monteath's inventory, are listed as "in the possession of George Marcy as Proprietor on the 28th day of June 1820".[95] The issues over ownership as well as the indeterminacy of Kep's geographical/parish ascription are reflected in the remarks in a longitudinal scroll that accompanies the list in the Returns of Slaves for 1817 in respect of Westmoreland. It reads: "Enrolled in the parish of St. Elizabeths in the possession of Peter Campbell Esquire then considered as Owner and purchased from Taylor Cathcart Esq. Executor to the late John Monteath Esquire deceased."

George Marcy may have been the son of George Marcy by Ann Evans. He may also have been the same George Marcy who in 1817 owned Geneva Sugar Estate in Westmoreland with a labour force of seventy-seven, fifty of whom were male.[96] His name recurs in the Moravian diaries for the church at Carmel as an owner who kept classes for his slaves and who attended the Carmel services. He was, however, buried by Anglican rites at "The Kepp" on 31 December 1857, aged eighty-six years old.[97] The prelude to his will of 10 December 1857 certainly bears the imprint of his piety, as he prefaces his instructions regarding his property with the submission: "I resign my Soul to God in humble hope of its future happiness through the alone merits and righteousness of his Dear Lord Jesus Christ our Lord and Saviour to whom I dedicate my Children beseeching him to steep them in all estates and events of their lives and to dispose of them and whatever concerns them as may be most to his own Glory and their Salvation."[98] His will also reveals that Taylor Cathcart, one of his own executors, was his son-in-law, and indeed Cathcart had married Frances Anne Davis Marcy, spinster of Westmoreland, on 23 July 1823.[99] Part of the acrimony over John's will perhaps lay in a competition between the executor and his relative against the seller and his relation (Archibald Douglas Monteath and Campbell). In the end, the former parties won the day, and the Glasgow Monteaths had to settle for a very graduated payment schedule.

The prominence of Archibald Douglas Monteath in these negotiations is of some interest. He was not mentioned in John Monteath's several wills and codicils, but emerges as legally entitled to act in these testamentary matters as "brother and heir at law of John Monteath", according to the wording of the deeds of 1818 and 1819 concerning the sale of Kep. This is most likely because

Walter Monteath, John's father, who was to be the ultimate recipient of the residue of John's fortune, had involved Archibald Douglas Monteath in negotiations for the disposal of John's property. Furthermore, in Walter I's brief will of 15 April 1817, he appointed both James and Archibald as his "sole executors and universal legators . . . with power to conform my moveable subjects and estate and to do everything competent to the office of executry".[100] But since James appears to have been John's man-of-business in Glasgow, we wonder why he seems to play no role in the Glasgow end of matters pertaining to the winding up of John's estate. Was it because James was abroad at this time? Or had he been upstaged by his brother, the major? Was he in fact Archibald's junior, thus having to yield to Archibald's rights of seniority? Even more intriguing is the remark in one of the preambles to the 1819 deed that in his will "John Monteath had directed the residue . . . to be remitted to his brother James Monteath in Glasgow since deceased". This is belied by James's decease three decades later. Were the lawyers duped? Was this a deliberate ploy? Was it part of the conspiracy to keep Walter Monteath's creditors at bay? Or merely the lawyer's misunderstanding of the reasons – concealed from us – relating to the perhaps innocent explanation as to why Archibald was so prominent in the pursuit of these affairs? For instance, Archibald was a retired major, while James would have at this time been at the height of his legal and business career, without the time to devote to winding up his father's affairs, which were interconnected with the provisions of John's estate. On the other hand, in the closing years of the 1700s and at the turn of the nineteenth century, James had been occupied, among other things, with sorting out the entanglements of his father's American finances. It would appear that Major Archibald Douglas Monteath was at this earlier period still out in the East Indies. He must still have been on the other side of the world when John wrote his wills and codicils and thus was not mentioned as a possible functionary for John's affairs, but he must have returned to Scotland by 1815 or 1816 when he became active in the disposal of Kep.

As for Nancy, on 7 April 1820, almost five years after John's passing, she received the sterling £500 left her according to John's will. Its value was now Jamaican £700.[101] A year later, on 28 March 1821, she was in a position to purchase the 431 acres called Dumbarton for Jamaican £500.[102] She seems to have passed managerial responsibility for this property over to her eldest son, James, which is probably why Archibald, our subject, believed that James was his new owner. Additionally, by the early 1830s, there seems to be some evidence of a liaison between Nancy and one of the witnesses to John Monteath's first will. This was James McGregor, who may have been a brother or relative to Alexander McGregor, but this is as yet unclear. As a matter of fact, there existed another James McGregor who made his will in 1822 and who might also have been the witness in question.[103] Also unclear is the nature of the liaison, which could have been purely business-related: for instance, was he Nancy's overseer or attorney? Or could the relationship have been sexual? By 1830 Nancy would have been around fifty, a woman with property in land and a few slaves, though perhaps with insufficient working capital. The incidence of the remarriage of widows in the documentation on eighteenth-century Jamaica[104] leads one to realize that widows with property had high repurchase value since their property became their husband's by right. Nancy could not expect that a white man would have married her, but she and her property would have attracted attachments of various sorts. Nancy's 431 acres of Rosehall and 117 acres of Dumbarton were appealing propositions, apart from whatever attractions were inherently hers. McGregor himself possessed very few slaves by 1817 – three females and one male; by 1820 he had bought a thirty-three-year-old African male to add to his complement.[105] But McGregor's will of 13 December 1831 does not include any reference to Nancy. Rather, it calls on his executors to arrange for the manumission of Charlotte Porter and his three sons by her – John, Alexander and Roderick – and provides money for the education of three other children by Sarah Wilson – Margaret, Alexander and James. As with Dr Ford and Nancy, no specific provision was made for his married daughter whom he considered already "settled" by her marriage.

The evidence, however, of McGregor's acting in concert with Nancy stems from the manumission of a black named Robert Smith. In the manumission records, the entry is listed intriguingly under the names "Nancy Monteath et al".[106] But it reads that on 2 March 1832 James MacGregor of St Elizabeth Esquire "for and in consideration of the faithful services of a certain negro man Slave named Robert Smith have manumizzed Enfranchised and for ever set free" the said Robert Smith "as if he had been born of free parents". Had Robert Smith saved James McGregor from death, or from some wounding loss of property? Whatever the case, the witness to the manumission deed, Duncan Robertson, a doctor, declared that "[t]he said manumission was not given for the purpose of relieving the owner from the obligation of maintaining an aged or infirm Slave". McGregor made an X for his signature; strange, given that he had put his signature to other documents, but he supplies the explanation for this in his will made some months earlier, on 13 December 1831 where he says that he makes a mark, "being unable to sign my name from infirmity in my hands". Perhaps he had suffered a stroke. In this will, McGregor intimates that it "is my desire that my Negro Man Named Robert shall serve my friend James Hall for three years after my decease and at the Expiration of that period if he has conducted himself with propriety it is my wish that he be manumized by my Executor and let free from

Bondage".[107] By March of the next year, McGregor had changed his mind as to having Robert Smith remain enslaved for an unspecified length of time, since the date of McGregor's own passing was uncertain. Perhaps the earlier wording had been devised when McGregor felt certain he was on the point of death, but having recovered, he saw the implausibility of his suggestion. What influence the restlessness of the enslaved at the turn of 1832 had on this decision, we cannot be sure. But this appears to be the same Robert Smith who is recorded in the 1832 Returns of Slaves for Nancy Monteath's cohort as having been manumitted, even though McGregor had referred to him in his 1831 will as "my Negro Man". This suggests that Nancy and James McGregor were acting in concert and owning certain assets, such as slaves, in common. For several people could have part ownership in a slave, as occurred with the Hartshall slaves who were owned conjointly by Mary Scott and her four mulatto daughters, the Harts,[108] and later some were owned jointly by the daughter Sarah Hart and her daughter.[109] Seven months after his manumission, by 17 October 1832, Robert Smith bought 30 acres of Rosehall land from Nancy for £150.[110] But there is still some uncertainty over the identity of Robert Smith, seeing that the 1832 Returns of Slaves lists him as being only eight years old and in 1826 he had been registered as having been born to the enslaved Peggy of Rosehall two years before. This apparent overlap either suggests some chicanery or scribe's error, or that the boy Robert was the son of the adult Robert Smith and that his manumission had been secured at the same time as his father's.

As for the eventual demise of Nancy and her son James, we have been unable to locate data about this in the Anglican records for St Elizabeth, Westmoreland or St James.

5

Colonial Commercial Networks

The Monteaths

THE NAME MONTEATH DERIVED from southwest Perthshire in Scotland and since its first appearance in written form in 1237 it carried a variety of spellings: Monteath, Monteith, Mandtheth, Mineteth, Menetech, Mentheith, Mynteith, Manteeth, Mentayth, Montecht, Munteith and so on.[1]

John Monteath's paternal grandfather, Archibald Walter Monteath, had been born circa 1699, and died circa 1776. He had also apparently been knighted.[2] He had inherited from his brother, William Monteith, the lands of Ardmore or Arnmore on 8 February 1739 and had succeeded another brother, John, as "heir of line and conquest general"[3] on 20 November 1765. This succession brought under his control the lands at Kep in Stirlingshire, southwest of Perthshire. The fact that some documents place Kep lands in Stirlingshire and others in Perthshire suggests that it straddled the border in some sense. As for Ardmore, it was described as "a beautiful wooded promontory in Cardross parish, Dumbartonshire. . . . It connects with the mainland by a narrow isthmus . . . [and] forms a fine feature in the magnificent lagoon-like scenery of the Firth [of Clyde]. Ardmore House stands upon it, amid pleasant grounds." With Ardmore came Pow, a place name given to "any one of numerous sluggish rivulets or stagnant burns in marshy or alluvial districts of Scotland".[4]

Archibald Walter thus belonged to the landed gentry. But it was a class which by the eighteenth century was becoming heavily drawn into commerce. They represented "the 'middling' elements in Scottish society", so that between "1730–90 the fathers of only four tobacco merchants were craftsmen, while on the other hand not one, as far as is known, was the scion of a noble or aristocratic family. The vast majority were sons of the well-to-do in lowland Scotland below the ranks of the aristocracy." This merchant group was relatively small, thus concentrating in its hands power and economic control by way of "[i]nterlinked partnerships and massive expansion among certain firms", creating a virtual web of investment in domestic and overseas agricultural activity, in shipping, banking and domestic mining and manufacture, "a series of compatible and suitably inter-locking investments".[5]

Like others of his class during the eighteenth century, John Monteath's father, Walter I, would likely have "spent some time at the University of Glasgow", meaning one or two years, learning, among other subjects, Latin, Greek, classical antiquities, history, geography, and moral philosophy.[6] Apparently, it was not expected that this type of student should graduate; rather, attendance at classes was the point of it all, with the "class ticket" being "a kind of minor degree parchment".[7] This level of educational involvement was built upon a grammar school training in reading, writing, the classics, arithmetic and bookkeeping. This wide range of mental preparation was considered useful even for those desirous of entering the world of commerce; indeed, "[b]etween 1728 and 1800, at least sixty-eight tobacco and West India merchants had been students at Glasgow University".[8] In addition, travel either in Europe or the colonies was thought helpful and it was customary for merchant aspirants to spend time in apprenticeship as a storekeeper, factor or accounting clerk.

Walter I registered in the Burgesses and Guild Brethren of Glasgow on 3 June 1760, a month later than his father, who had neglected to do so earlier, probably because he felt that he was more a country gentleman than a merchant.[9] His son's generation, however, saw its fortunes more solidly linked to entrepreneurial activity than to inherited farmland and feudal rents. As such, one of the trajectories of Walter Monteath I's commercial ventures concerned the leather industry; he was a partner in Glasgow Tanwork during the 1770s and 1780s.[10] But his principal hope lay in the tobacco trade with the American colonies. Tobacco as a cash crop and maize as a subsistence crop were being produced by both large and small white planters in the Chesapeake Bay and James River basin of Maryland and the Virginia side of the Potomac as well as in the Cape Fear hinterland of North and South Carolina. White indentured servants and enslaved blacks comprised the main source of labourers on these plantations and farms. But the unhealthy tidewater location of many plantations, slave resistance, poor labour supervision, high overseer turnover, tired soils and poor technology all affected yields over time.[11]

From at least the 1770s Walter I followed the current practice of entering business co-partnerships with other merchants, manufacturers and land-owners. Of the partners in many tobacco firms, for instance, only a minority were actively involved in the day-to-day running of the firm, while the managing partner resided in Glasgow. In some cases, there was a manager in charge of the Glasgow end of the business and another in command of American operations. The role of the other partners was to put up capital, to draw interest from shares and to participate in policy decisions. Partnership deeds were effective for fixed limits of time and strict control was exercised over the reallocation of shares belonging to a deceased or bankrupt partner. This was because if a bankrupt's share was extracted by his creditors it would destabilize the firm and also because firms were obligated to pay the trustees of a sequestrated estate if even they prolonged the process of repayment. Meanwhile, the bankrupt's share "could not be withdrawn until his debts to the company and *all* its debts were paid".[12]

By 1 November 1771, Walter I entered a projected seven-year co-partnership with other Glasgow merchants. These were John Glassford and James Gordon; Neil Jamieson and James Glassford largely stationed in Norfolk, Virginia; William Robertson mainly located in Antigua; and Adam Fleming at Cabinsport, or Cabinspoint, on the James River, Virginia. The firm would carry the name Glassford Gordon Monteath and Co. and would establish in Virginia a series of merchandising stores that would also serve as collection points for tobacco leaves. The proposed stores were to be located at Norfolk, Falmouth, Fredericksburg, Petersburg and Cabinsport.[13] Others were set up at Stafford County, Culpepper County and Spottsylvania County. The firm was capitalized with sterling £24,000. Four-sixteenths of the shares went to John Glassford and Neil Jamieson each, Walter Monteath put up three-sixteenths, James Gordon two-sixteenths, and one-sixteenth part came from each of the other partners. As for John Glassford's main company, in its "most successful years . . . the company owned a fleet of twenty-five ships and imported ten percent of all tobacco received in Gt. Britain". Together with this mainstay, "[t]he sale of goods such as hardware, rum, wine, sugar, salt, and slaves became a major source of revenue for the branch stores".[14]

By 27 January 1772, Walter was involved in yet another co-partnership, this time with Andrew Ramsay. This firm was called Ramsay Monteath and Co. The shares were as follows: Andrew and Patrick Ramsay, three-twentieths each, Walter Monteath and Richard Allan two-twentieths each, Richard Marshall together with Walter and Archibald Robertson one-twentieth, with the remaining seven-twentieths belonging to the company according to the respective ratios of each party. Four of the merchants were resident in Glasgow, whereas both Robertsons and Patrick Ramsay were based in Virginia.[15] This arrangement accorded with the pattern by which a network of stores was established as collection points for tobacco as well as sales outlets for goods imported from England and Scotland. The stores were run by factors or "store boys" who operated a system of credit for small planters and bartered goods for tobacco deliveries. The stores operated by Ramsay Monteath and Co. were located at Blandford and Pitsylvania in Virginia. As such it was one of the small- to medium-sized players in the Chesapeake tobacco trade. For instance, in early 1775, whereas Glassford, Gordon and Monteath exported 1,359 hogsheads of tobacco to Holland, 989 to German ports, 703 to France, and 163 to Ireland, Ramsay and Monteath sent only 87 to France, its sole outlet apparently;[16] this fact also indicates that the firm's tobacco was the sweet-scented variety grown in Virginia and preferred in France as against Maryland's strong-flavoured oronoco species popular in Holland and Northern Europe.[17]

The major blow to these businesses came from the outbreak of the American War of Independence in 1775. As the Scots were largely loyalists to the British Crown, they were either forced out of the territory by the American insurgents, or they adopted several subterfuges, such as moving into "back country" beyond the war lines, or even taking out Danish citizenship as a decoy meant to signal political neutrality.[18] But by December 1777 the large firms of

> Buchanan, Hastie and Co., and its sister concerns Bogle Jamieson and Co. and James Jamieson and Co. failed for over £62,000. The repercussions of this disaster were felt among the moneyed classes of lowland Scotland because the Buchanan firms had been borrowing heavily on bond for several years and had had to default on many of the loans.[19]

The negative effects of the American War, combined with years of credit crises such as 1762–63, 1772 and 1793, meant that some of the most respected families in Glasgow experienced a collapse of fortunes. This led to the bankruptcy of such figures as Provost Andrew Buchanan, George McCall, William French, Hugh Wylie and Walter Monteath.[20]

After the war ended in 1783, overseas investors such as the Scots attempted to secure compensation for business losses incurred on account of the hostilities. But the new American states took several measures to evade the payment of these debts. In May 1787 the Virginia Assembly "passed a law which provided that no debt due a British merchant should be recoverable in any court in the state". Earlier, in 1784, the South Carolina State Assembly had ruled that "no suit could be instituted for a debt incurred previous to

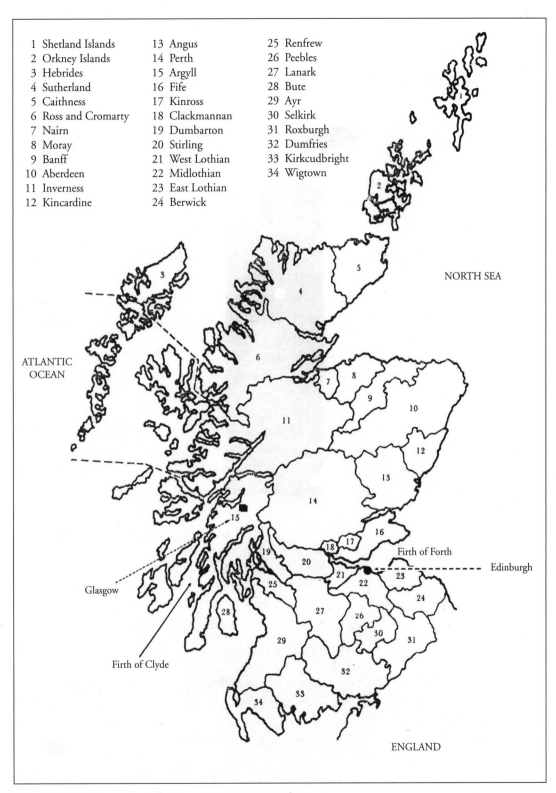

1 Shetland Islands
2 Orkney Islands
3 Hebrides
4 Sutherland
5 Caithness
6 Ross and Cromarty
7 Nairn
8 Moray
9 Banff
10 Aberdeen
11 Inverness
12 Kincardine
13 Angus
14 Perth
15 Argyll
16 Fife
17 Kinross
18 Clackmannan
19 Dumbarton
20 Stirling
21 West Lothian
22 Midlothian
23 East Lothian
24 Berwick
25 Renfrew
26 Peebles
27 Lanark
28 Bute
29 Ayr
30 Selkirk
31 Roxburgh
32 Dumfries
33 Kirkcudbright
34 Wigtown

NORTH SEA

ATLANTIC OCEAN

Glasgow

Firth of Clyde

Firth of Forth

Edinburgh

ENGLAND

Map 6 Scotland: its counties. After Cory, *Tracing Your Scottish Ancestry.*

1782 until 1 January, 1786". However, the Congress of the United States, in compliance with Article IV of its ratification of the Treaty of Paris in early 1784, recommended each state "to repeal all existing laws against loyalists and recovery of debt".[21] Virginia and Maryland refused to comply, and it was only in 1796 that "the U.S. Supreme Court annulled all state legislation which was contrary to the Treaty of Paris", thus enabling several merchants to successfully win their claims, including those in respect of pre-war debts. In 1802 a commission was appointed by act of British Parliament under the Convention with the United States of America, which "provided that the United States should pay Britain £600,000 in compensation to be distributed among those who still had outstanding claims". By 1811, £415,921 had been awarded "to those creditors who had proven their cases satisfactorily" but there was of course dissatisfaction over the length of time it had taken to arrive at settlements, and for their part the many claimants chafed at the disappointing level of their settlements and the failure of several of their suits.[22]

For example, Glassford Gordon Monteath and Co. claimed £11,543 in the 1780s, of which only £2,205 was settled.[23] On 1 January 1798, a claim was made for £13,604 17s. 9d. Virginia currency or sterling £10,883 18s. 2½d. in principal and interest with respect to the Blandford and Pitsylvania stores of Ramsay Monteath.[24] Again, in 1804, Gilbert Hamilton, trustee for Walter Monteath, claimed for debts of £6,520 13s. 7¼d. Virginia currency in respect of principal and interest due in the 1780s to Ramsay Monteath and Co., but compounded to £12,553 10s. 3d.[25] By 1809, Hamilton's son was appointed the new trustee, no doubt because Hamilton senior had died or was seriously incapacitated.[26] In fact, an affidavit dated 14 August 1806 and signed by Patrick Colquhoun, formerly of Glasgow, but currently in London, was sent to the commissioners, stating that all the partners in Ramsay Monteath and Co. were now dead except for Richard Allan and Walter Monteath.[27] However, an affidavit by James MacKenzie, dated 27 May 1806, had claimed that Walter Monteath was the sole surviving partner and that MacKenzie had seen him "in good health" the day before.[28]

All this litigation from the 1780s till the 1810s meant that money had to be spent on lawyers' fees both in the United States and in Glasgow and on data-collection by agents whose job it was to scour the Maryland and Virginia counties where past debtors were to be detected as well as past storekeepers who still retained credit bills; all these had to be collated, entered and computed.[29] No wonder then that John Monteath instructed in his 1809 will:

> My Executors are empowered to sell all my Negroes land, Stock in fact every thing
> I am possessed of and after my Legacies above mentioned are carried into effect the

residue of my fortune is to be remitted to my Brother James Monteath in Glasgow who will deliver it to my father Walter Monteath in the manner he may think adviseable, so as his Creditors shall have nothing to do with the same.[30]

This caveat was an echo of the disclaimer in Captain Walter Monteath II's will of 1799 where he wrote:

> Now as my father owes Considerable Sums of Money to Different People I think it necessary to explain that I do not design any part of money of Interest or Money thus bequeathed to be applied to the payment of my fathers debts, with which I have no connection. My intention is that the Interest of the money which I have directed to be placed at Interest shall be Bona fide applied as I have directed to the use and comfort of my father and mother During the term of their natural lives and I hereby cut off the claim of any other person or persons whatever.

Walter I's creditors were likely to have been, on the one hand, his erstwhile co-partners in business and, on the other, the banks and businesses from which he had obtained credit.

John Monteath's stipulation indicates that one of his main financial targets was to assist his father to survive his bankrupt status, but also, in the course of doing that, to sequester his father's assets from inroads by his creditors. Thus, at Walter I's death on 7 June 1817, his bank balance with Carrick, Brown and Co. was given as a mere £271 10s.[31] But in the years following the American debacle, Walter had also become a partner in Hill and Monteath for which there is evidence that the company lent two sums, £96 11s. 10d. and £22 9s. 7d. to the Glasgow merchants, Thomas Donald and Co, and Robert and Thomas Donald and Hugh Colquhoun. These loans seem indirectly implicated in the American trade, since James, one of Walter's sons, had appeared for Hill and Monteath before the America Loyalists Claim Commission in Glasgow on 17 April 1787.[32] Besides, the implication of letters sent by Walter to a Mr McFarlane, probably James McFarlane of the Glasgow firm McFarlane, Marshall and Co., between October 1779 and January 1780 is that he was involved in stockbrokerage, providing money on credit to companies such as Colin Campbell and Co. and Shafland Williams and Co., importers of olives, and in trading goods, including puncheon rum, between Glasgow and Ireland.[33]

These activities, however, seem low-keyed. On the other hand, Walter I had enterprising sons to shield him from total dereliction: John, a prospering Jamaica landowner; the very wealthy ex-military man Archibald Douglas Monteath, "the recognized arbiter of beauty in Glasgow";[34] and a merchant son, James Monteath, who bought up land and properties in Glasgow and Lanarkshire in the 1810s and 1820s, and was to become Distributor of Stamps for the counties of Lanark and Dumbarton, a post from which he retired in

1843. The thumbnail sketches of James speak affectionately of him. "He was a man universally liked and respected, with a kind heart and gentle manners."[35] One of the "burgher aristocracy" of Glasgow, he was for years a member of a whist and supper club called The Board of Green Cloth that at the beginning of the nineteenth century provided entertainment and opportunity for vigorous conversation among the city's leading businessmen and local landed gentry. Much rum and wine flowed and were used as the basis of both prankish and serious bets. As a businessman, James was a partner together with Archibald Hamilton in the firm Hamilton, Monteath and Co., wine merchants. He had also become a lawyer in 1812, partnering with Archibald Lithan Cuthill of Kelvinside, the firm being called Cuthill and Monteath. About 1821, "this respectable firm amalgamated with Mr. Thomas Graham, an old and equally respectable lawyer [since 1793], and the firm became Graham, Cuthill and Monteath".[36]

Archibald Douglas Monteath passed away on 15 June 1842 at Helensburgh near or at Ardmore. While his furniture, books and moveable effects were valued only at just above £100, his investments in Scotland's industrial sector were substantial. His stocks and shares in Monkland Navigation, Glasgow Water Works, Glasgow Light Company, Edinburgh and Glasgow Railway, the Glasgow, Paisley, Kilmarnock and Ayr Railway, the Wilsontown and Morningside Railway, and the Ardrossan rail line, at the time of death amounted to a value of £28,453. Further stocks and shares were invested in Bank of England Stock, East India Stock and Bengal Bank Stock. Cash in the Glasgow Bank of Scotland and at Ferguson Brothers and Co., Calcutta accounted for just under £2,000. James Monteath was nominated as sole executor and with power of attorney to carry out "certain written directions and instructions" that were separate from the will itself.[37] One of James's assignments was to deploy £1,000 for the construction of "monumental tables in the [Glasgow] Necropolis to the memory of his father, mother, sister, and brother Capt Walter Monteath".[38] Instead, a mausoleum was constructed where "the two brothers were interred side by side [in] two covered vaults in the centre of the mausoleum . . . without slab or inscription. There is not a single letter or date either internally or externally, about the whole structure, although it is completely covered over with so much elaborate ornament."[39] One wonders, though, why this monument was not also dedicated to John Monteath? Was it only because his body was not interred there? But then, it is unlikely that the body of Captain Walter Monteath rested there, as he had died in India. John was buried at Kep; to the best of our knowledge, he lies in an unmarked grave.

Figure 5.1 Monteath Mausoleum, Glasgow Necropolis. Photo: Alan Wilson.

The Monteaths in Jamaica's West

Four of Walter I's brothers came to Jamaica to make their fortune. But they were merely following a track that had already been beaten by other Scots. "By the latter part of the seventeenth century Scots merchants, planters, seafarers, and transportees were to be found throughout the English and Dutch colonies of the Caribbean."[40] In addition, thousands of Scots had been lured by plans to colonize the narrow neck of land in Central America north of present-day Colombia and flanked to the east by the Gulf of Darien and to the west by the Gulf of Panama. This was the Darien Peninsula, and the plan was to establish there an entrepôt on the route of a canal that would link the Atlantic to the Pacific. The idea, whose conceptualizer was the Scot, William Paterson, began with the exodus of colonists from Leith in Scotland in 1698 and was followed up by other boatloads in 1699. But the hardships of climate and terrain, as well as the hostility of Spanish precursors, led to the major financial disaster of the so-called Darien Scheme. After less than two years attempting to colonize the area, survivors abandoned the location and "dispersed: some to Jamaica and other islands of the West Indies; some to Charleston, South Carolina and other ports up to Philadelphia, New York and Boston; and others returned home to Scotland".[41]

In Jamaica they found a tropical island some 146 miles long by 22 to 55 miles wide. One of the islands of the Greater Antilles in the Caribbean archipelago between North and South America, it was a land of exquisite beauty and variety of landscape, once peopled by native Americans known as Taino, who lived in hunting and gathering communities. Their settlements along the coastline, in caves and in highland fastnesses had been disturbed by the intrusion of the Spaniards under Christopher Columbus in 1494. He was looking for sea routes to Asia and was desperate for gold. Neither could be found, so the Spaniards had established a few urban settlements, largely as stopover points for vessels moving out from the Atlantic into Central and South America. The Spaniards were routed by an English expeditionary force led by Captains Penn and Venables in 1655 and the island was formally ceded by Spain to England in 1670.[42]

The British, coming in partly from Barbados, Montserrat, Nevis and St Kitts (formerly St Christopher),[43] had put the land into sugar cane cultivation, following on the success of such enterprises in Barbados and Antigua. A century and a half later, the land had only been partially cleared for agriculture and vistas of pristine vegetation were much in evidence.

> We rode through a luxuriant valley, between the St. Elizabeth and Manchester mountains, which were covered with thick forests, often most beautifully interwoven with cactuses of different kinds. . . . We ascended, with slow paces, the Manchester mountains; having reached the summit of the ridge, our eyes feasted on the beautiful view which appeared in sight; declivities, shaded with rich foliage, afford the weary traveller a covering from the beams of a tropical sun, while rocky precipices, in every direction, often exhibiting very grotesque forms, give variety and interest to the landscape.[44]

Another view from the Dom Figuerero Mountains in the southwest describes the panorama from the road along Ambey, Silver-Grove and Huntly:

> Every turn up the mountains struck out some new beauty. Though well acquainted with the scenery of Cumberland and Westmoreland [in England], and with the lakes of Scotland, they were almost tempted to declare, the views of this day superior to any thing they had yet seen. Mountains that in the valley appeared of great height, sunk into comparative insignificance amidst the numbers, and more commanding aspect of their fellows. The plain below presented a varied picture of wild savannah, tracts of brushwood, and extensive cane-fields of the most delicious green; in the distance, was ocean girting the scene, and flashing its silver light, while rocks crowded with ferns and shrubs, and trees of stupendous growth, loaded with the most beautiful parasitical creepers, adorned the ground in front, and displayed all the richness and luxuriance peculiar to a tropical climate.[45]

No wonder a European would later confess, "Jamaica appeared to me one of the most beautiful countries I have ever seen",[46] and another would express the opinion that the parish of "St. James's is the most beautiful part of the island I have yet seen, and the land is in the best cultivation".[47]

One of the early Scots who settled in Jamaica was John Campbell, who had emigrated to the Darien Peninsula in Central America in 1699. With the failure of the settlement, he took refuge in Jamaica in 1700, eventually becoming an assemblyman, a militia officer and custos of St Elizabeth parish. He died in Jamaica on 29 January 1740.[48] Among the estates he owned was Holland Estate, St Elizabeth,[49] which was inherited by his son, Colin Campbell. By the 1820s Holland was owned by Peter Campbell, who had thoughts of purchasing Kep, John Monteath's principal property.

There were yet other Scots who took advantage of the opportunities for overseas settlement and the administrative, military and land-endowment privileges afforded by the union of England and Scotland in 1707. For Europeans, landholding was the index of wealth, and ample fortunes and enhanced status by way of landholding and wealth could be made overseas. Among persons who sought this leverage were maternal relatives of John Monteath. These were the Douglases, Campbells and Wallaces. There were the brothers of Jean Douglas, who had married Archibald Walter Monteath. There was the maternal great-uncle Campbell Douglas who had property in St Thomas parish in southeastern Jamaica and who made his will on 9 June 1775. There was another great-uncle, Colin Douglas, who predeceased his wife, Margaret Douglass or Douglas, identified in her will as resident in Westmoreland parish.[50] Colin had a mulatto son, named James, an apprentice mason in 1775. Much later, on 1 June 1803 John Graham Douglass "at present of the parish of St. Catherine" made a deed of gift, probably in settlement of some legal matter or to circumvent legal taxes, for the cost of 10s., to Dugald Campbell of Salt Spring in Hanover involving the 826 acres of that sugar estate, with its boiling, curing, still and trash houses, together with another 97 acres in Hanover "bounding north on Prospect Estate East on Saxham Estate South on Green River Estate and west on Hopewell Estate". There were approximately 340 slaves thrown in for good measure.[51]

The Wallaces too owned lands in Jamaica. The mother of Colin, Jean and Campbell Douglas had been Rebecca Wallace. Her will is dated 10 May 1766.[52] It would also appear that John Monteath's great-aunt, Elizabeth Douglas, daughter of James Campbell Douglas and Rebecca Wallace, and who had been christened on 2 December 1720 at New Kilpatrick, Dunbartonshire, had married the merchant Thomas Wallace around 1735. Thomas was the third son of Thomas Wallace of Cairnhill and had registered as a burgess in 1745.[53] Thomas's eldest brother, Hugh, had secured a loan of sterling £630 2s. 3d. from Thomas and Elizabeth's son Thomas Wallace on 1

April 1772, through the mediation of the merchant Arthur Connell. Connell was an in-law to the Wallace brothers[54] and was also a factor or agent for young Thomas, in addition to being a "tutor", that is, a "guardian" or more specifically in this case, "the administrator of the estate of a person legally incapable". Since Thomas would have been in his mid- to late thirties by the time the loan was given, there is a suggestion here that Thomas was ill, incapacitated, or even deceased. The loan was to have been repaid by 1 September 1774, on 5 per cent interest, with a penalty of £150 for failure to pay. Hugh Wallace had inherited lands in Jamaica, such as Biscany Estate and Eldersley in St Elizabeth, just as he was owner of Biscony in Renfrewshire. Apart from being a planter and pen-keeper, Hugh was a merchant with business in Savanna-la-Mar, and was custos of Westmoreland when he died in October 1774, being buried on 24 October.[55] But he had defaulted on the loan, which was then inherited by his son, also Hugh, an army captain. Recovery of the monies became a legal matter when Elizabeth, acting in concert with Walter Monteath I, her brother-in-law, on 6 June 1781, secured power of attorney for her son (again suggesting some incapacity on his part). Some years later, on 18 September 1788, they both granted power of attorney to the firms of Walter's Jamaica-based brothers, Thomas and David Monteath and their business partners James Millar and William Sinclair, to obtain yearly repayments from Hugh Wallace as the eldest son of his father. By 1 January 1789, the outstanding sum amounted to sterling £1,152 11s. 8d., representing principal, interest and penalty.[56]

With regard to John Monteath's paternal uncles who made their living in Jamaica, James, the second son of Archibald Walter and Jean, also became a merchant, and by 1779 was based in Kingstown, capital of the island of St Vincent, but transferred to Jamaica by the 1780s. He owned Belfield or Bellfield Estate in Trelawny parish, and died on 18 September 1798 in Jamaica.[57] William, the third son, became a merchant too, having left Glasgow some time before 1777.[58] He died in Jamaica on 15 July 1782 and was buried two days later.[59] John, the fourth son of Archibald Walter and Jean, became a mariner, yet seems towards the end of his life to have become a merchant in Jamaica. He died on 30 June 1779 in Hanover parish, his interment being on 1 July.[60] David was the eighth and last son of Archibald Walter and Jean. He was baptized in 1759 and died in Glasgow in May 1804.[61] However, we know more about Thomas, very likely the person who migrated from Glasgow to Jamaica in 1774 on the *Janet*. He was the sixth son of Archibald Walter and Jean and had been born in 1759.[62] Thomas was married to Amelia Murray, who negotiated business either together with Thomas or in her own right. The couple named James Smyth junior of Edinburgh as their attorney on 12 October 1795, and by 10 April 1799 she was a widow in

Jamaica, issuing a will in favour of her grandfather, John Schaw, an Edinburgh merchant.[63] Thomas and Amelia had a daughter, Margaret, born on 25 August 1788 and baptized on 3 November 1788, followed by a son, Thomas, baptized on 7 June 1796.[64] By the 1840s this latter Thomas rose to be lieutenant-colonel and brigadier in the East India Company, seeing action in Peshawar and in Kabul in Afghanistan. Indeed, he retired as General Sir Thomas Monteath Douglas, having been decorated for his services during the First Afghan War when he "distinguished himself in the defence of Jellalabad with Sir Robert Sale in 1841".[65]

However, Thomas Monteath senior had other children as well: he fathered a "reputed daughter", Jesse Monteath, registered as a mulatto in the Hanover church register. She was baptized on 26 November 1779, together with Colin, reputed son of George Scott, and George, reputed son of George White.[66] Other documentation indicates that Jesse's mother was Sarah Donaldson, "a Mulattoe".[67] This means that Jesse was a quadroon, rather than a mulatto. Another of Thomas's children by Sarah Donaldson was John Monteath who was born on 25 June 1781. He became a mariner, owning a sloop called the *Francis Ann*. He bought land in Savanna-la-Mar from his mother, and died in June 1840 as harbour master of Black River.[68] His will of 9 April 1839, left the proceeds from the sale of his sloop to be shared equally between his nephew John Nevins and his housekeeper, Mary Hugh Williams; the latter also received all his household furniture.[69] Both Nevins and Williams were executors, and among witnesses to his will was his second cousin, Archibald John Monteath, the Scotsman John Monteath's son.[70] Other children of Sarah Donaldson[71] with Thomas Monteath were William Monteath, born 1 May 1893, and Rebecca Monteath. Rebecca was baptized on 30 January 1795, and made her will on 6 March 1861.[72] In John the harbour master's will, he makes bequests to both a Jessy Monteith, identified as his adopted daughter, and to a nephew, John Monteith Stephens. This "Jessy Monteeth", resident at Black River, is listed as baptized on 21 February 1841, having been born in August 1832, but no parents are specified.[73] The structure of her name suggests that she may well have been the child of either Jesse or Rebecca Monteath, sisters of John the harbour master, and therefore his niece.

The earliest reference to the elder group of Monteath brothers is on 24 April 1773 when William, having already borrowed Jamaican £1024 6s. from Alexander Anderson, possibly another Scot, had to forfeit twenty-two slaves to acquit the debt. In the document of forfeiture, William is referred to as a planter of Hanover parish.[74] Ancillary data reveal that he purchased 1 puncheon, 121 gallons of rum in 1776 from Graunge Plantation in Hanover, owned by Alexander Miller.[75] Six years later, in 1782, Long Pond Estate in Trelawny sold both William and Thomas Monteath 7 puncheons, 775 gallons.[76] Indeed, William's business fortunes seem to have improved with the presence of Thomas, their emphasis now turning to retailing and to real estate. As regards the latter, as of 1773, and continuing into 1781, Thomas, and later both Thomas and William, were involved in the mortgage difficulties of John Robert James and his wife Mary, both of St James parish east of Green Island, Hanover parish, where the Monteaths were based. The Jameses had got a mortgage of £5,650 from Ephraim Dunn, a magistrate, to buy an estate called Prospect. By 1778, Dunn nominated the Monteaths as his attorneys to recover the sums owed him by the Jameses. In fact, the Monteaths paid Dunn £5,989 in 1778 on this matter, and in 1776 they had already succeeded in securing 6,000 acres of land in Negril (probably the very Prospect) from the beleaguered Jameses. Yet by 1781, the Jameses were still indebted to the Monteaths to the sum of £9,000. However, the Jameses were also owed monies and there were at least two court cases to recover these debts. Earlier, on 1 June 1776, the Jameses sold William and Thomas two parcels of land amounting to 600 acres near Negril in Westmoreland for £1,800.[77] In another matter, on 15 March 1777 William Monteath and Co. of Green Island invited a one-year or more rental on William Downes's upstairs four-bedroom house with out-offices, cellars and about 4 acres in "plantain walk" (grove). Two years later, the brothers bought "a negro woman slave named Dinah and future issue" for £60 from Dr Richard Brooke and his wife Frances of St Catherine parish,[78] and on 24 March 1780, they spent £100 to acquire two women slaves, Rose and Mary, from Lewis Cadot, a mariner.[79]

William passed away on 15 July 1782,[80] and in August that year a newspaper announcement gave notice of a change in business partnership of the firm.[81] Before this, on 1 March 1781, Thomas entered into an agreement with Mary James, now a widow, to lease 6¼ acres of land between the King's Road and the beach at Green Island Bay for fourteen years at a rent of £30 per annum in order to build a house and office.[82] By 1781, Thomas was in business with William Sinclair. Perhaps they were in merchandising as well since they held an auction. The profitability of this business is understood when we read that "Jamaica alone took off 40 percent of all Scottish linen exports to be made up into clothing for the planters and their slaves. Other Scottish exports to Jamaica consisted of haberdashery, goods of leather, iron, copper, tin, hats, ropes, delft and stoneware, herrings, and coaches."[83]

It also becomes evident that Thomas was involved in shipping, apart from real estate, moneylending and merchandising. In 1781 a newspaper article announced that "the schooner belonging to Mess. Monteaths of Green Island" had a week previously seized a Spanish sloop manned by eighteen hands and brought it into harbour. The sloop was on its twelfth raid along the Jamaican coast, during which it had taken twelve vessels with thirty-five

Figure 5.2 Lucea by Joseph Kidd. Courtesy National Library of Jamaica.

blacks, among its prizes being a "fine sloop, with a valuable cargo, from Kingston for Savanna-la-Mar". The newspaper invited "a general subscription throughout the County of Cornwall" to encourage "the gallant volunteers, who . . . have boldly stepped on board for the defence of the sea-coast of this country".[84] So the Monteaths were apparently involved in intra-island shipping, if not trade with nearby islands as well.

In 1785 a Jewish couple, Abraham and Rebecca Myers, forfeited their property to Thomas Monteath, James Miller and William Sinclair for indebtedness amounting to £1,560.[85] By 1787 there were newspaper notices warning debtors of William and Thomas Monteath, and Thomas Monteath in his own right. Thomas himself withdrew from his business partnerships, both Monteath Miller and Sinclair, and Monteath Sinclair and Co., in December 1785.[86] The renunciation document identifies Thomas and his associates as having "lately conducted and carried on a very considerable business as merchants and copartners under the two firms". Meanwhile, David had arrived in the colony at some stage, but he pulled up anchor from Jamaica, probably around 1790 when James advertised for sale a lot of land with a house owned by David. However, the business still retained David's name, as in 1792 and 1793 the firm of James and David Monteath was retailing food items and haberdashery at wharves in Trelawny, where these two were based. Items sold included flour, butter, men's and ladies' hats and coats. It would in fact appear that David had returned to Glasgow, where in August 1803 he entered a co-partnership in Monteath Dickson and Co., a rum and wine merchant house. However, he died the following year.

John Monteath: Economic Profile

We do not know the date of John Monteath's arrival in Jamaica, nor the circumstances of his early years in the island. He may have arrived in the early to mid-1790s, in his twenties. Had it not been for his father's vicissitudes on account of the American Revolution, John may well have made his way to the American colonies to seek his fortune there. But by the 1790s the main economic engines of Britain lay either in the East Indies or the West Indies, and by the 1780s Jamaica had surpassed both Antigua and Barbados as the principal driver of sugar fortunes.

On the basis of established practice, John may have proceeded from Greenock, the transatlantic waterfront near Glasgow, with letters of recommendation from persons who had trading or legal contacts in Jamaica, to help him secure a post as bookkeeper or overseer.[87] But since John had two or three uncles at any one time in western Jamaica in the 1770s through to the 1790s, it is quite possible that they had already made local contact with persons seeking to employ a young Scotsman with reputable family connections. Or it is possible that even while in Scotland, the British network of returnee investors in Jamaica had attracted or solicited his interest in employment there. The pattern of personal relationships oiling the way for building careers had been well established.

Even more, these "patronage networks . . . designed to facilitate living and working in unfamiliar surroundings in the tropics" were in fact a reinvention of the Scottish clan system, reinvigorating kinship ties and reproducing the geographical proximity of clan members' lands.[88] Instances of the workings of one network centre on Dr James Paterson of Perthshire, a cousin of the Wedderburns. Paterson took responsibility for the welfare of the minor, Sir John Wedderburn, whose father had been executed for his part in the Jacobite rebellion in Scotland in 1746. "At eighteen Wedderburn was too young to have been on his own and Paterson apparently arranged for apprenticeship as an apothecary. By 1752, at 23, he was described as a 'surgeon in Jamaica'."[89] Another protégé of Dr Paterson was David Fyfe, of whom Wedderburn wrote in 1747: "Davie Fyfe has been here too 4 or 5 months he is with a Surgeon now who is very Sickly and if he shou'd go off the Island he has a good Chance to fall in to his Business." In addition, there was John

Kinloch, a cousin of the Olyphants, Paterson's in-laws, and who, within three months of his arrival in Jamaica, Paterson had made "[o]verseer to a small Plantation he is Attorney for and will gett him into better Business when he has seen a little more of the Planting trade".[90]

As for John Monteath, had he started off working in the merchandising and real estate business of his uncles in Green Island in Hanover parish? This might have been unlikely, given that the most active merchant brother, Thomas, had already withdrawn from his co-partnership business in 1785. So had he begun as a bookkeeper? Was he then one of the white administrative personnel at Lower Works Pen on the waterfront in St Elizabeth, owned by Joseph Royal in the 1780s and 1790s? Joseph Royal or Royall had by the 1780s retired to Great Cumberland Street in Marylebone in Middlesex, a wealthy man,[91] Middlesex being a quiet county outside the hustle and bustle of London and apparently a favourite residential location for persons with West India business interests. During the 1770s to 1790s Royal appears to have been in co-partnered ownerships of various estates, such as Sunderland Estate in St James, Unity Plantation and Pleasant Pen in Trelawny,[92] as well as Y.S. Estate in St Elizabeth. Before leaving Jamaica, he had been custos of St Elizabeth in 1768 when he married the widow of Robert Delap.[93] He was at the same time chief judge of the Court of Common Pleas for St Elizabeth.[94] Lower Works Pen produced cotton for export, as well as supplying pasturage to the St Elizabeth regiment horses and selling other landowners milk, stallions and other types of livestock. The Pen, described as "near Black River bay",[95] also hired out "negro labour" to work on board several ships while in harbour.

If John Monteath were stationed at Lower Works, this could account for his liaison with the slave Phillis with whom he had a daughter, Charlotte, in 1796; but he may just have had a visiting relationship with her if he was based on a nearby pen or plantation. Had he, like Thomas Thistlewood thirty or so years before him,[96] begun his Jamaican career as an overseer? We do know that he was the overseer on William Harriott's Mexico Plantation in St Elizabeth as of 1796 thereabouts, witnessing between 1796 to 1800 to the veracity of statements regarding the income, local sales and overseas shipments of the plantation's sugar and rum produce.[97] Then by 1802 and until 1803, he became overseer for the joint Fonthill and Hampstead Estates owned by Thomas Smith, Fonthill producing sugar and rum, while Hampstead yielded coffee.[98]

That John was in touch with his uncles is clear from the fact that he bought a black male in 1800 from the same party to whom his uncle Thomas had earlier sold some slaves.[99] Jean Monteath, more likely John's aunt than his paternal grandmother, had also sold the same Charles James Clarke of

Figure 5.3 Overseer. Sketch by Robert "Quizem" Hawkins. Courtesy National Library of Jamaica.

Hanover eight slaves in 1796.[100] In addition, one of the mothers of Dr Thomas Ford's children, Sarah Ford, was also the property of Clarke, at his Enfield Estate in Westmoreland. Dr Ford became John Monteath's doctor and was also the father of John's principal concubine, Nancy.

Credit: The India Connection

John was to profit from the financial assets of his brother, Walter Monteath. Walter II apparently had earlier negotiated that his uncle, Robert Douglas, would, on Walter's behalf, advance monies that he intended to give to John. This was some time before 1799 because Walter mentions in his will the need for his executors to use a sum he had placed on loan to the Madras Government to repay Robert Douglas the debt. We are not told the figure of this loan. Furthermore, even after Walter's death, John was able to negotiate with the executors of Walter's estate to raise a one-year loan of sterling £1,000 in 1801, and in 1804 for another loan of the same value for a three-year period.

In 1785 Walter Monteath II's name entered the officer list as cornet in the Nineteenth Light Dragoons. Cornet was the fifth grade of commissioned officer in a British cavalry troop and also the standard bearer. The Nineteenth regiment had previously carried the banner as the Twenty-third Light Dragoons and had been raised in 1781 for service in India, the first British cavalry regiment that had been sent out to India and for fourteen years the only one. This regiment was, however, disbanded in 1783 and then redeployed as the Nineteenth. Monteath retained the rank of cornet until 1789. As of 1780 he was promoted to lieutenant, and then in 1795 to captain.[101] Walter therefore saw action for at least fourteen years in India, a fact which helps explain the strong showing of his estate, given the prize money won in various campaigns.

The Nineteenth Light Dragoons were based in southern India in order to clear the way for the trading interests of the East India Company. In so doing, they had to prosecute several campaigns against Moslem state holders who had subjugated previous Hindu monarchs. One of their chief targets was the state of Mysore, which produced agricultural surpluses of rice, sandalwood, betel nut, black pepper, cardamom and both raw cotton and cotton cloth.[102] When Britain first clashed with Mysore, it was ruled by Hyder Ali who on his death in December 1782 was succeeded by his son, Tipu Sultan. The latter continued the war with the East India Company till 1784.

After another campaign that began in 1790, Tipu's headquarters at Bangalore were eventually overrun by the British under Lord Cornwallis in 1792,[103] but not before loss and injury to Walter Monteath's co-officers. Subsequently Tipu established an alliance with French troops, an alliance complicated by Napoleon's declaration of war against Britain in February 1793. The Nineteenth Light Dragoons then participated, under Colonel John Floyd, the battalion's lieutenant colonel, in the seizure from the French of the enclave of Pondicherry in August of the same year. Already, however, the "gallant bearing of the 19th Light Dragoons" in the 1790 campaign against Tipu had "made an impression that spread to every Native Court in southern India, and gained them a reputation for fighting, that clung to them during the whole of their service in India".[104]

The storming and capture in May 1799 of Seringapatam Island, the site of Tipu's fort and palace, resulted in Tipu's eventual demise. But the April–May 1799 action resulted in 192 British troops killed and 657 wounded.[105] The fact that Walter Monteath's will was made up in March 1799 might indicate some pre-existing injury or decline in health or that he died in one of the skirmishes leading up to the larger offensive. But in the words of the colonel of the Nineteenth Light Dragoons, Sir John Burgoyne, service in India was "not less honourable than lucrative". If the prize money gained during the war earned every private soldier £14 11s. 9d., then it was even greater for the senior officers who received advantages and power over and above those granted East India Company officers.[106] "Prize money was one of the great attractions of eighteenth-century military service in general and Indian service in particular, since in India, where hoarding of precious metals was common, even a minor fort taken during a small campaign might well yield a great windfall to a lucky officer." Cornwallis's Mysore War yielded £93,584 in prize money, to which Cornwallis added a gratuity from the money paid by Tipu as an indemnity; and this was matched by an equal amount from the East India Company. Nevertheless, "Cornwallis' war with Mysore paled . . . before the sum distributed when Seringapatam was taken by assault in 1799. The treasure and jewels found in the fort amounted to £1,142,216."[107]

Walter II seems not to have lived to participate in and profit from this last action, although he may have earned posthumous prize money. Whether or not this was so, his will gives evidence of a methodical cast of mind, precise and clear, given that he wrote it (perhaps wounded or otherwise ill, or preparatory to a military encounter which he felt would be fatal to him) "in presence of Almighty God and of no person whatsoever in Camp a few miles from Bangalore". His carefulness is also apparent in his prefatory remarks nominating his executors where he sets out his intention to include with "this paper a statement of [his] circumstances", but if this was not possible "a paper book marked *Private account*" among his documents "would be found useful" (emphasis his).[108]

His will made provisions for his siblings, as well as a bequest of sterling £500 for the welfare of a son born at Trichinopoly and the child's mother, an

Indian "girl now at Madras". This was to be realized from the sale of his two "grays", an Arabian horse and other effects. He owned a bungalow on Trichinopoly Plain far south of Bangalore that was left to his brother Archibald Douglas Monteath, then a cornet in the same regiment, and destined to rise to the position of major. This brother was also to have his compass, pistols, their canteens and their contents, together with a large China chest. Archibald Douglas was also to have charge of his child. His staff and regimental swords, and a silver medal bearing the impression of Marquis Cornwallis, were bequeathed to other officers, as well as his spy glass. Sterling £300 was left for Agnes, his sister, and the balance of his monies was to be "placed at interest on good security" by his trustees in Scotland: his maternal uncles Robert and Campbell Douglas, his brother James Monteath, and the lawyer John Maxwell, who may have been related.[109] His father and mother were to receive monies from the interest, in addition to which he bequeathed his father his gold watch and chain.

The monies to be invested from Walter II's estate constituted the source of a loan of sterling £1,000, equivalent to Jamaican £1,400, that John Monteath was able to access at an interest of 6 per cent per annum or sterling £60 per year in January 1801. The monies were lent by Captain Monteath's executors and fell due on 1 January 1802 "on the Exchanges in the City of Glasgow". To secure repayment of the principal and interest, John mortgaged to the trustees eleven "Negro and other slaves" who were his property, namely Campbell, Jack, Douglas, Glasgow, Guy, Jonathan, Sophy, Fanny, Yabba, Marianne and Juliet.[110] On 1 August 1804 John was again to call upon family financial support when he negotiated a loan of sterling £700 from the captain's account through his sister, Agnes Monteath, acting as attorney for Walter II's estate. He offered eight of his slaves as security for this loan,[111] which was worth Jamaican £1,000.

John Monteath's Investment Trajectories

It was in 1800, when he was still overseer at Mexico, that John began a series of land purchases in the same St Elizabeth parish in southwestern Jamaica. The lands he acquired were in the neighbourhood of Hampstead Estate for which he was to become overseer in 1802. For the price of £456 on 14 August 1800, he bought 114 acres from James Downie, overseer at Forest in 1797. It was identified as "part of a run of land called Mocoe".[112] He followed this up on 7 February 1801 by acquiring an adjoining 32½ acres, also from Downie, for £165;[113] then for £500 on 29 June 1803 he took control of another adjoining 116 acre premises, either seized or bought from Downie by the now seller, Peter McGregor of the adjoining Westmoreland parish. These

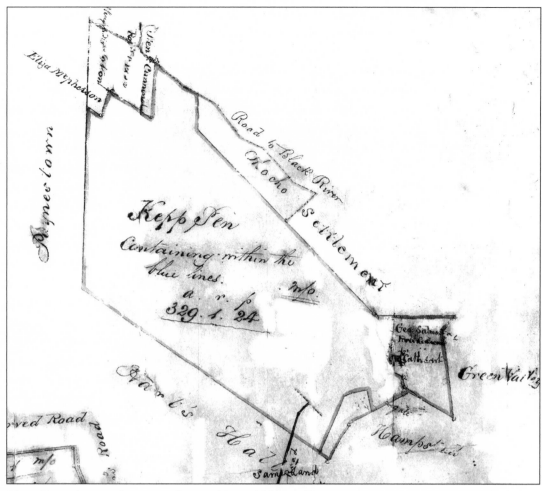

Map 7 Kep and surrounding estates. Courtesy National Library of Jamaica.

lands he amalgamated and named Kep, in remembrance and re-creation of his paternal landholding in Perthshire, and using a Scots word which in Perth meant a "porridge bowl", but which in the adjacent counties of Renfrew and Lanark slightly south of Perth referred to "horizontal frames laid over a cart for carrying hay etc.". In fact, in some other parts of Scotland it meant a "pen" or cattle pasture,[114] which is what John intended it for. The word was variously spelled "kep" or "kepp" and occurred as "keps" between the counties of Renfrew and Lanark.[115] Not surprisingly, however, there is evidence that someone else had earlier invoked this Scots word to endow a piece of land in the general vicinity of John Monteath's own Kep. For James Hart, another Scotsman, had in 1792 purchased from James Crow a 50-acre swathe of land in the parish of Westmoreland between Deans Valley and Lenox Estate, a piece of land already "commonly called Kippens",[116] and listed as "Kipping" owned by Margaret Hart on page thirty-four of the *Jamaica Almanack* of 1817. This name can be deconstructed as Kip or Kep Pens. This place name occurs in north Stirling, and is also pluralized as "kippeens" in Northern Ireland, meaning "wood for kindling".[117]

It would seem then that Monteath was retaining increasingly rewarding employment from established landowners while he was gradually building up his assets. And by taking on overseer responsibilities and by 1804 attorney directorship of estates not very far from his own land acquisitions, he was in a position to cast an eye on the development of his own holdings while earning income elsewhere. For instance, on 4 March 1804 John paid £132 to William Green of Trelawny parish, attorney to Edward Gregory Morant Gale of Great Britain, for 30 acres of Gale's land in the vicinity of Kep, on resurvey found to contain 44 acres.[118] So by 1804 he owned a small property in his own name.

At death John owned some ninety slaves, according to the advertisement for sale of the property, though the list in his official inventory at death named eighty-five people. But not all of his human acquisitions are accounted for in the documents so far found. The largest number of these purchases was made in October 1802 when he bought from Thomas Hardin, deputy marshal for Westmoreland, St Elizabeth and Hanover parishes, fifty-two slaves lost by Downie in a legal case brought against him by one Rodgers. Monteath paid the sizeable sum of £4,275 for this large acquisition.[119] The gender proportion of this group of enslaved persons was roughly equally divided but the ages are not given. The date of these acquisitions coincides with the time when Monteath was centrally consolidating a nuclear family unit around Ann or Annie or Nancy and the three children already born to them both, and when he was also involved in clearing and preparing the estate at Kep. One notices that it was only in the two years after his death – 1816 and 1817 – that Kep is listed in the crop accounts records as one of the business concerns that was in a position to export produce. His earlier purchase, on 1 May 1800, of an adult male named Ned from Charles James Clarke of Hanover for Jamaican £125 may have been an acquisition connected with building a modest house and business premises for his livestock farm.[120] Ned must have been a skilled and responsible person to have cost so much. Then, on 21 January 1803 he acquired a woman named Leah and her child named Helena from Catherine Bowes of St Elizabeth for £130.[121] Was she to perform household duties, most likely to be a wet nurse for Rose and a nanny for the four children to date? On 1 February 1810 he purchased eight "negro and other slaves" for Jamaican £810 from William Channer of St Elizabeth,[122] and on 10 May 1813 a boy named Harry and a woman named Eliza, together costing £300, from George Channer.[123]

John Monteath's stature as a rising landowner was paralleled by his public appointments. On 8 January 1800 he was appointed as a lieutenant in the St Elizabeth parish foot regiment, moving up to captain in 1804–8, and between 1811 and 1813 holding an appointment as a lieutenant colonel.[124] Such militia had come into existence after the disbanding of the Cromwellian army that had dispossessed Spain of Jamaica in 1655. These militias were activated in various important settlements of the island in order to address invasion threats, to assist resident army platoons in putting down slave uprisings and in raiding maroon and runaway slave hideouts. Similarly, John was one of the three commissioners of the St Elizabeth Workhouse between 1806 and 1807, and again in 1813.[125]

His interaction with important landowners and his resident status also equipped him to assume the responsibilities of attorney for some large estates. Attorneys or estate managers

> usually with more than one property under their direction, performed a remarkable variety of duties. They not only hired and fired overseers, bookkeepers, and other white personnel, but they also decided, wherever they were allowed to, how many slaves to purchase and how to use them to insure maximum productivity. They were responsible for buying plantation supplies, keeping everyone well fed, and selling the crops, or arranging for their consignment. They had to advise the owner of what needed to be invested in order to raise production levels, as well as whether or not the crop matched expectations. They were also responsible for making sure that governmental regulations were honored and the proper forms filed in Spanish Town [the administrative capital].[126]

Attorneys usually received a 6 per cent commission on all sales and purchases for the estate, and as such it was more profitable to be "attorney of an estate of a non-resident . . . than to be its owner, the first receiving benefits without the least risque". Another perk was that the attorney was entitled to take up residence on one of the estates he oversaw. A cynical view was that the attorney's greater interest was "to save expense to himself. . . . He looks about for a healthy eligible situation . . . a kitchen garden to furnish his table; but above all where small stock are numerous and thriving, that he may have an abundant supply for his own table without expense."[127] The option of residing at the estate house of a property for which one was an attorney is the reason why John Monteath, in his 1809 will, declared that he had a bedstead at Forest Estate.

In the capacity of attorney, from 1804 to 1807, John succeeded John Graham (1797), and later persons such as William Brown, Patrick Miller, Samuel Forrester (1800–1802) to manage the Jamaican affairs of David Fyfe of Drumgath in county Fiofar or Fofar in Scotland. By 1804 Fyfe was deceased, but he had owned Forest or Forrest Estate in Westmoreland parish, which sent sugar and rum to Wedderburn Webster and Co. in London and to America. During John's tenure as attorney, Forest exported sugar, rum, punch and logwood to Wedderburn and Co. in London, to Sterling Gordon and Co. in Glasgow, and to Bristol as well.[128] Logwood had been introduced into Jamaica in 1715 from Honduras by the botanist John Bartram, and yielded a purple-black dye for wool or silk. This was its main commercial purpose, but it also served as fence posts and to provide hedges, while its smaller stems were used as barrel hoops.[129] In addition, by 1818 Forest housed 168 slaves and 404 livestock, which suggests that it operated as a pen as well, all quite possible given the 1,373 acres it covered. The Wedderburns, both James and his brother John, were owners of extensive estates in western Jamaica. They too were Scots, from Inveresk near Edinburgh. The first in the family to come out to Jamaica had been a Sir John Wedderburn, whose father had been executed for Jacobite sympathies. John arrived as a late teenager either in the latter part of 1746 or early in 1747. The James of Archibald's biography was probably the great-grandnephew of Sir John. The latter's brothers, James, Peter and Alexander had gone out to Jamaica around 1755 and had prospered. One of James's sons was the radical anti-slavery activist, Robert Wedderburn, who wrote *The Horrors of Slavery.*[130] Another of these Wedderburns, named John, born on 18 August 1776, had been educated at Glasgow University in 1789, gone to Jamaica in 1794, and died in Westmoreland on 19 May 1799.[131] Either his son or a cousin, also named John, owned, according to the 1817 *Jamaica Almanack,* several estates in Westmoreland, including Mount Edgecombe, which carried 242 slaves and 357 livestock.[132] In 1804 John Monteath was also attorney for Grandvale Estate in Westmoreland, owned by John Cunningham. Grandvale, adjoining Forest, sent sugar and logwood to Bristol and Glasgow; while rum was sold to various local planters.[133]

By 1806 John Monteath had clearly been able to secure the interest and investment of friends and relatives in Scotland in an animal husbandry business. Did he see it feeding into the leather and tanning industry in Scotland, or was its production solely for local consumption? What we do know is that John, together with a consortium consisting of David[134] and James Connell, Patrick Falconer, James Robertson, Andrew Buchanan, John Bannatyne, William Tate and John Kinnear of Scotland, bought into land being sold by James Morrison of St Elizabeth to offset a mortgage Morrison held with Thomas Johnston, a St Elizabeth planter. The 422 acres bought on 2 July 1806 lay "in St. Elizabeth in the mountains above Lancaster Estate" and cost in combined principal and interest Jamaican £2,557 10s. 10d. 3f.[135] This probably became the land later referred to as "Upland", though by 1825

Upland accounted for only 240 acres.[136] Had Monteath misled his co-partners as to the size of this land, or had he himself been misinformed? As we have seen, in the changeover of ownership, it was not unusual that errors were discovered regarding the size of parcels of land. Or had part of Upland been sold off by the time John's son, James, acquired it, by purchase, in 1825? In any case, it is not known how John or his executor eventually satisfied the claims of those who had partnered with him in this particular venture.

Business networks in Scotland were consolidated through marriage and co-partnered enterprises, and financed by intra-family and bank credit. These networks extended overseas by way of the migration of individuals to both North and Central America, including the Caribbean. Trade expansion likewise followed this out-migration, which also took place eastwards, into India, with the opportunities for military and commercial adventures in the service of and alongside the rise of the East India Company.

6

Entrapped within
Colour as Caste

PLANTATION SOCIETY IN JAMAICA was structured along caste distinctions. Two principal caste categorizations were in operation: one was based on colour; the other on personal freedom. Somewhat less significant than these two was the caste created by place of birth: Europe or the Caribbean. This latter parameter had cultural rather than legal implications. The two major caste categories largely coincided, but there were discrepancies that produced conflicting and contradictory paradigms. For instance, within the two parameters of colour and freedom, there was class stratification, which introduced slight complications into the other social hierarchies. The colour caste placed Africans, by and large, on the lowest level, even though there may have been gradations within this, given that Africans bore many skin-colour variations between yellow and jet black. Evidence of shade awareness in Africa has received scant consideration in written sources, and little evidence of it is currently available from documented oral sources among the Africans themselves.[1] On the other hand, a preoccupation with colour shading became a peculiarity deriving from close and prolonged contact with the European ideology that skin colour was an index of moral and personal value.

What made colour a caste category was that there was an almost exact correlation between blackness of skin colour and slavery. It was for this reason that by the post-slavery period it was observed that "the black people do not like to be called Negroes, but preferably, coloured or black".[2] To top this, Europeans linked colour intimately with physical features: with respect to the face, there was breadth of nose-bridge and tip, cheekbone height and width, forehead protrusion, lip evertedness and thickness; in respect of hair texture, it mattered whether hair was tightly curled or wavy.[3] Body markers included the protrusion or slant of the behind and the presence or absence of decorative body markings such as filed teeth, and facial or other body scarifications. The last group of markers was evidently more important to the Africans than colour gradation, precisely because such marks indicated subethnic and ethnic affiliation and, as in the Nri case, class status. But it was all these, together with general darkness of skin colour, which identified for Europeans the African, and this category of person was ideologically placed on the lowest rung of the aesthetic and biological evolutionary ladder. The European placed himself on the highest, most evolved, rung. Of course, there were gradations of beauty among Europeans, based on the negative or positive value placed in different eras on dark as against blonde hair, lankness or waviness of hair, nose-bridge height and curvature. Mulattos fitted into intervening scales based on approximations to one or other of the polar extremes: "essential" African versus "essential" European. While this judgement would have varied according to individual cases, an official generalized recognition of ethnic gradations based on quantification of the European element in the mixture was instituted. This system was most elaborated by the Spanish and Portuguese.[4] The British recognized only the following: A "mulatto" was the offspring of white + black; a "sambo", the offspring of black + mulatto; a "quadroon" or "quateroon" or "quaderoon", the offspring of white + mulatto; and "mustee", also known as "mustize" and "mestize", the product of white + quadroon. Another category, known as "reputed white" or "white by law", was the offpring of white + mustee.[5] These categories defined persons listed in church and legal records.

Another cultural categorization concerned locus of birth and social conditioning. It was a non-legal, more descriptive, category, which may be considered a subordinate caste category. It was the difference between "African" and "Creole". It distinguished the Africa-born from the Caribbean-born, and inferred cultural differences, such as mother-tongue, and therefore facility with the European language, and it implied a differential level of acculturation to the hypotheses on which plantation life and slave society rested. It was also semantically extended to infer level of intelligence, for since mature enslaved Africans had difficulty understanding European languages, they obviously gave the impression of dim-wittedness for, typical of ethnically arrogant perceptions, no allowance was made for African linguistic alienation. Thus one Moravian missionary adjudged the "poor Africans" with whom he was trying to communicate "ignorant and stupid".[6] In the literature connected with the Monteath story, the term "Creole" was used as a distinguishing category for blacks only, though in other contexts of the period it was used also of Europeans, categorizing those born in the Caribbean against those born in Europe.[7]

An even more important caste distinction was that between free and non-free. While persons had not necessarily been born into these castes, they entered plantation society on the basis of this caste differentiation. For instance, most of the Africans had been born free citizens in their home societies – even though some may have become slaves there because of debt or ritual classification – but such distinctions became irrelevant once they entered the process of transatlantic slavery. The new social framework into which they entered operated on the premise that some human beings were the economic property of others.

Ownership of a slave was virtually the prime signal of an individual's wealth. It was even more significant than land as a unit of wealth. Such a status symbol invited in the owner an acute awareness of the high economic value of his chattel property: it was property that could be bought, it could be sold if the slave was habitually troublesome, but also if one had debts to defray. It could also be moved according to the owner's convenience, for instance when a white woman married, her personal slaves would be transferred with her to her husband's premises as part of her dowry. Slaves could also be willed to another, and could be given as presents. The significance of their economic value explains why so few slaves were manumitted, even by Europeans who were very devoted Christians. It also explains why free blacks themselves owned slaves; and why some of the Moravian missionaries and Anglican clergymen of the seventeenth, eighteenth and nineteenth centuries also owned slaves. The fact is that the economic ideology of the society did not include the notion of paid labour for non-white ethnic groups, especially for persons with African physiological properties.

Ironically, it might be thought that awareness of the economic value of ownership over someone else's person and labour might have led to the slave's enjoyment of particular care. However, the excessive authority exercised over the slave by his or her owner bred a contradiction: it led to a negative evaluation of the treasured object since that commodity was as human as its owner, possessed reactive agency and thus invited provocation. It was not dead, dumb or insensate. This commodification of a living creature drew contempt:

> It is not possible to speak in too strong language of the utter contempt with which the . . . slave master looked upon his slaves! If we say that he regarded them as beasts and chattels, it is doubtful whether we do not take too favourable a view of his conduct; for there was frequently a harshness and cruelty exercised towards the slaves, which was not shown to dumb animals. And even those whose naturally

kind disposition did not allow them to illtreat the slave, nevertheless despised him from their very heart. The slave was to them their beast of burden, the tool of their lust, and sometimes their plaything.[8]

All the same, a few Africans were able to procure free status, which afforded them an asset denied to the mass of persons in the black caste category. Freedom was acquired in a number of ways: Some persons were freed because of particular assistance to whites, for example, in leaking information regarding an insurrection or an attack from the Maroons. Or because of particular personal attachment over a long period, a slave may have been freed by an owner who was about to die, or who was leaving the island, or who had already left the colony and sent instructions to his legal representative in Jamaica with respect to the particular servant. Some slaves, both black and mulatto, were freed because of their intimate sexual relationship with a European, usually a male, and in such cases, freedom was also arranged for the particular issue or issues of the slave female. However, the converse did not always apply: the mixed-blood offspring of the European male could be freed without that privilege being extended to the mother. Other slaves bought their own freedom by dint of saving money earned from farming plots of land on the periphery of the estate and trading in its excess produce, or from trading some skill they possessed, such as at fishing, or smithing, and so on. Freed persons sometimes contrived to save money to buy the freedom of relatives or loved ones.

A classification just above that of unfree was that of indentured or bond-servant. This latter category affected Europeans recruited, whether in families, as individuals or en bloc, to serve indentureship with European employers. "The white servant, contracted as a bondsman or bondswoman, for a period of four to seven years, was a significant member of the majority of early Jamaican households. . . . Servants were originally needed in the Caribbean as general labourers, in agriculture, trades, and domestic service: as the number of black slaves grew, white labour specialised, and came to mean almost exclusively supervisory work on estates, and artisans' skills."[9] These skills included trades such as those of millwright, wheelwright, cooper, carpenter, ship's carpenter, bricklayer, mason, butcher, printer, blacksmith, coppersmith, distiller, wharfinger, mariner, shoemaker, tavern keeper and shopkeeper. White women servants were cooks, nurses and nannies, and those who outlasted the climate "graduated in time to the ranks of the free, and the respectable".[10] Those who remained as house servants were employed in making and mending clothes, and if "in addition to her domestic skills" she was also "handsome and kind", "she could fairly confidently plan to become mistress".[11]

So class differences were a factor in white society in plantation Jamaica, but "[t]he consciousness of being a small minority helped to develop a strong sense of cohesion and interdependence among white creoles", a trend "strengthened by the entrenched practice of inter-marriage among local families".[12]

The Coloureds or Browns

What was the condition of the products of miscegenation and more specifically of such women, in eighteenth- and nineteenth-century society in southwestern Jamaica? Because of their ethnic hybridity, it is not possible to discuss mulattos or browns in isolation from their diverse ethnic antecedents: broadly speaking, whites and blacks. Whites included European Caucasians as well as Jews, while blacks included the Africans of various ethnic origins as well as their hybrid amalgams, black Creoles.

Those mulattos fathered by whites financially unable or emotionally unwilling to buy their freedom were left to live out their lives as enslaved persons. Since it could cost considerable sums to buy the freedom of a person, the person seeking to liberate a slave from bondage had to be prepared to put up the required funds to satisfy the slave's owner, and further monies to secure a bond with the vestry of the parish to which the slave belonged in order to safeguard against the freed person becoming a charge on the state. Otherwise, by and large,

> planters tended to remove [ethnic hybrids] from the lowest category of workers, to make tradesmen out of the males, to promote females from the field to the great house. Preferential treatment, designed to make white allies out of brown slaves, applied particularly to women, who as domestics and housekeepers, served many functions.[13]

Fulfilment of such roles was no doubt responsible for the pharaonic treatment accorded a slave mother who had passed away. Her queenly treatment was in part because of her longevity, in part because of the fruitfulness of her line, and in part out of acknowledgement of her foresight and no doubt self-sacrifice in securing upward mobility for her offspring by genetically altering their colour. A missionary put it this way: "As she had a great number of mulatto children and grand-children, her funeral was conducted with as much pomp, as if she had been one of the richest people. The coffin was covered with gold tinsel, and all the other furniture was of a similar description."[14] More overt evidence of the power of the colour caste system in fostering distorted social attitudes is detected in a particular instance related by the missionary Jacob Zorn. He observed a young mulatto named John who, interestingly, is noted as owning no slaves – perhaps this implied that not only did he not work, but also that he had not bestirred himself to purchase others to labour for him. Rather, a "brown woman" whom the missionary had questioned "as to the character and abilities of several of the neighbours" in Middle Quarters remarked, "[h]e likes to lie down all day, and his old mother works for him". The missionary then comments that "even among slaves, it is customary for the fairer offspring to be called massa, and missis, and their mothers are content to work for these would-be gentry, even when grown up to manhood".[15] The contempt with which John treated his mother and her toleration of his abuse – attitudes that were in part due to his colour – were the warp and woof of generalized discriminatory behaviour in interpersonal relations. For instance, the remarks below illustrate the power of the hierarchy of colour as reinforced by the other caste paradigm based on freedom and its negation:

> Free coloreds not only adopted white values but also tended to compensate for their lower status by abusing slaves. Many travelers reported that brown men were harsher masters than whites and were more likely to mistreat their slaves. A common Jamaican saying reflected the feeling that slaves preferred white owners: "If me for have massa or misses, give me Buckra one – no give me mulatto, dem no use neega well."[16]

In the eighteenth century and up to the first decade of the nineteenth, the ethnic gradations of persons were recorded in official documents such as baptismal, marriage, death and manumission records. But the British, unlike the Spanish and Portuguese, apparently found the niceties of these gradations too burdensome and bewildering to calculate, so the broad terminologies "brown" and "of colour" came to be applied to ethnic hybrids. These wide spectrum categories collapsed transethnic combinations that produced various skin shades and phenotypical characteristics. Close examination of the records reveals inaccuracies of colour labelling, given the taxonomy of ethnic cross-breeding conventionally recognized and set out above. For example, several of the white Dr Thomas Ford's children are described by himself and by Anglican pastors as "of colour" rather than as quadroons, given that their mothers were mulatto. On the other hand, two of his children baptized in 1821 are officially recorded as quadroons. Then, since Nancy Monteath, one of Ford's daughters, was technically a quadroon, as her father was white and her mother a mulatto, her children by the white John Monteath rendered them mestize or mustees, but this term is not applied to them in the church records. Does this terminological blurring indicate that persons whose skin tone and hair quality showed more elements of African derivation were more likely to be referred to as being "of colour", "quadroon"

Figure 6.1 A woman of colour. Photo: Brennan. Courtesy Michael Gardner.

or "mulatto" even though they technically were mestize? These are only some of the instances of terminological inconsistency on the part of British writers. It may have been that semantic practices varied from person to person, or perhaps they varied according to the subject being assessed. For instance, whereas in 1819 the recorder of the marriage of Edward Dunkley and Sarah Pight describes them as "free coloured", in 1820 both Benjamin and Martha Ebanks are specified as "free mustees".

The St Elizabeth–Westmoreland region showed much evidence of the growing economic salience of this intermediate group during the second half of the eighteenth century into the nineteenth. For instance, the Returns of Slaves for these two parishes contain a noticeable number of persons of colour as owners of slaves and property in the first three decades of the nineteenth century. At the same time, the detrimental effects of the dominant colour ideology of the period become patent in the views and bequests of James Hart, a wealthy planter who died in 1800.[17] His will, dated 27 September 1793, and its codicils of 13 February 1796 and 10 August 1800, make handsome provisions for several persons – some servants, some themselves landowners, as well as for enslaved mulatto women with whom he had meaningful liaisons, and for two free black women with whom he had children. But he stipulates that his daughters – who were mulattos – should only inherit if their children were either "lawfully or unlawfully begotten" for a white man. No similar stringency was laid upon his mulatto sons![18] This attitude was a variation upon that which had prompted the Jamaica Assembly, composed of planters, to take measures during the eighteenth century to limit the access to wealth of ethnic hybrids. In 1701 it had passed an act "to prevent the inconveniences arising from exorbitant grants and devises made by white persons to negroes and the issue of negroes, and to restrain and limit such grants and devises". Despite this effort, having realized by 1761 that four sugar estates and other property worth £200,000 had been inherited by mulattos, the Assembly voted to forbid legacies of more than sterling £1,200 to Negroes and mulattos.[19]

White male privilege was, in the case of the Harts and similar families, enforced by legal sanctions. Not surprisingly therefore, perusal of the St Elizabeth church records for this period show the parallel sexual activity of white males among females white and black and brown. With "an overwhelming slave population and a scarcity of white females, intercourse between white males and black slave women became common".[20] Whether concurrent or sequential, these unions with women produced individuals and family groups that were mirrors of each other, at least in respect of names, which makes it sometimes very difficult to disentangle identities. The colour ascriptions used in official records, despite their original motive of reinforcing hierarchical distinctions in the social order, prove the sole basis of differentiating identities centuries later.

For instance, Jeremiah Meyler, apparently Jewish to judge by the name, a merchant and landowner, parented four children with Cloe, a black slave belonging to John Hunter. The Meyler sons of this union, Richard, Jeremiah and James were born between 1755 and 1759. Meyler senior then had two girls, Ann and Frances, with a white woman, Ann Williams, in 1761 and 1762. He subsequently married Ann Williams in 1764, reproducing another Jeremiah and Richard Meyler in 1764 and 1765 respectively. In 1771 Francis Cook, also Cooke, had a daughter, Catherine Gale, with Bessy Wallace, probably a quadroon. He was at the time married to his second wife, the widow Mary Armstrong, a marriage that had produced Edward Francis Cooke in 1767. This Edward is the grandfather of the Edward Cook or Coke who owned Paynestown Estate where Archibald attended his first religious services. Thomas Boyd had six children with Rebecca Allen, a free mulatto, between 1773 and 1785. Dr Alexander Rose, one of the witnesses to John Monteath's will, had William and Elizabeth, born 1793 and 1796 respectively, from his relationship with Eve Solomons, a free quadroon; and Robert Dellap in union with Elizabeth Alexander, a free quadroon, had two girls in 1801 and 1802. James Hart had two parallel families with free black women, to the extent that he had two daughters named Elizabeth: one born on 31 August 1789 to Elizabeth Green and another born 29 March 1792 to Mary Scott. The parallels go even further. Mary bore him Rebecca on 7 February 1782, while Elizabeth had William on 29 November 1782; Mary had Nancy on 21 October 1785 and Elizabeth produced Robert a few weeks later, on 12 November 1785. A wider space separates Mary's Sally, born on 1 January 1788, from Elizabeth's Elizabeth born in August 1789. The 1790s brought more children from Mary Scott: after Elizabeth in 1792, there was Thomas on 5 August 1794 and George on 2 September 1797.[21] Isaac Allen, colonel of the militia, married Cecilia Rankin in 1806; however, he produced Alexander Allen in 1807 by a freed mestize, Rebecca Beavers. In 1810 he had three children: one, Isaac, with his wife; William, with Beavers; and James Thomas Allen with Sarah Dixon, presumably white since the record carries no colour assignation. Similarly, James Daly had two children in 1807: James Daly born of Margaret Rawlins a mulatto slave who died, perhaps in childbirth, and Sarah Daly born to Sarah Mendez, another mulatto slave. And in 1812, the year that Daly married Marianne Smyth from a well-connected family, he also had a son, Frederic Daly, born to Mary Scott's daughter, Sarah Hart, a free mulatto. The three "outside" children were all baptized together at Sarah Hart's family residence, Harts Hall, on 25 October 1813. In February that same year, a daughter, Bridget, was born to his wife, Marrianne. Sarah Hart had yet another son with James Daly; and both George and Frederick were abroad in England when their mother made her will on 24 May 1822.[22]

John Monteath's own promiscuity replicates his uncle Thomas's performance. Thomas's first recorded child is a daughter, Jesse, mothered by Sarah Donaldson, "a mulattoe". Jesse was baptized on 26 November 1779.[23] Then he had two sons with Sarah: John, born on 25 June 1781, and William, born on 1 May 1783. Both were christened on 23 December 1783.[24] Sarah bore him another daughter, Rebecca, whose baptism took place on 30 January 1795[25] together with another son of Sarah's, Robert Benjamin, a "free Quateroon". His father was John Benjamin Downes.[26] Sarah had yet another son, James Wilson, who became a saddler in Hanover.[27] Thomas Monteath himself also had two children with his wife Amelia: Margaret and Thomas.[28]

There are also mixed-race males who married or mated with either white or coloured women. George Brooks, white, and Mary Powell, a free mulatto, produced Jane Brooks, a free quadroon, who became the wife of the white Abraham Sables Cole in 1772.[29] George David Harriott, a mestize, married the white Mary Goodfellow in 1800. The latter couple is listed in the Whites section of the register since the minister considered Harriott sufficiently and therefore "reputedly white", and he explained this positioning of the record by the parenthetical justification that "the children will be white".[30]

Africans

Archibald's biography indicates a lateral network of relationships among enslaved persons on the same property, others on neighbouring estates and some at a distance of about fifteen to twenty miles. He speaks of holding conversations with "Christina" of Paynestown, adjacent to Kep, as he was returning to Dumbarton and as she was fetching water at a pond or well. He exchanged opinions with freed blacks near Petersville Estate and with workers at Woodlands and Hampstead. He himself courted Rebecca at Hampstead, where she lived, and at the prayer meetings at Paynestown and Hopeton. Vertical relationships among slaves are tangentially treated, as for instance, where reference to Archibald's status as overseer suggests difference in rank and responsibility. An individual like Archibald, though a slave, had the authority to upbraid and punish the workers under him; in addition, his role as helper in the New Carmel Moravian church augmented his scope of authority as he had to keep himself informed about the moral conduct of church members, and to report conformity as well as infringements to the missionaries. Archibald's standing in the church, for example, accounts for the number of infants whom he sponsored for baptism,[31] and the number of couples for whose weddings he acted as witness. Needless to say, vertical work, religious and social interactions took place between slave owners, officials and missionaries on the one hand, and the unfree on the other. These independent and interdependent vertical and lateral relationships served to constitute plantation society, which itself was a matrix in the evolution of Caribbean society.

One of the stages in this evolution in the British Caribbean colonies was the period of "amelioration" in the conduct of the slave system. The period took effect during the second decade of the nineteenth century but was an outgrowth of the anti-slave trade and anti-slavery proposals that were very heatedly debated in Britain and in planter circles in the West Indies. As part of what some saw as a gradual disengagement from the system, and what others regarded as a more palatable dilution of the system, amelioration addressed issues such as

> the encouragement of religious instruction, marriage, child-bearing, and education among the slaves; the attachment of slaves to the plantations and provisions against the separation of slave families; the recognition and security of the property of slaves; regulations defining the slaves' minimum allowances of food, clothing, land, and free time, especially on Sundays; protection of old or wornout slaves; restrictions on the master's powers of punishing slaves, and for preventing cruelty to slaves; the appointment of protectors of slaves to ensure enforcement of the laws in their favour; and the facilitation of the manumission of individual slaves and also of slaves' families.[32]

Among the provisions of amelioration was a three-yearly census or register of slaves. The initial 1817 listing for any one estate stayed constant insofar as slaves remained in the ownership of the holder or holders indicated, so that a slave was not named in the registers or returns after 1817 if she or he continued in the holding of the 1817 owner over the fifteen-year period during which the registration was exercised, or had not died or given birth. These returns of slaves according to owner and plantation break down slave holdings into gender and ethnic type, the latter erroneously designated as "Colour", the categories thereunder being African, Creole, sambo and mulatto (see p. 119). An age is provided, but as it relates to slaves born much before 1817, this turns out to be highly speculative, given the poverty of the slave diet, the harsh work routines, their largely outdoor life, regional differences in build among differing African ethnicities, the imprecise dating techniques of non-literate peoples, and the lack of interest on the part of owners in precision over personal matters such as these. The column called Remarks provides useful information regarding the maternal parentage of minors; unfortunately, paternity is not addressed.[33] Remarks also allow for information regarding the acquisition or loss of slaves by purchase or litigation, the individual's death during the intervening three years, or maternal identification of a child born within the same time period. Other important information to be gleaned concerns the literacy status of the owner, as he or she was required to sign the entry or to make a mark; further information concerns the joint or single ownership of a slave, and the identity of guardians, attorneys, or deputies of the owners.

The Enslaved Population on Rosehall Estate

Thanks to the innovation of slave registers, called returns, albeit late in coming, it is possible to know more than had previously been possible of the hitherto anonymous mass that were slaves.[34] Even so, the data provide only the barest outlines of their individuality. We are severely limited to specific events and can guess little about the personalities and emotional lives of these subjects. But at least it is possible to identify Archibald's fellow slaves, owned by Nancy Monteath at Rosehall, on 28 June of the years 1817, 1820, 1823, 1826, 1829 and 1832. Toby remained hers during these years because after 1817 his name never appears under remarks as sold or in any way alienated from her. The data from these registers, together with those from church records of baptismal, marriage, death and membership status, allow us skeletal profiles of the slave community at Rosehall and its social and religious inter-connections with surrounding estates. As such, the returns allow us to know that in 1817 Nancy Monteath owned a very small muster of ten males and fifteen females. Of the males, four were African; of the females, nine. The rest were Creoles. Four males and ten females were listed as above twenty years of age; of the minors, eleven were born to her female African slaves: Juliet, Jeany, Darby and Bella each had two, while Phillis, Ellen and Peggy had one each. We now offer commentary on some, though not all, of these individuals.

Among the male adults was Toby, whose age was given as twenty. This is the later Archibald Monteath. Estimating that he may have been between nine and eleven at the time he was snatched from his home, and further guessing that he may have been acquired by John Monteath around 1802, he would have been about twenty-five in 1817. In his baptismal record of 1821 he is reckoned as being thirty-eight.[35] The nine-year difference between our estimate of his age and the parson's may well be an indication of the maturity of his air, his height, on which one missionary remarked,[36] and the inattention to personal details concerning non-whites evident in the sparse notations made by the Anglican parsons who baptized large quantities of slaves at the same time. In any case, the unreliability of these official age quantifications is also shown up by the discrepancy between the estate attorney's estimate that Toby was twenty years old in 1817 (and the owner and her attorney are likely to have known him more intimately) as against Reverend McIntire's reckoning of thirty-eight only four years later!

On the same day, 24 June 1821, that Archibald was baptized by the Anglican Church, a fellow Igbo made the formal transition to Christianity. This was Richard of Rosehall, who was estimated at twenty-two years old in the 1817 register, and who became James Monteith on baptism. He was only two years older than Archibald by the estate hierarchy's reckoning; however, for whatever reason,[37] he was not received into the Moravian congregation until 22 August 1830, whereas Archy had been admitted on 18 November 1827. There was even further delay, as James became a communicant only on 20 January 1833.[38] He had married a Jane of Rosehall on 16 May 1830, but she died at Cool Retreat on 17 August 1850.[39] This may have been the Jane Monteath who was about thirty-five, according to the parson, when she was baptized at Black River on 18 June 1821.[40] A year after her passing, on 2 August 1851, James remarried, now to the blind Cecilia Thompson. Identified now as a widower and labourer of Nightengale Grove, his marriage to Cecilia of the same district was witnessed by Archibald together with Elvelina Clemens, the parties all making an X, except for Archy who affixed his signature.[41] Cecilia's surname is given as Thompson in the church entry in O-Carmel, but she was also known by the surname of her mother's second husband, Dickenson. Cecilia Dickenson of Nightingale Grove had been baptized by the Anglicans, and later by the Moravian, John Collis, on 15 September 1831.[42] The marriage to James produced a child, Mary Elizabeth, at Cool Retreat, on 15 April 1860, the child being baptized at Carmel on 17 June 1860. James eventually passed away on 26 February 1865, the year following Archy's decease and two weeks after the death of Archy's wife, Rebecca.

It is suggestive that James gave consent for the marriage of Juliana Marcy of Happy Hall and William Richardson, stone mason of Nightingale Grove, on 7 May 1842.[43] Was the bride his child, biological or fictive? Archy was a witness at this marriage. Juliana had been received by the Moravians on 6 December 1840.[44] James also stood as godfather for "Edward David Montieth", son of Edward and Frances Monteath, born on December 6, 1844 and christened on May 19, 1845.[45] The adults had been co-slaves on the Kep and Rosehall Estates for many years.

The other African males in Nancy Monteath's 1817 returns were mature, Jack and John both being cited as forty years old. Named as John Hebbard belonging to James Monteith, Nancy's son, John is stated to have been baptized in the Anglican Church at age fifty on 9 October 1825.[46] As for the Moravian records, John appears as an Igbo received among them on 15 September 1831 as John Ebbert.[47] A few weeks later, on 9 October, he married Rachel Edwards who belonged to Margaret Edwards, owner of Cool Retreat.[48] In this record he is identified as the property of "Miss Nancy Monteath", contradicting at surface level James Monteith's ownership of him in 1825. Or had Nancy bought him back from James? In his marriage record, his name was given as John Hibbert, an indication that some ministers decoded the dropped initial "h", common in Jamaican pronunciation, while another did not.

Figure 6.2 Peasants with their mules bearing hampers. After Macmillan, *The West Indies and Bermuda, Illustrated.*

While James and Archibald were in their twenties, Robin and Quamin were ten and twelve respectively in 1817. Robin was the son of Bella, and Quamin the son of Jeany. Both Bella and Jeany were among the eight African females at Rosehall. In 1817 Bella's age was given as forty, while Jeany's was thirty. In addition, both Bella and Jeany had been willed to Nancy Monteath by John Monteath in 1809, a wish repeated in his 1814 deed of gift. Bella was a Congo. She had given birth in 1800 to Judy, and to Robin around 1807. But Judy had died before 1820 and by 1832 both Bella and Robin were dead, Robin being already in his early twenties. Bella had taken the name Isabella Palmer when she became an Anglican, then she joined the Moravians on 7 January 1830.[49] It is recorded that she married Thomas Allen. But a Thomas Palmer, aged thirty-one, of Rosehall married an Isabella, also of Rosehall, "in congregation meeting", apparently in December 1830.[50] There were psychological as well as legal difficulties presented by this form of marriage. John Buchner was of the opinion that such marriages, "not being regarded as legal, several who had thus been united, appeared inclined to take advantage of this to gratify their sensual appetites. . . . However in 1835, the Brethren called upon all in their connexion who had been privately united, to have their marriages regularly legalized."[51] One wonders if that marriage was dissolved and whether Isabella remarried, this time to Allen. But there was another Thomas Palmer who married Mary Ann Monteath of Rosehall on 20 February 1831.[52] Palmer, a Congo, had carried the name Cesar at Nightingale Grove, a property owned by William Finlay and which adjoined Dumbarton.[53] He had been baptized originally by the Anglicans, but joined the Moravians on 5 April 1829 and received his first communion on 8 August 1830.[54] Mary Ann for her part became a Moravian on 29 May 1831.[55]

As for Jeany's offspring, Quamin was said to be twelve years old in 1817, giving him a birthdate of 1805. He became Edward Monteath when he was baptized by Reverend Williams of the Anglican Church in November 1828, taking his first communion on 30 March 1831.[56] Edward became a very active member of the Carmel church and earned the following remembrance from the missionary John Elliott:

> Br. Edward Monteath . . . has always been faithful in doing all he could to instruct the children, to question and catechise them. Asking the question, 'Where is God?' and receiving the answer 'God is everywhere,' to my astonishment he said, 'That cannot be—you do not know what you say.' Again he put the question, and he received the same answer. 'Well,' he said, 'it must be so. The Psalmist, in the 139th Psalm, thought so himself. I think so also, but although you say, God is everywhere, you do not all believe it. When you speak bad words, you do not think He hears you: when you do bad things, you do not think he sees you. Even some of you in this room, do not know that God is here, for I have observed you amusing yourselves, instead of listening to the Good Word. So, you see, children, it is one thing to say, God is everywhere, and another thing, to believe it. In this way he spoke on several subjects, on the fifth commandment, etc., etc. He added, 'You say you are free, and will not obey anybody. My dear children, I thank God, that the text I heard from the pulpit, that day when the *free first stepped in,* sounds in my ears every day I rise: 'If the Son shall make you free, you shall be free indeed.' Our Saviour was no slave, but He honoured his parents; He was subject unto them.[57] (italics his)

On 12 December 1830 Edward married Franky of Hartshall,[58] one of the neighbouring estates. Franky had been the child of Maria, an African, also of Hartshall. In 1817 Maria was estimated to be twenty-two years old and seems to have had Sancho later that year, since his age in the June 1820 return is given as two years eleven months. Franky, born in 1811, had been renamed Frances Johnson or Johnstone when baptized by Reverend McIntyre the first day of 1822 on the same occasion that her mother assumed the name Ann Johnstone. Frances was received into the Moravian congregation on 26 July 1829 and confirmed on 13 June 1830.[59] Together Edward and Frances parented nine children. The first two, Thomas Hart Monteith and James Edward Monteith, were born at Hartshall in 1831 and 1835 respectively. The third child, Mary Elizabeth, was born on her father's estate, Rosehall, in 1837. But, with slavery abolished by 1839 when George Robert was born, the family seems to have removed to Nightingale Grove, probably to premises they called Happy Lodge, which is where Ann Maria and Edward David were born in 1841 and 1844 respectively. John Buckner, born in 1848, Edward Archibald, in 1850, and Margeret Alicia, in 1853, were all born at Cool Retreat, which is where the family is listed in the 1859 Register of Families in the Carmel congregation.[60]

A brother of Quamin, being another of Jeany's sons, was Duke who, like Frances, was born in 1811. He became David Monteath when baptized in the Anglican Church aged ten, according to the baptismal record on 11 September 1825, which would mean that he was born in 1815, but if the 1817 return is used as a basis of reckoning, then he would have been born in 1803, an appallingly wide time difference of twelve years. He officially joined the Moravians on 15 September 1831 and became a communicant in July 1837.[61] On 28 July 1838, a few days before emancipation, he married a Creole by name Eleanor or Eleana or Eleaner Smith of Woodlands.[62] Witnesses to the marriage were Edward "Montieth", David's brother; Thomas Vassel, who had bought land near to Archy; Sarah Shakespeare, and Margaret Blackwood. Eleanor had been received by the Moravians on 1 March 1840 and admitted to Holy Communion on 15 October 1843. Between 1839 and 1865 the couple had fourteen children – eight sons and six daughters, and also adopted a son in 1885.

Jeany's third son, George, born in 1820, fades from the records, as does Jeany herself. So too does Darby whose age is entered as twenty-eight in 1817, just two years younger than Jeany. But James, Darby's first recorded child, apparently born between 1814 and 1815, became James Campbell, who was baptized by the Anglicans at about seven years of age on 18 June 1821.[63] He joined the Moravian brethren on 22 April 1830, beginning communion on 17 March 1833. He and Felicia Williams of "Nightengale Grove" were married on 12 March 1837.[64] Apart from James, Darby had earlier given birth to Ann in 1810. After James she had had Eliza in 1818. Ann came to be known as Ann Clark of Rosehall who was received on 3 April 1831 at Carmel,[65] bore William Clarke in 1832, and married John Monteith or Monteeth, twenty-four, of Rosehall in 1839.[66] The emblem of a cross above John's name in the C-Carmel Register indicates that he subsequently died, though no date is given.

Another adult female was the Igbo, Juliet, who later became Juliana Hart. She had been originally baptized as an Anglican, but was received by the Moravians on 18 September 1831 and admitted to Holy Communion on 6 July 1834.[67] In 1802 she mothered Charlotte, a sambo, and in 1807 another sambo named Prudence. By 1826 Prudence was dead. Alexander, black, arrived in 1821. Charlotte, the surviving sambo, was baptized as Henrietta Monteath in June 1821.[68] She later married George Woodstock, a free Creole black, on 30 July 1826, the same day he was received within the Moravian fold.[69] Both had been baptized as Anglicans, but she was received into the Moravian Church on 16 November 1828 and joined their communicant assembly on 8 August 1830. Before marriage, Charlotte had produced William in 1821 and Elizabeth in 1824. Margaret was born in 1826 and Susanna in 1828, the same Susan Woodstock of Rosehall baptized by Brother Scholefield on 6 July 1828.[70] Another of George and Henrietta's children, Robert, was baptized by Brother Pfeiffer on 17 February 1833.

Phillis, a thirty-year-old African in 1817, had had a daughter, Frances, in 1810. Frances in turn birthed Anna Ebanks in 1829 and Isabella Ebanks in 1832. Peggy, another African, estimated to be twenty-six in 1817, bore Robert in 1824, but by 1929 Peggy was dead. Robert is noted as having been manumitted by 1832, but this represents either deliberate or genuine error, for in 1832 Nancy Monteath et al. did liberate a Robert Smith, who bought land from her some months later, so this would not have been the child of eight in the 1832 return. Was it then Robert Smith's son, who was also being freed because he was, under the stipulations of amelioration, just two years above the age at which children born to slave mothers were given their freedom? Or was the age given in error for eighteen or twenty-eight? Or was there a conflation of Peggy's son who had died, with the Robert Smith who had been emancipated?

Ellen, listed as a twenty-eight-year-old African in 1817, but as a Creole in the Moravian baptismal records, was baptized Ann Monteath at the Black River Anglican church on 18 June 1821. She had already given birth to a sambo child, Thomas, in 1810. She joined the Moravians on 10 June 1827, started Holy Communion on 8 August 1830,[71] and on 27 December 1829 married the Creole, Adam Hart, of the neighbouring Hartshall Estate.[72] Adam was listed in the 1817 Hartshall returns as aged thirty-two, the son of Amy, herself a fifty-six-year-old African on that same property. Before becoming a Christian, Adam had been called Blackwall and was listed as belonging to the adjacent Hampstead Estate, previously owned by James Hart, in the Moravian baptismal record for 25 September 1825 (though entered for Hartshall in the 1817 return with an age of thirty-two). Hampstead and Hartshall were, however, adjacent properties with prior joint ownership. Adam officially joined the Moravians on 26 July 1829, was confirmed on 20 March 1831, and by the early 1830s was already a helper at New Carmel. Adam and Ann are listed in the Carmel Register of Families, entry 5, as residing at Cool Retreat, with children born at an average of three-year intervals between

Figure 6.3 "Spanish wall" of limestone, mortar of earth and lime, framed by timber uprights, in cellar at Huntly plantation house, 2004.

1847 and 1856, with a four-year gap before the last child in 1860. Ann and Adam died within a year of each other, Ann, aged seventy, on 21 January 1869 and Adam on 18 August 1870. In the remarks column of the church record, he is noted as having been a church member for forty-one years and to have died of old age.[73]

A long-time friend of Archibald's, and one who was identified as his shipmate, was Mary Brown.[74] She was the Rose in the possession of Nancy Monteath and she appears in the Anglican baptismal register on 18 June 1821, virtually a week before Archy's reception in the Christian community. Here her age is estimated as thirty, fairly consistent with her age as twenty-eight in the 1817 Return of Slaves. Mary was, like Archy, an Igbo, and Archy helped her build her home, which was ready to be blessed[75] on 27 February 1839, within two months of a 12-acre plot being sold by Ann Monteath to Thomas and Mary Brown, agriculturalists, for Jamaican £64 on 9 January 1839.[76] In terms of gender relations, it is of interest to note, in a narrative where so many of the female personalities are submerged, that the property title was issued jointly in the names of both husband and wife. They had married on 13 December 1829 in the Anglican Church.[77]

Another shipmate of Archibald's was an unnamed male tied to Archy by the bonds of loyalty, affection and nostalgia which stamped that special personal relationship. As Bryan Edwards remarked, the use of the term "shipmate" signified "a relationship of the most endearing nature".[78] The individual in this case was "a boy brought over from Africa with [Archibald]"[79] who appears to have been stationed at Woodlands Estate, bordering on Rosehall. The Woodlands connection is indirectly revealed in a comment about this friend made in the context of Archibald's pastoral work:

> I also often went to Woodlands, to invite the people there to come to church; kept meetings and read the Bible. . . . But the manager soon forbad this to be done in future. Still, the desire to hear of Jesus was so great, that only a few allowed themselves to be kept from the meetings. . . . Among them was one man, who always excused himself for staying away, by lying, and to this day, that man is a poor wandering sheep who does not know nor love Jesus.[80]

This denunciation made in the 1850s is rehearsed in Lichtenthaeler's summary of Archibald's physical decline. The minister observed that "the death of a friend, apparently in a state of spiritual darkness, proved a severe blow to him". In fact, three versions of the biography make reference to this friend in the context of a foreshadowing of Archibald's death. "After the emancipation of slaves, the one grew rich in this world's goods, the other 'rich toward God'. By the sudden death of his friend, A.M. was so deeply moved, that he was ill for some months, and the signs of old age became at once more visible."[81] "Experiences" gives further details about the identity of this person: "after he gained his freedom, he settled in the town of Black River and through fortunate business transactions became a very prosperous Negro. . . . Both had become important men, but in very different ways. One was rich in earthly goods, the other rich in God." We may understand the depth of Archibald's grief by grasping the significance of companionship forged during the Middle Passage experience that was the crucible in which individuals were remade into new beings, and also by lingering on the meaning which Archy admits to ascribing initially to Christian baptism: "I imagined that as a result of the act I would go to a good place when I died."[82] Archibald looked forward to death as a reunion with those he valued. By his friend's recalcitrance, he would not be there in the glorious company.

Another group of persons with whom Archibald would have been quite close was his church brethren, particularly his helper colleagues at Carmel church. One such person was clearly the mother of Cecilia Thompson or Dickenson or Monteith. Cecilia's mother was a Creole called Clary as a slave. In 1817 Clary was registered as the thirty-two-year-old daughter of Venus, a forty-seven-year-old Creole, who had another daughter called Cicy. The latter must have been close in age to Elizabeth since she too is posited as being thirty-two years of age.[83] Clary became Elizabeth Ricketts as the wife of James Ricketts, also of Lenox, when they were married by Brother John Ellis "at

Hopeton (before New Carmel Chapel was built)" on 16 July 1827.[84] While J-Carmel Adult Male Baptisms, entry 20, lists her as belonging to Hopeton, the C-Carmel marriage entry cites her as belonging to Lenox Estate. In any case, both estates were contiguous and owned by Edward Francis Coke or Cook, and in the 1817 Return of Slaves the enslaved population of both estates is combined. Elizabeth was received into the Moravian congregation on 13 January 1827, first took Holy Communion on 27 May the same year, and died on 9 November 1878. In J-Carmel, Adult Female Baptisms, entry 14, she is recorded as a widow residing at "Nightengale Grove". Her formal name is given there as Elizabeth Rickets, and her slave name as the familiar Betsy, but Rickets was subsequently crossed out. This erasure must have been done after she had married her second husband, Thomas Dickinson or Dickenson of Happy Grove, previously known as Tom. He likewise became a helper at Carmel,[85] and died at Bigwoods on 28 February 1849.

Elizabeth's first husband, James Rickets, estimated as twenty-five in 1817, had been the son of Franky, a Creole, aged forty-six. Franky also had a daughter, Bessy, who was ten years younger than James. For his part, James Rickets fathered Rowland Rickets with Charlotte, also of Lenox. Charlotte had been nineteen in 1817, the daughter of Bell, a fifty-year-old African. Rowland was baptized on 28 November 1824 and lived until 28 April 1895.[86] Another son of James and Charlotte was Leander, baptized on 30 July 1826.[87] Charlotte must have died soon after Leander was born, since James and Elizabeth were married in 1827. Elizabeth's second husband, Thomas Dickenson, had been married before to Evelena or Evelina Cunningham, a Creole of Cruse Estate, who had Cate as her plantation name. They married in the Anglican Church on 11 December 1825.[88]

The high esteem in which both Elizabeth and her daughter Cecilia were held is reflected in frequent mention of them in missionaries' written commentaries. This is because Cecilia had demonstrated the courage to confront challenges. In about March 1839 Cecilia had begun to learn to read Braille and Brother Elliott reported how he taught her to read on Sunday mornings after worship.[89] She mastered the Gospel of St John, "which she read through several times", before receiving further literature from the British and Foreign Bible Society in the form of "the embossed Gospels of St. Matthew and Luke, and the book of Psalms in two parts".[90] Further citations include one in which John Ellis quotes from a letter written to him by Mrs Coke of Paynestown, in which she reports that Betsey Rickets and her daughter had acted as interpreters of the Christian message to an elderly African woman.[91] Another anecdote again emphasizes the close relationship between mother and daughter:

> Old Elizabeth, Cecilia's mother, is now a teacher in our Sunday school, but she complains, that her daughter has a great advantage over her in the learning to read at home. "When the rain causes the house to be shut up, and all is dark, Cecilia can read. And at night, when we have no oil, Cecilia can read, and me, poor ting, cannot read a word, unless with good day-light, or a good lamp".[92]

Indeed, an annotation in Elizabeth's baptismal entry carries the following comments on her death: "She was one of the first who began to seek her soul's salvation when our Brn. [Brethren] first preached at Hopeton",[93] a reference to the advent of Moravian missionaries in the locality during the 1820s. And the report from Carmel for the year 1878 echoes this encomium when it records the death of "the good old sister . . . who was received into the congregation here in 1827, before the church was opened for public worship".[94] In fact, Elizabeth had been encouraged by Archibald himself to join the Paynestown group of worshippers in the mid-1820s. He recounts meeting her the day after he had an epiphanic experience of religious awakening. He confided in her his sensations, "and she took it in with interest". It turned out that she "did have some knowledge of Christian teachings" because her parents had attended some of the Moravian services at the Old Carmel mission on Bogue plantation. So Elizabeth began accompanying Archibald to the Sunday services at Paynestown, and after a while they went every evening to prayers. Then others joined them on Sundays, and soon they "were a little crowd that went to Paynestown to the meeting".[95] That was to be the beginning of a long relationship cemented by the dedication of these two to the religious life.

Both Elizabeth's husbands, James Ricketts and Thomas Dickenson, were helpers at New Carmel in the early 1830s. Another helper was Fredrick Daily or Daly, who was Archey or Archy of Hartshall, a Moko or Moco, an umbrella term designating persons from the hinterland of the Bight of Biafra, such as the Igbo, Efik, Ibibio, Kalabari, Ijaw, Sobo and Ejagham. He was gauged at twenty-six years of age in the 1817 Returns of Slaves. Together with a large number of slaves from Hartshall, he was baptized on 20 September 1817. He married Mary Ann Kelly, Creole, formerly named Julina, the property of Rebecca Allen, owner of Pleasant Hill, at the Black River Anglican church on 16 December 1827.[96] Mary Ann had been baptized as an Anglican, received among the Moravians on 16 November 1828, and took first communion on 8 August 1830.[97] In the 1859 register of families, Fredrick and Mary Ann were resident at Kilmarnock.[98]

Yet another African helper was William Foster, an Igbo, known as Castila or Castilla of Winsor or Windsor Forest, a large estate of 107 men and 77 women workers. In 1817 Castilla was thought to be forty.[99] He was married to

Ann, also of Windsor Forest, who had been baptized as a Moravian on 2 March 1834.[100] But as a widower, William Foster, now resident at Jacob's Hope, married Mary Wade of Hopeton on 15 May 1841.[101] Foster died at Bigwoods on 28 February 1849.[102] Another Foster, Samuel, had also been a helper; he worked as a carpenter at Elim. Already in his seventies, he died of a "sudden bursting of blood" on the road as he journeyed to work on 9 December 1856.[103] And when Edward Hunt of Flint Valley died on 3 October 1848,[104] he was eulogized as one of the first converts at New Carmel. He had served as helper for many years.[105]

Another helper, William Thom(p)son was a Creole called Beddy belonging to Hartshall. He had been baptized as an Anglican together with William Smith and Frederick Daly of Hartshall by the Black River Anglican church on 20 September 1817.[106] William Thompson married Margaret Barrett of Woodlands Plantation at Black River Anglican church on 27 April 1828.[107] The Creole Samson of Hampstead had become William Smith when he was baptized as an Anglican on 20 September 1817. At an age estimated as twenty-five in 1817, he is identified as the son of Fressa, a fifty-three-year-old African who was also the mother of Cambridge, aged fifteen.[108] William married Abby Johnson in February 1830, was received by the Moravians on 27 June 1830, and first took Holy Communion on 7 July 1833. Yet another Creole, Robert Coke, was from the Cruse and bore the slave identity of Ceasar. In the 1817 Return he is reckoned to be thirty and identified as the son of Phibba, sixty-two, herself Creole. Phibba also had a twenty-year-old daughter called Margaret Brown. Robert Coke's official Christian journey began in the Anglican Church, but he transferred to the Moravians on 23 September 1827, receiving his first communion on 4 October 1828. He married Rebecca Coke at the Black River Church on 23 July 1826. Her address is given in the Anglican records as Cottage in Westmoreland and in the Moravian records as Coke Cottage.[109]

Another helper was Alexander Pinnock of whom Archibald spoke in connection with the opposition he encountered in his ministry at Mount Edgecombe Estate. Pinnock had married Marcia Darling of the same property on 17 April 1830.[110] It was Pinnock who led the prayers and read the Bible as a means of celebrating the visit to the estate of its owner, James Wedderburn.[111] Another helper of this period was Thomas Laird, known as Neptune at Prospect Woodlands, who was baptized in the Moravian Church on 14 October 1832 and took Holy Communion on 26 March 1834. He married a woman named Rebecca.[112] Also from Prospect Woodlands came Robert Beckford, later of Grange Hill. Robert's slave name had been Emperor; his wife was Jane Shakespeare, formerly named January, also of Woodlands Property. She was Creole, and had been baptized as an Anglican,

Figure 6.4 Peasant family. From Hark and Westphal, *The Breaking of the Dawn.*

then received as a Moravian on 29 May 1831. The relationship between these Beckfords and Archibald showed itself in the fact that Archy was godfather for Cicilia Beckford, a daughter of Robert and Jane born on 15 May 1840, and christened on 20 June 1842. By the 1840s Julines Garwood or Gerwood, a labourer of Paradise, became a helper. He married Margaret Holyness, a domestic of Happy Grove, on 19 June 1845.[113]

By 1847, in addition to Elizabeth Dickenson, female helpers would have included Catherine Williams and Elizabeth Wilmot.[114] Elizabeth Warren of Pleasant Land became the wife of George Wilmot or Wilmott, a labourer of Freely Mountain; they were married on 9 November 1849,[115] the legal documents being witnessed by George Hart and Catherine Williams. All parties made an X. By 1859 the couple had three sons and two daughters.[116] George Robert Wilmot had during slavery been known as Cuffy, a Creole, of Lenox Plantation. He passed away on 2 May 1868, aged seventy, but his wife was listed then as Mary,[117] suggesting that Elizabeth may have pre-deceased him. For her part, Catherine Williams may have been Catherine Holdness before her marriage on 20 March 1836 to Joseph Williams. Both were from Rose Hill.[118]

Not surprisingly, there were differences among these churchgoers, and the strictness of control observed by the Moravian hierarchy meant that exclusions were part of church life. For instance, the diary for New Carmel on 18 July 1844 recalls "the painful duty . . . of excluding five persons, 2 from the Congregation Class, for Adultery & Sin and three from the Communicant Class for Africanish practices". As regards adultery, Richard Williams of Pleasant Hill and Maria of Cottage had been married on 3 August 1834, but a note beside their marriage record reads that "one if not both have been guilty of adultery and they separated";[119] while the Congo, Ann Scott, formerly called Damsel, of Lenox, who had married George Grey, was excluded in 1827, a year after Moravian baptism "for living with a man who had two wives".[120] The reference to African forms of religious practice may well have been to Myal [ma-yal] worship that was in a resurgence during the 1840s (see chapter 7). Three helpers who offended, probably in this respect, were William Hamilton, William Salmon and Patrick Leslie.

Hamilton had been recorded by Brother Elliott as holding service in a schoolroom on 26 February 1837.[121] This was at a time when the New Carmel church was attracting a larger and larger membership: "the number was so great that outside of the church, under 3 separate trees, meetings were held by Br Laslie and Hamilton and myself".[122] In another text Archibald recalls: "Then our dear preacher, Brother Scholefield usually asked me to preach, along with Brother Hamilton. At that time poor Brother Hamilton seemed to be very moved, but later he became an unbeliever again",[123] clearly in reference to his apostasy and exclusion. Hamilton had been baptized by the Anglicans on 20 September 1817. The exclusion of Patrick Leslie and his wife as of 10 May 1829, deprived Archibald of another of his close co-workers. Leslie was married to the free Creole named Sarah Bell; she had been baptized as an Anglican, received by the Moravians on 5 April 1829, becoming a communicant by 1 November the same year.[124] The observation that Patrick Leslie, carpenter resident at Black River, died at about sixty-three years of age, and was buried at the Black River Anglican church on 19 August 1858[125] suggests that after his differences with the Moravians, he transferred either his practising or his official allegiance to the Anglican Church. William Salmon was a free man who had been baptized by the Anglicans at an estimated age of thirty as early as 25 June 1820, when he belonged to Hopeton Estate.[126] He was received into the Moravian Church on 27 September 1829, and made his first communion on 23 January 1831. His wife Mary[127] seems to have belonged to a Mrs Millar, but Mary is also listed as a free Mandingo who was baptized as an Anglican, then became a Moravian on 26 July 1829 and received first communion on 4 August 1832.[128] Perhaps her husband negotiated her manumission.

Even Alexander Black, the teacher-in-charge at New Carmel school in the 1860s, who was received on 29 July 1860, was excluded by June 1862.[129] The date of this event suggests that Black may have been active among the Myalists whose movement was again in its ascendancy around the early 1860s. On the other hand, the exclusion of Archibald's own son-in-law, William George Holness, seems to have been less of a doctrinal than a lifestyle matter for, after having denied some offence, it was thought justified to exclude him on 23 September 1883 for "extreme carelessness".[130]

7

Messages and Implications for Blacks of Christianization

THE PROFILES OF MORAVIAN converts among the enslaved population provide only rough outlines of the estate membership and Christianization of slaves in a western sector of Jamaica in the early 1800s. The Anglican clergy mainly serviced the white population and linked into the official institutions of British colonial rulership,[1] which by the early decades of the 1800s sanctioned the mass baptism of enslaved persons as part of the official slave amelioration initiatives. However, evidence from the eighteenth century in the Anglican baptismal and marriage registers at the Black River Anglican church in St Elizabeth indicates that non-white individuals, both slave and free, were already being accepted into the English church and being married there.[2] All the same, the occurrence of black church marriages was sufficiently rare that in 1830 the Moravian minister Zorn could mention that Africans could "scarcely retain their gravity, when they see [such marriages] solemnized".[3]

Meanwhile, a few black evangelical preachers visited some estates and, we can imagine, also spread "the Word" at Sunday markets.[4] But the more sustained aspect of Christian life in southwestern Jamaica was recruitment into Moravian congregations. Moravian evangelists came among the enslaved population, establishing prayer meetings, Bible classes and chapels. Yet the route to Moravian membership was arduous and selective, as evidenced in the accounts of preparation for reception, and the testing period between reception into the church and first communion. Once the Moravian Brethren built up churches in districts where they attracted interest, Christians from

Figure 7.1 Black River Anglican church, side view, 1995.

the estates in close proximity to these churches gravitated toward these centres. The Moravians enhanced their presence by the schools that they began to open in the late 1820s and by the permission they received in 1835 to have their marriage services considered legal in the colony.[5] Prior to this time, the missionaries required their converts who wished to live together as man and wife "to promise faithfulness, when they joined their hands with prayer and the blessing of the Lord on their marriage state",[6] but the slaves' masters could ignore these extra-legal rituals and separate by sale parties to the contract, so that eventually the missionaries themselves came to view these "private" marriages as somewhat unsuccessful attempts to circumvent the law, since those so married also tended not to view them as binding.

Eurocentrism

The value system encouraged by the missionaries was presented as a slate of European recipes for raising the spiritual and also cultural level of black people. For the point was consistently and insistently made in the missionaries' writings – a point which must also have been reiterated to their flock – that the slaves constituted an "ignorant and depraved population".[7]

Indeed, the recurrence of the term "degraded" in nineteenth-century writings is worthy of attention. Archibald, or his amanuenses, used it in spiritual self-abasement towards the end of his narrative. And Thomas Harvey, the Quaker missionary, applies it to Archibald as well, echoing Shakespeare's polar oppositions of Prospero and Caliban. "What but the power of divine grace", he asks, "could raise this once dark and degraded heathen, this untutored being from the wilds of Africa, not merely to a level with the pious and the cultured, but 'made' with them even 'to sit together in heavenly places in Christ Jesus.' "[8] This notion was clearly part of the disparaging hegemonic discourse of the time, and one finds it as a signifier of non-European cultural actors, as when Joseph Kummer in his sermons alludes to the "poor and degraded" people of Greenland, and speaks of the "degraded and despised negro slaves" of the West Indies,[9] similar to Jacob Zorn lamenting the condition of "poor degraded Africa",[10] and referring to some of the blacks around Bethabara as "still very degraded. . . . [T]he midnight revelries and dancings of the people, accompanied with the most boisterous noise and heathenish yellings, are not uncommon."[11]

Apart from connoting powerlessness and illiteracy, depravity was linked with non-whiteness, so observations like the following were posited as contradictory: a fifteen-year-old female student, Fanny, was described as "quite black, but", we are told as if in ironic surprise, she was "of rather superior talent to the generality of them".[12] Africa, Africans and Africanness were sites of degradation, an opinion that became so internalized within the black church membership that we are pained, but not surprised, to read the sentiments of black volunteers for missionary work in West Africa. One of them imagined "the children in Africa . . . growing up like beasts, running about wild", and jumped to the assumption that Africans in general were "poor ignorant people"; others reported that "various members of their families [had] endeavoured to dissuade them, by representing the cannibalism of Africa, the horror of wild beasts, and by relating terrifying dreams"; and one, echoing no doubt the sentiments of the British military fighting to dismantle the power of the Ashanti kingdom in the Gold Coast at the time, assured the meeting "that in the strength of the Lord he would meet the horrors of Ashanti", while a member of the audience wished that the prospective travellers would be "brought in safety to the wild mountains of Africa".[13] Africa was a nightmare of wildness and horror. Feelings of superiority were thereby implanted in church congregations, taking root particularly among Jamaica-born Creoles and even among the Africans who had been dislodged at an early age from their native environments. Such deprecation and resulting snobbery also translated into disparaging social attitudes on the part of educated and Christian Jamaicans towards other Jamaicans, as reflected in the complaint of the "old untaught Negroes . . . that those who know *de book* look down upon them, and, however young or inexperienced they may be, will take no counsel or advice at their hand".[14] In general, this disdain fitted into the overall paradigm by which "creole negroes" were felt to be "much more intelligent, though, perhaps, not less depraved than the Africans".[15] One way or another, if black, you were depraved. While this was the opinion of Europeans, Christianized blacks imbibed this point of view, which coloured their intra-ethnic relations, and this attitude was compounded when the Christianized also happened to be educated as well.

Communication Barriers

Among difficulties faced in mission work was the matter of mutual unintelligibility – on the one hand, the Europeans' inability to comprehend the languages spoken by the Africans, and on the other hand, the challenge for blacks posed by the missionaries' ways of speaking. As their names indicate, many of the missionaries were continental Europeans, so they faced the task of learning to speak English. But with more humility than his written English suggests was warranted, John Hafa betrayed what he considered his language deficiencies: "Then the sermon follows; and though I am yet deficient in speaking the language, I experience the help of our Saviour."[16]

For his part, Zorn, himself of German descent though born in St Thomas in the Danish Antilles, privately rued in a letter that some fellow ministers, "excellent Brn from Germany take such a length of time to become masters of the language". He also looked forward to the pressures of communication in Jamaica breaking their habit of "high flown sermons" since he himself had discovered his "chief care" to be the ability "to be understood by [his] humble hearers".[17] Buchner learnt an important methodology from observing that Africans "use many comparisons and similes in their conversation, and the missionary who has a talent for illustrating all he has to say, by comparing it with common objects and events, will succeed best".[18] Exemplification of this method can be seen in this incident recalled by Brother Thomas Ward:

> One of the men said – "I also wish to love our Saviour."
>
> I replied: "But you curse and swear at the cattle."
>
> "Yes, Massa, but then it is only my tongue that curse them sometimes, but my heart is not bad."
>
> Q. – "What is the cause of the mill yonder, turning so many wheels, and working so fast?"
>
> A. – "The great wheel, Massa, which the water drives."
>
> "Well, your heart, like that great wheel, moves your tongue, and stirs up all your passions."[19]

Figure 7.2 Waterwheel at Worthy Park, Jamaica, 1997.

But if the former example was a matter of speech style, at a more fundamental level the issue of language vehicle remained. On several occasions, missionaries in their diaries confessed to realizing that their hearers had only caught a word or two of what had been preached. George Timaeus was disappointed to have new aspirants comment after church that "Massa speak sweet word". But they were then unable to explain the content of the sermon: "Me cannot say it like Massa."[20] Zorn admitted:

> It is frequently distressing, after explaining in the easiest language, some part of the gospel of salvation, to see their eyes fixed upon you with a vacant stare, their answers proving that they have not understood a single sentence. Then we must begin afresh and try to be understood, perhaps by the aid of a figure or simile; and sometimes we succeed in that manner, at least so far as to leave a faint impression in their memories.[21]

The obverse of the linguistic challenges faced by non-English Europeans was the "imperfect knowledge" of English on the part of the newly arrived or adult Africans. George Timaeus unknowingly confessed to the same strategy of pretending to understand that Zorn had accused the Africans of doing: "The negroes from the mountains speak very unintelligibly; we have to catch at some word, guess at its connection, and answer accordingly. . . . When we do not comprehend what they say, they seem discouraged."[22] John Ellis attempted to sympathetically rationalize his frustrations over the language difficulties of the Africans: "Like many more in these newly settled mountains, [the African] has had little opportunity to learn the language, and consequently, can neither speak nor understand plain English words and phrases, even where it refers to every day's concerns, much less such as are used to express those of a spiritual Nature."[23] Mrs Coke of Paynestown marvelled at the conversion of "[p]oor old Flora" who could understand so little English that "Betsey Rickets, and her own daughter interpret to her what she does not comprehend".[24] But some of the Africans made more rapid adjustment to the new language, whether because of innate linguistic skills, or because they came from multilingual crucibles, or because they began this language transition at a more tender age than older people. There was, for instance, the case of the helper sister Rebecca at Hazlegrove who "[t]hough an African . . . had learnt to read very well", so much so that "her Bible is her treasure. She is very useful in her office, for, to the sensibility of a female she adds a sound judgment, and her heart is truly devoted to the Lord."[25]

A third factor impeding mutual comprehension is revealed when two English speakers commented on their difficulties with Jamaican English: George Heath "found a slight difficulty at first, in understanding the broken English spoken by the Negroes; but it did not last long"; and Blandford commented on the problems encountered by converts in expressing themselves as clearly as they would have wished.[26] As such, there was concern over the use by educated young people of this Creole language, which came to be called "patois" or "patwa". Sonderman faced difficulty in getting his students "to adopt a mode of speaking, different from that which is generally used by the common people". While it was clear to him that the trainee teachers were "not deficient in their knowledge of [English] grammar . . . we could wish, that this knowledge were put to a practical use, in their intercourse with each other".[27]

African Beliefs and Ritual Behaviour

If the forms of speech were obstacles to communication by speakers and to comprehension on the part of hearers, the content of the religious cultures of Europeans and Africans presented difficulties on both sides.

The maintenance of African religious thinking presented the missionaries with a great hurdle. Belief that spirit force could manifest in the physical self made the body a site of spiritual conflict. Obeah, an African-based belief system operated by part-time priests or priestesses, was credited with producing both negative and restorative effects. In the instance reported by Francis Holland at Lititz on 25 November 1846, belief in this spirit force had induced a sense of helplessness and a reluctance to apply European treatment to a condition that had been popularly diagnosed as a spiritual sickness with a physical manifestation:

> A young married woman . . . had been afflicted with disease of a dropsical nature. . . . I was unable to prevail upon her husband to employ a medical man. . . . At last his wife died. . . . On occasion of my visit to his wife, I had sufficient evidence to convince me, that the husband was not devoid of sensibility or affection; and while I could not account for his neglect in one particular, it never entered into my mind, that it was owing to any superstitious belief. When too late to counteract it, I learnt that his relatives had persuaded him "not to throw away his money" – the woman was "obeahed", and no medicine could do her any good.[28]

For his part, Jacob Zorn inveighed against one of several of the obeahmen with whom the church came into conflict. In this case it was a "cunning old African" who "maintained a degree of respect among our people". He made "strange and delusive professions, e.g. that he was able to see the soul of the departed when they came out of hell, on which occasion they were to make a feast, etc.". This individual was excluded from the church by John Ellis.[29] Decades later, the church took the same measures against a former helper in the Bethany congregation who maintained "that he [was] specially endowed with that spirit 'which searcheth all things, even the deep things of God' ". He received "special revelations by means of visions and dreams. . . . [T]his blind guide of the blind frequently [kept] meetings which last[ed] through the greater part of the night."[30]

There was a close link between well-being or disaster in this world and the condition of the spirits of the dead. This constant awareness of an otherworld of spirits, particularly ancestral spirits, was an aspect of traditional African religion. For instance, the "little house-idols of a foot in length"[31] of which Lang had been told were probably representations of ancestral family *lares* such as are found in Igbo, Yoruba and other African religions. From the outline of Igbo religious practice given in chapter 9, it will be seen that libations would be made every morning to such a shrine by the eldest person in the family compound. This was because ancestral spirits could be beneficent and secure good for their descendants. But they could also be malignant, as in the case of the man "ridden"[32] by his mother, and in the instance of a Williamsfield (St James) woman who "was persuaded by the Myal people that the shadow (soul) of her departed daughter had no rest, but was upon a cotton-tree in the pasture". To bring peace to the daughter's soul, a white fowl had been sacrificed at the tree and its trunk sprinkled with the blood; another ritual had involved about twenty persons singing and dancing for hours round the tree, the mother having procured a little coffin covered with black merino, in which was trapped a firefly found on the tree into which the woman's soul had transmigrated. The coffin was then closed and buried.[33]

The motifs of the wandering, restless spirits of the dead were to come more forcibly to attention during the Myal revivals of the early 1840s and mid-1860s, when Myal practitioners whirled in a circle around large silk cotton trees as a means of communing with the spirits they believed inhabited the trees. Myal was an elaboration of the homage paid to the spirits of the dead, who were believed to haunt the cavernous roots of silk cotton trees, and John Lang had been informed about worship in Manchester of a silk cotton tree, but such devotion was less about the tree itself than the spirits thought to inhabit the tree. "Ma-yal" is a Kongo term referring to spiritual power; and the exercise of "mayal" was intended to access that power, and discharge it, for largely curative purposes, in the interest of its believers. Myal syncretized elements of Central African, West African and Christian religions.[34] Its public ceremonies took place in natural surroundings, where those seeking solutions to their problems danced in a circle around a spirit site such as a sacred tree, singing rhythmic, repetitive music of "wild and inharmonious songs" that produced trances when devotees became possessed by spirits of the deceased. The cries of one man in such a trance that his mother should let him go[35] implied that her spirit lingered with him to the detriment of his desire to pursue an independent path and consciousness.

The door to the spirit world was the trance, and the trance could be induced by movement of the dance and by music. Sleep was another trance-like state and was the door to dreams that could be inhabited by spirits as well. Spirits brought messages. To counter the reliance on this spirit world, a missionary felt himself bound "to reprove a man, who, in consequence of a dream, was harbouring the idea, that another person had bewitched his sick son".[36] Other dream instances recounted were of a happier nature. John Elliott narrated the happiness of his church members when, during floods in the New Carmel area, he made his way to them "through narrow tracks that had been cut in the vicinity of the flooded road". On this occasion, an old man welcomed him triumphantly with the words "Dream cheat me, two, tree [three] nights; but him no do cheat me last night, for I been seen you come, through de middle of de water on a dry pass, like the Lord's people in formerly time". Elliott then tried to disabuse him of his reliance on dream-messages: " 'Well,' I said, 'I have sometimes strange dreams too; but we cannot depend generally on such things, and even your last night's dream cheated you in one respect, for I did not come through the middle of the water; but through the track which is cut by the hillside.' " The old man, however, stuck to his line, carefully refuting the literalness of Elliott's reasoning, while exercising tactfulness by evasive reproof of his pastor's rationality: " 'True,' said he, 'dream no know every ting; but Jesus know all, and if He bring you by fire, or by water, or by bush, we tank [thank] Him all the same.' "[37]

The encounter between these different systems of thought precipitated inner turmoil. This took moral, cultural, psychic and cosmological dimensions: it was the struggle between the individual's good and negative tendencies, as well as between African and European religious and cultural ideologies. The "outbreaks" of Myal activity were public expressions of these inner crises as well as heightened responses to external pressures on the individual and on groups. So that the resolution of these struggles in the "conviction" of moral good, or their irresolution, manifested themselves physically in the form of deafness, dumbness and darkness. In the latter case, Theodore Sonderman had been told by Myal adherents who were also Moravian church members that "a sudden weakness came over their whole body . . . [T]heir eyes . . . would start from their sockets, and . . . this was accompanied by distressing inward uneasiness. Some stated, that a sudden, awful darkness came over them, whilst others lost all consciousness, and could not tell what happened to them."[38] August Clemens had been told of "strange fits of trembling, which generally seize females, but occasionally also strong men", with "some of the converts being suddenly struck dumb" for two to three weeks.[39] And as early as 1816 Brother Lang had had the experience of delivering a sermon at Peru Estate during which "a heathen woman began to twist her body about, and make all manner of grimaces". He had one of the assistants take her outside the church since he thought she was in pain, but he was afterwards told that "it was a usual thing with the Negroes on M[esopotamia] estate, and called by them *Conviction*".[40] A related term was "the Convince", which suggested an epiphanic or conversion experience.[41] When first confronted with this ecstatic or violent form of religious devotion, the missionaries were deluded into thinking that it was a purely Christian experience, but when they realized that this behaviour was an intrinsic part of Myal rituals, they condemned it as devilish possession and excluded many of their church members on this account.

Preferred Religious and Cultural Values

Through their preaching and teaching the missionaries attempted to inculcate in their charges their own attitudes and values. Exposure of the naked body was repulsive. On 4 April 1846, Edwin Reinke turned off the road to give his horse water. "A boy was standing in the pond naked washing his Frock, a young woman and some little girls being present and apparently thinking nothing of the matter. I reproved them sharply." More of the same was to follow. His diary entry continues: "In riding thro the negro village was a woman washing cloaths from her waist upward quite naked yet seemed thoughtless of the impropriety." One notices that the last word – with its connotation of cultural behaviour – is crossed out and in another ink, but in the same handwriting, the word "indecency", with its moral undertone, is substituted.[42] To counter such naive display of the body, the missionaries insisted not only on body covering, but further on modesty in dress and spending.

Similarly, another minister admitted encouraging early marriages by young people, at the same time "opposing grand weddings, and admonishing them to put their money to better uses". It appears that such lavish spending had been common in the 1840s, perhaps a psychological expression of freedom from all pre-1838 restraints. But by the mid-1850s this "extravagance . . . [was] no more to be seen". The minister himself attributed the change to "the want of means" as the hardships of the decades following emancipation in 1838 took greater and greater hold upon the new peasantry.[43] Extravagance had been earlier condemned when, in 1813, the funeral of a slave woman of Elim Plantation took place amid much pomp. Because Agnes had borne "a great number of mulatto children and grand-children", her coffin had been covered with gold tinsel, "and all the other furniture was of a similar description". In the face of this opulence, the missionaries announced themselves "pleased to hear our Christian Negroes expressing their contempt of this ridiculous finery" but the reason for this condemnation by fellow slaves was given as the opinion that such pomp and circumstance "was quite inconsistent with the situation of a negroe", that is, a slave.[44] Opulence was not considered consistent with Christian whites either, as emerges in Zorn's denunciation of the acquisition of lavish dress by some ministers and their wives.[45]

African-type funerals involved drumming, blowing of conch shells and dancing, rituals which were repeated to commemorate the anniversaries of death, as well as, no doubt, three or nine days subsequent to the passing.[46] The main drum mentioned in connection with these rites was the gumbah or gumbiah, "a kind of drum with feet".[47] While the missionaries gave no description of the funerary dances, from which they obviously distanced themselves, another source indicated that at the funerals of those held in great respect, the mourners engage in a warlike dance, in which they display great agility, by running, leaping, and jumping, accompanied with many violent, and frantic gestures and contortions. Here also they sing funeral songs of an heroic nature, considering death as a welcome release from the calamities of life, and as a passport to the delightful, and never-to-be forgotten, scenes of their nativity; an event, which while it frees them from bondage, restores them to the society of their dear, long-lost relatives of Africa.[48]

The memory of the dead was prolonged and their spirits assuaged by the continued attentions of the living, so that "dances for the dead" were held, during which "food was placed on the grave of the departed". Francis Holland deplored this practice which, in November 1846, he considered as belonging to "the 'old time' of slavery and ignorance". Furthermore, these were occasions on which "rum was freely used. Drumming, the blowing of conchs, dancing, and other more secret works of darkness, are, in some districts, the regular order, not of the 'day,' but of the 'night.' Verily, this is more like *Heathen Africa* than '*Christian Jamaica*'!" (emphases his).[49]

Christian funerals had a different tenor and inculcated a divergent concept of the afterworld. Before the establishment of churches in a locality, funerals took place on the estates themselves. When in 1817 Old Peter of the Island Estate died, the corpse of this head driver and faithful church assistant was enclosed in a very neat coffin that was "set down on the green before his house". A large number of blacks arranged themselves on either side of the coffin, the funeral also being attended by four white men. A hymn was sung, a prayer offered, after which Brother Ward sermonized on the theme "Prepare to meet thy God". Thomas Ward was obviously impressed by the fact that the "greatest silence and solemnity prevailed",[50] in contrast to the noisy celebrations of the afrocentric funerary rites. A similar scenario played out at the funeral of John Abraham, master mason of Two-Mile-Wood Estate. It was the overseer of the estate who called at John Becker's home immediately after Abraham's death to request the missionary to preach the sermon at the final rites. The overseer spoke highly of Abraham, giving "a most excellent testimony for faithfulness and diligence in his employment". On the basis of this testimony and Becker's own good opinion of the communicant brother, Becker "preached to an attentive auditory, consisting of nearly thirty white people and Mulattos, and 200 negroes".[51]

Jacob Zorn condemned liquor, even what he considered the "invidious seduction" of brethren ministers to add rum to their water as an antidote to illness, the West Indian custom by which fevers were broken by the drinking of rum mixed with lime juice.[52] Zorn also denounced the drinking of brandy, gin, wine, and, ironically, rum and porter, the West Indian staple products of the sugar estates among which he worked and whose producers were his

Figure 7.3 Composite of Isaac Belisario prints of house jonkunu and its musical band accompaniment. Courtesy National Library of Jamaica.

personal friends and patrons! He also deplored the drinking that accompanied "digging-matches" held by blacks, that is, competitive work-teams performing tasks such as hoeing fields and building structures.[53] That condemnation is also present in the following commentary on the conduct of "a string of laborers of both sexes" who at five o'clock on the evening of 12 June 1846 passed through the Paynestown Pastures on their way from work back to Bog Estate. "They were singing in a noisy way. The ringing of our Bell . . . for evening service appeared to cause a moment's halt, which was followed by a fresh burst of jollity and all seemed to hurry away from the sound of God's house. . . . Liquor was in their *heads* and the Tempter in their *hearts*" (emphases his).[54]

Drinking and drumming were closely associated with jonkunu, a Christmas festival that was consistently denounced. Its public manifestation took the form of a procession consisting of a man "gaily dressed in red flannel, carrying on his head a little wooden house, and holding a conch-shell, which he often blows". This "house jonkunu" was the dancing centre of a circle of masqueraders who had originally congregated in front of a neighbouring shop or other public building. Brother Hennig considered it a "wild heathenish amusement" that he quite rightly interpreted as "derived from the custom of the heathen, to carry about their idols at certain seasons".[55] The depth of antipathy to jonkunu on both religious and aesthetic grounds was such that one of the missionaries professed:

> Were I not certified that I am in a so-called Christian land, the sounds that I hear would almost constrain me to believe, that Satan and his host were holding their midnight orgies around some of Afric's bloody rites, so fiend-like are the yells that, mingled with the blowing of conch-shells, come wafted through the air.[56]

His imagery and choice of words speak to the conflation of Africa with hell. Indeed, at Lititz in 1861, church confirmation was deferred "in order that we might see how they would pass through the Christmas ordeal, in case there should be a recurrence to those orgies which marked that season in days past".[57] As early as 1813, Christmas Day for Brother and Sister Becker was ruined by the residents of Bogue Estate who "made a dreadful noise, which lasted from seven till midnight". Unable to sleep, Brother Becker "went down to the people, to see what could be done to put a stop to it, especially as his wife was taken very ill". When he did get a hearing and requested a stop, the people protested, "What, will you take from us even our Christmas joys? It is the only time in the year that we may thus make merry, and are we to be deprived of that too?" Becker's reply was the admonition "that the true cause of joy at Christmas led to no such extravagancies, which were sinful, and hurtful to their health". They were also invited to attend church the next day. Becker's words seemed to make some impression (or was it because the revellers were winding down their festivities?) for "the uproar gradually ceased".[58] Drumming was also normal during non-Christian funerary rites, and also in celebration of Emancipation Day, 1 August. But one pastor, echoing the sentiments of his colleagues, complained in the New Carmel diary on 5 August 1845 about the "evil-minded people" who had been beating drums for two days in commemoration of their day of liberty.[59]

The confrontation between Becker and the music makers is an indication that some Africans correctly perceived that the missionaries attempted to control both the public and private spaces of their lives. The proprietorial nature of their control is evident in the recurrent phrase "our people" in the missionaries' accounts of their congregations, and their diligent inquiry into the personal choices and sociopolitical conduct of their parishioners. These inquiries ranged from mating arrangements to political disaffection, and to latent antagonisms between blacks and German immigrants that, at least on one occasion, erupted in a sequence of fights.[60] Apart from factors such as personal inertia and a discomfort with change, it was no doubt also a conscious desire to preserve a private space, a self unknown and unknowable to the Other, which led some Africans to stay far from the missions' reach. The following account from W.S. Blandford provides one indication of the determination by some to hold to *their* way, outside of what they saw as the *further* involvement of people they distrusted and who were their enemies:

> I offered a tract some time ago to an African Negro, when the following conversation took place:
>
> – "Good afternoon, old man".
>
> "How de, Massa?"
>
> "Do you go to God's house on the Sabbath-day?"
>
> "Yes, me Massa".
>
> "Where do you go?"
>
> "Me go to de cross-church, me Buckra". [61]
>
> "Well, here is a little book for you".
>
> "Massa, me no know paper" [I don't know how to read].
>
> "Shew it to your minister, and he will tell you about it".
>
> "Me no go da on Sunday."
>
> "Where will you go?"
>
> "Me go to de church on the plains".
>
> "You can shew the book to the minister there, and he will kindly read it to you".
>
> "No! me no want de book; me top at home Sunday".
>
> And, at last, the poor old man turned his back on me and the book: I could not prevail on him to take it. My boy, who was with me, said, of his own accord, "Hie! him foolish, for true!"
>
> I cannot account for the conduct of this poor old Mocho[62] man. I was never treated so unceremoniously before. My sable friends have generally received the tracts readily, and expressed their thanks for them. [63]

As far as the Europeans were concerned, musical instruments and rhythms that were foreign to them were viewed with grave suspicion. Even fifes of bamboo reeds were disparaged as "these wretched things" by Brother Renkewitz,[64] perhaps because they were integral to the musical accompaniment of processing jonkunu bands. Brother Prince of Lititz was offended when visiting the home of a non-believer where he "saw a drum, tambourine, etc.". And as if a drum and a tambourine were not sufficient evidence of debauchery, Brother Prince had heard that the sinners at Lititz attended the Mandeville racecourse for good measure![65] So betting and gambling were clearly on the list of deadly sins. Another noxious practice was dancing. When he began frequenting prayer meetings in the mid-1820s, Archibald was to learn to his horror, since he "was passionately fond of dancing", that dancing was "wild" and thereby sinful.[66] Having imbibed this point of view, Archibald was many years later to oversee the abstention from these "heathenish diversions"[67] at a particular estate where an absentee master was visiting. Archibald knew it was a plantation custom for the slaves to welcome such a master "with dancing, and noisy demonstrations of joy".[68] Indeed, the missionaries themselves were aware that one of their benefactors, John Foster, proprietor of Bogue and Elim, was favourable to "the obnoxious custom of dancing" and they planned to "make known to him their objections" when he came out from England in early 1831.[69]

Convinced of the rightness of the missionaries' stance on the matter of dancing, Archibald "warned the people . . . not to receive and welcome their master in such a heathenish manner", and then he had stayed at a nearby plantation to ascertain how his followership would comport themselves. He was therefore greatly heartened when the master's invitation to the slaves to "Come up to my house this evening, then you can dance and play" was countered with the response, "Massa we are Christians, we will not play and dance before you, but we will pray for you." The master's reply met with Archibald's approval as well, for he said "Good. . . . then come up and pray for me!" So they "sang hymns, and then Br Pinnock a Helper, read the Bible, made an address, and kneeled down and prayed. The Master and Inspector [attorney] also kneeled down with them, and afterwards all went quietly home."[70] This particular episode in the late 1830s had a fortunate outcome for Archibald, but it had turned bitter for an earlier convert at Elim Estate who, one Christmas

> had been sent for by the overseer . . . and commanded to come and dance for him, with other Negroes. Upon his objecting, that he had learnt that such practices were sinful, his master was very angry, and said he should not go any longer to Mr. Becker's church, where he had such things put into his head. The Negro persisting that he could not do otherwise than go where he heard what was good for his soul, he was severely punished.[71]

Religious devotion, attentiveness and stillness of manner were considered signs of great decorum.[72] On 4 May 1845, the "choir" of single sisters and girls at New Bethlehem held their memorial day communal tea-drinking and meal. "Fifty-four were present, seated in an open square before the desk, all clothed in white. . . . 16 were brown young women, superior in birth and education to the Negroes; the rest were blacks, but, being steady young persons, and mostly members of our congregations, they appeared, both in manner and dress, becoming the church and people to which they belong."[73]

As a corollary, industry at work was highly praised. Brother Elliott commended some settlers at New Savannah in 1843 where the cottages and their occupants evinced a "very cheerful appearance". Cane-grinding and sugar-boiling were going on "briskly". A mill with one horizontal lever and three vertical rollers propelled by two men and attended by a man and a heifer were all producing "a considerable quantity of work", while the women were engaged in sugar-boiling activities.[74] By contrast, the missionaries were extremely averse to the habit of congregation members camping out in their ginger-grounds away from their villages. There they were "exposed to temptations of no ordinary kind, and [fell] an easy prey to the seductive power of sin".[75] These sins of commission were "adultery and fornication", which in 1842 Zorn identified as "still form[ing] the chain, by which the devil 'leads many captive' ".[76]

Again and again the pastors noted the circumvention of the marriage ritual. They made frequent complaints about adultery and fornication constituting "the besetting sins of these people", resulting in "frequent quarrels and fightings".[77] Part of the basis for interpersonal mistrust and a sense of injustice lay in the fact that gender relations were clearly paternalistic, not unlike European practice indeed. But the contrast between the chivalric aspect of middle- and upper-class European gender attitudes and the androcentric patterns of African gender relations caught the attention of the missionaries, so that in the mid-1850s one of them commented on the practice of husbands riding on horseback to market and church while wives followed on foot. Furthermore, "among the older people, it is very common, that the wife will wait upon her husband at table, and then sit down in the kitchen to take her dinner".[78] Having as a boy lived in a society where polygamy had been practised, and having witnessed the multiple partnerships of European personnel on Jamaican plantations, Archibald was quite taken aback to hear from a white nurse in the employ of Mrs Eliza Coke, a planter's wife, that a man cohabiting with several women was an instance of "bad living". The nurse had similarly denounced dancing, so this new matter "also struck my conscience, for I was living with 4 women. . . . In Africa this was done, and here in Jamaica we saw many white men, who were called gentlemen, and seemed to be respected, do the same."[79] The breaches of fidelity and the marriage contract led Zorn in 1830 to lament that drunkenness and fornication were "deplorably prevalent" among the residents of Lacovia who were "mostly free persons of colour".[80] And Brother Prince recalled visiting "from twenty-five to thirty families of browns and blacks" among whom he found "only *one* married couple". A congregation member found it necessary to seek the missionaries' counsel for her daughter who was "living with a man, by whom she ha[d] nine children, but who ha[d] another woman living five miles away".[81] Zorn lamented the "dreadfully depraved . . . lives of the negros, brown people and whites"; in the six years previous to his writing "you might have wandered the whole length of the land and found not a single married couple, white, brown or black. . . . [They were] all living in promiscuous concubinage." He relented though, in parenthesis, that there *were* legally married couples.[82]

The pastors were also dismayed by the cohabitation of black women with white men, a practice about which they seem to have exerted more moral pressure on the black participant than on the white men involved. This unequal blame is to be seen in the manner in which the missionaries failed to bring their complaint against cohabitation to the white sea captain who was living with a black woman. Instead, the moral suasion seems to have been directed to her on this occasion. We have no indication as to whether the topic was ever raised with the male partner, who carried the social and economic leverage. The incident in question occurred on 21 September 1846, when Brother and Sister Heath and their little daughter set off from New Carmel for New Fulnec. But the rain "obliged them to take shelter in a house on the road side". Here they were

> kindly accomodated [sic] by the mistress, a Negress Concubine of—who was just leaving for England. She was very humble and endeavoured to make us comfortable—when her manner of life was alluded to she express'd her hope that her "Saviour" would enable her henceforth to live better. She gladly allowed us to keep evening worship with her household. She had lived 12 years with Cap—and had one little girl who was being educated in England. Whilst we sat at her table to dinner and Tea She stood at a distance to wait on us Her quiet humble and very respectful behaviour attracted our notice and excited the earnest desire that she might be converted to God.[83]

The next morning their "kind hostess" provided them coffee before they set off again for breakfast at Fulnec. Report on a comparable situation in 1845 allows us some background to the implausibility of a black–white union being church-sanctioned. John Buchner provided a synopsis of the life of an English adventurer who had been born in Jamaica, educated in England, become a seaman and naval lieutenant, and then gone into slave trading in the Gambia. There he "became attached to a young Negro woman whom he purchased, and promised her marriage, sent her home to Jamaica, and followed soon after, but found that she was already sold to another". He bought her manumission, "but . . . he was a white man, and at that time could not be married to her by a clergyman". Now aged eighty-five and living in Manchester parish, he appealed to Buchner to marry them, and "upon my representation of the case, he came to church, and was legally married by me".[84] While there was no legal prohibition against such a union, it was outlawed by a strong cultural embargo, one which was upheld in practice by the established Anglican Church. It was only the non-established religious organizations that allowed it, and even then, we note that Buchner found it necessary to confer with his co-pastors or his church superiors over the matter. The prevailing plantation culture did not provide an encouraging

Figure 7.4 Gravestone for John Henry Buchner, Carmel Moravian churchyard, 1995.

environment for marriage in any case, and its attitude toward interethnic marriage was even less tolerant. While the St Elizabeth and Westmoreland Anglican church registers give evidence of several marriages between gradations of coloured people, and between them and whites, there is no evidence there of black–white or black–near-white alliances.[85]

The Work of the Ministry

During the week, missionaries made tours of various estates. In January 1835 Zorn reported visiting "Kepp", then Hampstead, opening there a "new Negro house with prayer", then holding catechism classes in the evening, and returning home to New Fulnec next morning.[86] But even along the route, attempts at proselytization were made. The tireless Zorn admitted that "[w]hen, on a journey, I overtake any Negroes, I generally rein in my horse, and proceed along slowly with them, in order that I may have an opportunity of addressing a word to them about their immortal soul. The seed thus scattered on the highways is not altogether in vain."[87]

In locations where there was no church but an eager congregation base, services were held at two- or three-monthly intervals at the premises of certain plantation owners. Such sites were assembly points for slaves from nearby properties: Hopeton attracted blacks "from nine or ten different estates in the vicinity" who were permitted by their owners to attend. A similar situation obtained at Isle, Edward Peart's coffee plantation, in Manchester's May Day

Hills, further to which the proprietors of several of these neighbouring estates had invited the Moravians "to come and repeat our instructions on their respective properties".[88]

Then there were out-station meetings in between the communion Sundays that were spaced at five-week intervals. These meetings were held either at "the house of the Helper of the district, or a school-house. We go out, for this purpose, about twice a week."[89] Such an occasion began with hymn singing, then passages of scripture were read by various people, followed by explanations and discussions of these. This was followed by further hymns and there was a closing prayer.

The mission stations were sometimes visited by congregation members who might "come in the evening for further instruction" in reading or for marriage counselling, and who were welcomed into the mission family's worship.[90] A minister reported in 1855 that three couples came "to settle their differences" during a one-week period.[91] Some marital problems had their basis in personality conflicts, as in the case of the disputes between John and Luna Richards. According to the diarist, John was miserly to the extent that he wanted the wife, "a sickly woman", to "support the family and let all his earnings be laid up in store". What must have been a long-standing problem reached its climax when Luna "took off her marriage ring and put it on his horse bridle".[92] This was certainly an indication that she had done with the marriage, but was it also an indication that the husband could offer the ring to another person whom he visited on horseback? Or that he could marry the horse since it apparently meant more to him than she did?

Before 1835, the year when the Moravian marriages were legally recognized in the colony, the missionaries devised a type of marriage ceremony that took place within the congregational meetings. The ambiguous status of these marriages was to compound the personal and economic problems that beset the best of unions. Peter Ricksecker was to regret:

> The private marriages have done much injury, as many do not consider them binding, and act accordingly, which gives rise to quarrels, and occasions us much trouble. To make an end of these sinful, and to us painful practices, we now expect all to be publicly married, as we may be called upon by Government for a list of our marriages. Those who are members of our church, are now united in the presence of the whole congregation.[93]

Apart from marriage disputes, several ministers alluded to "frequent quarrels" among the peasants, bred of "[v]indictiveness, passion, bad language, and a most shocking perversion of right and wrong", in addition to "a certain degree of intellectual imperfection . . . owing to the total absence of educational influence during the time of slavery".[94]

Apart from weddings and funerals, grand occasions for the church community included separate "lovefeasts" for widows, married couples and school children.[95] Also at times like Easter, church members, "who sometimes do not see each other for months, being employed in the cane-pieces and woods, meet again with such delight, shaking hands and wishing each other God's blessing, that it is a real pleasure to see what Christianity has effected among them".[96]

Ordinarily on Sundays, members "who live at a great distance bring their breakfast in a pan, and eat it in the church-yard, during the intervals of the meetings. The public service is followed by a meeting for catechization and instruction of adults as well as of children."[97] And by the late 1840s there was evidence of a certain display of well-being among the Fulnec congregation. At the church, a long shed had been built for the accommodation of the horses which they rode to church. "Ninety-four saddle-horses and mules were counted the Sunday we spent there", wrote William Mallalieu, "either in the shed . . . or under the shade of a large fustic-tree." But he cautioned, "Horse-keeping is no criterion of wealth; for many keep them on the properties on which they are settled, and make them shift for themselves on the road-sides, and in the uncleared bush on the mountain slopes."[98]

Sometimes congregation members visited the manse to assist in agricultural or domestic labour. "The Negroes came and sowed corn on our land", reports John Becker, stationed at Old Carmel in September 1814,[99] though it seems they had slaves or servants as well, since in August he reported working together with "our three Negroes, in planting our new land with sweet potatoes, cassava-roots, cocoa [coco], and plantain".[100] Congregation members also gave of their physical labour in helping missionaries settle in to new premises:

> We had much trouble to move the goods from Carmel to this place [Fairfield]. The ascent from the Low-lands is uncommonly steep; and our cart could not get farther than to the foot of the [Dom Figuerero] mountains. But our church-people exerted themselves with the greatest willingness, on their own Saturdays, to bring the various things up the hill. Our neighbours likewise very kindly assisted us with their mules.[101]

In the post-slavery period some kinds of labour could apparently earn wages, as when in 1842 the Blandfords

> were received by the people [at Parker's Bay] with every expression of joy and thankfulness. Some Brethren, with a large canoe, volunteered to go to Black River to fetch our baggage: carpenters, masons, and field-labourers, to the number of

240, came forward to put the Missionary premises in order, their labour being worth about 18*l.* sterling [pounds]. Some negroes brought young breadfruit trees in their hands, and planted them in rows. The fishermen brought fish; and some came with a present of vegetables.[102]

Voluntary help clearly continued to be available. On the return to New Eden from convalescence at Beaufort, Kiergaard and his wife were greeted by the church members:

The people, learning that we were on the road, came in numbers to meet us, some even as far as twelve miles, before we reached the place, so that we had quite a little band of horse and mule-riders behind our gig. When passing through the estates adjoining New-Eden, the people came leaning on their staffs, the blind being led by the others to the road-side, who with tears of joy exclaimed, 'Bless de Lord, who so good to send we old Massa back again, to we poor sinners.' Thus we arrived, on the 21st of November.[103]

Similarly, on his removal from New Bethlehem to New Carmel in February 1846, George Heath and his family were grateful for the assistance of the welcoming flock who, "coming on horseback or foot as far as New Fulneck, ten miles", helped carry his children and luggage over the mountain.[104]

Furthermore, congregations assisted in church building. In one such example, the timber was donated by the white landowner, but the labour to turn it from trees to lumber was the slave sweat and skill of Africans:

all the heavy timber [for construction of a church there] has been cut and brought hither out of the woods, without any material injury to the work-people, though some of the trees grew among craggy rocks, and in other scarcely accessible situations. Such light materials as boards and shingles, the negroes gladly carry upon their heads, whenever they have time at their disposal.[105]

Anywhere between fifty and one hundred people were reported as engaged in building a large lime-kiln and exerting themselves on other preparations for the erection of the church at Mile Gully.[106]

Despite their straightened financial circumstances, they also made monetary contributions to purchase items for church services, as when the Parker's Bay congregation "subscribed for a chapel-bell, communion vessels, and a seraphine".[107] They also put towards church building as well as towards missionary activity overseas. They pledged: "Massa, we will give money, and help to build a church."[108] And having heard of the Moravian mission in Greenland, they pledged one and a half pennies per month for overseas missions.[109] The larger world that first-generation migrants knew, and to which church affiliation had further introduced them, provided a focus for their public prayers, even in 1860, exemplifying the framework of community

Figure 7.5 Chimney-sweep, by Isaac Belisario. Courtesy National Library of Jamaica.

in which they placed themselves: "Some of our older congregation-brethren . . . offered most heart-affecting prayers. . . . The minister of the congregation, the teachers of the schools, their own families and districts, the Brethren's Church, the Island of Jamaica, their 'slave-brethren' in Cuba, the heathen world, particularly Africa, are subjects which are continually brought by them in their prayers before the throne of grace."[110]

In their labours the missionaries were greatly assisted by the devoted help of some converts. In the first decade of the nineteenth century, Thomas Ward regretted the passing of "old Peter at the Island [Estate] . . . a faithful assistant; for having been head-driver for many years, and highly respected by all the

Figure 7.6 Nineteenth-century Jamaican villagers. Photographer unknown. Courtesy Michael Gardner.

Negroes, his influence among them was very great. He was indeed blunt and rough in his manner of expressing his thoughts, but firm, upright, and sincere in wishing well to all his countrymen."[111] Similarly, at the October 1820 death of Peter of Two-Mile-Wood Estate, Brother Becker recalled that Peter "had been baptized by Brother Planta, in 1777, and was admitted to the Communion in 1813. He was a man of few words; but his walk was worthy of the gospel. His age was generally supposed to amount to 100 years."[112] Another eighteenth-century convert was Sister Patience of Bogue Estate who was baptized in 1799 and became a communicant in 1801. "It was her delight to assist her poorer Brethren and Sisters, as far as she was able; and as she was unable latterly to work in the fields, she made a practice to visit the sick and aged on the estate, and to speak a word of comfort, when needful. She was highly respected by the whole congregation, and her funeral was numerously attended."[113]

In their own simple way too, the less prominent church members offered hospitality to the strangers at their humble homes. By the 1840s Africans were sufficiently self-confident to invite the European missionaries to breakfast with them after out-station meetings. F.W. Hennig's report on 8 January 1857 conveys the qualified "prosperity" of the new peasantry during the 1850s:

> In some places, the Missionary is invited to take a breakfast after the meeting. This
> consists of a roast fowl with yam, to which a cup of coffee is sometimes added. The

cookery, as well as the cleanliness of knife, fork, and table-cloth would do credit to the housekeeping of a respectable European villager. Some of our people have whitewashed houses, really very neat and clean; and, in most cases, neatness and cleanliness are a sign, that there is a taste and desire for moral and spiritual improvement.[114]

A decade earlier the approach had been more tentative and less ritualized than the full breakfast board of the 1850s, as in May 1846 when two members of the very same "Nightengale Grove" settlement "brought us sweet and juicy Pines which refreshed us and the poor people rejoiced that we eat in their house. They counted this an unusual favour."[115]

Schools

The liberal ideas opened up by the anti-slave trade and slave amelioration debates fed efforts by religious-minded persons to educate a cadre of black persons. In Britain social welfare organizations such as the Ladies' Negro Education Society were formed, one of their functions being to raise funds for the salaries of teachers and the establishment of schools in overseas territories. But there were also local initiatives, such as private schools run by white female members of slave-owning families – owners' wives, daughters and in-laws. People like Mrs Eliza Scott of Hopeton and Mrs Mary Cooper of the Cruse had begun to teach reading and writing as an extension of their proselytizing mission that seems to have started in the 1820s. The Scotts were Creole whites, resident in Jamaica for several generations. Mr Scott's sister was Mary Cooper, which helps explain her depth of involvement in the educational project. Their mission took the form of prayer meetings at their homes and the hosting of visiting parsons who delivered sermons to assemblies of neighbouring white and mulatto families along with their slaves. The Scott school was financed by Mr and Mrs Scott, while Mrs Cooper's school was financed by the Ladies' Negro Education Society in England.[116] By October 1830 another independently funded school along the lines of the Scott school was being operated by Matthew Farquharson at Spring Vale in St Elizabeth where the estate's slave children under eight years of age "receive[d] daily instruction in reading, learning the Catechism, and a number of suitable hymns" through the "unwearied exertions" of their teachers, relatives of the owner.[117] At Hopewell, nine miles to the west of New Carmel, Samuel Spence "encourage[d his] negros to go to church", and the Spence daughters taught the more than forty slave children on the property.[118] It is clear then that the functions of these private schools and the proselytizing missions of their proprietors overlapped. Archibald himself began in 1824 to attend Christian services at Paynestown Estate led by Edward Francis Coke or Cook or Cooke, its owner, who after some time encouraged his congregation to attend Moravian services at the neighbouring Scotts' Hopeton. There Mrs Cooper,[119] "a pious white lady who also always went to Hopeton", approached Archibald with an offer "to teach [him] to read". To take up such an offer and persist with it between the 1824–26 period, Archibald "had to bear with much mockery" from his fellow blacks who accused him of presumptuously wishing "to read the white peoples book", but "this did not confuse me, and disturb or hinder me from going for instruction to Mrs. Cooper as often as possible".[120]

Similar private educational initiatives took place within Moravian missionary circles themselves, probably dependent on the family infrastructure and the time availability of particular ministers. In this way, as early as 1826 the Moravian missionary wives at Fairfield began to operate a school for children.[121] Ellis wrote enthusiastically for help to readers in England asking them to send out "a few copies of the four large lessons, for scholars of the lowest class, for pasting on boards, and about one hundred copies of part 1 of the Union Spelling Book".[122] Indeed, even before the declaration of emancipation in 1834, the children of free black people could attend day schools. This change of affairs meant that whereas "the idea of schools for Negro-children was [once] ridiculed",[123] by 1834 embryonic efforts at educating young black people were already underway.

During the slavery era, the Moravians established both day and evening classes, catering in the daytime to the now freed children of slaves under six years of age,[124] according to the new provisions of the Amelioration code, and in after-work hours to those enslaved persons who wished to do book-learning. By 1830 there was already at New Eden a day school for twenty-seven enslaved children together with eight free children, while ninety people attended the evening school. At Somerset in New Savannah, there were twenty-six children and two enslaved persons in the day. At Fairfield there was a day school comprising fifteen slaves and five free people, while evening classes were held for twenty slaves in irregular attendance. Zorn's school contained fifty slaves and twenty-eight free people. Sunday school, however, attracted eighty-six people.[125] By 1845 the school at New Fulnec catered to seventy-nine boys and fifty-eight girls. In 1860 the Belmont school was sited on Holland's Estate, near New Fulnec at the encouragement of the estate's proprietor who had "thankfully acknowledged our efforts on behalf of the heathen Africans on that property".[126] The success of the church's educational enterprise was such that by 1840 a missionary based at Fairfield could remark: "Some years ago, it would have been a difficult matter, to find a dozen Negroes who could read, out of a congregation of 500 persons. . . . I am happy . . . that there are about 150 adults of both sexes, belonging to the church at this place, who read the inspired volume."[127]

The subjects taught at day school were reading, writing, scripture, geography and grammar.[128] It is clear that repetition and memorization played significant roles in learning, as gleaned from one pastor's astonishment at the students' satisfactory progress in reading and writing; furthermore, "[t]hose who can read, continue to commit to memory two or three verses out of the Bible, and one hymn during the week; and a few, of their own free will, learn six or seven verses every day, and sometimes more".[129] We also know that the blind Cecilia Dickenson kept her own school of about a dozen infants where she taught them "to repeat and sing hymns, and recite scripture texts".[130]

The supply of a larger clientele during apprenticeship, 1834–38, served to make the institution of church schools a viable proposition. Such schools were also a weekday adjunct to the Sunday schools that were kept in small schoolhouses beside the churches or under trees in the churchyard while adult services were being conducted. In some cases estates made individual religious and educational provisions for their workers. Mr Marsey or Marcy, the owner of Kep, was found to "regularly instruct the negroes on Sundays, and a number of children during the week".[131] At the same time, the "indefatigable" Scott and Senior women were lauded for their teaching of "young persons unconnected with their school". These students comprised persons who attended evening classes in their after work hours.[132] Among the teachers was "the most active and efficient teacher in our Sunday school", Isabella Senior, the youngest sister of Mrs Scott, who in May 1829 had become the wife of the Anglican minister, Seymour Yates. She was, however, to "[enter] into her eternal rest after giving birth to a child" on 11 February 1839, coincidentally preceding the death of her mother Mrs Senior by only a few hours.[133]

In time these home-based schools were complemented and later superseded by church-sponsored and -supervised schools, which in some cases shared the same teaching personnel. But in those vicinities where the church schools opened, the private schools became feeder schools for the larger enterprises. Those who transferred were a few of the older children from Mrs Cooper and a number from Mrs Scott. Among the reasons were, apparently, the older ages of these women and their consequent ill-health, combined with competition with the church schools for teaching personnel. So although in 1834 Hopeton's enrolment was almost a hundred, and Cruse's around sixty, by 1839 they were described as "almost abandoned" as "[u]nder less regular instruction than formerly, there are about thirty children still at the Cruse school, and not quite so many . . . at Hopetown".[134] Apart from the reasons advanced above, the decline of these schools was partly a response to changes in the political balance of forces by which new legal entitlements were added to bolster the demographic weight of blacks. This must have caused some social discomfiture to whites. For it emerges that shortly after emancipation in August 1838, the two elderly white planters' wives, in the circumlocutious explanation of one missionary, "resolved on partially giving up their respective schools, not that they felt less interest in training the rising generation in the knowledge of God's holy Word, but because they saw plainly, that the feelings and circumstances of the emancipated Negroes, were such as to render such a change expedient".[135]

The weight of the demographic representation of Africans in the society was also responsible for the eventual replacement of white and mulatto teachers by blacks at the formal Moravian schools. So that by the 1850s, as the programme expanded, a number of young black men became schoolmasters. New Carmel's school opened in January 1839 with a complement of seventy to a hundred children. It was headed by James Macfarlane, son of a helper sister. He had been "trained at the Mico Institutions in Kingston".[136] Margaret Isabella Gale (probably coloured) instructed the girls in sewing for one hour a day.[137] By 1859 Joseph Turner had taken over the New Carmel School, while David McFarlane headed the Benashurts School in Kilmarnock, and Archibald Clarke the Union School in Chantilly. The probably "brown" females, Rose Ann Parchment and Amelia Briscoe, headed schools: in the case of the former, the St Mary's Hull School at Hopeton; and the latter, the Tunbridge Wells Infant School at Carr. In 1860 Alexander Black had taken over at New Carmel, and in 1861 Robert White had succeeded at Benashurts; in 1862 William Sanderson went to Union School; and at New Carmel Seymour Wynter replaced Black (now excluded from the church). By 1864 James Walters was in charge at Carmel, and by 1865 Kilmarnock received Joseph Thompson, who was accompanied in 1866 by H.M. James; Alexander Wright took over Kilmarnock in 1867. George Wellington Sill or Scill went to New Roads in 1867, being replaced two years later by James Barratt or Barrett. Chantilly received Thomas Parker in 1868, and Joseph Henry was the new man at Kilmarnock in 1870.[138]

The delivery of education was dependent on religious persons who, if not equipped to teach, were yet prepared to provide land and locations for classes. The Woodlands schoolhouse was built in the mountains five miles east of New Carmel on land "given for this purpose by two brown women, members of our congregation", possibly the Gales.[139] Brother Zorn, instrumental in establishing the Moravian school system in the early 1830s, records riding out from Spring Vale on 2 April 1830 to the house of a Mr Lock, "a free brown person of some property" where "it was proposed to begin a school".[140] Then in early September 1850 when the "old cottage" where a school was held had

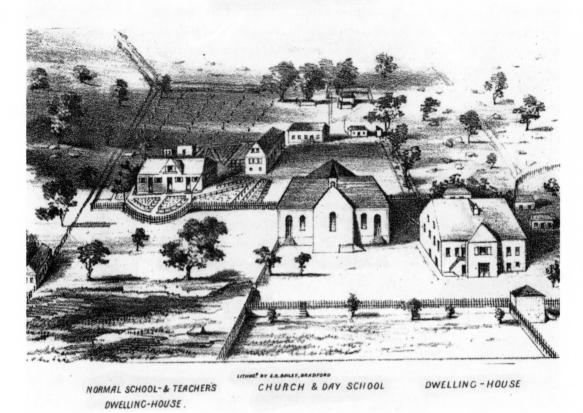

FAIRFIELD, JAMAICA.

LITHOG. BY S.O.BAILEY, BRADFORD

NORMAL SCHOOL- & TEACHER'S
DWELLING-HOUSE.

CHURCH & DAY SCHOOL

DWELLING - HOUSE

Figure 7.7 Mission station at Fairfield, Manchester. From Buchner, *The Moravians in Jamaica.*

become "too small and tottering", Archibald Monteath allowed the Rose Hall or Pitts' school space to operate in his own home.[141] The schools also benefited from gifts in money and in kind offered by persons both in Jamaica and overseas. The Religious Tract Society in 1835 sent from England a supply of children's books for general distribution and also donated items for the libraries of missionary families at New Carmel.[142] By 1860, a lady in Hastings, England, sent £10 for the establishment of an infant school at Fairfield.[143]

In several locations there was enthusiasm for the classes, with parents willing to pay school fees, and prepare lunches that children carried on their heads to school. The latter practice made for what Brother Blandford called "a very picturesque" sight, as on 6 May 1843 a group of young people and adults passed "before my window . . . on their way to the Friday-school, all dressed in neat clean clothes, with their breakfasts and dinners on their heads, in little baskets or small wooden trays".[144] Parents also provided "bread kind" or ground provisions for the meals of trainee teachers at the Manual Labour and Training School.[145] The yams and coco were supplemented with crops that the boys cultivated during three hours of the five-day school week.[146] By 1847 enrolment at the training school consisted of about twelve males between the ages of fourteen and eighteen who also acted as monitors in the nearby day school.[147]

But the picture did not continue so uniformly rosy, what with Francis Holland at Lititz reporting in the late 1840s on parental reluctance towards sending their children to school and non-payment of school fees in the early 1850s.[148] As the combination of epidemics, drought, and land hunger incrementally weighed heavily on the people, it is obvious that adults in particular districts perceived impediments to freeing their children from economic tasks or to financing less immediate benefits such as their children's education. In fact, complaints about the black community's lukewarm support of the church's educational efforts became more sustained in the decade of the 1860s. "It is the custom of even respectable families to send their children only in rotation, and in consequence our schools which might be a means of elevating the people, scarcely suffice to prevent the next generation from relapsing into barbarism", wrote Allan Hamilton at Bethany in part of his remarks concerning 1866,[149] and J.P. Pulkrabek's report about Nazareth in 1865 called attention to "bad attendance at church and school . . . ascribed to want of provisions, of clothes, and of water for washing".[150] Another reason from the Bethany district was the priority given to the agriculturally based economic lifelines of the people. These involved the employment of young people as ginger peelers on distant cultivation grounds, and coffee-picking in the autumn which "afforded many an excuse for neglecting the schools".[151]

Despite these setbacks, by 1853, with financial underpinning through a bequest from W. Taylor,[152] the Manual Labour and Training School was upgraded to a training institution that offered a higher level of instruction. The Institution had opened at Fairfield in 1842, enlarging on a kernel project begun in 1837 by Zorn with funds from Bristol in England, and which was then further expanded in 1840. The subjects taught at the new teacher training school included church history, and vocal and instrumental music.[153] Theodore Sonderman, however, thought that "comparatively few of the scholars . . . have a good ear for music, though many have a natural liking for it", an observation that may reflect differences in culturally conditioned vocal and tonal aesthetics regarding dominant scale types, harmony, voice timbre, and the treatment of notes, which among Africans involved "scooping", that is, attacking a note by way of its half-tones. Interestingly, he contended against the theory that "Negroes" were "naturally deficient in powers of reasoning and argument", given the "ample testimony" afforded by the monthly helpers' meetings; what he considered problematic, however, was what he considered the incorrectness of the inferences which they drew from data, a deficiency which he ascribed to logic that was not "true".[154] Zorn had earlier voiced other related reservations about the thinking habits of the young students generally: "Their memories have been cultivated, and their fingers have been tutored, but the higher powers of the mind have not been sufficiently called forth."[155]

Indeed, the expatriates were uneasy about the future prospects of their charges, in light of some evidence of moral lapses. And by the 1850s Brother Plessing voiced the complaint that "Our young people . . . feel themselves free, without having a correct idea of liberty. . . . They hardly listen to the accounts, given by the older people, of the difficulties and trials they had to undergo in former times, or, at best, smile at them as idle talk."[156] Brother Sonderman too was later to admit that "the young people give much cause for anxiety and even alarm for the future. Disregard of parental authority, a self-conceited display of a certain degree of worldly wisdom, a disinclination for settled occupation, and wasteful pursuit of foolish novelties"[157] were myriad causes for concern. Here was a grim warning about psychological and, no doubt, domestic instability, and intimations of generational and attitudinal gaps in the society at large. Despite these drawbacks, the early endeavours of Christian planter families and the Moravian missions began the tradition whereby the western half of Jamaica became the site of many educational institutions, some of which have not only been long established but also have had excellent reputations.

8

Planters and Missionaries

Tensions and Alliances

"Between Scylla and Charybdis"

JACOB ZORN BORROWED THIS Greek, later English, idiom to encapsulate the concept of the pitfalls that the missionaries negotiated between the freedom so ardently wished for by the enslaved and the suspicions of the whites whose well-being lay in control of the unpaid labour of their drudges.[1] As such, the idiom also sums up the consequent precarious and conflicted relationship between the planter class and the Euro-American Christianizing missionaries whose prime concern was the spiritual welfare of the enslaved.

Indeed, it was the initiative of planters to foster Christian outreach towards the enslaved that laid the foundation for a tradition of collaboration between slave owners and Moravian clergy in Jamaica's western parishes. Two brothers, William Foster and Joseph Foster Barham of Northumberland in England,[2] had inherited some nine hundred slaves stationed on several large sugar estates in Jamaica: Lancaster, Elim, Two-Mile-Wood and Bogue at the eastern end of St Elizabeth, together with Mesopotamia in Westmoreland. However, the Fosters had come under the influence of John Cennick, an evangelical Moravian preacher in Britain, and sought to reconcile their economic advantage by the charitable endeavour of enabling the message of spiritual redemption to uplift "these poor souls—the Negroes in this part of the world, where Providence ha[d] cast [their] share of temporal blessings".[3]

Under their aegis, then, the first missionaries specifically dedicated to the conversion of Africans set foot in Jamaica in December 1754. They were

Zacharias George Caries, Thomas Shallcross and Gottlieb Haberecht. The Fosters made them a grant of 300 acres, about half of which was marsh, and a very small stipend, but the obstruction of overseers on these absentee-owned estates and the newness of the enterprise made the venture painful and laborious. Added to this, internal wranglings over strategy with an additional team of missionaries in 1756 effectively stymied the project, even involving the departure of Caries and Haberecht by 1760. The advent, however, in 1805 of John Lang infused new life, boldness and direction into the establishment of Moravianism in Jamaica. Yet by 28 November 1816, Lang himself reached a nadir of frustration over the accumulated discrepancies between promises made by the church's planter sponsors and the realization of these intentions. In his diary he "grieved" over the Fosters' lack of support for Eden, the name of the mission at the Bogue, and the similar experience of the other missionaries, Thomas Ward and John Light, at the hands of Barham and the Halls, respectively. The "Fosters have promised to do one third at Eden Building & 1/9th only is performed. Halls promised every comfort to Br. Light & the Negroes are threadned [sic] with flocking [sic] if they come to church. Barham Sends Br. Ward without any thing to live on."[4] Thomas Kirkpatrick Hall who owned Tryall in St James eventually made land available for the mission station at Irwin.

Further aggravation for Lang came from attempts to incriminate him in anti-government and anti-planter agitation. As a result of the ongoing opposition of the Spice Grove overseer to the Christian conversion of his charges,[5] Robert Peart,[6] headman of Spice Grove Estate and first convert in the Fairfield area of Manchester, was questioned by the estate's attorneys about the manner and content of Moravian religious teaching. The hearing, quite probably in mid-1817, was part of a generalized disapproval by whites in the area to the proselytization being done by George Lewis, an itinerant enslaved preacher-cum-trader, who had gained the support of John Lang. In the diary of Bogue Mission, Lang had reported on 31 March 1816 that the whites had threatened to bring him before a court of justice on account of his association with Lewis. They chose to make the hub of their opposition an allegation that Lang had, during a particular service at Peru Estate, pronounced "dangerous" words jeopardizing "the safety of the Island". A further damning circumstance was concocted out of the allegation that an enslaved man who had been hanged at Mile Gully – "some say for praying and others say for Rebelion [sic]" – had, before he died, uttered the incriminating words "God Bless Parson Lang".[7] Lang was most uneasy about all these charges and the false witness that was being hatched against him. This inquiry into Lang's ministry did, apparently, take place, with Peart, along with others, being taken before a bench of magistrates, and examined as to the nature of the instructions they received. His answers convinced his judges, that religion will make a man a more valuable servant and member of society, and they sent him away in silence. To the first question, as to the nature of the instructions they received, he replied: "We are told to believe in God, who sees us every where, and in His Son, Jesus Christ, and to pray to Him to take us to heaven". "Well, what more?" "We must not tell lie". "What more?" "We must not steal from massa". "What more?" "We must not run away and rob massa of his work." "What more?" "We must not pretend to be sick, when we are not, and neglect massa's work". "What more?" "We must not have two wives, for by-and-by they will get jealous, and hurt one another, and massa's work will fall back". "What more?" "We must pray for busher,[8] and every body". "Well, go along".[9]

In contrast with later non-conformist churches, such as the Wesleyans and Baptists, the silence of the Moravians with regard to the economic and moral degradation of slavery has long been noted. The policy of the Moravian Church had been traditionally very guarded, even in Europe, with respect to its intervention in civilian and political matters. The individual who had most extensively charted their doctrines and codes was Count Nicholas Ludwig von Zinzendorf of Saxony and he had consistently instructed that they should in no way oppose the laws of the countries in which they operated. This position was further endorsed by Zinzendorf's successor, August Gottlieb Spangenberg, who instructed that in slave societies the enslaved " 'must be taught to be obedient to their masters', and learn to 'patiently submit' to their lot".[10] As such, Moravian "principles were suitable for the preservation of the existing social order".[11] Basing this position on Romans 13:1, "Let every soul be subject to higher powers", they considered it "imperative to obey the state authorities, no matter the latter's qualities".[12]

These conciliatory teachings, however, gained the Moravian positions little approval from most of the West Indian plantocracy, and also earned them the opprobrium of the later Protestants, such as the Wesleyans and Baptists. But these positions were to win them acceptance by significant segments of the plantocracy when the tide of British public opinion in the closing decades of the eighteenth century eventually turned towards abolition of the slave trade or, as an alternative, the amelioration of the conditions of life of the enslaved. The careful diplomacy and lobbying of the English Moravian Ignatius La Trobe (1758–1836) during the British government's 1788 Enquiry into the Slave Trade assisted the compromise conclusion that the institution of slavery would continue but that its conditions would be improved. In this improvement, Christianization would play a major role since the methods of the Moravians in particular showed that "converts became better workers and more moral beings".[13] As William Wilberforce asserted, the planters of

Figure 8.1 King's House, Spanish Town. Daguerrotype by Adolphe Duperly, *c.* 1845. Courtesy National Library of Jamaica.

Antigua, where there were thriving Moravian missions, had confessed to him the increased value to them of their slaves because of the latters' "increased habits of regularity and industry".[14] As a result, "there would be less punishment; more work done, and better done; more marriages, more issue, and more attachment to their masters and to government".[15]

Apart from the general principles of church policy towards enslavement, the Moravians were keenly aware that their presence in slave societies and the success of their missions there depended on the goodwill and cooperation of the ruling class. They had suffered much from non-cooperation and broken promises at the beginning of their mission in the second half of the eighteenth century; worse than that, one of their missionaries – a German, Heinrich Pfeiffer, then stationed at New Eden in western Manchester – had been arrested, tried and was within hours of losing his life on the charge of inciting rebellion during the slave uprising of 1831–32. The Moravian Church therefore felt justified in their adoption of a hands-off policy towards property owners, the manner in which they conducted their lives, and their conduct toward their human property. Their conciliatory posture attracted the cooperation of several slave owners who invited them to evangelize on their plantations, donated lands for church construction and living quarters for missionaries, financed school buildings, organized schools and taught in them. It is this type of slave owner whom Archibald regarded as making a positive impact on his life, imparting to him their moral standards, advancing his skills, and promoting him socially.

Ironically, we may note that some of the missionaries in the Moravian Brethren circuit also employed slaves. The late eighteenth-century missionaries agonized about this, but they were caught on the horns of a dilemma in a society where labour was almost one hundred per cent slave. To put it another way, there was little way of hiring *paid* labour.[16] According to caste specifications, if the labourers were black, then they were slaves. This economic culture continued to present the missionaries with a moral problem even into the first decades of the nineteenth century. So that the following minutes of the Mission Conference held at Fairfield, 30 November 1831 are noteworthy, whereby a decision was made to

> recommend to the UEC [Unity[17] Elders Conference] to manumit the 6 slaves belonging to the mission in Jamaica, who are all attached to Fairfield, *without delay*, as the expense of manumission is trifling, the opposition of white neighbours not to be heeded . . . and further as it is probable that the negros . . . from their affection to the place [Fairfield], will prefer remaining at a hire which will not increase the annual expenditure more than £30 currency. (emphasis theirs)

The matter was still up for discussion at the next Mission Conference at New Carmel on 11 July 1832 when it was decided to free these slaves "quietly and regularly, and charge upon the liberated not to spread the report abroad".[18]

But during the seven-month delay, the fulcrum of change had shifted radically. The dispatch with which the matter was concluded in July 1832 may be read as a response to the unmistakable December 1831 signs of agitation for freedom among the enslaved themselves. Not surprisingly, violent agitation was viewed as frightening by those who valued peace, so John Ellis, writing from Fairfield in Manchester parish, condemned "the late disturbances", apparently around 1824, as "the works of darkness and confusion":

> Not one of the members of our congregation, either at Fairfield, New Eden, or Irwin, has in any way joined, or been connected with, the insurgents. Even at Hopeton and Lennox Estates, which lie in the immediate vicinity of the place where the insurrection broke out, and where we have lately begun to preach, not one negro joined the rebels.[19]

From his point of view, "the pure light of the Gospel" had shone and routed evil. Whether or not a metaphorical matter, the fact was that the economic and social environment did not lend itself to sustained peace, even though it was underpinned by massive physical force.[20] For all that, the number of attempted revolts in Jamaica's history was impressive.[21]

For the very reason of the unsustainability of such a repressive system, the moral climate of the times was changing in Europe, and there is some evidence that among the Jamaican Moravian hierarchy there were closet abolitionists, who had clearly come under the intellectual and ethical influences of libertarians in the British Isles. At least one of these was Jacob Zorn, born on the island of St Thomas to a missionary father. Jacob served in Jamaica from 1828 and was for nine years superintendent of the Moravian mission in Jamaica till his death on 25 May 1843. Zorn's mother, having been widowed, became the wife of John Kummer. As such, one of Jacob Zorn's stepbrothers was John Gottlob Kummer, who married Sarah Hinchcliffe of Yorkshire, England. Perhaps this British connection accounts for the presence among the papers of the Kummer family of a printed pamphlet in the form of a letter put out by the Bradford Anti-Slavery Association and dated 24 November 1832. It was addressed to Mr Hinchcliffe of Horton Academy, probably the father of the later Sarah Kummer. The Hinchcliffes were resident near Fulneck, a settlement of the United Brethren in Yorkshire. The 1832 letter notes "with great satisfaction, that the cause of Emancipation has become very generally, what it should ever have been considered, a test of moral and political worth, in respect to Candidates for Parliamentary distinction" and demands "the TOTAL ABOLITION" of the "iniquitous

system" of slavery. The enslaved soul, meanwhile, "looks over the sea, and yet waits, impatiently waits, to see if the righteousness of the English nation will accord him as a BOON, that which . . . he will shortly vindicate as his INALIENABLE RIGHT".[22]

There seems yet another connection between Zorn and the anti-slavery school. It was a connection that also embraced Joseph Horsfield Kummer, Zorn's first cousin, whose manuscript of Archibald Monteath's biography is reproduced in appendix 2 of this work. Joseph's father was John Jacob Kummer, who had been a missionary in the Danish West Indies, today the Virgin Islands. He married Maria Horsfield, whose mother, Elizabeth (1754–1836), had been a Benezet before her marriage to Joseph Horsfield. Elizabeth's grandfather, John Stephen Benezet, had been a Huguenot who sought refuge in Holland during the religious persecutions of Protestants in Louis XIV's France. John Stephen moved his family from Holland to England, where they lived for sixteen years, and where he became acquainted with the United Brethren's Church [the Moravians]. In 1731 he crossed the Atlantic to Philadelphia, befriended Count Zinzendorf and August Spangenberg there, and allowed his son, Daniel, Elizabeth's father, later a Philadelphia merchant, to accompany the Moravians on their missions among the Native Americans. Another son became the "Quaker antislavery writer Anthony Benezet, whose works on Africa and the slave trade were widely read in the 1770s and 1780s".[23] His influence "extended from Pennsylvania across the Atlantic", and he was "a major inspiration for the first important British abolitionist, Granville Sharpe".[24] Apart from founding the first school exclusively for girls, Anthony Benezet set about teaching enslaved children in Philadelphia in 1750, continuing this practice until 1770. As Joseph Kummer's great-uncle, it is therefore quite likely that both Joseph Kummer and Jacob Zorn were familiar with and perhaps influenced by Anthony Benezet's works and sentiments.

Judging from the warmth and frankness of the letters sent by Jacob Zorn to John Gottlob Kummer, it would appear that they shared a close relationship, and it is therefore instructive to note the anti-slavery sentiments that emerge from Zorn. In a letter dated 7 May 1833, he fulminated over the continuing traffic in slaves even after the British Parliament had outlawed the trade in 1807 and set up naval anti-slave trade embargos in the Gulf of Guinea, off the Central African coasts, and in the sea lanes to ports in Latin America, North America and the Caribbean where slave ships were headed: "Last week as if to open the eyes of the British Public to the shameful extent to which the Slave trade is still carried on by the Spaniards & Portuguese, a Schooner of the latter country was wrecked on our shores, near Kingston, with 230 negroes on board."[25] In another letter dated 15 September 1835, he adverted to the scare of black unrest that was expected in 1834 in the wake of the announcement of projected freedom for the slaves after six further years: "the lies of the newspapers notwithstanding, the negros are behaving as well, and doing as much work as can reasonably be expected". In another letter written on 23 November 1841, he admitted that he held differences with Americans on the subject of slavery. This position is reiterated in a letter written from Newfield or Bethabara on 24 June 1841, in which the slaveholding states of the American South are challenged:

> As to the working of *freedom,* we can, on the *whole,* give a very cheering testimony, such as should encourage our Southern Citizens to take the subject of Emancipation with serious consideration. . . . As to the *industry* of free negros, – they are as other people, some lazy, some very industrious; – on the whole I should estimate the quantity of work performed as *greater* than in slavery; but their industry is in part turned into new Channels.[26] (emphases his)

In another letter, penned on 21 December 1838, a few months after full emancipation had been declared on 1 August that year, he updated his brother that "In our Parish, Manchester, (entirely a coffee parish) things were going on very well, till in November rent began to be enforced; – this rather unsettled their minds". This was an allusion to the decision by many of the landowners to demand rent from their former slaves for the cottages that they had occupied under slavery and those that they had built on the estate peripheries. As discussed in Wilmot ("Emancipation") and Monteith

("Emancipation and Labour"), this provoked great resentment among the ex-slaves, who, injustice of injustices, had received no compensation whatsoever for their years of landlessness, unpaid labour, and mental and physical anguish and injury. Zorn continued: "Most of them having built their cottages themselves, think it very hard now to pay rent for them, and some ejectments have been the consequences and in other instances the rent has been enforced in Court." Despite all these provocations, Zorn testified that, "[o]n the whole . . . the negroes have conducted themselves with great propriety, considering the greatness of the change, and the variety of new duties they have to learn".[27] The injustice of the purveyors of the plantation system was so consistent that even one year after emancipation people were jittery and highly suspicious of their liberty being retracted. For example, in 1839 Zorn alerted his readers that

> A foolish report was spread among the credulous negroes, that the whites would attempt to reduce them to slavery again; and, in consequence, numbers have armed themselves with fowling-pieces. Our people about Nazareth believe this so firmly, that they might have got into serious difficulty had I not heard of it, and gone there to speak with the communicants, and disabuse their minds.[28]

Injustice past and injustice continued gave rise to economic and psychological uncertainties with their potential for violent flashpoints. Zorn, however, advocated a gradual process of co-opting the workers into a commodity-based capitalist economy through wages, exchange and trade:

> The way to induce them to work well, is to increase their *wants,* to make them consider other things, besides yams and an osnaburg dress as *necessaries.* The better clothing of their children, paying for their schooling, supporting their ministers, paying for doctor's attendance, making their houses more comfortable etc. (emphases his)

Conversely, some of the planters wished to deprive the ex-slave force of some of the resources to which they had had access under slavery, such as provision grounds where they could keep stock and raise subsistence as well as surplus produce for market. Withdrawal of these resources would, such planters reasoned, compel the labour force to work on the estates for money with which to purchase their necessities. Zorn condemned this policy as too akin to "slavery and despotism", and later was even so inflamed as to denounce it as not so much "absurdity or insanity" as "roguery". The immediate cause of the latter outburst was the absurd situation by which a labourer had been offered a wage of $18 a year to watch a corn and provision ground at the same time that he was being charged $72 a year in hut rent![29]

Zorn's abolitionist positions were not public, and they very likely had a more philosophic and ethical base to them than the rationale of most of the open-minded planters, such as they were. The conciliatory attitude of the landowner James Wedderburn towards Archibald Monteath, giving him licence to proselytize among his slaves, was not unconnected to the "winds of change" blowing in England regarding the advantages to planters of a Christianized workforce.

Opposition to the Missionary Agenda

The slave system was morally threatening, especially on large sugar estates that had hundreds of slaves and were therefore large enterprises in which the weak were either marginalized, or deliberately abused. Moreover, the large percentage of absentee landlords enjoying in Britain the fruits of their Jamaica investments left the chattel slaves exposed to myriad abuses from intermediaries who themselves bore no financial loss from maltreating the work force. On large and on otherwise ill-supervised estates, "the little flock of Christian negroes . . . are as sheep among wolves; for, in their situations, they hear and see nothing but what is sin and evil, by day and night".[30] Archibald himself condemned the sexual laxity encouraged by an overseer at Mount Edgecombe, who was himself married.[31] The sugar estates were considered by the missionaries as "far from being favourable places for . . . growth in grace", as the Christians were "exposed to more than ordinary temptation" particularly during holiday festivities when "heathenish abominations" flourished.[32] Human life there had much to disgust the sensibilities, not only morally, but physically as well. Even the Barhams' slaves were acknowledged to be "in a destitute state".[33] Several years after emancipation, poor health and sanitary conditions on some estates continued to typify the condition of their working inhabitants. Brother Heath on a visit to Bog Estate south of Hopeton in June 1846 indicated: "There were plenty of people. *Careless Ignorant dirty ragged lame sick old and young, bck* [black] Brown and White. . . . Satan seems to reign there."[34] With regard to the same estate, Brother Elliott was constrained to take along "some Chloride of soda to disinfect the house" of a church member who was ill with dysentery and fever. "Their *little dark dirty* rooms" were "generally very close and bad".[35]

Where there were absentee landlords, the "attorneys and overseers were the real masters, and threw obstacles in the way of the missionary, entirely out of his power to remove. In most instances, they put him to such annoyances, to such inconvenience, scorn and ridicule, that it required on his part no small degree of humility, forbearance, and self-denial" to cope. The attorneys and overseers, belonging to the same caste as the missionaries, saw the latter as "another officer added to the staff of agents on the plantation; to him the overseer complained of the laziness and disobedience of the slaves; he was expected to reprove them, to tell them to obey and work diligently".[36]

Duplicity upon duplicity was the corrupt moral fabric woven out of the original theft and degradation of human beings for economic profit. The missionaries themselves could not completely avoid the taint. Although George Timaeus reported in September 1826 the passing of Mr Morrice, the manager of the Bogue Estate, and commented: "To us he behaved in the most friendly manner. We experience the same friendly disposition in Mr. R., of Mesopotamia"[37], this was a deliberate massaging of the truth as a public relations ploy. It is in the manuscript diaries that one reads how on 19 August 1826, "Br. Ellis . . . called on Mr. Morrice to see if he would pay the yearly stipend which the owners of Bogue and Elim Estates have kindly awarded to our mission, but the unwillingness of that gentleman to part with one farthing towards a missionary cause remains unchanged although he is to all appearances hastening to the grave". True enough, by 9 September "Mr Morrice had departed this life".[38] This cat-and-mouse game was played by both sides, as Brother Ellis, writing on 5 May 1826, had reported that both himself and Brother Timaeus had visited Mesopotamia Estate, where the attorney was "very kind and attentive to us" and "made it convenient for those negroes, who wished to have an interview and a confidential conversation with me, to come to me".[39] But in the privacy of their Mission Conference meetings, such as that on 5 January 1831, they noted that the estate's owner, "Br. John Foster . . . is soon expected to arrive in this island and take charge of the Foster and Barhams properties. . . . When he . . . arrives we will without reserve relate to him a true account of the hindrances we have met with on those properties."[40] Another instance of double-speak on the part of estate management is encountered in the narrative of John Hafa: he reports visiting the attorney at Peru Estate, who promised "to put the church in order, and to permit negroes from other estates to attend the service".[41] That was on 6 June 1819. On the 23, Hafa "accordingly" went to Peru and "had the pleasure to see a great number of negroes arrive". But before the service began, "there was a report spread among the people, that this was the last Sunday, on which strange negroes would be permitted to attend". When the service was over, the head driver "then informed the people, that he had orders to warn off all the strange negroes in future". He did not make the remark directly to Hafa. But "[b]y this measure" Hafa understood that he was "in fact prevented from visiting Peru any longer", where, it would seem, quite a number of enslaved persons from neighbouring plantations had come to join in the worship.[42]

Problems raised by the hindrances put in the way of the missionaries by locally based agents of the plantation owners were discussed at the Mission Conference of 27 April 1830. On this occasion, missionaries' discussions revealed that an expanded role for helpers was being thwarted "as the overseers do not allow negroes to visit on neighbouring properties even in the night if they can possibly prevent it. Their present condition make [*sic*] them afraid to tell anything to Br. Light of the misconduct of congregation members if it be of a nature to cause investigations before the overseer."[43]

But even as late as 1833 the custos of St Elizabeth opined "that evening meetings were illegal, & that no master could give his consent to such an assemblage without incurring the penalties of the law".[44] By August another Mission Conference heard from Brother Renkewitz "that the attorney for the Bogue continues to refuse his consent to the evening meetings at New Eden, & would not even permit as many as 12 catechumens to go to the Chapel of an evening to be prepared for Holy Baptism! In consequence Br. Renkewitz wishes to go into the negro village during the *negro* time of shell blow to impart instructions" (emphasis his).[45]

There were other obstacles. In Brother Becker's recounting of the experience of enslaved persons on Elim Estate who wished in 1820 to be baptized by the Moravians, the purposeful thwarting of the Moravian mission by an overseer in favour of Anglicanism is patent. Becker was peeved that "some of the overseers had resorted again to the practice of having their Negroes baptized by the clergyman of the parish".[46] Such mass baptisms were largely a formality, since there was no prior indoctrination and no follow-up ministrations. It was a pragmatic measure to "Christianize" the enslaved while avoiding subsequent demands from them for personal time to devote to catechism and worship activities. So the attorneys or overseers or masters would invite the Anglican rector of the parish to come to the estate to baptize the blacks, on the agreement that each individual's baptism would cost the estate an agreed amount. "The slaves being all assembled, generally in the mill-house, the minister went round, accompanied by the housekeeper, or concubine, of the overseer, carrying a basin of water, and naming each slave by a new name, while he sprinkled the water upon them. After this followed a dance, with a large allowance of rum."[47] Archibald Monteath's account apprises us that the eight-shilling fee for baptism was paid by the candidates themselves, not the estate.

Planter Hospitality

Given their newness to the strange physical and social environment, and the general hostility and suspicion with which non-Anglican clergymen were regarded by the secular establishment, the missionaries who subsequently arrived were more than grateful for the hospitality and assistance of members of the plantocracy. We detect a sigh of relief when one missionary recounts in the 1820s that the family of Farquharsons at Spring Vale in St Elizabeth was one of about five places "where the doors of respectable proprietors in the neighbourhood have been opened to us".[48] The foreigners had great need of this support. They needed the permission of estate owners to carry their message of the Gospel to the slaves, as when Robert Keith Senior and his wife, Mary Dunn Senior,[49] at "Musquito-cove" in Hanover parish invited a missionary to visit their estate regularly for this purpose. For want of personnel, it was an invitation that was at the time impractical to act upon.[50] And as they moved on horseback and carriage from one property to another, the inconveniences of travel were relieved by the existence of welcoming households where they shared some modicum of cultural and religious fraternity. "[W]e spent Sunday with [the Hopeton Scotts], when I had the favour to address from two to three hundred Negroes, who gladly assembled to hear the Word of God."[51] Sister Timaeus had the convivial company of "our kind christian friend Mrs. Wright the owner of a coffee plantation called Kensworth" in the Mayday Hills of Manchester.[52] Hospitality was also forthcoming from some overseers, such as the one at Devon Estate in Manchester parish with whom, after ministering to the blacks, Becker had dinner. He ruminated: "I felt on this occasion the advantages afforded to travellers, by the prevalence of hospitality in this great island. Wherever you travel, you are at no loss for refreshments, it being the custom to enter into the nearest house, and to sit down to table without invitation."[53]

Moreover, missionaries frequently fell ill, and their diaries are replete with information regarding the rescue of the health of themselves and their family members by the visits and advice of friendly planters and their provision of accommodation in more salubrious locations than at some of the mission stations. As one example, John Ellis, convalescing from a combination of illness and bereavement, revealed in a letter that "Our kind friend, E.P Esq., [probably Edward Peart] invited us to come, for some time, and live with him at Lincoln, a place noted for its healthy situation."[54] Mrs Tomlinson came from Huntly with her nurse to minister to Mrs Collis "for upwards of a week, as assiduously as if she had been her own sister".[55] And Mrs Renkewitz remained at Huntly for several weeks as of December 1836 when she, Brother Renkewitz and their children came down with yellow fever.[56] Apart from these convalescences in hilly locations, seaside situations were also available to them. Both Jacob Zorn and his wife spent a few days benefiting from the sea air at Belmont, a Hanover property belonging to Hutchison Mure Scott.[57]

Facilitating Pastoral Work

At first, services were held in buildings on the estates, such as the coffee-store[58] or the overseer's house,[59] or "in the open air on the barbecue, a terraced square for drying the coffee",[60] even "under the shade of some fig and mango trees".[61] Zorn was clearly exhilarated by the venue at Bethany in Manchester:

> The place of assembling (it is neither house nor chapel), is quite unique: the whole resembling an infant settlement in the American back-woods. Imagine a long shed, partly covered with shingles, but principally with boards overlapping each other, among stumps and stones, and logs of timber, only a part of which have been consumed in burning lime. At one end are a few rooms for Br. Scholefield and his family; and the rest, closed on two sides with boards tacked in their rough state against the posts which go into the ground, forms the place of meeting. A few of the people are accommodated with benches, but the majority find a seat on boards placed on blocks in the ground, some higher, some lower. . . . For the evening meetings, they are requested to bring their small tin lamps with them, the place being too open to admit of the use of candles; and these being suspended on the beams and rafters, throw around a fitful glare, as the breeze sports with their flame.[62]

Before the building of the church at New Carmel, Brother Light recalled officiating to "crowded auditories, both in the morning and afternoon" at the house of Edward Francis Coke at Paynestown.[63] Similarly, prior to the establishment of a chapel at Parker's Bay in Westmoreland, eight miles west of New Carmel, use was made of Hutchison Mure Scott's wharf-house on the bay.[64] Later, John Collis was to speak of the commencement of worship on 13 August 1836 at their "new place of worship at Parker's Bay, on the ground presented to us by our worthy friends, Mr. and Mrs. Scott".[65] Mr Tomlinson of Huntly, described as "[o]ur esteemed friend and neighbour", took "an active part" in the "lately renewed" Sunday school at Fairfield, "which is held in the church, and at present attended by between two and three hundred scholars". Tomlinson "ha[d] also occasionally read prayers and a sermon to the hundreds of negroes, who could not find entrance in the church, or when one of the Missionaries was preaching in Mile-Gully".[66]

Another helpful intervention occurred during the time while the missionaries awaited the erection of premises on designated church grounds. At such times, they were sometimes housed on nearby plantations. So "by the kindness of Matthew Farquharson, Esq., clerk of the peace and vestry" for St Elizabeth, Zorn and his family were resident in "a small but convenient house" at the Spring Vale property from March up to his writing in October 1830.[67] By 1833 Matthew Farquharson offered "the gift of a building, formerly

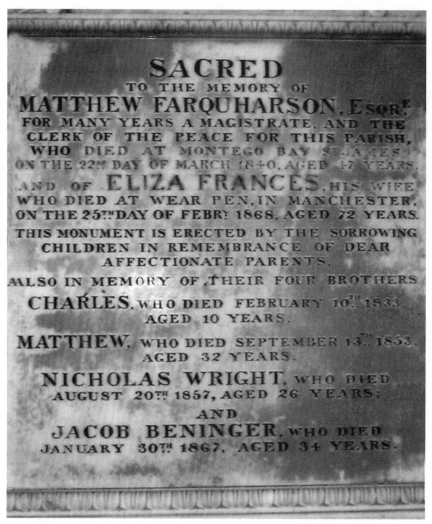

Figure 8.3 Memorial tablet for Matthew Farquharson, Black River Anglican church.

used as a butchery, which might with comparatively small expense be removed to New Fulneck Chapel, & form 2 rooms for the Missionary's residence".[68] The Hamans occupied the overseer's house at Malvern in the Santa Cruz mountains of St Elizabeth while they awaited the completion of "the little cottage" being built close to the New Bethlehem Chapel.[69] But the inadequacy of space and the desire for autonomy dictated the need to detach the church from the plantation ambit; it was a strategy to which the Moravian benefactor, Joseph Foster Barham, "had been brought somewhat tardily".[70] On the other hand, John Light expressed himself forcibly on this matter: "I am more and more convinced, that until we have a station detached from the buildings on a sugar estate, we shall not see any very extensive benefit result to the negro population."[71] If truth be told, while attached to the estates, missionaries performed as estate chaplains "for which they received some small allowance from the proprietors". Their likely demeanour of dependency would have been transparent to the enslaved, who would in turn have been suspicious of the missionaries.[72] As it was, the missionaries were dependent on owners and attorneys for permission to proselytize on their properties.

Sympathetic planters contributed substantially to the provision of materials for the physical structures of churches, church manses and schoolhouses. In the 1820s Edward Peart at Isle, a coffee estate in Manchester, made a gift of timber for the church roof, pulpit and communion table at Fairfield,[73] the church being opened and dedicated on 15 January 1825.[74] Edward Peart, Andrew and James Miller, and Matthew Farquharson visited the Fairfield station on 3 March 1826 and "expressed their approbation at the substantial manner in which our church is built".[75] Peart had, in fact, given the missionaries "invaluable assistance by his counsel when contracting for the erection of the church".[76] Peart also provided mahogany for the Irwin church outside Montego Bay.[77] In addition, planter families made donations towards the construction of the chapel at New Carmel. These included £30 from Mr and Mrs John Salmon; £20 from Edward Francis Coke; and a similar amount from Mr and Mrs Frederick Cooper; from R.H. Senior and family £10; E. Marcy £5 6s. 8d.; and from A. Miller and C. Miller £1 6s. 8d. each.[78] The missionary home at Spring Vale was built with aid from the Farquharsons; from Mrs Spence of Hopewell, who loaned the services of a mason for several months; and from James Daly, who loaned working steers over three or four weeks gratis.[79] Both William Peart and David Robertson subscribed £50 each towards construction of a chapel at Mile Gully, with Joseph Bramwell donating several acres of land. The Honourable David Skaife, custos of the parish of St Elizabeth, granted the Moravians 469 acres between Fairfield and New Bethlehem, where Lititz was eventually established.[80] Edmund Francis Green, who owned Y.S. Estate, granted a lease of 26 acres for 999 years to the United Brethren for the purpose of forming the settlement of New Fulnec.[81] "Its elevation, and the extensive view of the lowlands of St. Elizabeth, with the Santa Cruz and May-day mountains, like large breast-works, in front, and Fairfield, though upwards of twenty miles distant, plainly discernible with a glass [telescope]" made it "a very pleasant spot".[82] William Farquharson, the proprietor of Hazel Grove in St Elizabeth, and brother to Matthew, donated both roof shingles and timber for the New Fulnec vestry along with £50 for the construction of the chapel.[83] The gift of land on which New Bethlehem or Malvern was founded in 1833 as a teachers' training school was made from a part of the property of James Miller.[84] In addition, "the walls which are 50 feet by 30 would, according to the regular prices of building, have cost several hundred pounds, but a hundred will be all we shall have to pay for them". Zorn then explained the deal with Miller as follows: "we have bought 40 acres of land for the sum of 200*l.* [pounds] currency (about 140*l.* sterling), and on giving one half of the said land to Mr. Miller, he has built the walls of the school (or church) of substantial stone-work, reckoning what it comes to above 100*l.* as his subscription".[85] The land and the school on Tryall Estate in Hanover were also planter-donated: the school opened on 17 June 1838 and had been "built at the entire expense of the worthy proprietor, Mr. Hall".[86] Already, by 1835, an "excellent friend", Benjamin Angell of Manchester, had offered land at Adam's Valley for the erection of a schoolhouse.[87] And just as Hutchison Mure Scott donated the land for the New Carmel church out of lands from his Hopeton Estate, he also donated lands from his Culloden Estate towards the New Hope station, which was "within a few yards of the sea, at Parker's Bay".[88] The gratitude felt by the missionaries towards these benefactors was such that Zorn, for example, encouraged John Kummer, his stepfather, who was the Warden at Nazareth, one of the Moravian centres in Pennsylvania, to reciprocate on his behalf the hospitality that he had enjoyed at the hands of "our excellent friend Mr. Farquharson Esqre.". Farquharson had gone to the United States "for the benefit of his health" since he had been "very unwell".[89] Zorn encouraged his stepfather: "if he should visit Nazareth, you will find him of decided piety; he is one of our warmest friends, and a liberal supporter, as far as his limited means will allow".[90]

Among the practical considerations that led planters to promote church construction was an attempt to respond to their slaves' fervent desire for Christian fellowship while ensuring that this labour force was still sufficiently refreshed to perform their tasks. As the distance between estate and church could be as much as eighteen miles, "the poor people cannot do it without much fatigue, and this necessarily creates uneasiness in the minds of their masters. But the desire to hear the word of God is so great among them, that they are willing to submit to the fatigue and trouble." So to ensure that their slaves were not too weary to perform their tasks, some planters saw it in their own interest to bring the church nearer to the flock. As Samuel Hoch confided: "I have . . . had much conversation with planters and proprietors, who are willing to lend assistance, that their negroes may not go so far from home, and by fatigue render themselves unable to work with the same activity as when they had had proper rest."[91]

In addition to the material benefits derived from members of the plantocracy, the evangelists appreciated the overt manifestations of Christian brotherhood this association involved. Not only did the planters act in the interest of the well-being of their slaves but they also fellowshipped with them, even though they probably, as in the Anglican Church, took the front church seats. Church fellowship did not infer or engineer social equality. But Brother Scholefield commented favourably about the regular attendance at New Carmel services of Mr and Mrs Cooper of the Cruse or Cruze, Mrs Coke of Paynestown, and Mrs "Hutcheson" Scott's sisters, the Misses Mary and Isabella Senior of Hopeton.[92] Another missionary was more explicit: "Our public services on the 2d, were attended not only by a great concourse of Negroes, but also by some of the white inhabitants, whom we are always glad to see joining their black Christian Brethren in worship of their common Redeemer."[93]

Hazards of the Ministry

Travel

The missionaries' difficulties started with the sea journey to Jamaica, usually from England, but sometimes from other Caribbean islands, or from the United States. Between delays, storms and pirates, the voyages were very uncertain: during the Napoleonic Wars two missionaries found it very difficult to get a place on a vessel out of Philadelphia because "they are So afraid to take English people". Perhaps the presence of Englishmen would prove compromising to the safety of the ship and crew if the vessel was intercepted or seized by French privateers operating out of Haiti. Towle and two other church brothers wanted to get to Black River in southwestern Jamaica, but three ships in Philadelphia refused them on 2 June 1796. One ship asked fifteen guineas a person exclusive of rations, another was taking no passengers for fear of privateers, and yet another was "bound to Mantegua bay" but could give them no assurance of room aboard unless they went to "Mantigua bay", but Towle knew that Montego Bay "Lyes on the other Side of the Island from Black river".[94]

Bad weather and high seas were nearly the ruin of Samuel Hoch who in March 1821 arrived in Jamaica "after a tedious voyage of sixty days. Of nearly nine weeks, five were spent in combating the most violent gales and contrary winds . . . the waves frequently breaking over the ship and pouring into the cabin."[95] Similarly, on 2 January 1843, "Br. And Sr. Feurig arrived in safety at Black River . . . after a long and dangerous voyage, their boats having been swept away, and the bulwarks of the vessel broken in".[96] Lewis Stobwasser traced a less horrendous journey from England:

> We left the Downs on the 6th of June. . . . On the 19th we passed Madeira, and on the 7th of July . . . the Island of Antigua. . . . [A] squall came on and hid the

island from our view. We were now rapidly carried towards Montserrat and Rodonda, the latter a barren rock, inhabited only by innumerable birds. For fear of the pirates we kept much to the southward, so that, excepting the islands of Nevis and St. Kitts, we did not see any land till the 14th, when the east end of Jamaica and the towering Blue Mountains, presented themselves before us.[97]

Hazards of the voyage could persist even into harbour:

> When passing between Hayti and Jamaica, the sea was rough, and we all felt very ill, but this lasted only twenty-four hours; when we found ourselves on the north side of Jamaica, passing St. Ann's Bay, Falmouth, and about two o'clock, p.m., entered Montego Bay. Here the pilot came on board, and we had passed all the vessels in the harbour except one, when a tremendous crash was heard, and the Berkeley received a fearful shock. The napper of our anchor broke just as they were lowering it, and the helm of the Berkeley was making its way through the left side of the ship Fairfield. But for the anchor, which at once stopped the ship from going further, both ships would have been dashed to pieces. The jib-boom of our ship was broken, and the spar entirely gone; and some slight damage was done to the Fairfield also.[98]

In contrast, Adam Haman endured a tedious, but not dangerous, arrival in the island. Having arrived at Greenbay in the environs of Kingston on 22 October 1832,

> after a favourable & agreeable passage of 17 Days, all to the two last days which were very stormy accompanied by rain & repeated squalls . . . to our great sorrow we were detained here a whole week on quarantine laying at anchor in the Bay there being no quarantine ground here allotted for Ships. At length on Monday the 19th we were released the flag being hoisted at Port Royal as a signal soon after which the Doctor & an Officer arived [*sic*] in a canoe to inform us of our being released. Anchor was imediately [*sic*] hoisted & sails struck & being favoured . . . with a . . . breeze we made up the Bay & entered into the narrow Bay that leads to Kingston at which place we arrived, it being already dusk. Here we were obliged to remain on board till the next day towards noon waiting for the customhouse officer to come & inspect our trunks, after this was done without any charges made attended with the kindest treatment, our good Joe the second Steward went on shore & hired a dray for us to convey our trunks to Mrs. Clarks lodging house.[99]

Having set foot on terra firma, however, one had to face the rigours of settling in. In 1848, H.R. Wullschlaegel experienced a great delay in getting his luggage from Kingston to Fairfield in Manchester.[100] Over this experience he was advised that "Jamaica is the land where one may learn 'to have patience' ".[101]

Passengers did not always land at Kingston, since the boats might proceed to other ports along the island's coasts. Black River was St Elizabeth's seaport, just as Alligator Pond was the port serving Manchester. The Hamans, having landed in Kingston in late 1832, were faced with an overland journey to Fairfield in Manchester of "no less than 100$", whereas by schooner from Kingston to Alligator Pond two passages and luggage charges cost them only $8.[102] Alligator Pond was also the destination of the Kiergaards after their eight-day journey from Barbados, via a three-day stopover in Kingston, in June 1841. Having lodged the night at "a Negro house" in Alligator Pond, "Next morning, horses were sent by Br. Prince, for our conveyance to Lititz."[103]

Ever so frequently ecstatic comments flow from the pens of the church diarists. Lewis Stobwasser elegantly recaptures the sights and sounds that struck him on his first approach to the island from the sea:

> A black pilot soon came on board to bring us in. . . . Near the shore, from the effects of the late rains, the verdure was delightful; fields, cane-pieces, cocoa plantations, and pleasant copses, with buildings of various kinds, formed a charming foreground, bounded by woody hills, and in the back-ground the lofty chain of the Blue Mountains, here and there covered with clouds. About noon we reached Port-Royal, at the entrance of the vast basin which forms the harbour of Kingston, where we arrived two hours after. . . . From [Kingston] I went to Spanish Town to deliver my passport to the Governor. The scenery throughout the whole journey delighted me. I was particularly struck with the singing of blackbirds which I had never heard in Antigua. At Spanish Town there is a handsome iron bridge over the Rio Cobra.[104]

The following year in a similarly structured passage, he exulted over the "picturesque and romantic scenery" on the mountain road between Hopeton in St Elizabeth and Montego Bay.

> For fourteen miles the carriage-road lies along a ridge, now on the right, and again on the left, presenting dangerous precipices. The beauty of the glens and gullies, and the luxuriance of growth of every species of known and unknown plants, bushes and trees constantly attracted our attention. . . . [T]he road to Montego-bay [from Bonavista] exhibits some very beautiful prospects, descending along a picturesque glen, through which a brook flows rapidly, forming several small cascades. To one, who has resided so long in Antigua, the murmuring of springs and brooks, clear as crystal, which abound in Jamaica, is a great treat. About a mile from the town of Montego-bay, a handsome stone bridge crosses the river, when the road turns to the right along its banks to Irwin.[105]

But the journeys were not always so pleasantly awe-inspiring. The poor condition of the roads, the defects and age of the horses and carriages, the inclemency of the weather, and the length of the routes all made for risk to

Figure 8.4 Stone bridge over the White River, St Mary, by James Hakewill. Courtesy The Mill Press.

life and limb. It could even prove challenging to keep one's eyes on the landscape, given the treacherous conditions of the roads.

> The road [to Windsor from Williamsfield in St. James] was frightful. . . . I could hardly keep my seat on horseback both in ascending and descending the mountains, and the poor beast frequently stopt, hesitating whether he should venture to proceed.
>
> In some places the path was so narrow on the side of the hills, that it just admitted the horse's feet, the steepnesses above and below being upwards of half a mile each. Here and there immense fragments of rock seem to hang over one's head, suspended merely by old roots of trees, which spring from every crevice in them. Indeed, very large trees seem to gather all their nourishment from one huge stone, into the cracks of which their roots are inserted.[106]

The ascent from St Elizabeth to Manchester, either the later Spur Tree Hill or a track adjacent to it, was and remains so precipitous, that we are not surprised to learn that the missionaries "had much trouble to move the goods from [Old] Carmel to [Fairfield]. The ascent from the Low-lands is uncommonly steep; and our cart could not get farther than to the foot of the mountains."[107] Rough roads caused Clemens to be thrown out of a gig on the way from New Fulnec to Lititz,[108] just as Brother Becker and his wife had suffered an accident on 17 August 1813:

> As they were going down a short hill, the wheel passed over a stone, and at the same time one of the shafts broke. A few minutes after, the other shaft broke

Figure 8.5 Treacherous paths. Pencil sketch by B. Hassick. Courtesy National Library of Jamaica.

likewise, and the whisky fell down, over their heads, and upon the horse's hind-legs. This made him quite wild, and, springing forward, he dragged them along about fifty yards. . . . [T]he remaining part of the shaft breaking off, they got disengaged from the whisky, yet not without some slight hurt, and Brother Becker's leg began to swell much. Meanwhile the horse, with part of the broken shaft and harness upon him, ran on, and arrived at Carmel, to the no small terror of their friends.[109]

On another occasion, he reported how: "My horse reared and fell with me; in rising, his fore-foot struck my head; but as fortunately the chief weight of it rested upon my hat, I escaped any serious injury. My right foot, however, upon which the animal likewise trod was bruised considerably. When I got up my foot had swelled much."[110]

When accidents did not occur, the discomforts and tedium of travel left the travellers totally exhausted. Pfeiffer chafed over the discomforts of the trip from Fairfield to Irwin Hill in Montego Bay, sentiments echoed by Herman in 1846 regarding the journey from Fairfield northwards to Bethany.[111] A ten-mile ride from Fairfield to Lititz could take four hours.[112] A few years later, in March 1847, Brother Herman and party

left Bethabara between five and six, a.m., and rode as far as Fairfield to breakfast. . . . Thence we were transported hither by Br. Pfeiffer, the twenty-seven year old horse, Hazard, an old but faithful pensioner, being pressed into extra service to drag me and Br. P. in one of their crazy chaises over the most hilly and rugged roads imaginable; the consequence of which was, that good Br. P. had to walk and lead the horse nearly half the journey, myself experimenting a little that way on steep or precipitous places of the roads. . . . The church at Nazareth, about two miles distant from the Mission-house at Maidstone, lies on the summit of the opposite ridge; a deep and rocky valley has to be crossed, and the sides of both ridges are rough and exceedingly steep. It took me and Br. Feurig nearly an hour's fatiguing walking to accomplish it; the rest went on horseback, which I could not venture again; and about half-past four, the meeting being over, we walked home again, rather tired.[113]

Perhaps in order to pack a large number of activities into their schedules, the missionaries sometimes travelled at night. Zorn reported in May 1830 leaving Mesopotamia soon after midnight and reaching Spring Vale at 11 o'clock next morning, "having accomplished thirty miles of rugged mountain road, on horseback, besides stopping at New Carmel for breakfast".[114] Night riding was perhaps a means of avoiding the blistering sun that was yet another hostile factor in maintaining links between the mission posts. Mallalieu, for instance, recalls a ride from Lacovia to Parker's Bay in February 1847 when "[r]ain having fallen the day before, the sandy road was heavy, and though we started by 6 a.m., we had two or three hours of very hot sun, and were glad to shelter ourselves with Br. Kieldson".[115]

There were no wild animals to confront, and no poisonous snakes. The most fearsome beast in their environment was the alligator, and this was confined to mangrove wetlands where the missionaries' business generally did not carry them. However, in 1816, when the only mission was near the marshy lands at Bogue Estate, a missionary did encounter one of these "most destructive animals", which was eventually killed by a slave's discharge of well aimed rifle bullets to the eyes. The alligator had attacked a pig belonging to one of the mission's workers. "He measured 9 feet in length, and 3 feet 2 inches in circumference. . . . When they get to a negroe village, they hide . . . themselves quietly in the mud, till a dog, a pig, or a fowl, comes within their reach. They then open their jaw, which is a full foot long, and furnished with a dreadful quantity of sharp teeth, and the poor creature is soon devoured."[116] But the most consistent ecological annoyances were presented by the heat and the perils of journeys over sea and land.

However, these were offset by the compensations of physical beauty in the vistas from their own manses or from the homes of their friends. John Collis admitted to being uplifted by the beauty of Jamaica: "Such . . . is the beauty of the country and so varied its features, as frequently to arrest attention, and form subjects of contemplation, even in hours of great weariness and languor."[117] There was, for instance, a breathtaking view looking to the east of Manchester.

From the dwelling-house of Mrs. Wright, at Kensworth, is a most extensive view, comprising the fertile low lands of Vere, with its cane-pieces, and sugar works; the peninsula of Port Royal, and its harbour, full of shipping, and on the Eastern horizon the majestic Blue Mountains. The latter are 8000 feet high.[118]

Spring Vale in St Elizabeth was described as "situated in a most romantic and beautiful valley".[119] Enchanted by Jamaica's inland beauty, Zorn described the scenery of north St Elizabeth:

Passing the falls on the Y.S. river, which are by no means contemptible, whether as to height, or beauty of scenery, they proceeded up a wild pass, and then descended into the remote gulley [sic] of Ipswich, surrounded by precipitous mountains, resembling huge pyramids piled beside or upon each other. The valley is narrow, winding, and perfectly level, and intersected by a small stream; it was a beautiful sight. The luxuriance and regularity of the cane-pieces, contrasted with the savage grandeur of the forest-covered hills, strike the mind very forcibly.[120]

Zorn was likewise charmed by Fairfield itself in the Mayday Hills, primarily because of its "delightful climate, that of a fine May day, as its name implies".[121] Lititz, however, was situated in the St Elizabeth savannahs below the Mayday Hills. But even this was beautiful. "The appearance of the plain itself is diversified by numerous rocky elevations, varying in extent from less than a rood to several acres. These clumps are covered with low trees and tangled shrubbery, interspersed with thorny cactuses, agaves, etc. The soil of the savanna is of a bright red colour, very firm and hard, and yet so porous that it readily absorbs the heaviest rains almost as soon as they fall."[122] Stobwasser had also commented on the colour of the bauxitic loam in the Mayday Hills, which by 1952 was to become a major economic factor in the island: "The country abounds with a very hard limestone rock, singularly perforated. The earth is in most places of a deep red colour, soiling one's stockings and clothes."[123]

In the savannah lands between the Mayday Hills and the Santa Cruz Mountains, it had been noted then, as still persists, that "[n]o part of the island is more subject to drought". However, "[a] few showers of rain very soon change the appearance of the landscape. The short brown grass which covers the plains in a few days acquires a greenish tinge, and the clumps assume a bright green colour. . . . [I]mmediately after the spring rains had commenced falling. . . [i]nnumerable little delicate flowers were open among the grass, and the tall scape of the agaves overtopping the dwarfish trees in the clumps, flauntingly hung out its hundreds of nectariferous bells."[124]

Despite its visual beauty, climatically Jamaica was a land characterized by cycles of drought followed by tempest, and it was also prone to earthquakes and hurricanes. John Lang experienced "a trementous [sic] Shock of an

Figure 8.6 The Pedro Plains, south St Elizabeth, 1995.

Earthquake" at 1:45 p.m. on 15 February 1813.[125] Slight tremors were reported during the sermon at Mesopotamia on 18 July 1830, accompanied by thunder and lightning;[126] and an earthquake was felt on 25 September 1832.[127] That same year there was a total eclipse of the sun on 27 July.[128] Earthquakes also occurred at about 8 p.m. on 12 June 1839 and at the same hour on 1 November the same year. Three years on, in the night between 6 and 7 March 1842, a "violent shock" was experienced. "The next day, we heard of the dreadful earthquake on the 8th of February, in Guadaloupe, and the neighbouring islands."[129] Twice in the same month in 1843, quakes were felt – a slight but prolonged shock between 3 and 4 a.m. of 7 March that rattled the bedroom windows and "Jealousies [window slats]" and again at about 10 p.m. on 30 March.[130]

Droughts and floods were more spectacular. In 1843 Elliott remarked that there had not been "so dry a Season for Seven years at least".[131] Again in the mid-1850s the same churchman bewailed the fact that the people of the Savannah around Lititz had been "bordering on starvation ever since Midsummer".[132] "Drought and consequent scarcity of provisions were the cause of much distress" in 1863, with the coffee crop failing, while the plundering of provision grounds and "an over-crowded jail" were among its "sad consequences".[133] Similarly, at Fairfield in 1863, yams and cocos were very scarce, with only "a very diminutive crop of sweet potatoes" being reaped by the male students at the training institution, "and of these the larger portion

Figure 8.7 Disused water tank on Huntly property, Manchester, 2004.

was stolen".[134] Thieves even "entered the mission-premises" twice in the latter part of 1866 "and stole coffee from the barbecue, fowls, and other articles, and likewise plundered the garden near the house".[135] In Manchester, the year 1864 was distinguished for its "[l]ong continued drought, followed by a heavy flood in May [that] did much damage". Further hardship was occasioned by "the fearful increase of theft in the provision-grounds . . . and the high price of materials for clothing".[136] By 1866 the drought was described as "very trying" and, as was to occur again in 1868, those who could afford it were obliged to buy water. Those who could not, foraged in the woods or travelled for miles to rivers and ponds. But the sale of water in the New Carmel district where the several ponds at the estates dried up, was a phenomenon "which had not happened in the memory of the oldest people".[137] At New Bethlehem, the early months of the year were characterized by "much privation for want of water" by the mission family, who had to send their cows "to the Bogue, a distance of twenty miles, to keep them alive".[138]

After these terrible spells of drought came excessive flooding, with its drama and tragedy. Writing from Salem, formerly New Hope, the parson there noted that "1870 will long be remembered as the wet year, more rain having fallen in any one year in the memory of the oldest people. Large springs broke out, and continued flowing from May to the end of the year, where, in former wet seasons, there were only small rills flowing for a few weeks."[139] Apart from the over-ground effect of prolonged rain on hilly land, the limestone bedrock of the greater part of the island was responsible for many underground rivers that burst out of the caves, emerging overland or heaving up the waterlogged soil. Thomas Ward recalled a visit on 2 September 1817 to one such cavern on the property of Captain Stephenson between Carmel and New Fulnec: "we visited a place, where the river runs through a subteranean [sic] cavern in a mountain, into the opening of which, one may penetrate above an hundred yards. All the sides and roof are covered with calcareous incrustations."[140]

The pattern of severe droughts followed by flooding had earlier recurred in the New Carmel region in May 1842 and October 1844. On the latter occasion, "Paynestown was flooded and the main road closed but traffic could go thro' the commons".[141] The 1842 occurrence led to death and several near-death experiences. The Paynestown pastures were so flooded that Brother Kiergaard "missed the road and got into one of the Sinkholes in which, tho' he kept on horseback he was wetted to the neck". The rain obviously kept up for several days, so that few members of the congregation could come to church on 19 and 22 May "except some strong men who cut their way through . . . the bushes on the hillsides" since the low ground had been flooded some six fathoms deep in some places. By 23 May, Edward Monteath arrived at the manse "with the sad news that Thomas Collins must be drowned in Wormwood Bottom, a place so called, on the road about 1½ miles to the East of us. A drowned horse with saddle and bridle on was seen in the water and two other horses with [indecipherable] on them feeding by the water's edge." Collins and his wife Sarah,[142] both Hopeton employees, had journeyed to a property named Mayfield to attend the Hopeton family, the Scotts, who were staying there at the time. "In going they were obliged to ride far out of their way in order to avoid the Paynestown water", and on his return he had encountered an unexpected depth. "The horse had on a Martingale which pulled him down whenever he got beyond his depth." During the next few days search parties were looking for "poor Collings" until 27 May when a female church member discovered the body.[143] These events were repeated in 1870 when

> [o]wing to heavy rains in May and October, a lake three miles long was formed in our immediate neighbourhood. It is now decreasing, but for 7 long months prevented numbers from attending church and speaking. Whenever the weather permitted, some came through the bush, or by boats; but, as several met with accidents, the most courageous were detained at times, whilst the less willing remained frequently at home. Some damage was done to the provision-grounds of many of our people. Several of the latter had also to leave their homes, and two young candidates were drowned – one leaving a widow, whose father had also a short time before met with a watery grave.[144]

Figure 8.8 Pond in Westmoreland.

In their turn, hurricanes unleashed their fury. In October 1780 a combination of earthquake, tidal wave and hurricane had assailed the island's southwest coast.

> On Monday the 2nd inst. the weather being very close, the sky on a sudden became very much overcast & an uncommon elevation of the sea immediately followed – whilst the unhappy Settlers at Savanna-la-Mar were observing this extraordinary phenomenon, the sea broke suddenly in upon the town, and on its retreat swept everything away with it, so as not to leave the smallest vestige of Man, Beast or House behind—This most dreadful catastrophe was succeeded by the most terrible hurricane that was ever felt in the Country with repeated shocks of an earthquake, which has almost totally demolished every building in the parishes of Westmoreland, Hanover, part of St. James's and some part of St. Elizabeths.[145]

James Light details the "dreadful storm" in 1818, "which most unexpectedly visited the north-west and south-west part of this island" on 10 to 12 November, "after the so-called hurricane season was over".[146] The same issue of *Periodical Accounts* gives reports on the ravages of this storm from its Carmel and Savanna-la-Mar stations. In the latter case the report spoke of the continuation of the storm blowing "with considerable fury" and rain "from Sunday to Thursday", destroying "every planta-tree [plantain] and cane. A great deal of damage was done to the buildings, shipping, and wharfs." On this occasion, in somewhat less of a repeat of 1780, the town of Savanna-la-Mar was flooded to a depth of three feet.[147] Light's graphic account of this hurricane reads:

on the 7th and 9th we had incessant heavy rain, with dismal windy weather. On the 10th, towards evening, the wind increased from the north; at eight o'clock the sky exhibited every appearance of an approaching hurricane, the momentary puffs of wind gathering strength with each successive blast. At midnight, it appeared to be at its height, and our house shook to its foundation. At one o'clock in the morning of the 11th, the roof of our stable fell in, but being providentially driven towards the wall on the east end, it was thereby kept from the horses' backs, the principal beam falling between them.

The forenoon of the 11th, was calm with showers, thunder, and lightning. In the afternoon, the upper region of clouds began again to fly with great swiftness through the air, and at four in the afternoon, the wind rose to such a height, that it was with difficulty, that the people kept on their feet, walking from house to house. The wind was at east and north-east, but turned to the southward through the night. The roofs of two out-houses . . . fell into the yard, without hurting any body. This was another distressing night and morning. As the day began to dawn, the gusts of wind from the westward were dreadful. We expected every moment to see the roof of our house fly off, being more than once lifted up from the wall-plate, the stones and mortar falling into the room.

The beautiful appearance of an excellent sugar-crop, with abundance of provision, which we had beheld with so much delight, has, by this storm, been almost destroyed. Many of the negro-houses are unroofed; the fruit and foliage of the trees nearly all gone.[148]

There were also storms in November 1826,[149] and on 19 August 1827.[150] A decade later, on 26 September 1837 "dreadful wind and rain" commenced at midnight. Elliott arose "being afraid of the house coming down". The storm continued the next day, and by 29 September when the wind and rain had abated, many trees had been blown down.[151] Another storm, accompanied by much lightning, caused a delay in the opening of the New Carmel church.[152] A similar storm had been experienced at Bogue on 25 July 1817. It was "a very tremendous storm of thunder and lightning. There was scarcely any interval between the flashes, and the whole element seemed to be on fire; but no harm was done."[153]

Illness

John Light, reviewing 1831, recorded that "[a]fter the rains began, in the month of May, fevers and dysenteries soon followed. . . . With these came that fearful and contagious disease, the small-pox, which also carried off great numbers."[154] At the start of the 1850s, it was the turn of cholera to wreak its havoc. But, as we see in the case of Elizabeth Cornish, Rebecca II's godmother, smallpox was still causing fatalities in the early 1850s.[155] By mid-1863, measles were the scourge.[156] So apart from contending with the elements, one had to face the unseen viruses that brought sickness and could be fatal.

The tropical climate bred many insect-borne diseases; wind-borne viruses proliferated in the droughts; contaminated water bred stomach ailments; and a variety of epidemics made their periodic appearance. The loss of life was great. James Light recounted the last days of John Lang who had rekindled the ministry in the early years of the nineteenth century. His passing in mid-1818 coincided with the illness and passing of other missionary brethren. Light recalls receipt at Irwin of a letter on 4 May "communicating the painful intelligence of the serious illness of Brother Gründer of Mesopotamia [Estate], and requesting, that as soon as possible, I would come to see him, there being danger of his being shortly no longer able to speak". Having set out the same day from Irwin near Montego Bay, he reached Mesopotamia, thirty-six miles distant, at one o'clock. "I found brother Gründer still alive, but . . . he departed this life early on the sixth" at fifty-three years of age, and was buried the same afternoon. While still at Mesopotamia on 9 May, Light received information that Brothers Ward and Lang were ill. Lang had for several months been unable to take any nourishment but soup. Aware now of his impending departure, he had, on 23 May, "assembled the Carmel Negroes around his bed, and took a solemn leave of them; giving his directions, and entreating them faithfully to attend to the comfort of Sister Lang and her children". His end eventually came on 4 June.[157] Thomas Ward lingered into the following year, dying on 23 February 1819, aged twenty-nine.[158]

By 1837, Zorn, reporting on the past year, informed his readers of Brother Roemer's "shattered health", and Brother Kochte's loss of his wife and the child to which she was giving birth, as well as his young son, all in a twelve-month period.[159] Yet another "labourer in the vineyard" penned a prose elegy when, writing from his station at New Eden in 1841, he bared his sorrowful heart: "my harp has been tuned to notes of mourning and lamentation . . . the Lord having been pleased to call home to Himself my dear and valuable helpmate on the 3rd July, by means of an attack of bilious fever. This severe visitation has changed my joy into deep sorrow, and my Eden has become to me a dreary wilderness. My domestic horizon is covered with thick darkness."[160] Renkewitz had had to be relocated as of October 1835 at Shirehampton in Manchester for a "change of air" on account of his "very enfeebled state of health", his wife, his three children, and himself having "all taken dangerously ill of yellow fever" at the post at Nazareth.[161] They all fortunately recovered.

As if such illnesses were not enough, women often lost their lives during labour. This was the fate of Mrs Seymour Yates, the former Isabella Senior, who had given such sterling service to the early school efforts around the New Carmel area. John Collis's wife, Mary, however, survived such an ordeal with extra special care. After the birth of a baby in 1834, she entered into such a "critical state", that Mrs Tomlinson of Huntly and her nurse took up temporary residence at the manse to administer to her needs.[162] The Tomlinsons were described as "very good friends of the Brethren, and constant attendants at Fairfield on Sundays".[163]

Political Unrest

Another life-threatening factor was posed by the constant tensions of a society built and sustained on coercion. This was exacerbated by the fact that it was the few who denied personal freedom to the many. While various mechanisms of consensus served to win the compliance of the servile, among which figured some of the doctrines of Christianity itself, the psychological and social glue that held the social fabric in peace could become dysfunctional under certain pressures. One such pressure lay in countervailing doctrines of Christianity: from the New Testament came the message regarding the brotherhood of mankind, while the Old Testament contained the saga of the liberation of the Jews from Egyptian bondage. The potential "political volcano" created by ideological and social contradictions vented itself in "violent heavings"[164] for the period of almost a year extending from 1831 to 1832. The immediate cause of the fuelling of this fire lay in the graduated steps toward a liberalization of the slave system (another contradiction) and the anxieties that these bred in people who in any case thirsted for their individual freedom. There had already been rebellions, both minor and major, in addition to which there had been a steady stream of runaway individuals[165] and the contestations between the British militia and various bands of Maroons, slaves who had abrogated their condition by taking up residence in village settlements in inaccessible fastnesses. But as the slave system began to unravel and to be ideologically challenged in Europe, the frequency of slave revolts increased.

This unrest must have stemmed from a heightening of consciousness among the enslaved regarding their economic, legal and social disadvantages, and the grave anxieties they felt over their material conditions. This disaffection was remarked on by Jacob Zorn who, in recapping the advent of the final great uprising, wrote that around the middle of 1831 "a rumour became prevalent in various parts of the island, that the slaves intended to rebel on November 1st, which was the day they were admitted to the privilege of witnessing against whites in criminal cases".[166] Any concession of civil rights to the enslaved by the metropolitan political directorate was felt by whites with local interests as an incentive for the enslaved to riot and seize more freedoms.

9

Outwardly Bound
but Inwardly Free

"BY THE GRACE OF THE LORD, although I was outwardly bound [äuserlich ein gebundener], I had now become inwardly free [innerlich frei]."[1] This is Archibald Monteath's credo of faith in his Saviour together with the avowal of an inner capacity to withstand sexual urges, the opposition of friends and partners to his new chosen way of life, and the sufferings he endured in the early days of his commitment to Christianity. The words echo the psalmist's exhortation that Edward Monteath had quoted to his Sunday school class: "If the Son shall make you free, you shall be free indeed."[2] The phrases carry resonance with the Moravian teachings to the enslaved in that the Moravian Church counselled the subjugated to serve Jesus in their slavery, and to obey their masters as part of their legal and moral commitment. As George Robbins recorded in his church diary for 1836 on "the second anniversary of the abolition of slavery in the British dominions", the preachers "made use of the opportunity to exhort all present, to shew themselves grateful for this boon by their willing obedience to those who are placed over them, and by an unreserved surrender of body, soul, and spirit to the Lord Jesus Christ".[3] In sum, the Moravians "focused on what they considered the spiritual liberation of the slaves".[4] This was the prime objective of the Christian path, whether for enslaved or free. It was a creed that allowed the sufferer to transcend the physical brutalities of worldly existence and to strengthen the spiritual dimension. But it was a path that was bound to produce tensions within the enslaved individual. Archibald's attainment of spiritual freedom did not, in the long run, quench his desire for physical release. At the same time, he was determined to use his legal disengagement from bondage to further the quest of others for spiritual liberation, and to confirm in himself that liberation of his own spirit that he had achieved when he carved out for himself an agenda separate from the routine work demands which tied him to the dictates of Dumbarton.

Freedom of the Spirit

Spiritual Foundations

Speaking as a mature man who had dedicated his life to spiritual matters, Archibald in his life story had made mention of a few aspects of Igbo spiritual life of which he was aware before his removal from his family home.

Being a child, Aniaso understood little of his society's religious ideas and habits. But he was pleased to equate the Igbo and Christian conceptions of a great divine spirit. He declared that the Igbo understood there to be a "God or Being in whose existence every heathen believes, because the works of creation declare this". The greatness of the divine presence in the concrete and temporal world is manifest in nature and the works of natural forces. This Being "was called Tschuku, or Tschuku-damma". As a northern Igbo saying asserts: *Chukwu selu aka, uwa agwu,* "Should the Great Chi take away his hand, the world would end."[5] In some texts of the Monteath story, the initial consonant of the name is given a German spelling "tsch", whereas contemporary Igbo uses the English spelling for this sound as "ch".

Aniaso understood Chukwu to be male: he specified the properties of this presence by saying: "He makes the thunder and lightning."[6] In the 1895 biography, "Chukudama" is glossed as "thunderer". Chukwu, a syncopation of *chi ukwu,* means "vast god, highest god" and is associated with the power of the sun and creation, hence its attributive, *Anyanwu,* "the sun". This entity is also referenced as *Agbala,* "knowledge". Then, as a power conceptualized by a patriarchal society, the presence was personalized as a being of male gender. Another appellation, *Chukwu Abiam(a),* was either mispronounced by Archibald as *Tschuku-damma,* or heard by his interpreters as such. But the second element is incontrovertibly recognized by Igbo speakers as *abiam(a),* an attributive meaning "person who is a visitor among you". The term is, however, another cryptic phrase. Nwoga, following the line that Chukwu was an introduction from Aro country, understands *Chukwu Abiami,* a variant of *Chukwu Abiama,* to mean "The Great Deity of the Strangers", a reference to the Aro people.[7] Interpreted more in a theological sense, however, *abiama,* "one who comes to visit", would refer to the force or presence that human knowledge or understanding can only fitfully grasp.[8]

It is of some semantic interest that Archibald glossed the creator of aerial phenomena and of creation in general as *Chukwu*. There has been contention among African scholars over the indigenous terms which were co-opted to translate European concepts of "spirit", "soul" and "Supreme Being". A major and recurrent problem in attempting to disentangle African from European semantic fields regarding spirituality is that the African discussants, together with the earliest European writers on these matters, all contest their points within the paradigms of European knowledge. Several African commentators are themselves Christian theologians who seek to correlate African belief systems with Christian hierarchies of spirit, thus fitting African polytheism within a Christian monotheistic paradigm. Where other Africans contest these positions, they too are reacting to Euro-Christian and Islamic concepts.[9] Issues debated are: Did particular African societies conceive of a divinity who embodied the greatest of all spirit-force? Did such a supreme divinity create lesser divinities, or did the latter create themselves, or did humankind create them? Did a supreme divinity control daily human experiences? If and where this was so, what then was the function of the lesser gods and other spirits? Was there an overlap between the concept of a High God and that of the earliest founder of the ethnic group, or the spirit-force of the ancestral collective?[10] Was the creative source conceived of as male or female, or both, or neither? Was it singular or twinned?[11] Was there symbolic representation of a High God? If not, what did this absence of concrete representation imply? If yes, why was it less overt, even less grand and more abstract than the representations of lesser gods?

Archibald's identification of Chukwu with the Christian God reminds us of the role which African-language speakers must have played in formulating the parallels that are so hotly contested today. Archibald first encountered Christianity in Jamaica, and even if this were not so, it is not likely that he had heard of such a correspondence before he left his compound. Nor is it likely that Igbo speakers he encountered later in Jamaica knew of the Christian God prior to their advent to the Caribbean, since Christianity penetrated Igboland from the second half of the nineteenth century.[12] But whether within or outside his native environment, the speaker of Language 1 (Igbo in this case) is very apt to co-opt a familiar terminology with which to comprehend the terminology of Language 2 (English in this case). This is so even though the semantic fields of the two languages do not mesh completely. Missionary attempts to identify in Igbo a suitable term for the Christian concept of God led them to use *Chi*, *Chukwu* and *Chineke* interchangeably. Later, *Chi* was dropped, *Chineke* became associated with the Creator aspect of the divine, and *Chukwu* eventually became the established term for the concept of omnipotence and omnipresence.[13]

Archibald's choice of the name Chukwu leads one to question the validity of the present-day assertion by some scholars that Chukwu was the name used originally by the Aro subgroup for their national god. According to that thesis, the name diffused to other subethnic Igbo groups in the course of the assiduous trading activities of the Aro.[14] Apart from the hypothesis that Aniaso was sold to or by an agent of the Aro, there is not much else that links him to them. And the details of his enslavement do not, as in the case of Equiano, suggest that there was a time lapse of months before he was shipped out of the Bight of Biafra. During such a hiatus the captive would spend months in various locations and so would likely absorb some cultural influences from them. Rather, Archibald's co-optation of the nomenclature here supports the idea that it is an autochthonous Igbo term, and also that it refers to a superior deity. Of course, that correspondence may have been made to him in Jamaica by other Igbo who had come into contact with the Aro. On the other hand, Archibald does associate Chukwu with prayer in his compound: "We only prayed to him when we were sick, so that he should make us well."[15] Of further interest is the gender ascribed to Chukwu. Was this a result of Archibald's Christian conditioning, or was it reflective of the association between civic leadership and male gender in his original patrilineal society?

Further, the associations Archibald ascribes to Chukwu are informative. Chukwu is linked to creation. Another name for this principle is *Chineke (Okike),* which some interpret as "the chi which creates", but which others understand as the syncopated form of an Igbo phrase, *chi na eke. Eke* is "creative force", but is complementary to *chi*; "*eke* is what *chi* gives to every person – that is, one's 'destiny' or 'fate' ".[16] Green, Achebe and Nwoga interpret *chi na eke* as "totality of the person (reincarnation and destiny)".[17]

The term *chi* has been a most troubling one for both lay and professional intellectuals to disentangle and comprehend. Insightfully, Manfredi points to the fact that almost every noun in Igbo carries a prefix composed either of a vowel or a syllabic nasal ("n", "m", or "ng" pronounced as a separate syllable). "Besides distinguishing nouns from verbs categorically, a prefix may provide lexical-semantic information, such as whether the noun is animate or agentive." By comparative dialectology, Manfredi identifies

> the etymological source for the cosmologically analogous, pan-Igbo item *chi* as the verb *chi(azu)* "(re)turn". The parallel is strengthened by the association of this verb with *no/lo/yo*, "arrive home" . . . in the compound verb *loghachi/yoghachi* "come back again". . . . In this way, the analytic meaning of the noun *chi* would be an agent noun "returner/reincarnator". From this point of departure, it is but a small step to the cosmological meaning of one's "reincarnating personal spirit", and thence to the related meaning "dawn" as in the return of daylight.[18]

By another analogy, adverting to the Igbo dialect, Ehugbo, he points out that the noun *uwa,* derived from the verb *wa* "arrive home", means "male personal spirit", whereas *uwa* in pan-Igbo means "world, universe". The connection between these two apparently diverse meanings is that "the subjectively experiential, visible world is the one into which one reincarnates (*wa*) from the invisible, non-experiential world of the ancestors".[19]

This interpretation reveals the link between *chi* and the sun and daylight evident in ritual and in Chukwu's symbol, Anyanwu, the sun, the source of life-giving power,[20] or as Archibald intimated, the source of the "works of creation".[21] As in other African societies, the supreme divine force is not physically externalized, because nature is already its external sign. This self-engendered force also bears no time constraint, so that no particular day is sacred to it, since all days were caused by and therefore belong to it.[22] Achebe records that in the area of Awka the *chi* shrine is established by a priest invoking the spirit from the face of the sun at the break of dawn.[23] Manfredi's interpretation also uncovers the link between *chi,* age and gender. Thus "although in theory every Igbo individual has his or her *chi,* in practice only adults, especially males who have married and females who have borne children, establish their own *chi* symbol. . . . [O]nce the *chi* shrine is established it serves as the 'protector' and altar for all minors and protégés under the particular adult owner. In this sense the *chi* of a newly wed bride remains her husband's until she gets her first child." *Chi* is also related to *ikenga,* "the cult of strength and success", and to the belief in *iyo uwa,* "reincarnation".[24]

Aniaso was too young to know the religious rituals of his native society. Furthermore, his Christian conversion influenced him to belittle the little he had observed. Speaking of Chukwu, he asserts that once a sick person regained health "then there was an end to prayer".[25] However, this is not likely to have been so. The practice is for the eldest father of the resident family very early each morning to pour libations at the shrine for the ancestors in a corner of the compound. This shrine contains carved wooden insignia representing: the face, a chalice; the tongue, a long and flat wooden representation; the feet, also representational; a saucer with a flat handle; and the *ikenga,* an anthropomorphic figure with ram's horns projecting backwards. The face symbolizes charm; the tongue, the power of persuasion; the feet, safe travel; the saucer, accumulated wealth; and the *ikenga,* the power of the right hand with which a man makes his living.[26] At this shrine, the elder calls on "the supreme God who lives in the sky" (*Chukwu/Obasi bi nigwe*), "the gods or deities of our ancestors" (*umu agbara nnayi ha*), "our ancestors" (*ndi iche*) and "god of the morning" (*ututu*), inviting them to drink the palm wine and eat the kola nut offered. He then proceeds to ask for protection and guidance during that day for himself and the family. This ritual is also performed when family members are ill, prior to family and village discussions, before embarking on journeys or ventures, during festivals and ceremonies, and also before offering kola nut in welcome to guests.[27]

Regarding the place of the ancestors in his sensibility, some of Archibald's sentiments in the conclusion of Kummer's 1853 text carry with them a ring of African reverence for the elders. His words are in fact rather paradoxical, suggesting multiple layers of religious belief, and marking him as an individual who imbibed and lived Christianity, yet retained bonds of affect and aspects of spiritual understanding from his origins. For as he prays earnestly that his "black brethren and sisters, may soon hear the precious word of God, and follow its teachings", and that they like himself would "make good use of the opportunities . . . to hear the precious gospel proclaimed in all its purity and take it to heart", he positions these laudable attitudes within the framework of action pleasing to the ancestors. By this sleight of thought he acknowledges that repentance and faith are of utmost importance to salvation on the Day of Judgement; but judgement will also be exercised by "our fathers in Africa who are still living in darkness and the shadow of death".[28] He is saying that failure to accept the Christian teachings will meet with rebuke from "our fathers in Africa" even though they themselves are ignorant of the "good news" of spiritual salvation! One of the implications is that, had they heard the Christian message, they would have recognized its veracity.[29] Like several other Africans in the West Atlantic, he no doubt also perceived his rupture from Africa as the sacrificial experience by which he was brought to knowledge of the true Light;[30] while those left in Africa remained "in darkness" and therefore in spiritual death. Another implication is that Archibald still measured his actions and achievements against the will and wishes of his family, certainly of his parents and grandparents. The latter were by the 1850s long dead, though his parents might still have been alive and nearing their end. Their earthly existence was being played out thousands of miles across the seas. Meanwhile, Archibald's statement carried covert African spiritual application, in that, both as an African and as a Christian, he conceived of his ancestors as occupying the "nearer presence of God".[31] His assertion also allows us an indirect clue to some of the well-springs of his motivations to action, intimating, as they do, some of the guidelines for his secular status and mission in life.

Christian Vocation

A turning point in Archibald's life came in 1824 when he accepted the invitation of an enslaved woman from the adjacent Paynestown Estate to attend Christian services at the home of her owner, Edward Francis Coke or Cooke. Coke had been born on 10 January 1795 and had married Juliana Harriott on 9 August 1814.[32] Both husband and wife were active evangelicals; as Archibald asserted: "Mr. Cook was a revivalist, and his wife shared his beliefs."[33] In other words, like the Foster brothers who had invited the Moravians to send missionaries to convert their slaves in Jamaica, the Cokes were part of the evangelical movements connected with the rise of Methodism that swept England in the late eighteenth century and again in the 1820s.[34] In fact, Mrs Coke's father appears to have been a clergyman, Reverend William Harriott of Clifton near Bristol, who had inherited Jamaican property from his father, William Harriott.[35] A William Harriott is listed in 1817 as owning Mexico and Santa-Cruz Park, the first with 192 slaves and 87 stock, the latter with 144 slaves and 194 livestock.[36] By 1832, Harriott retained only Mexico, with as many as 343 slaves and 197 livestock.[37] Ironically, one of these William Harriotts owned Nancy, the main concubine of John Monteath, Archibald's first owner, and Archibald was to become the slave of Nancy herself as of 1814.

Figure 9.1
Memorial tablet to Edward Francis Coke and his wife, Juliana, Black River Anglican church.

Archibald's learning about the religious services took place soon after the Cokes' return from abroad, and it would seem that they were fairly often away, seeing that the 1817, 1820 and 1823 Returns of Slaves for Paynestown were submitted by their attorney – in 1817 by John Salmon, in 1820 and 1823 by Charles Farquharson. No doubt Juliana Harriott's close ties with England may have accounted for their frequent stays overseas. But it was at the Cokes' residence at Paynestown that Archibald was first "awakened" to the spiritual life. The moment of epiphany and conversion came on the day he entered the "doorway of the big grand house" at Paynestown, and was welcomed inside by a black servant and Mrs Coke.

> Very shyly I came into the house and waited outside the hall until a little bell announced the beginning of the prayers. . . . Mr. Cook held the prayers. People sang, then he read a little from the Bible, and finally he prayed. . . . I understood little or nothing of it because I still knew nothing of the Saviour. Nevertheless, I will never, never forget this hour. It was one of the deciding hours of my whole life. I felt the presence of the almighty God, my Lord. I was deeply terrified; my limbs trembled. Unable to say a single word, I rushed away afterwards and stayed very quietly at home.[38]

The morning prayer that he had attended formed one of the events in the "customary movements of the Jamaica proprietor", the practising Christian proprietor, we may well assume. As described by one of them: "It is seldom that most of the family do not mount their horses very soon after daylight, and take that recreative exercise till between seven and eight. Sometime, during the subsequent hour, the family and guests assemble to morning prayer; after which comes the breakfast, at about nine."[39]

The slave woman who had invited Archibald to the prayer session was Casteen, though the biographical texts record her name as Christina.[40] Like other names in the biographical texts, there are slight phonological discrepancies between the names as they might conventionally be pronounced and their articulation by an African-born speaker and again as filtered through the comprehension of a non-English hearer like Hermine Geissler and an American English hearer like Joseph Kummer; furthermore, these intermediaries did not know the third parties personally and therefore arrived at their own personal interpretations of their names. In any case, Casteen was an unusual name and therefore not easily recognizable to the amanuenses; but its spelling is consistent in the Returns of Slaves for Paynestown. In 1817, she is listed as a Creole of thirty-five years.[41] And in 1826, she is again listed as a Creole, her age being given as forty-three at the time of her death on 4 September 1825, which is recorded in the remarks column.[42] Archibald might have been about thirty-two at the time that he met her one evening fetching water at a well and as he was returning to Dumbarton from Lenox. Perhaps he had gone there to do some hired labour or was on some mission for his owners. She indicated that her mistress wished to have people from other plantations attend the religious services Mr Coke held every morning for the slaves. Archibald received this information "as though something had pierced [his] heart". He therefore took up the offer, and thereafter Casteen held a special place in his regard. "I always since that time had a particular affection for her, and visited her every Sunday." But one Sunday he found her very sick. He then spiritually ministered to her; indeed, she was on her deathbed.

> I asked; "Christina, do you pray? and what do you pray?" She answered, I pray, *if* I have done sin, Jesus forgive me." I told her, You must not say, *if* I have sinned. You *have* sinned, we all sin and are the cause of the death of Jesus, and so also *you*; say rather, Lord Jesus have mercy upon me and forgive my sins." I moved nearer to her bed, and said, "say this after me Christina." She said it; "Lord Jesus etc. etc.["] "Oh, say it again"—she did so, but had hardly finished the last word, when she sank back, and expired! Her soul was gone—[43]

For Moravians, "eternal life was a possibility for all those who would recognize the depths of their own corruption and their absolute dependence on the Heiland [Saviour]".[44]

Some time after Archibald joined the Christian fraternity, the evening singing and prayers at Paynestown became yoked to the embryonic Moravian mission encouraged by Paynestown's neighbour, Hutchison Mure Scott who owned Hopeton Pen and Lenox or Lennox Sugar Works, two contiguous properties. In addition, Archibald accepted the invitation from Mrs Mary Cooper, sister of Edward Coke[45] and wife of Frederick Cooper who owned The Cruse or Cruze, to attend literacy classes at Paynestown. This was an aspect of the outreach activities of the religious group. As part of this fledgling community, Archibald met Brother Ellis who held services every eight weeks until the New Carmel Moravian church was established in 1827 on land donated by Hutchison Mure Scott. Archibald's regular attendance at these Christian services was followed by his reception into the Moravian fold on 18 November 1827; he then made his first communion on 6 September 1829.[46] Soon afterwards, he was nominated a helper for the New Carmel church. Native assistants or helpers were "an important body of native laborers. They are appointed by the Mission Conference", that is, "all the Missionaries belonging to a Province, who meet in order to discuss the progress and necessities of the Mission". Helpers normally received no monetary compensation, but when Archibald became a free man and took up full-time work as a missionary himself, he was paid as the only full-time helper in his period, thus becoming a national assistant. The duties of helpers were:

> to visit the converts from house to house and make themselves acquainted with their spiritual progress; to call upon the sick and report them to the Missionaries; to labor among such heathens as they meet with and bring them to the notice of the Missionaries; to exhort those converts who neglect the means of grace and report such cases to the Missionaries; to settle differences and disagreements among their people, and in case they do not succeed in doing this, to call in the aid of the Missionaries; to urge on the attention of parents the duty of sending their children to school; and to go after those who are under church-discipline and entreat them to forsake their sins and return to Jesus. . . . The Female Assistants labor among their own sex.[47]

Needless to say, all this religious activity was a new trajectory in Archibald's life and brought strains between himself and the unidentified woman with whom he lived at the time, between him and his fellow workers who mocked him for associating with whites outside the necessities of work, and between himself and his master, the young mestize James Monteath, who had been born in 1798 and who was therefore about six years Archibald's junior. Archibald had doubtless acted in the role of elder brother to James as the latter moved from infancy into childhood, but James would eventually have come to identify himself as Archibald's "young master". The distorted social and psychological relationship between the two was a classic example of how "the degradation of the slave nurtured the master's sense of honor, both in his childhood training by slave nannies and, throughout his life, as a ready object for the exercise of his sense of power".[48] James had apparently been sent abroad, to Scotland, since his father's will in 1809 stated as much. We have no idea how long he stayed there, what he did, apart, no doubt, from meeting members of his father's family. We can imagine that on his return he relished the overlordship that he considered his inheritance. Although born a slave, the social advantages he acquired by virtue of his colour, his lineage and class are likely to have made him arrogant, if even he tried not to be. We have no idea whether he knew that he had been born a slave, as the son of a slave woman, but his release from this status as a small child of four years of age came too early for the mentality of the enslaved to have shaped his personality to any great extent; indeed the fact of his early origins may have been secreted from him, itself part of the pathology of the social fabric, and any such allegation in his adult life may have served as a severe embarrassment brought on by the unclosetting of an unsavoury secret. In any case, the psychosocial environment would have shaped tensions and hostility between the two adults, master and slave, these being well captured in Archibald's complaint:

> The whole time since I had become acquainted with Jesus my Saviour, and was in my first love to him, Mr Monteeth my master, was very hard towards me. If I was sick, or if every thing on the plantation did not go according to his wish, he said, "This comes from your walking to Paynestown to prayer!" he could not bear to think that I should become pious.[49]

How did James Monteath show harshness toward Archibald? Was Archy on the receiving end of abusive language, wrongful accusations, or floggings? Was he boxed in his face or on his ears? Was he humiliated in front of others? Even as a driver, an agent of the master's will, he was still an underling, and if crossed, the master would let the slave know who called the shots. The incident reported by John Lang on 17 March 1816 was not a singular case: it concerned the head driver at Phantilands or Phantillands or Fantillands Estate who had been put into the stocks for attending religious services. This naturally made the driver's subordinates fearful of going to church themselves.[50] For other reasons, the conduct of James Monteath did eventually cause his slaves fear, but it was the terror of being kidnapped when on the roads. Archibald was able to detect that "as his riches seemed to dwindle down more and more, and grow less and less . . . he had many debts". One of the results of this was that "we were no more allowed to go out of the place in the evenings, as it would have been easy for the creditors to catch us up, and sell us".[51] This would have effected the break-up of the community that had been fostered at Kep and Rosehall or Dumbarton.

As an aspect of his conflicted emotions regarding James, Archibald confesses his regret at losing the affections of his master.[52] Clearly, a love–hate relationship existed between Archibald and James Monteath, his boss. On one hand, Archibald had reason to think that "my master, to whom I had clung from my youth on, really did not like me".[53] Yet James admitted during his conflict with Archibald over the latter's manumission that he and his family "have loved you from the time you were small",[54] suggesting a special relationship that seems acted upon when, during Archy's arthritic crisis of 1827 or thereabouts, Archibald reported that "My master had me cared for well and called white doctors himself for their advice".[55] After the patient had regained the use of his arms and legs, James arranged for him to stay at the seaside "where I had to bathe twice a day in order to regain my earlier strength".[56] Archibald's emotional loyalty to his master meant that "in an emergency", that is, an uprising, he was prepared to protect him and his family,[57] but this loyalty did not preclude his desire to be free of his "legal" obligations towards them.

By 8 January 1826, after having gone through several sexual relationships, and having severed an existing partnership with someone who chose not to follow the Christian or Moravian path, Archibald married Rebecca Hart, owned by Mary Scott of Hartshall.[58] Rebecca had formerly been named Anne and was listed as a Creole belonging to Hartshall.[59] It was most likely she who, on 18 June 1821, just a week prior to Archibald's baptism at the Black River Anglican church, was the Creole Hartshall slave called Anne, christened Rebecca Hart by Reverend Stewart; but the issue is confused by the baptism of a Rebecca Hart of Hartshall, aged twenty-four, recorded as taking place at Black River Anglican church on 20 September 1817, the same day as that of William Smith and Frederick Daly.[60] Although we cannot be adamant about it, the 1821 date of initial christening appears more plausible, suggesting as it does, some element of collaboration among the similar age cohorts. Archibald mentions that she was a devout member of the Paynestown fellowship, an environment in which he was able to observe and admire her piety. She was eventually received into the Moravian Church on 8 February 1829, and into their communicant assembly on 13 June 1830.[61] However, it has not proved possible to find Anne listed among the workers at Hartshall or the contiguous and larger property of Hampstead[62] (which had previously been owned by James Hart), or in the possession of either Hart's concubine Mary Scott or one of her four mulatto daughters: Rebecca, Sarah, Elizabeth, and Ann. Yet Mary Scott was her owner who gave permission for the marriage, which took place in the Anglican church at Black River,[63] because the Moravians had yet to officially establish a church district in the neighbourhood of Kep and Hampstead. Archibald relates that this cross-plantation marriage was initially resisted by his owners. He used the plural in this instance, and seems to have made reference to Nancy Monteath, apart from James Monteath, unless we surmise that James had a wife or concubine, which was quite likely as well. But since we know that Archibald was officially owned by Nancy, we might assume that she was the one most likely to have taken objection to his proposal. Archibald recorded that he made known his choice of marriage partner "to my mistress Mrs. Monteeth, but she dissuaded me from marrying any one except a person from the same Estate as myself". Such an objection was a way of preventing the slave from spending time away from the home property, and most likely as well, it was a way of securing an increase of hands on the home estate that would be forfeited if the female slave belonged to another property, the female and her issue being her owner's belongings. It was only when the Monteaths heard the banns of two of his friends, Elizabeth Ricketts and Thomas Dickenson, being read out in the Black River Anglican church that "God changed their minds, and they allowed me to be married".[64] Again we may wonder, how many times did he broach with his owners the matter of his intention to marry? And what was his reaction, his mood, when they refused him? What did they think of his proposal? That he was uppity, that "he fly past his nest"[65] in aspiring to a type of relationship that few persons in plantation society indulged, even whites? That this intent to keep blacks psychologically in their place was part of the overall opposition to Archibald's marriage is supported by the report of attitudes displayed at the church on the occasion of the wedding:

> Since it was an especially popular market day, the church was more full than usual. As the wedding ceremony for us and a few other black couples who followed our example went on, the white spectators broke out in laughter. In loud voices they made fun of us, that now black people were so pretentious as to consider themselves equal to whites. The agitation was so great by the end that the pastor could barely restore the peace of the holy place, even with the most serious words. His rebuke did work, however, and the wedding ceremony could be carried out.[66]

We can well imagine though that the Monteaths' objections must have made Archibald sullen, and they must have sensed the obstinacy of his resolve – a situation that we had already seen in his behaviour toward the ship's captain decades before.

It was another ten years before Rebecca had a child, named Rebecca after her mother, and born in 1836, being baptized by John Collis on 23 October 1836 when she was six weeks old, with godparents John Collis himself, Mary Ann Collis, the minister's wife, and Elizabeth Cornish.[67] In other words, little Rebecca had been born while slavery was still in force, during the period officially known as apprenticeship. She was therefore born free. But both her parents were still de facto enslaved and living on separate estates, obviously in a visiting relationship rather than in a co-residential unit as they were likely to have enjoyed after slavery was completely abolished on 1 August 1838.

Young Rebecca was received into the Moravian Church on 9 December 1855 by Brother E.E. Reinke, and took first communion in November 1857.[68] Three years later, on 19 December 1860, she married George William Holness, a widower and shoemaker, residing at New Savannah, a neighbouring community to Frazer where Rebecca lived. She was literate, as both herself and her husband signed their wedding certificate.[69] We know nothing about Archibald's reaction to her marriage, whether he and his wife were supportive of it. But we know that Rebecca gave birth to Archibald Monteith Holness, born 10 August 1861 and baptized on 15 December 1861. His godparents were Robert Morris and Susan Myreh. Anna Elizabeth Holness was born on 12 June 1863 and baptized on 23 August 1863, with godparents John and Rachel Holness and Mary Jane Holness. This child eventually died some months short of ten years old, passing away on 22 April 1873.[70] Furthermore, we are shocked to learn that her mother, Rebecca, died in December 1863, the very year of Anna's birth. Her cause of death and its effect on her husband, her children and her parents, we are never told. For his part, George William, probably unable to cope with five motherless children, remarried almost exactly one year after Rebecca's death. He married Mary Elizabeth Kelly, a spinster of Brunti, on 15 December 1864.[71] But he already had three children by his first wife, Hannah Cooper, a free woman, whom he had married in 1830, on the same day that he married Rebecca, 19 December.[72]

But Archibald had another daughter, born earlier than Rebecca, and unfortunately not named in the biographies or by the missionaries. In fact, it is only in the Kummer version and "Experiences" that we are allowed to hear him acknowledge "another daughter born in the time of ignorance, and who is married to a teacher of one of our schools".[73] Our conjectures on the identity of this daughter are speculative, but we will present what hard evidence we have dredged up on the matter. There was a Robert White, the teacher in charge of the Benashurts School in Kilmarnock in 1861. A Robert and Sarah White were stationed at Hampstead in 1843 when they had Robert, born on 26 March. But by 1847 they were at Kilmarnock when their second child, Rachell, was baptized. She had been born on 12 February that year.[74] For Sarah to have delivered her son, Robert, in 1843, she would very likely have been born in the 1820s perhaps, before 1824 when Archibald had his first conversion experience and before 1825–26 when he came to think his sexual mores abhorrent.

Nevertheless, and here there is more compelling evidence, there was a Robert White married to an Elizabeth Woodstock in the 1850s, the couple being resident at Rosehall.[75] Perusal of the Rosehall slave list for 1826 indicates that Elizabeth had been born in 1824 to Charlotte, a sambo daughter of the Igbo Juliet. Charlotte's baptismal name was Henrietta Monteath; she had married George Woodstock in 1826, but had given birth to Elizabeth in 1824, which is consistent with Archibald's pre-Christian phase. It would further seem significant that Robert and Elizabeth White had a child, Emma Frances Felicia White, born on 19 March 1853 and baptized the 10 July following. The child's godparents were none other than "Archie Monteeth", together with Margaret Lind, a missionary, and Margaret Senior, no doubt of the Hopeton family.[76] This was a composition of sponsors similar to that assembled by Archibald for his daughter Rebecca in 1836. A second child, Jabez Emmanuel or Immanuel was born on 7 January 1857 at Rosehall, baptized on 22 March that year, with witnesses Archibald and James Monteath, together with Elizabeth Dickenson.[77] A circle of best friends. By 26 March 1861 when Samuel James was born, the Whites were resident at Beeston Spring. At the baptism on 19 May 1861, the child's sponsors were Robert's fellow teacher, Archibald Clarke, together with Elisha McGrowder and Chaunce or Channer Edmondson.[78] William Richard arrived on 9 May 1863 and was baptized on 5 July; the family was now residing at Chantilly, another of the Moravian school sites.[79] The last child, born on 19 November 1865, was John Archibald, evidently named for the grandfather who had died in 1864. The family was still at Chantilly when the baptism by Augustus Geissler took place on 11 February 1866.[80]

Was it then that there were two Robert Whites in the Carmel vicinity, and that one was married to Sarah, another to Elizabeth? Or had Sarah died and Elizabeth become Robert's second wife? Unfortunately, searches for the marriage record(s) of Robert White have so far proved futile. However, we know that Robert had been received into the Moravian Church in October 1853 and confirmed in March the following year, having, according to a note in the remarks column of his baptismal entry, been recommended to the Carmel congregation from the New Hope congregation. This notation was written in April 1861 when Robert was resident at Beeston Spring. Elizabeth, for her part, had been received on 24 November 1844, and had made her first communion on 9 April 1854. Her residence was given as Rosehall. Given the appropriateness of the dates, then, and the correspondences shown by her children's names, it would appear that Elizabeth may have been the daughter whom the Quakers Harvey and Brewin met at Carmel a year or so after the funeral of Archibald Monteath in 1864. For Rebecca, his daughter within wedlock, had passed away the previous December.

Soon after Archibald had been received into the Moravian Church in late 1827, he was struck down with a severe attack of rheumatism.

> Rheumatism had so seized upon me, that I was quite contracted and crippled, so that I could neither move, nor use either hands or feet, and had to be fed like a little child. No one thought it possible that I could recover. All counsel, advise [*sic*], and means of various kinds seemed useless, though I had the best nursing and attention from my Master and Mistress and Mrs Cooper.

He must have been highly valued to have received such personal care. And we may note that his caregivers and facilitators were both estate- and church-related. But he was eventually cured, he was convinced, by "a tea prepared from a bush that grows here" that made his mouth sore. "I felt very bad, but when the mouth got better, I also felt better otherwise and was able to walk, and again received the use of my limbs." The infusion had been given to him by "a coloured man". Unfortunately for us, the precise identities of both the healer and the cure are not given. This recovery was further helped by the subsequent treatment of sea baths. In this, his owners were again cooperative and caring. "For the perfect strengthening of my body and limbs, Mr Monteeth advised me to go and bathe daily in the sea; to this the Lord added his blessing, and I became well and strong."[81] It is quite possible that this course of sea baths might have been facilitated by his convalescence at Nancy's seaside home at Whitehouse, if a building had been put on the property, or by his stay with her relatives at the seaport, Savanna-la-Mar, further west.

This bout of illness probably occurred during 1828–29, because he says that "[a]s soon as I got better I was confirmed at Carmel, and appointed and accepted as a Native Assistant or Helper". That confirmation was no doubt his reception of Holy Communion, which took place in September 1829. This illness was to recur and there might have been other ailments as well. On 12 June 1839, John Elliott spoke of visiting Archy who was ill. Some years later, on 10 October 1846, when Archibald was very likely already in his late fifties, Brother Reinke "visited Br. A. Monteith who ha[d] been laid down suddenly and [was] very sick".[82] Even when he signed the marriage register for James Monteeth and Cecilia Thompson on 2 August 1851, his shaky script suggests that his arthritic problems were posing an impediment, since other samples of his writing show a steadier hand. A year later, on 8 July 1852 John Buchner reported paying "a visit to our well-known Helper-brother Archy Monteith. He has been latterly complaining much, and has not been able to visit as frequently in our congregations as he did before." Furthermore, his

Figure 9.2 Gravestone for Archibald Monteith, Carmel Moravian churchyard, 1995.

"wife and daughter are both in a very poor state of health, and he has much domestic affliction".[83] His daughter was already a teenager. But Archibald viewed his illnesses as the Saviour's visitations upon him for the purpose of testing and ultimately renewing his faith. Of his first attack, he said that "the faithful Saviour deemed it good, in this time of spiritual refreshing, to visit me with severe trial and affliction. He laid me upon a sick bed, on which I suffered and lingered for 10 months."[84] And in 1846 "he expressed himself clearly and surely as to his entire trust on the Lord Jesus and his hope of being with Him".[85] Given the centrality of Christ's Passion in Moravian liturgy, "[d]eath became all-important both because it replayed the experience of the Heiland in death and because it represented the ultimate union with the Heiland".[86] He must have thought that his end was now near. Given the high mortality rates of the time and the relatively short life expectancy of most, Archibald's body and spirit seem able to have withstood many a shock. We need also to remember that he outlived epidemics of the time. In the New Carmel listing of deaths during 1852, most had died of the smallpox. One of those who passed away in this epidemic was the widow Elizabeth Cornish of Bigwoods, godmother of Archibald's daughter, Rebecca.[87] Furthermore, during the early years of the 1850s, cholera swept the lands of the Caribbean. On a trip from New Hope in the southwest to Montego Bay in the northwest, Buchner recalled, "[t]his part of the island has been heavily visited by the cholera, and nearly every person whom we met wore a black coat, or a black ribbon round the hat, as a sign of mourning".[88] And in the early 1860s "[m]uch sickness prevailed. . . . [I]n addition to common fevers and whooping cough, several cases of typhoid fever occurred."[89] In the middle of 1863 there was an outbreak of measles.[90]

For Archibald, however, the end began around November 1863 when he "was seized with a rheumatic affection, which soon increased to such an extent that his right leg was rendered useless, and he was racked with severe pains". Nevertheless, in early December he was still able to conduct a service in the absence of Brother Lichtenthaeler, minister at New Carmel, "though he spoke as though convinced that it would be the last time he would have an opportunity of addressing the congregation. This proved to be the case, for he was never again able to leave his house."[91] Lichtenthaeler idealized Archibald's health record by claiming that "the dear sufferer . . . had not been ill for a period of twenty-six years", and the editor of the 1864 *Missions-Blatt* referred to his "otherwise iron-clad good health",[92] but the minutiae in the missionaries' diaries tell a somewhat different story.

Old age, toil, the cumulative physical deterioration brought on by illnesses and personal griefs eventually took their toll, and Archibald John Monteath, formerly Aniaso of Igboland, passed away on 3 July 1864, aged about seventy-two.[93] His departure "claim[ed] special remembrance", acknowledged Lichtenthaeler in his annual report for 1864. Describing Archibald as "our long-tried and faithful helper-brother", he recorded for posterity the church's "testimony to his faithfulness and worth".[94] For his wide-ranging services to the church, the 1854 "Retrospect" singled him out among the survivors of the 1820s membership. He was lauded as "the most eminent for his truly Christian character, spiritual experience, and varied usefulness" and hailed as "the well-known Br Archy Monteith, of New-Carmel congregation, who for many years past has been a true apostle among his countrymen".[95]

Archibald was buried at the Carmel church the day following his death. The loss of husband, daughter, and God knows what other hardships and illnesses took their toll on the shadowy Rebecca Monteith senior, whose passing took place less than a year after Archibald's, on 13 February 1865, at an age given as sixty-five.[96]

Archibald's Pastoral Work

References to Archibald 's Christian evangelism recur from time to time in the missionaries' diaries and reports of the period. As early as 1837, the year he gained freedom and began full-time ministry, Brother Elliott rode out to Hampstead Estate "accompanied by Archey Montieth who served as interpreter at the baptism of three old Africans", most likely Igbo, who understood very little English. The account continued:

> They seemed however to understand (what all Christians do not appear to know) that it was their duty to be useful to one another. The cottage in which the baptism was to be held was a few paces from where the old creatures resided so the one that had most strength took up the one that had least on his back, but being blind he could scarcely have found the way had not the third led him. In this manner they entered.[97]

In August 1843, there was an early morning prayer meeting conducted by John Buchner and at which both Brother Elliott and Brother A. Monteath prayed.[98] On Good Friday of 1846, Brother Reinke kept an instruction meeting at which "Br Monteith spoke and prayed".[99] In 1846 too, Brother Reinke recorded that he had "held the usual services in the Chapel", while "Br. A. Monteith kept Meeting in the Schoolroom".[100] On Emancipation anniversary, 1 August 1846, George Robbins recorded that Archibald and R. Smith spoke "with good effect" at the second public service; but about the 1855 anniversary Edwin Reinke was ecstatic: the "excellent addresses from our worthy helpers, T. Jones and Archy Monteith" were worthy of "a very interesting and truthful report". Monteith, he said, "was in his happiest mood, and I do not recollect having heard him speak better and more effectively".[101] Earlier, in 1845, Archy, having accompanied Brother Holland on out-station visits, had reported to Holland that "a number of brn. and srs. [brethren and sisters] felt themselves incited" by what they had heard the previous Sunday regarding the church's missionary outreach in icy Greenland, and were willing to commit themselves to contributing 1½ pence monthly toward the Moravian Missions.[102]

In a repetition of the excursion of 1837 with Brother Elliott, and no doubt several times repeated, Brother Heath rode up to Hampstead on 7 April 1846 "accompanied by Archy Monteith. The poor infirm and blind ones were assembled in a Negro house where we held a meeting and the holy Comn. [communion] which appeared to refresh their understanding." On this occasion, they also visited an old woman in her hut as she was leprous and therefore quarantined. "In the house on the ground a bundle of rags seemed lying and from it a weak crying voice was heard. This was the poor old leper Sr. quite covered up and crying about her pain and sickness." On hearing them, "she sat up and listened to [Heath's] remarks expressing her hope in the Lord and her daily dependence on him. A small gratuity on leaving spread pleasure over her countenance on which the recently shed tears still trembled."[103]

Figure 9.3 Petersville plantation house, 2004.

In 1847 Archibald was still engaged in visiting "various Estates and Settlements every week".[104] In Archy's own words: "I often visited the places now belonging to the New Hope district; and here the people were particularly hungry to hear of Jesus Christ."[105] He "also often went to Woodlands, to invite the people there to come to church; kept meetings and read the Bible, which they liked very much. . . . In Hampstead also, the home of my wife, I often held meetings." Before that, while encouraging a man on Petersvale or Petersville Estate to enter the married state, rather, no doubt, than remain in concubinage, "a third person was listening, and he was persuaded to come to Carmel the next Sunday, where the proclamation of the gospel he heard, made such an impression on him, that he and his wife immediately had their names entered as Candidates, & asked me to come to Petersvale to keep meetings".[106] Many new congregation members for New Carmel were recruited in this way.

Brother William Mallalieu's report on his visit to New Carmel from Irwin Hill in the north on 15 February 1847 obliquely intimates that Archibald's fame had preceded him. Mallalieu wrote: "There we saw Arch. Monteith, a fine coal-black man, full of life and zeal. He offered up a very fervent prayer at the close of the meeting."[107] Some years earlier, John Buchner who was then stationed at Irwin Hill wrote commendably of his renewed contact with Archibald in 1842: "One Helper, Brother Archibald Monteith, spent a whole week with us, and I was again much pleased with his sound faith, solid judgment, and child-like simplicity, strangely combined with shrewdness and ready wit."[108] During this week, the missionaries had gathered to consider the challenges posed to them by the "rise and spread of Myalism" – the resurgence of African-Christian religious fervour that their church was hard put to bring under their control. Myal posed such a challenge to the authority of the European hierarchy of church personnel and to the European manner of restraint in worship that a meeting of Mission Conference held in 1860 endorsed an observation that had been made at an earlier conference in 1831 regarding the choice of church helpers:

> With regard to the Helpers we feel it increasingly needful to select in future for the office only such as are able to read, and otherwise give proofs of an intelligent piety and true devotedness to the cause. Doubtless a few of our Helpers are as good and useful as can be met with anywhere, but their number is small. More than one instance has recently been brought to our notice of Helpers, whose want of capability to read the Scriptures disabled them from meeting and refuting the arguments of fanatics by correct scriptural references, so that they were obliged to give up the debated point.[109]

But Archibald seems never to have been at a loss for words. A memorable *bon mot* of his was recalled by John Elliott when Archibald first saw a blind church-sister reading:

> Archey Monteath, when he first saw Cecilia reading, stood for a few moments in astonishment, and then exclaimed, "Massa, the English people should love the Lord more than all others, for He gives them wonderful wisdom." And then, before I had time to say any thing, he added, "As sure as the Queen of the South[110] shall stand up in the judgment, to condemn those who will not take the trouble of coming to Jesus, so sure will this poor blind thing stand up in the judgment, to condemn those who will not take the trouble to learn to read the Bible, though they have two eyes to see?"[111]

Another instance, though unattributed to him, has the ring of an Archibald analogy, especially since a narrative subsequently attributed to the same speaker is corroborated by comments in the biography itself. For instance, Archibald had recounted in his story:

> When I was once busily occupied on a Sunday digging holes to plant my yams, the thought suddenly came into my mind! "How is this; a commandment of God says; Remember the Sabbath day to keep it holy etc. etc. and how do you keep that commandment, missing the morning prayer, and doing work you might do on Saturday?" While I was thinking over this, and reflecting, I felt the presence of God so powerfully, that I threw down my hoe, and seemed to be necessitated and could not do otherwise then fall down on my knees in the hole I had dug, and earnestly prayed my Saviour, to let me find his way and will, and begged him to counsel and help me! He heard me. I arose with a feeling and strong conviction that my laboring on Sunday was displeasing to him, for the Sabbath was given to be kept

holy, and he gave me the firm assurance, that if I would follow him, he would supply my needs, and provide for me that I should never want. And this the faithful Saviour has done until this day. I never again from that day to this touched my hoe on Sunday, but rose up very early on Saturdays and labored diligently, and this the Lord has blessed much more than when I labored on Sunday.

He goes on to exult:

Oh, its wonderful how I have been prospered! In every thing that concerns temporal things too. Why only think! I now own 15 acres of good land right around my house, that is more than any other negro in this whole neighbourhood, and all good land, and brings forth wonderfully! I have been richly rewarded![112]

The corollary to this tale is contained in John Collis's entry in the "Diary of New-Carmel, for the Year 1836" in respect of late July. Here he recapitulated that

This brother was converted about 12 years ago, and since that period, has never been known to labour upon a Sunday. He relates, that, while cultivating his grounds one Lord's day, and meditating upon what he had heard the preceding week, his heart began to feel warmer and warmer; that, after some time, the thought entered into his mind, "What, am I working to-day? Has not Jesus said, if any one will do His will, and trust in Him, he *shall never want?*" And that he then felt so assured of the presence of God, and of his future help, that he threw aside his hoe, knelt down upon the very spot, and, after earnest prayer, vowed to the Lord that he would never work again upon the Sabbath.

Collis comments on this subject: "His faith has not been put to shame; and though derided at the time, so abundantly has his ground yielded its increase during this long period, that he has not only had sufficient provision for the maintenance of his family, but frequently large supplies for sale in the public market." Thanks to this synchrony of narrative content between Archibald's life story and Collis's remarks, we know that Archy traded agricultural goods in the market, though we are unsure exactly what these goods were. That there were yams, the Igbo staple, among them, we can be sure.

From his material blessings, Archibald contributed towards the furtherance of the church's work. For instance, by early September 1850, the Rose Hall or Pitts' School had had to move to Archy's house, as the old cottage where it had previously convened had become "far too small" and "tottering". The minister therefore called together the parents of the schoolchildren for the purpose of organizing them to rebuild a proper schoolhouse. "Every one subscribed a dollar or two, besides promising their labour. Br. A. Monteith gave half an acre of land, which we at once measured off."[113] We have no indication whatever that Archibald himself taught school,

Figure 9.4 Market at Falmouth. Lithograph from daguerrotype by Adolphe Duperly, *c. 1845*. Courtesy National Library of Jamaica.

but he did teach at Sunday schools. In this connection he was specifically named: In the 1850s it was reported that the congregation at New Carmel was so numerous, "and the attendance in the house of God, which [would] seat 700 [was] so great, that above 200 children [had to] be kept . . . in the school-house, by one of the teachers, or by the helper Br Archy Monteith".[114] He also took charge of church meetings of various kinds, and assisted the white missionaries on their tours of various chapels and estates.

In John Collis's 1836 reminiscences, he had spoken about an unnamed congregation member who had forsaken work on Sundays. He had begun by recounting that

> The remarks of some of our people, during the speakings of the present week, were interesting and edifying. One of our Helpers, an African, being asked, if he thought his countrymen would receive the gospel, in case a minister should be sent among them, replied, "Massa, if God put it into the heart of the minister to go and to preach the gospel, will He not also open the hearts of the people to receive it?"[115]

That shrewdness of judgement and sharpness of wit were gifts that Archibald was to display again in his confrontation with the estate owner, James Wedderburn, recounted later in this chapter. These talents were combined with what appears to be a formidably strong personality and steadfastness of opinion, the latter being suggested in an entry on Christmas Day 1846, when "Br Arch Monteith" read the circular letter from the missionary conference to congregations, "enforc[ing] the principles of the letter in his usual way. The people appeared to receive it well."[116] John Collis too attested to Archibald's powers of conviction and persuasion when he commented: "The effect of his spiritual conversations among his negro brethren, touching, as many of them declare, almost immediately the heart, will only be developed in eternity; while his conduct on the property on which he is an apprentice has been so exemplary, that to it, his master informed us, he attributes the fact, that he has not been necessitated to call for a special magistrate's interference since the commencement of the present system."[117] So James Monteath, Archibald's de facto master, had testified regarding his confidence in Archibald's leadership of his workforce and good judgement in adjudicating conflicts on his estate.

These qualities were likewise in evidence in his supervisory responsibilities within the church. A series of incidents that took place in 1846 demonstrate Archibald's faithfulness to his missionary superiors, and his penchant for leadership roles and disciplinarian attitudes. On 30 June Brother Robbins had heard that "Susan F[ord] (of Bog)" was delirious: "her mind was not at peace. She complained of 'sin sin'." It appeared that she had recently been involved in a quarrel and fight with another female "in which she had shamefully stript up [the clothes off] another woman". She had been put out of the congregation for this misconduct. Robbins continued: "Subsequently I hear of adulterous courses and taking medicine to procure Abortion and thus bringing on herself her present serious illness." By 8 July, Elliott's diary records the death of Susan the previous day. He commented that it was "an awful instance of the bitter and melancholy consequences of sin. Her adultery and other wickedness has [sic] issued in her untimely wretched death, without hope." He then gives us the sequel:

> Br. A Monteith rode over to the Estate, not to bury her, but to try and improve the sad event. The husbd [husband], a commt Br [communicant Brother], and other neighbours were expecting "their Minister" would come to inter the Corpse. Monteith said "Minister will not be here" In a short time the husd came to him, supposing he was come to bury his wife, and said "it is all ready sir" Monteith ansd [answered] "I cannot bury her how can I read the burial service over one who has died so" The man then exclaimed angrily "Somebody has told Parson that I inveigled my wife. he forced her" He then went to a wicked brown man, who was afraid to interfere finally a half drunk wicked man came along and encouraged and aided them in burying her Much concern and feeling was manifested. Many of the females cryed and mourned and it is hoped that this mournful event will be sanctified to many of the Sinners there. After the grave was filled, without any ceremony, Monteith spoke earnestly to many who assembled in a house near. The husbd *curs'd* and *swore* mad. Alas! And hitherto a Comt![118] (emphases his)

Freedom of the Body

The grand celebratory day for Archibald came on 1 June 1837, when, aged about forty-five, he paid James Monteath and his mother the £50 they demanded for his right to manumit himself. They obviously considered him trustworthy and valuable, and so had initially set a figure of sterling £90, which they considered would have made it difficult for him to produce. He had worked with the family for over thirty-five years and had, to all intents and purposes, become a fixture. Considering the high esteem in which he was held by the church authorities, one has every reason to believe that Archibald was a hard, unrelenting worker, who lived up to his superiors' expectations of his reliability. When other estate owners learnt of his discharge, they offered him paid positions on their establishments, which serves as testimony to his good reputation as an employee and leader.

Archibald fell within that category of enslaved person who was most likely to make a bid for manumission.

> [S]lave domestics and tradesmen generally had greater chances for manumission than did field slaves. This was so not only because domestics and artisans had more personal contact with their masters but also because they had relatively greater opportunities to acquire cash resources to effect self-purchase. (In addition, a slave's personal relationship with his or her master could also have been a causative factor which permitted the slave to attempt self-purchase in the first place.)[119]

Furthermore, the 1834 Emancipation Act "permitted ex-slaves to buy themselves out of apprenticeship if they could pay their masters the value of the remaining years of their service. Thus, self-purchase was made somewhat easier than it had been under slavery, and, as a result, the number of self-purchases increased."[120]

In addition to personal contact with owners, the chances of an enslaved person winning manumission were enhanced where there was a track record of loyalty to owners on the part of the enslaved, or where a singular act of loyalty had preserved the life and property of the owner. Archibald had kept faith with the Monteath family, no doubt on many occasions, but no more so than during the events of 1831–32 recounted in chapter 3. These levels of complicity were the price exacted by a system in which a great majority was subjugated by a minority. To achieve this asymmetrical balance of power, crushing force was deployed. "Terror, or naked power, was at the core of the institution of slavery. Jamaican slavery was especially brutal even by the elevated standards of New World brutality. Whites were encouraged to keep firm discipline and to punish slaves frequently and harshly."[121] And the daily experience of the enslaved provided ample pre-figurations of what massive deployment of arms would enforce. Floggings, mutilations, food and sleep deprivation, solitary confinement, rape, even the humiliation of being force-fed another slave's faeces[122] – these were the daily enactments of violence against the person and personhood of the individual. To incur the institutional wrath of the secular establishment would bring far worse. It was a price that many enslaved persons were not willing to pay. They heeded the proverbial commonsense that "coward man keep soun' bone" and "short cut draw blood [Short-cut paths are dangerous]", so they resisted rebellion. This did not, however, translate into an unconcern with achieving their individual liberty. It is clear from Archibald's account that he had been working patiently and single-mindedly towards this goal. And in "Experiences", Archibald expresses relief and joy "to see everyone who had been under the same yoke" as himself released from bondage in August 1838.[123] His wife and his friends, and all black people in Jamaica received this right.

Figure 9.5
Emancipation, 1834.
Poster by Ripingille
and Gleadah.
Courtesy National
Library of Jamaica.

The detail and length of treatment that are given to Archibald's attainment of freedom in 1837 convey the significance of this event for him. In fact, it forms the emotional climax of the narrative. His prelude to the actual manumission is an account of a debate between himself and two white men, one a Dr Gilpin, the other, a "Mr. Weddesburn", the very wealthy "master of several plantations".[124] By inference, one conjectures that this must have been James Wedderburn.[125] In 1817 a John Wedderburn had owned several properties that had passed to James: Spring Garden (439 slaves, 318 stock), Jerusalem (285 slaves, 254 stock), Mint (240 slaves, 210 stock), Retreat (363 slaves, 260 stock), Moreland (266 slaves, 209 stock), Paradise (145 slaves, 548 stock), and Mount Edgecombe (242 slaves, 357 stock), adding to these by 1821 with Endeavour and Kiter Inverness.[126] By 1832, James had succeeded to these estates.[127] He also owned Prospect, which was in Hanover, the rest of the pens and estates being in Westmoreland, further west of the Carmel/ Dumbarton area where Archy lived and worked.

Wedderburn had been cornered in the debate over whose authority was supreme, that of an original owner or a present owner. When Wedderburn conceded that the present owner's word was superior, Archibald had exulted at his own guile: "now I have you where I want you Mr W.", and had gone on to claim that God had passed authority to his son Jesus, whose will his adherents ought to obey. Archibald's argument was counterfactual, being based on faith: "God has given all into the hands of his son who died for us and rose again . . . and governs all." Either Wedderburn also deeply shared this faith or he was swayed to yield to the argumentation of this black underling by the profit for himself that he detected in the man's line of reasoning: "we must seek out and follow that which is written in [Galatians] V.22 to 24. [']But the fruit of the Spirit is love, joy, peace, longsuffering, gentleness, goodness, faith, meekness, temperance; against such there is no law.' " If this was the ideology that the enslaved were being taught through Christianity, then Wedderburn could expect peace and compliance on his estates. No wonder he reacted by shaking Archibald's hand, as he "exhorted [him] to visit and teach on all his plantations as much as [he] could, or would desire to do". Soon after, Wedderburn got into his carriage, called Archibald, once more shook his hand, and drove off. Archibald understood this episode to mean that "[t]hrough this permission a clear way was opened to me, to have access to a number of Estates".[128]

As we have already seen, Archibald had, in fact, in his capacity as New Carmel helper, already begun to proselytize among Africans on several estates in his general vicinity. But James Wedderburn's endorsement was the crowning entrée to a full-time occupation as an evangelist. If obstacles had been put in his way by overseers and attorneys, he now knew he had Wedderburn's backing and that opened up to him a wider field of proselytization. Further assistance for Archibald came by way of legal advice from John Daughtrey, whose name occurs as "Dodridge" in the Kummer text, suggesting either that Archibald pronounced it like that or that Kummer heard Archibald's rendition as that. During 1837 Daughtrey was one of the stipendiary magistrates for St Elizabeth. His address is given in the 1838 *Jamaica Almanack* as Lacovia,[129] but he no doubt had an office at Black River, the administrative capital of St Elizabeth, since he was one of the officials appointed by the British government to monitor the implementation of the slave amelioration laws. Archibald referred to him as "first magistrate in Black River, who was a dear Christian man, and always showed himself as a friend of the Mission, and as *my* friend".[130] Daughtrey's predecessor, Captain Oldrey, had also had a good relationship with the Moravians, as is recounted by Jacob Zorn regarding the approach of the initial emancipation date in August 1834: "Captain Oldrey, R.N., stipendiary magistrate for St. Elizabeth, was present at our chapel, and after the public service entered on some explanations of the new system [apprenticeship]. He expressed himself gratified with the order that prevailed, and the softened expression of the countenances of the negroes present."[131] Later, in 1836, John Collis recorded a love-feast for children followed by a meeting with many aged Africans on Boxing Day, 26 December. At the latter, "a small sum of money" was presented to each of the senior congregants, money "which we had been kindly furnished for the purpose by a worthy gentleman and special magistrate".[132] It must have been this connection between Oldrey, Daughtrey, and the Moravian missionaries that facilitated Archibald's access to Daughtrey and his legal advice. It would appear that Archibald had broached the matter of his self-manumission with Daughtrey and had been advised on the one hand to wait, and on the other to avoid appraisal in the courts as this would result in a much higher evaluation than appraisal by his owners. The basis of this piece of advice was that

> [t]here were two ways by which self-purchase could be effected during the Apprenticeship period: one involved the apprentice paying the value of his remaining years of service as this value was determined by the master and approved by judges charged with appraisal; the other way avoided formal appraisal and simply involved a personal financial agreement made directly between the master and apprentice. The "amicable arrangement" and "appraisal" appear to have accounted for the majority of manumissions during the Apprenticeship period.

All the same, "[m]any apprentices were unable to pay their appraised value, and others were so discouraged by the high prices that they never attempted self-purchase".[133] As we shall see, James Monteath initially computed Archibald's value based on his "remaining years of service". This was de facto rejected by Archibald, and the owner Monteaths eventually had to settle on the "amicable arrangement" basis.

Daughtrey's other caution to Archibald was in regard to biding time, in that "as a free man, [he] would sooner be hindered from keeping meetings on the properties, than as a slave".[134] This opinion gives some insight into the anomalous position of the free black, who was viewed by whites as subverting, by his free condition, the caste parameters of the society, as discussed in chapter 6. The free black was a physical representation of the discrepancy between "negro", that is, slave, and citizen, that is, free person. So much so that a parliamentary commission investigating Barbados's legal and judicial system in 1823 observed that "[i]t was admitted to be a rule that every Negro is presumed to be a slave, unless he can legally prove the contrary".[135] In this light, "[a] freedman could be arrested for violating a slave law and confined as a slave until his free status was established; or wages might be withheld from a skilled workman by claiming that he was a slave, thus forcing him to prove his free status".[136] In addition, as a free black moving among persons still enslaved, Archibald would have been perceived by nervous whites as likely to incite his fellow blacks to rebel, he would be in a position to carry seditious messages, or even serve as a living example of the possibility of self-manumission.

Despite Daughtrey's two provisos, Archibald felt that his chance for freedom was now! He would face the humiliations and injustices of being a free black man, and he would take a chance with the goodwill of the quadroon and mestize Monteath family, "even though masters were often reluctant to manumit their best and oldest servants".[137] Having decided to seize the moment, he wasted no time after gaining the permission of James Wedderburn to proselytize on his estates. He immediately brought this new licence to the attention of Mr Daughtrey, and the very same evening he received Daughtrey's approval, he approached James Monteath on the matter of his freedom. But James

> tried in every possible way to bring me off from my plan and desire; promised me all possible liberties if I would remain just as hitherto etc. etc.—Still I longed for liberty, and although I knew that in 3 years, apprentice time would be over, and my freedom would come, my spirit still longed for immediate liberty.[138]

Not surprisingly, the next morning, Archibald was unwell. Was this a ruse, was it psychosomatic, or had he become depressed because of his disappointment, the affront to his desire for personhood and liberty?[139] The second stage in this tense confrontation was that the foreman's absence from work caused James Monteath to leave his home and come to Archibald's hut. "Archie," he said, "I have spoken with my family about your wish to become free. We always loved you, and you have been of great service to us; hence we will give you freedom for £90. Sterling." At an exchange of Jamaican £1.4 to sterling £1, the figure stipulated amounted to Jamaican £126. Archy "gave no answer" to this suggestion. James was forced to rationalize: "You see, your services in one year are of more value to us than £30. That makes in 3 years £90." Archibald records: "I was still silent & thoughtful, for I had not expected that he would ask so much, and I was disappointed, and felt grieved!" Strong emotional words. Feelings so strong he could not speak. Ever ready with words and wit, Archibald was now silent. So much so that James Monteath was forced to retire. Clearly there was a stand-off, and we are led to assume that Archibald continued to be ill. The third stage came next morning. James returned. His bargaining position had been made to shift considerably: "Archie we have thought over the matter still further. You shall be free for £50." Archibald resumes his story: "Hardly had my master left me, when I took £40. that I had ready[,] went to Mr Monteeth and bought my liberty. The remaining £10. I paid soon after. He gave me my free paper, and herewith my slavery had an end." Not only had Archibald got better as soon as he saw freedom on the horizon, but his narrative shows how he had been preparing financially for his self-manumission. In the negotiations, he showed himself to be a man of guile as well as a man of planning and

Figure 9.6 Gravestone for John Collis, Carmel Moravian churchyard, 1995.

forward-thinking. He also tactfully refrained from indicating the source of the £10 balance on his manumission fee. One may surmise that it might have been sourced from Mr Daughtrey, but this would have been compromising for the government official. Rather, one is led to point a finger towards the missionaries, who a few months later revealed that they had advanced monies for two young men of Zorn's congregation "to purchase out the unexpired term of their apprenticeship, in order to train them for teachers".[140] We may also take note of the phrasing by Jacob Zorn of his public appeal for contributions to enable Archibald to take up full-time mission work: he indicated that Archibald had, "by the help of some kind friends, obtained his full liberty".[141] For his part, Archibald himself specially thanked Brother Collis for his support, an indication perhaps that John Collis had helped grant or advance the manumission sum that Archibald lacked.

> Oh, how full was my heart of thanks and praise that at length I had attained unto the blessing of *Liberty*. This day always remained to me a holy day. It was the *lst day of June 1837*. Soon after I had come from my masters presence, I dressed myself in my Sunday clothes, and rode to Carmel, where Br Collis as our minister lived and labored. All at Carmel were surprised to see me thus on a week day; all the people present looked at me with astonishment, as I stepped near the house; I took off my hat and waved it about my head, and cried out with a loud voice. THANK GOD! I AM FREE! – All rejoiced with me but especially my dear minister Brother Collis![142]

Collis seems to have been genuinely loved by his associates and his flock, as we detect from the wording of an obituary.[143] He served New Carmel for two-and-a-half years, after having worked at Fairfield for eighteen months. At New Carmel, "his conduct soon won the confidence of the people of his charge, and the esteem of all around. His labours among them were indeed abundant, and the cheerfulness of his disposition, as well as the warmth of his affection, drew all hearts towards him." John Collis died, aged thirty-eight years and two months, on 14 August 1837, just a month and a half after Archibald's self-purchase! No wonder Archibald specially mentioned his gratitude to his then minister, who had so soon after Archibald's great day shut his eyes to the world.

10

Shaping Identities

THE ORIGINAL DISPLACEMENT OF peoples from their native communities in Africa and their relocation in strange lands, without their parents, mates, or family members, meant that such persons would need to reconstitute social relationships by building new alliances, creating new friendships, establishing fictive families, and through their own bodies birthing offspring whom they would attempt to emotionally claim as their own, even though their children were also by law the property of the person or persons who owned the female parent. The effort to reconstruct self was so daunting that some preferred not to try. An old African woman narrated to Brother Holland's wife how, soon after her arrival in Jamaica, she had made an unsuccessful bid to take her own life.[1]

Persons born into slavery grew up to experience for themselves no other condition of being. They had a shallower past to use as reference point, a narrower resource of personal interaction. This would have made them more malleable to the plantation system, less locked into traditional codes and less goal oriented. But these qualities could be vitiated by socialization into the values of those who had come out of African societies, by the influence of character traits in both enslaved colleagues and Europeans with whom they came into close contact, and by the moral sensibility and ideational directions in which traditional African religions, Christianity and Islam[2] pointed them. So that a Creole born into slavery could, given the examples of freedom around him, place a high value on "personal autonomy"[3] and the honour that flows from this condition, and undo that "inability to defend oneself or to secure one's livelihood",[4] which epitomized slavery. Matthew Lewis narrates how a mulatto carpenter gave him as his reasons for pursuing manumission:

"It is not that I wish to go away, sir; it is only for the name and honour of being free; but I would always stay here and be your servant; and I had rather be an underworkman on Cornwall, than a head carpenter anywhere else."[5]

Whether or not the slaves had a substantial past reference point or a shallow sense of heritage, they were legally not their own master. It was only human that the enslaved individual would try to rehabilitate in some measure that alienation from the self. We try then, from the Monteath texts, to examine the mechanisms that enslaved persons harnessed to attempt the reinvention of themselves as persons outside the ambit of their masters' orders, intentions and control.

Traditions and Innovations of Naming

An important marker of identity is one's name. An individual's name or names are given and used by relatives and the community. Abducted and sold away from these anchors, and in most cases denied one's previous name, the slave's named identity, inasmuch as it remained an African label, was tied to its most generalized, least place- or family- or event-specific, integer: the day on which the individual had been born. Or was the day-name in every case the day of birth? Or might it also have been the day on which the name was being conferred by the estate administrator?

Brother Elliott commented on the failure of the enslaved to know the date on which a child was born: "There used to be . . . difficulty in finding out when the children were born. They always knew the day of the week, because the child was named according to the day on which it was born."[6] This difficulty for the literate needs of European official accounting derived from the illiteracy of the church's African constituents. For the Africans, lacking systems for calendrical exactitude, births were associated with other events – in nature, in marital relationships and in family and communal matters. Since these latter three requirements could not easily be met in the chaotic affective world of chattel slavery, the most accessible marker was the association of a child's birth with the day of the week, which had been an automatic association whether or not the name was later appropriated either by the child and its relatives. The tradition of day-names came to enjoy currency in the Caribbean because the Akan and adjacent Ewe peoples of the Gold, Ivory, and Slave Coasts were well represented among the earliest British imports, and their cultural habits were thus likely to chart the behaviours that later arrivals would follow.[7] In fact, the weekday associations adopted in Jamaica applied regardless of the ethnic origin of the enslaved, with the result that *it is not possible to assume that the bearing of an Akan day-name is a marker of the individual's ethnicity.* Evidence, for instance, from the

St Elizabeth/Westmoreland regions shows that Creoles also bore these names, as obtained with two young men at Rosehall named Quamin and Quashie. In addition, the Akan-Ewe, like the Europeans, broke up time into cycles of seven-day weeks, so that there was a synchrony of time progression which was not possible with some other African societies, such as the Kongo, the Igbo and the Yoruba, for example, who counted the week as four days. So ease of time correspondence allowed European owners and overseers to include these Twi (Akan) and Ewe names as part of their onomastic inventory for their workers, whether African or Creole. Another facilitating element was that the Akan-Ewe day-names were for the most part di-syllabic and therefore easy to pronounce and remember. John Elliott listed the correspondences, which were categorized not only for day but also for gender:

Day	Male	Female
Sunday	Quashie	Quasheba
Monday	Cujo	Feiba[8]
Tuesday	Cubanna	Benba
Wednesday	Quacco	Cuba
Thursday	Quao	Abba
Friday	Cuffe	Feba
Saturday	Quamin	Memba

Other names selected by the estate hierarchy were largely British names. Some were familiar and normal personal names, like Anne, Emma, Phillis, Lucy, Priscilla, Robert, Richard or Thomas. Some names were diminutive forms of British personal names, like Nanny, Nancy, Sally, Franky, Sophy, Bessy, Tom or Dick. Others applied mainly to adult males were place names. The Hampstead Estate list noticeably, but not exclusively, features such labels: Blackwall, Edinburgh, London, Glasgow, Canterbury, Aberdeen, Devonshire, Colchester, Waterford, Surry [Surrey], Dundee, Dublin, Jamaica, Essex, Ipswich and Bristol. Some other names were suggested by classical literature and mythology: for males – Ajax, Plato, Hercules, Vulcan, Titus, Homer, Cato, Horatio, Pompey, Hector and Jupiter; for females – Chloe, Ophelia, Lucinda, Cassandra, Parthenea, Diana and Phoebe. Then there were biblical names like David, Mary and Eve. A demeaning name like Bumkin was rather rare. In fact, most names, rather than being pejorative as the literature suggests was the general rule, were in fact common British eighteenth- and nineteenth-century names.[9] It is noticeable, however, that in most cases, like the Akan day-names, labels were monosyllabic or di-syllabic; very rarely tri-syllabic and longer.

Unbaptized slaves carried a single name. Exceptions to this practice occurred when an adjective was used to precede the name, such as "Old Jane". Or an African ethnic name may have been pre- or post-fixed to the name in order to distinguish persons with the same name on the same estate. So there was "Congo Sam" and "Jane Congo". In documents, however, we notice the writers' recourse to periphrases that distinguish one person from another with the same name. Such appositional structures comprised the single name followed by a relative phrase, for example, "Anne of Hartshall" and "Adam of Happy Grove". Since there was a limited pool of first names from which the British of the seventeenth to nineteenth centuries drew, it was clearly useful, as the official documents illustrate over and over, to establish particular identities by appending the name of the estate to which a person belonged. While the associative "of" is used on several occasions, there are instances where the associative is suppressed and the estate location operates in apposition to the first name, thus effectively functioning as a surname, for example, William Springvale and Adam Hazelgrove;[10] Henry Carmel;[11] Thomas Tombuctoo;[12] Elizabeth Peru;[13] Robin Spicegrove, Ruthy Spicegrove;[14] and Edward Nottingham.[15] All these second names were names of estates. But the enslaved realized that these locative associatives or surnames were markers of chattel identities. Free persons did not bear such nomenclatures.

Figure 10.1 Loosening the topsoil in preparation for planting. From Renault, *Bons baisers de la Colonie.*

The Social Significance of Baptism

Baptism carried several metaphysical meanings for blacks. Particularly in its immersion form, it served as a resurrection rite whereby the individual was passed through the realm of the ancestral dead in water, emerging into a new life and persona; it was also understood as guaranteeing a safe passage to a happier existence with the spirits.[16] Part of this metaphysical renewal was the assumption of a new name, and herein lay some of the social significance of the ritual. A new persona was born, with a label that the whites considered normative, because the names were like the ones they themselves carried. The possession of two European names was therefore a status symbol, an "escape from the stigma of slavery".[17] When we consider the affective difference between the same individual's identity as Philly or Phyllis, as against Felecia Richardson, we appreciate the expectation of higher social status attached to the last named individual in the list. And when we read of a Jannet Ramsay Ford or a Sarah Wilson, "free women of colour", one is not likely to conceive of them as erstwhile slaves, hoeing beds in the cane fields, planting cane ratoons, breaking stones, toting buckets, scrubbing floors, sweating in kitchens and washing clothes on river stones! Indeed, Collis records a slave's rationale for wishing baptism. He was tired of being treated like a nonentity "Massa, me go up and down the country, and people take me for *nobody!*"[18] Christian nomenclature, then, for a black person, conferred visibility against the backdrop of a mass of indistinguishable Fibbas and Neds and Blackwalls. Indeed, "[b]aptism clearly heralded the conferral of Christian names".[19] By this means, non-whites were rehabilitated into "honour and respectability".[20]

To understand in part the role of baptism in social evolution requires an appreciation that church membership had become one of the important indices of class status. This held for mulattos as well as for blacks, even though they were in differential caste categories. "[T]he people of color formed the largest church-going group in Jamaica in proportion to their numbers", church membership constituting part of the habitus deployed to counteract the stigma of their colour.[21] *Christian baptism, together with property, were important assets in the quest for recognition as a citizen.*[22] They entitled the illiterate ex-slave Nancy Monteath to be referred to as "Ann Monteath of St. Elizabeth gentlewoman" in the 1839 sale agreement regarding the land being bought from her by Archibald.[23] The insistence of Nancy Monteath's mother, Jannet Ramsay Ford, on having her name entered in a church register was tantamount to registering her citizenship in the island, having her presence officially recognized, much as the man speaking with John Buchner wished to emerge from invisibility into visibility, from chrysalis into butterfly. Baptism birthed a new persona. Other behaviours involving legal affairs also distinguished the free mulatto: the purchase or inheritance of a slave or slaves, the buying of property, and the making of a will.

We note, in contrast, Archibald's failure to make a will, even though he could write, and even though he did not seem shy to approach certain white lawyers, planters and ministers who might have helped him make one. What then were the inhibiting personal, social, cultural and psychological factors that prevented him, and many other black peasants, from legally passing on their real estate and belongings to others? Was it that Archibald, as a male headman in his peasant and church communities, had *already* achieved the social status that people like Jannet Ramsay Ford and Sarah Wilson craved and wished to have cemented by their fulfilling certain official and legal requirements? Or was the contrast between the habits of the urban free mulatto woman and the rural free black male concretized in the differential extent of their connection with legal papers and entitlements? We lack sufficient data to be sure of the answers to these questions.

Certainly, however, for blacks as well as mulattos, social respectability was tied up with church affiliation. It gave the enslaved individual a focus of activity and affiliation away from the plantation, another locus for his association with equally oppressed kindred and with Europeans, a site in which he was the putative brother, not servant or even slave, of other church members. We may recall Archibald's own remarks on the social distance between slaves and white people: "The difference or contrast between Master and slave, between white and black, was so great, that I did not venture to ask. I was timid and backward to do so."[24] Years later, when he was called to speak with James Wedderburn, he was able to display a less timorous attitude. But when in the early 1820s he was first invited into the hall of the Paynestown house for prayer meeting, he had felt awkward and out of place. By 1837 he must have felt more self-confident, but also surprised, when the attorney for the Wedderburn estates asked him to come and be interviewed about his evangelization of the workforce, and shook his hand at the end. Some time after, the landlord, James Wedderburn, summoned him, offered him a chair to sit, and furthermore initiated a handshake with him. In those intervening years, he had worked closely with foreigners by way of personal conversations and meetings in the mission of God's work; as foreman and overseer he would have had business dealings with not only his own master and mistress, but also with white overseers and personnel on other farms; he had developed a confidential relationship with Magistrate Daughtrey; and had been persuaded, as the letter acknowledges, to reply in writing during November 1855 to a letter of August 1854 sent to him by John Jacob Kummer, Joseph Kummer's father, in Pennsylvania.[25]

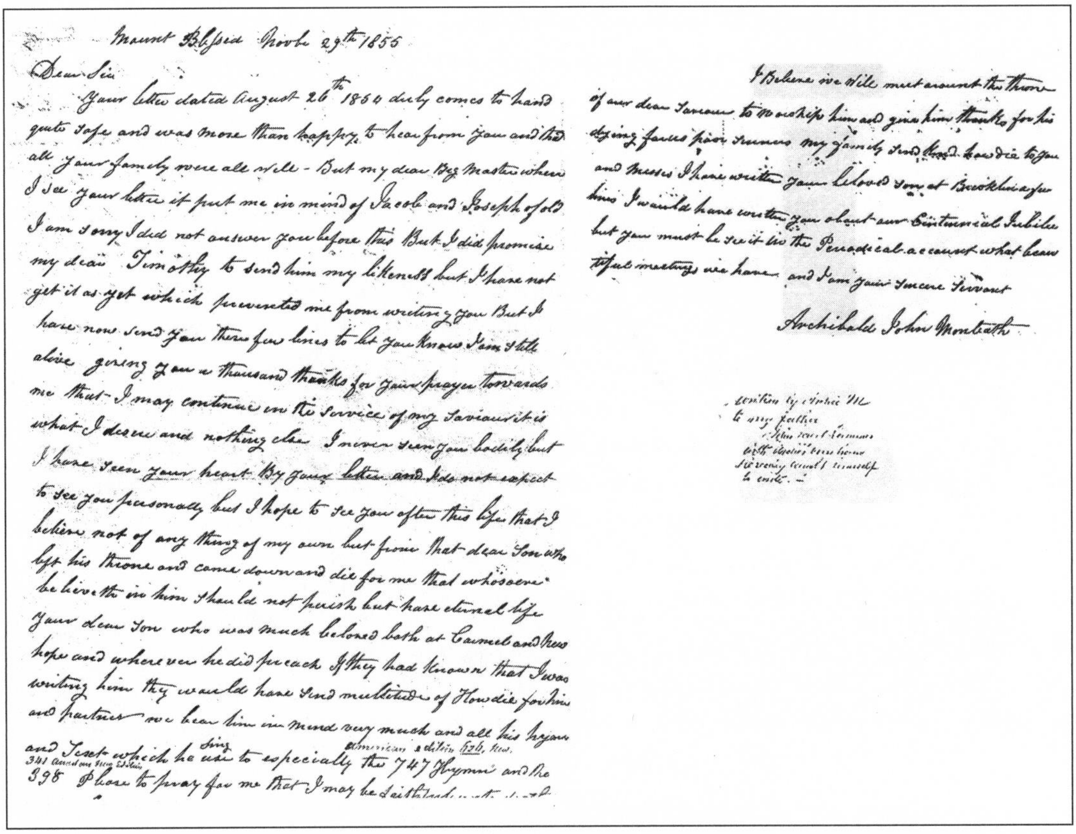

Mount Blessed Novbr 29th 1855
Dear Sir
Your letter dated August 26th 1854 duly comes to hand
quite safe and was more than happy to hear from you and that
all your family were all well - But my dear Bro Master when
I see your letter it put me in mind of Jacob and Joseph of old
I am sorry I did not answer you before this But I did promise
my dear Timothy to send him my likeness but I have not
get it as yet which prevented me from writing you But I
have now send you these few lines to let you know I am still
alive giving you a thousand thanks for your prayer towards
me that I may continue in the service of my Saviour it is
what I desire and nothing else I never seen you bodily but
I have seen your heart By your letter and I do not expect
to see you personally but I hope to see you after this life that I
believe not of any thing of my own but from that dear Son who
left his throne and came down and die for me that whosoever
believeth in him should not perish but have eternal life
Your dear Son who was much beloved both at Carmel and New
hope and wherever he did preach If they had known that I was
writing him they would have send multitude of Howdie for him
and partner we bear him in mind very much and all his hymn
and Text which he use to sing especially the 747 Hymn American edition 626 New and the
341 American New Edition
398 Please to pray for me that I may be faithful ...

I Believe we will meet around the throne
of our dear Saviour to worship him and give him thanks for his
dying for us poor sinners my family send their howdie to you
and Misses I have written your beloved son at Brooklin a few
lines I would have written you about our Centennial Jubilee
but you must be see it in the Periodical account what beau
tiful meetings we have and I am your sincere Servant

Archibald John Monteath

Figure 10.2 Archibald's letter to the Kummers. Courtesy Moravian Archives, Bethlehem, Pennsylvania.

Name Choice as Signifier of Fictive Kinship

As baptism involved the acquisition of a new name or names, it would seem that it afforded the adult an opportunity to choose his or her own labels. Just as the estate management's distribution of farming plots enabled individuals to plant what they liked and to dedicate themselves as assiduously as they wished, in the same way, naming for purposes of baptism lay within the province of the individual fancy.

Yet ministers of religion may themselves have played some part in the naming process. Particularly in instances, as among the Moravians, where converts were tutored in catechism classes, there must have been room for discussion regarding choice of names, whether for adults or newborns. In fact, Brother Herman commented on differences over naming when he spoke of having bestowed a name on a child "whom I had reluctantly to baptize by the name of 'Billy,' my remonstrances being silenced by the assertion of my worthy colleague, that it was by no means unusual in England to christen by names of such construction as Betsy, Nancy, &c. To such authority I had, of course, to yield, though I must confess somewhat against the grain."[26] The use of familiar name-forms such as "Billy" for "William" may have a class basis, the familiar form replacing the official correlate among the British working and peasant classes. In the light of church supervision, however, Africans would have sought to minimize problems of name choice with parsons by electing to use names that were current and that were borne by persons acceptable to Europeans. But blacks might also in their new name choices try to avoid names that reminded them of the myriad unpleasant circumstances connected with their slave name. They may have come to hate the sound of the name whose reiteration by masters, mistresses, overseers and drivers must have been the cause of great irritation. So a new name was a type of makeover; it might even bring good or better luck. That the elements of ancestral favour and luck were associated with names is revealed in Matthew Lewis's experience with some of his slaves in 1818.

> Neptune came this morning to request that the name of his son, Oscar, might be changed for that of Julius, which (it seems) had been that of his own father. The child, he said, had always been weakly, and he was persuaded, that its ill-health proceeded from his deceased grandfather's being displeased, because it had not been called after him. The other day, too, a woman, who had a child sick in the hospital, begged me to change its name for any other which might please me best: she cared not what; but she was sure that it would never do well, as long as it should be called Lucia.[27]

One of the sentiments activated in these new names was that of kinship with an estate, even if the estate name itself was now relinquished. Still part of the estate property, the enslaved looked to select names from among the owners of estates and their families. For instance, this option seems to have been enacted when Archibald's friend, Richard, at the time he required a new name for baptismal purposes, took the name of the current male head of the Jamaica-based estate-owning Monteath family. The name "James" belonged to the eldest son of John Monteath. On the other hand, Archibald, Toby then, assumed the name of John Monteath's junior son, Archibald John Monteath. This pattern leads to the interpretation that both men were not only close in age and ethnicity, but also close in friendship; that Richard and Toby observed African age proprieties in the application of the two formal names: Richard the elder taking the name of the senior son, and Toby that of the junior son. Indeed, there may have been a deeper meaning to Archibald's statement that John Monteath, his first master, always treated him as a father would: "he always treated me the same as a father".[28] It might have alluded to the construction of a parallel family relationship among certain enslaved individuals as that which obtained in the master's household. Furthermore, if one reads coordination between Richard and Toby in the choice of their new names, then it reveals that names could be self-generated. This interpretation cuts across the passivity suggested by the statement in Archibald's autobiography where it reads: the minister "baptized me, and named me Archibald John Monteeth".[29] Such a phrasal formulation may represent a shorthand way of speaking about naming, a formulation that may well conceal the politics and processes of naming.

Indeed, there is further reason to believe that names were chosen by the candidates for baptism themselves. For one thing, given the number of persons who were baptized at the same time, a minister would have been hard pressed to choose names for each and every one of them. Besides, the names tended to echo those of the baptismal subject's current or previous owners, information that the minister did not have in every instance. So that it is highly likely that Toby, in relinquishing his slave name, submitted the more imposing labels, Archibald John Monteath, at his Anglican baptism on 24 June 1821.[30]

In opting for this baptism, Toby followed the pattern set by his owners of becoming baptized by a minister of the Anglican Church. The way Archibald narrates this gives the impression of casualness. The ceremony proceeded without the minister "saying one word to us, as to why we were baptised, and what it meant; this no one told us. It had become customary to baptise."[31] The ritual was connected to a prior sequence of events. Speaking apparently of John Monteath's offspring, he says that at Dumbarton "one day Mr. Monteeth's children were baptised, by the Parish Minister of the Church of England. On this occasion the minister said to me; 'Come Tobi, in 8 days I will baptise you, gratis.' "[32] This minister did not, however, return, but another minister came one week later, "and I was obliged to pay him 8/ [8 shillings] for the service". The curate recorded the occasion as follows: "Archibald John Monteath, negro man, 38, property of RoseHall, baptised June 24, 1821".[33] It might appear that, as in several other instances, the baptisms were performed at people's homes and on estate premises. The biography's wording, though, that it was "all done in the Church at Black River", gives the impression that the ceremony was performed in church. But we are also free to interpret the wording as indicating the officiating body rather than the site of performance. Since the Anglican Church was an established rather than a mission church, such mass baptisms were the "only professional contact" of Anglican ministers with the enslaved population, and these were arranged "at the request of the planters".[34]

As for the first of his Christian names, the young Igbo man of about twenty-nine years old must have learned that Archibald was the name of one of his master's brothers and of a paternal uncle as well. Toby would have been privy to this type of information, having worked for eight years, he says, as a house servant. It is further of significance that Toby chose to give himself two forenames. Burnard notes that of freed people in St Catherine parish before 1764 "[f]ew of them had more than one forename".[35] The self-imposition of two forenames indicates the grandeur that Aniaso felt was his inheritance as only son of Duru and grandson of his mother's father. African names, he knew, carried no purchase in the society into which his slave ship had sailed, but he would find surrogate means of conveying his inherent nobility, even if his culturally fractured social environment could not read all his signs.

The data in Archibald's story thus speaks to some level of agency on the part of the subject in the naming choice. The decision to take the surname of the subject's owner was part of the mapping of an identity that fixed the slave to a particular place, in a sense the surname replacing the locative appendage to a single name identity.

From Placename to Personal Name

As we have seen, one process in the evolution of slaves' names was the acquisition of a normative British surname, just as whites carried. Such a surname now replaced locative and ethnic identifications, and it linked the individual to a particular conjuncture of associates, both socially lateral – names of their friends and relatives – and socially vertical – surnames of those parents who carried them and of their present or past owners. All the same, contradictorily, there remained, in the new name, indices of that connection to a plantation or estate by way of an owner's surname: the form had changed but the substance was the same, in that, of the at least two names a baptized person received, a personal name, and a surname, the latter often replicated that belonging to their present master or mistress, or that of a past owner or overseer. As contradictory a behaviour as this replication must seem, we must recall that the enslaved persons, whether from Africa or born in the Caribbean, had no tradition of names on which to draw, apart from the languages and conventions of Africa. As part of the alienating processes of enslavement, it was necessary for the owners to reject in the enslaved the revival and embedding of mechanisms of language and connectedness that would allow the slave to conceive of her or himself as possessing the same identity she or he once had. "[I]n every slave society one of the first acts of the master has been to change the name of his new slave . . . almost universally a symbolic act of stripping a person of his former identity."[36] This denudation of former identity left the enslaved with no other option than, for purposes recognized by Europeans, to cull names from a borrowed tradition, the only accessible one being that of their masters and overseers.

So the new surname was that of one's owner or it could be the maiden surname of one's mistress, because when European women married, they often brought slaves with them into their husband's establishment as part of the marriage settlement. As for the personal name, this could be a version of their slave name, so Dick would become Richard, and Fanny or Franky would become Frances. But the personal name could be that of any European the slave may have wished to emulate, or it advertised the relationship with someone the slave considered a mentor: it could have been his master's name, or that of one of the master's sons. It could also be a biblical name.

It is possible that names may have been vetted by slave owners or supervisors before permission was given to have them entered for baptismal purposes, and indeed adjustments may have been made. But one must wonder at the fact that slaves chose to appropriate the forenames and surnames of members of their owners' households. Surely permission must have been granted for this, but it appears that it was a source of flattery for the owners since the recurrence of their names is so frequent. In any case, it becomes clear from the European personal names which occur in this study, that there was an extremely limited range of first names to choose from: there was a surfeit of Johns, Jameses, Williams, Thomases and Georges; and nearly every female was an Elizabeth, Eliza, Margaret or Sarah.

Even so, one must interrogate the reasons why baptismal first names could diverge sharply from slave names. One can understand the correspondence between Bella and Isabella, Lucy and Lucinda, Kitty and Catherine, Franky and Frances: in some cases these changes were merely the longer or the more formal versions of shortened or pet names, and it may have been possible that the individual continued to be called by the pet name in daily practice. But why the change from Anne to Rebecca, as is the case of Archibald's wife? Did this suggest resonance between the experience of this Anne and the biblical character, Rebecca? Or did it indicate a greater affective affinity between Anne and the eldest daughter of Mary Scott, her owner, than with another of her owner's daughters named Anne? And what accounted for the change from Lucy to Sarah? The Lucy who became Sarah in fact took the name of one of her owner's daughters. Similar factors of affinity may have been at work. We may further ask: why should Richard, one of the Rosehall slaves, have changed his name to James? After all, Richard was not an abbreviated or a pet name. Toby, on the other hand, carried more of a pet flavour by its "y" ending. "Archibald" was much more resonant and important-sounding, but even so, subsequent to his assumption of this name Archibald appears to have been called "Archy", at least by the missionaries.

We note, however, that two names seem to have been used to address him in friendly formality: the maid at Paynestown welcomed his presence by saying "[H]ere comes Archie Monteeth"; Mrs Senior, mother of Mrs Scott, addressed him as "Archie Monteeth" also;[37] and the Mount Edgecombe Christian community quoted his admonitions by saying "Archie Monteeth had told them". This contrasts with the distanced formality of the attorney's elliptical "Monteeth, the more I speak with you, the more I like you" in the same narrative section.[38] A more familiar and intimate form of address, following both Jamaican and Moravian traditional practice, would have been "Brodda (Brother) Archy", and we hear him so called on two occasions on pages 296 and 301 in appendix 2.

Shaping Community Life

One of the means of cultivating an affective life was by social and sexual association and bonding. Because of the limitations of the data sources with which we have had to work, we can know the mechanics of who married whom, but we have absolutely no idea what attracted them to each other, or what were the compelling factors that brought some marriages into being.

The profiles of Archibald's associates given in chapter 6 illustrate the occurrence of both same-plantation and cross-plantation marriage. The estates were contiguous, so that they covered districts that lay within a twenty-mile radius from present-day Newmarket. Slaves could not marry without the consent of their owners, yet despite owner objections, as evident in Archibald's case, cross-plantation mating among individuals from adjacent and nearby plantations was inevitable. These cross-plantation alliances were an index of the network of occupational, religious, social and trade relationships that brought together people of like interests and comparable experiences. Cooperation in labour-intensive tasks such as clearing pastures and paths, felling trees and building churches, schools and homes also helped to cement communal ties. Meanwhile, a network of fictive relationships, beginning with shipmate alliances, was further woven by reciprocal roles as baptismal sponsors, both among adults and vis-à-vis friends' children.[39]

One factor in social amalgamation was ethnic bonding, which may have been at work in the marriage of two Igbos: Kitty of Hartshall who became Catherine, to John Clark or Clarke, previously Adam of Happy Grove. And one may read such an interpretation into the apparently voluntary baptism of Archibald and James and Mary within a week of one another, this peer coordination being impelled by the fact that they were all Igbo; at least Archibald and Mary were shipmates, and all three had been acquired by the same owner. It would also appear that the closeness in age between James and

Archibald was yet another reason for close association, though Mary was apparently senior to both of them by about a decade. A detail, however, that may militate against a reading of ethnic bonding in the case of Archibald and James is the recognition that baptisms of enslaved persons took place, not only singly, but more often in groups, some large, some small, along lines of estate affiliation and, in some cases, blood connection. A counter-argument in favour of ethnic bonding, however, lies in the fact that the African notions of family went beyond blood lines, to include co-residence in a village, and the wider notion of clan bonds. Even slaves in African societies came to be incorporated into the families of their owners, though they were debarred from certain rituals that were exclusively for blood kin.[40]

Physical Enclaves and Networks

In the building of community, factors of personal compatibility, shared residence, estate proximity and shared religion must have come into play and each of these may have been more influential than, or as pertinent as, ethnic solidarity taken on its own. One notes, for instance, interethnic marriages, such as that between two Hartshall Africans: Bessy, a Congo, later to become Margaret Scott, and the Mandingo Jonny, who became John Hart at his Anglican baptism in 1817.[41] Another Hartshall couple comprised Lucy, a Congo, whose Christian name was Sarah, and John Scott, a Cromantee.[42] Yet another Hartshall marriage took place between the Igbo Eliza, baptized Eliza Johnson, and George Hart, previously simply George, a Creole, in 1829.[43]

It is instructive that after individual manumission and general emancipation, many slaves in the Westmoreland–St Elizabeth border area – and this may have been a more general pattern – established their residences and hamlets in the physical vicinity of their former estates. As distasteful as the plantation experience had been, its topography together with the lifestyle shaped by these features, and the human relationships fostered in that matrix – the shared happy times and disasters, the births and deaths that had taken place there, the navel strings[44] and the graves lodged in that space – all these had made of this place "home" for the enslaved community. These affective ties bred by place and interaction, and less so by blood, were among the considerations given weight in the mitigating codes of the slave system in the 1800s, ties that were sufficiently powerful to cause slaves to abscond from plantations whenever they had a strong sense that the scattering of an established community was imminent. One such time was when it was known that a master was heavily in debt and might sell off slaves to raise capital; another more obvious occasion was the death of the owner. As was

Figure 10.3 Limestone-strewn land used for vegetable cultivation by peasants, Huntly, Manchester, 2004.

commented on in the mid-eighteenth century with respect to an estate in eastern Jamaica and obviously relevant to slave behaviour in general: "The Negroes are all born on the place, and there would be great trouble in removing them . . . to a distant part of the island." The consequence was that many of them would pre-empt this possibility by running away.[45]

Sensitivity to "kinship" ties and to geographical loyalty must have played a part in the choice of land being purchased by ex-slaves in the years following 1838. There is some evidence that new villages were being formed by close associates, and that the missionaries also attempted some social engineering in this respect. The dormitory system of communal living that the Moravians fashioned for their European and early American settlements was clearly not considered appropriate in an environment where their congregants were locked into relations of ownership by and economic dependency on entities outside the church, namely, the plantations. On the other hand, the dormitory system required separate living quarters for unmarried women, unmarried men, married women, married men, widows, children and so on according to gender and stage of life. Instead, the missionaries sought to provide the means for their flock to co-habit in villages and thus establish a peasant existence. In 1838 there was a settlement at Parker's Bay, now named New Hope, which had been established on Culloden Estate land donated by Hutchison Mure Scott.[46] Another settlement was established at Lititz in 1839 on upwards of 400 acres of land on the "savannah", known presently as the

Pedro Plains.[47] Maidstone was also one of their projects, the energetic Jacob Zorn having purchased part of the Maidstone coffee estate near Nazareth "for the purpose of accommodating settlers after the building of the chapel at Nazareth had been begun, but not finished".[48] A schoolhouse that doubled as a chapel had been built at Nazareth, but "the ground being rocky and uneven, did not allow the formation of a settlement in regular streets and squares". Despite this failure of the limestone topography to yield to Teutonic plans for symmetry, "the land was parcelled out and sold to the Negroes, who soon built a large, but irregular village".[49] Yet by 1850 several of the people at Nazareth owed money for land that it had been understood they would purchase from Zorn. Another settlement was also planned for Beaufort where "the Brethren purchased some hundred acres of land, which were sold again in small lots to the people. These attempts have not been successful."[50] Elliott had put repayment problems down to people "being rather premature in purchasing land before they were either able to pay for it, or to occupy it".[51] It is not known if those financial obligations were ever totally met in the instances cited. This was a period immediately after emancipation when, among a number of other difficulties, people on the coffee properties in the mountains, for example, "were oppressed with heavy rents, and land was not to be purchased elsewhere". Under these circumstances, "numbers of the Negroes came down, bought a few acres each, including a clump or two [of tree groves], and are now permanently settled here. They still go to the mountains for work, as nothing of consequence is carried on in the savanna for which wages are paid."[52]

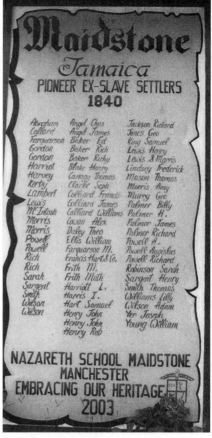

Figure 10.4 Memorial for first villagers, Maidstone, Manchester, 2004.

On the other hand, in the missionary diaries there are casual references to "settlements", which we are likely to overlook, except that the term turns up in respect of Archibald in a context which suggests that a community was taking shape in the vicinity of his cottage at Frazer, which lay above Cool Retreat. In this case, these were settlements where individuals had bought parcels of land from estate owners who were scaling back their operations. We note, for instance, that Archibald's title deed, in specifying his acreage, indicates that lands on his boundaries are "intended to be conveyed" to Mr Jasper Miller, Mr Thomas Vassall and "Mr. Robert Becford" from "a larger

Figure 10.5 Peasant house, St Elizabeth, by Susan Shirley.

run commonly called or known by the name of Rose Hall".[53] This fleshes out the reference on 6 July 1846, when George Robbins reported: "From [Flint Valley and Content] Br. R. rode up to the Settlement of our Br Archy Monteith where we met with a joyful welcome from our Br and his family."[54] The term "settlement" recurs in a reference to Nightingale Grove, and one notes that this was the residence of both Adam Hart and Edward Monteath, as revealed in John Elliott's diary entry of 27 February 1839.[55] Charlotte, an Igbo, who had been known as Old Jane, the Congo Thomas Palmer and his wife Mary Ann Monteath, and Robert Smith and his wife Henrietta Hart lived there. Another settlement had taken root on New Savannah property comprising persons such as the helper, Edward Hunt, John and William Richards, Eliza [indecipherable] and the elderly couple, John Adams and his wife. Even before the decisive moment of civic change, when freedom was a prospect three or four years on (since in 1834 the apprenticeship period was projected to last six years), large groups of people, in some cases as many as 200, were described as making roads, clearing pastures and building walls to segment pasture land.[56]

Buchner describes the landholdings, on which each house was "surrounded by a garden for the growth of vegetables or of the cotton tree, and generally shaded, or even hid, under the large foliage of the plantain". The smaller houses were 18 feet by 12 feet and "divided into two apartments, having no floor but the bare ground". The houses were plastered with mortar and covered with thatch. More often the houses contained three apartments, "decently floored with boards and covered with shingles; the rooms are generally well furnished, and kept clean and neat".[57]

The names people gave their properties are of some interest. They suggest piety on the one hand, and relief and release after long endurance. One might deduce that Archibald named his place "Mt. Blessed", the words across the top of his letter to the Kummers. Robert and Isabella Price's place was "Happy Be Thankful"; while Peter and Angelina Beckford were at "Rockland". In 1850 Robert and Jane Beckford lived at Rosehall, on a property called "Greenhill", but in 1843 they had been resident at "Ended".[58] How different was the perspective of these peasants from the somewhat disparaging, yet factually accurate, observation made by one missionary when he commented on the "universal anxiety of the Negroes" in the post-emancipation period "to make themselves masters of scraps of land, and to settle themselves thereon".[59]

Conclusion

IN THE AUTOBIOGRAPHY OF Archibald John Monteath, we are fortunate to have an account of the reclamation of a moral sense, of dignity and of personal identity. While not dedicated to the saga of political or economic overthrow of a pernicious system, this spiritual testament and conversion narrative attests to the will to overcome personal deficiencies in a corrupt political, economic and social system. Like most slave biographies, it concerns the realization of personal and individual freedom, but, as the product of a conservative missionary endeavour, it avoids insistence on the negative and life-denying aspects of the slave regime. Furthermore, as a post-slavery product, there was no longer a need for its tone to be hectoring. For these several reasons, it avoided concretizing the experience of a brutalized psychic and physical self.

In his autobiography, as told to the missionaries, Archibald John Monteath does not present himself as a particularly wounded individual, in the manner of Juan Francisco Manzano of Cuba,[1] Ashton Warner of St Vincent,[2] or Mary Prince of Bermuda, the Caicos and Antigua.[3] Rather, he speaks of himself as an individual with agency. He exudes a confidence that undercuts the prevailing image of the slave as an underling. He makes self-assurance normative, and indeed, were we to compare his personality in this regard with that of Equiano, or with some of the portrayals of subjugated persons emerging from the pages of Thomas Thistlewood's diaries,[4] we would need to concede that slaves possessed strength of character and opinion familiar to us in people we know today.

If carefully and sensitively read, Archibald's life story demonstrates a quest for honour lost in childhood, and honour regained through commitment to a spiritual cause, and later through the striving for redemption of the physical body from bondage and the recuperation of mental choice from compulsion. Ironically, adoption of a spiritual cause meant subjection of the body to abstinence of various sorts; it meant learning humility of the spirit; and religious adherence demanded some of the same principles of morality endorsed by his natal society, the Nri. Apart from a strong work ethos, centred on farming, the Nri were devoted to moral cleanliness in the individual and also in the social fabric. The reclamation of a moral code and centre-post was one of the reasons for the appeal of Christianity to some Africans. This point emerges in the confession of an elderly man who, about to be baptized, admitted to Jacob Zorn, the Moravian missionary: "Massa, aforetime me thief, me lie, me everything that is bad; me heart very wicked [previously, I stole, I lied, I was all that is bad]", but he hoped that his "sweet massa" Jesus would have mercy upon him, and forgive all that he had done.[5] On the verge of death, an elder named Robert expressed an anomie and world-weariness encountered in so many African-American spirituals: "I am the oldest negro on Elim estate, and have lived to see a great deal, but little that is good; I am weary of this life, and feel very desirous to reach my eternal home."[6] Archibald himself also mentions receiving endorsements after abolition from former slaves, "whose overseer I myself a slave, was", regarding his disciplining them to avoid stealing and "certain things which slaves on other places were not hindered from doing".[7] The inculcation of restraint and a moral underpinning to action were to stand them in good stead when the days of freedom and self-responsibility came along.

If there is a wounded bleeding figure in his narrative, it is the Saviour of Moravian eschatology, the crucified Lamb. The Christ, by "agreeing to become human . . . [had given] human beings a dignity which they had lacked before, and by sacrificing himself on the cross for their sins, he saved their souls from death. In this way he offered them a path out of their natural degraded state, and in return they owed him unending gratitude." As such, "Christ's sacrifice dominated their understanding of him. They called him the Heiland ('the Savior') and the Lämmlein ('the dear little lamb'). . . . Hymns and liturgies focused on Christ's wounds and his death."[8]

So here is an inversion of the portrayal of suffering. The inversion, however, then reverts when, for his part, Archibald is willing to serve as slave to this Saviour. The metaphor is, in fact, a figure of speech conventionally applied in African religions, allegiance to a deity or a king being expressed as human servitude.[9] In several versions of the biography, this image of religious self-surrender is invoked:

> My only wish and prayer is, that the Lord who bought me a lost and undone
> sinner, who purchased me with his precious blood and delivered me from the

Figure 11.1 Nazareth Moravian church at Maidstone, Manchester, 2004.

power of Satan, not with silver and gold, but with his holy and precious blood; may more and more gain ascendency in my heart, that I may *be and remain his property,* until he calls me from this earth.[10] (emphases mine)

I may <u>view myself as his own dearly purchased property</u>, that He has deemed *me* worthy to be made use of in the work of spreading his Gospel, and gaining souls for his kingdom![11] (italics his; underlined emphases mine)

That I may *see myself as his dearly bought possession,* that in faith through grace I have been reborn to a living hope in eternal life! That he deems me worthy to help spread the Gospel in his service![12] (emphases mine)

This was a willing service, a joyful, but not painless, surrender! How unlike the enforced service of the plantation and pen! This is an instance where a "freely established relation of dependence with a more powerful patron can be the basis for expanding one's honorific claims vis-à-vis one's equals. The client's attachment also firmly establishes him in a place within the hierarchy of honorable statuses. He belongs and is one with his patron as a member of *their* society."[13] African social systems powerfully entrenched notions of hierarchy, most fundamentally as age seniority. Therefore, the individual understood him- or herself as belonging within the social fabric, necessarily as the junior or servitor to higher echelons, ranks based on age, honour levels, family or caste ratings, and accessibility to supernatural powers. In addition, Igbo society considered some persons slaves, whether domestic slaves, *ohu,* or cult slaves, *osu.* The *ohu* was acquired by capture, kidnapping, or purchase from persons seeking to acquit a debt, and were alienated from their natal kin by absorption into the master's lineage.[14] The *osu* were created by "a village, a lineage, a family, or an individual dogged by illness, bad luck, or calamities and misfortunes . . . [to] become the deity's servitor and carry the sins of the dedicator".[15] The *osu* and his descendants suffer the social ostracism of the Hindu untouchables. But whether *ohu* or *osu,* in any society that marginalized a minority of persons designated as slaves, "the poorest free person took pride in the fact that he was not a slave". By sharing, then, in "the collective honor of the master class, all free persons legitimized the principle of honor and thereby recognized the members of the master class as those most adorned with honor and glory".[16] And while, in the main, traditional African societies were organized around "stratificatory systems [that] were not highly developed and classes were either absent or not 'well defined', . . . individual competition for honor and prestige was rampant. . . . The less centralized were such societies, the greater their emphasis on prestige ranking of individuals", the extreme being "the highly formalized recognition of honor found among the largely acephalous Ibos".[17] In Igbo society, title-taking was the goal of the male adult, but also the province only of the freeborn, the *diala.*

Enslavement had therefore made Aniaso less than a whole, freeborn male. Despite his avoidance of complaint against his secular servitude, we are nevertheless made keenly aware of how Archibald chafed under the circumscriptions and prescriptions of his bondage: whether it touched on his forcible ejection into the paddle-boat, or the delay in landing him at Jamaica, or his plans for marriage, his keenness to participate intensively in religious service, or his release from "legal" detention on Dumbarton Estate. How disgraceful was all this for one who knew that he was born into freedom, into respect, into honourable traditions, into the future prospect of community titles, material achievement, the responsibility of an adult for land, work, and family. As he passed into young manhood, the realization of what he ought to have been, what he ought at that stage in the life process to have been doing, must have figured forcibly in his psyche. The opportunity to become and identify himself as other than someone's slave must have been one of the factors that led him to seize the alternative that Christian affiliation presented. It led him into the skill of reading and writing; it led him into concourse with the superiors of the land in matters other than work-related drudgery.

Even though the recital of genealogy was a seminal element of the Moravian testimonial tradition, we feel sure that Archibald also thought it highly appropriate to include the information about his family origins and the status regime of his natal society because they held much resonance for him and his thrust toward high achievement goals. From a psychoanalytic point of view, Archibald is a contender for categorization as an *n*-achiever. Such a person "apparently perform[s] better only when an achievement incentive is present in the situation", an achievement incentive being "one in which a person gets satisfaction from doing something better *for its own sake,* or to show that he or she is more capable of doing something" (McClellan's italics). In other words, the individual finds "intrinsic satisfaction in achieving, without the need for external promptings".[18]

To reclaim his family ties at both the beginning and the end of his narrative was a counter to the mandatory system of "natal alienation" and physical exile that the transatlantic slave trade imposed.

> Alienated from all "rights" or claims of birth, [the slave] ceased to belong in his own right to any legitimate social order. . . . Formally isolated in his social relations with those [of his blood relations] who lived, he also was culturally isolated from the social heritage of his ancestors. He had a past, to be sure. But a past is not a heritage. . . . Slaves differed from other human beings in that they were not allowed freely to integrate the experience of their ancestors into their lives, to inform their understanding of social reality with the inherited meanings of their natural forebears, or to anchor the living present in any conscious community of memory.

We need to note the caveat here of the word "freely", and the further qualification that ends Patterson's paragraph: "That they reached back for the past, as they reached out for the related living, there can be no doubt. Unlike other persons, doing so meant struggling with and penetrating the iron curtain of the master, his community, his laws, his policemen or patrollers, and his heritage."[19] This countervailing assertion is reinforced in the observation that "To be dishonored – and to sense, however acutely, such dishonor – is not to lose the quintessential human urge to participate and to want a place."[20]

Archibald's sense of himself as belonging to a noble genealogical line is to be contrasted with a remark written in the diary of a black overseer, W.H., who comforted himself and his wife from whom he was being separated with the words: "Why should you cry? . . . and why should we murmur? We can neither make one hair black or white. *I am a slave, and I must be treated as a slave.* . . . I must only wait on the Lord our Saviour patiently"[21] (italics mine). While Archibald, his fellow helper, would agree with his doctrine of patience, one doubts if Archibald accepted his slave status with this degree of equanimity bordering on defeatism. Here is a classic instance of the expression of the "servile personality" that "is merely the outward expression of [the] loss of honor . . . the crushing and pervasive sense of knowing that one is considered a person without honor and that there simply is nothing that can be done about it".[22]

Archibald knew that there was a limited window of opportunity to do something about changing his state. But it had to be the slow, painful walk of the tortoise to get to the finishing line. Not only did it require the patience of Job, but one appreciates the consistency of effort it required to amass, like Archibald, £40 towards one's self-purchase, only to be told that one needed to treble the amount to meet the requirements of one's owner. Worse than this, it is clear that a court settlement would have demanded even more from him than the sterling £90 or Jamaican £126 being asked in a private arrangement. No wonder Archibald fell ill. Freedom was a very distant prospect.

This slow, laborious method of working towards one's freedom bore the outward lineaments of conformity; and Archibald was sufficiently conformist to have rejected the temptation to join in collective projects aimed at freedom which, as a pursuit exclusively to be achieved by the enslaved, was only possible through force. It was indeed the stance of many of the enslaved whose biographies we have been fortunate to retrieve. Such narratives reflect the biographies of "the great majority of slaves" who

> lived undistinguished lives in conformity with the plantation's rules. Few ever left the locality and fewer rebelled. Most worked quietly, if not industriously, in a limited range of jobs throughout their lives. Exceptional slaves demonstrated qualities that brought them into the small circle of the slave elite. Yet even this limited social mobility, with its small rewards of privilege and perquisite, was circumscribed by the needs of the plantation, the elite slave's usefulness, and his or her fidelity to the system and its code.[23]

Archibald's conformity is illustrative of the power of socialization on the susceptible mind of a nine- or ten-year old transplanted from his original culture. His formative teenage years were experienced in the crucible of the Caribbean plantation system, in which upward mobility meant making himself a useful cog in the wheels of the plantation hierarchy. Even when he tried to divorce himself from that tyranny, he found himself attached to another institution that was also alien to his natal society, but which nurtured his spiritual self and offered him outlets for personal development and fulfilment; these satisfactions, however, came at the expense of his being subject to the laws and tenets of that system and an efficient interpreter or intermediary between the missionaries and the people they wished to convert to their worldviews.

Despite the generalized conformity of Archibald and the majority of persons in his condition, there are indications that enslaved individuals sought ways and means of fashioning lives that subverted that "sense of debasement inherent in having no being except as an expression" of their masters.[24] The shipmate community offered them one such strategy of a new belonging. It was a response to the emotional deficit of the "motherless child". Africans of ethnicities other than the Kongo must have arrived at the same or similar mental formulations: that confined to the "house on water",[25] and furthermore penned down in the hold of the ship, they were as children being birthed within the womb of one mother. The fate of one was the fate of all.[26] As we see in Archibald's story, and detailed in chapter 6, there were at least two shipmates in his close vicinity, and given the fact that John Monteath purchased eleven slaves in Aniaso's batch, there were probably more. These relationships were taken seriously and were meant to last a lifetime. What were the celebrations like when shipmates recognized each other at market, at prayer meeting, by gushing springs, on errands along the roads, on work sites, at rites of passage? What was the story behind Archibald's discovery that a shipmate was stationed at Woodlands, a nearby plantation? We can only imagine the joy of mutual recognition when they discovered each other's presence in the same vicinity.

The churches offered another haven of kinship. Mary Prince testified to the new sense of community she found among the Moravian brethren in Antigua. Also in Antigua, Adam Domingo, an African, asserted: "When I left my native country, I lost my brothers and sisters, but when I found brothers and sisters in the Church, I was satisfied."[27] The church allowed the despised slave entry into an even wider community than he or she had experienced in their homeland. The sacrifice they paid for this was loss of kin. The necessities of capture and of adaptation demanded replacements, and these were to be found in shipmates, sexual mates and children, church brothers and sisters, trans-African co-workers, Creoles and the international church fellowship. These were now their a(d)-ffiliations:

> To belong to a community is to have a sense of one's position among one's fellow members, to feel the need to assert and defend that position, and to feel a sense of satisfaction if that claimed position is accepted by others and a sense of shame if it is rejected. It is also to feel that one has a right to take pride in past and current successes of the group, and to feel shame and dishonor in its past and present failures.[28]

However, as a slave, not only was power in the hands and mind-force of the owner/exploiter, but the slave's dishonour was the subjugator's honour; the indignity of the underling's status lent his owner the dignity of manhood or personhood. One notes, for instance, the acquisition of at least one slave by freed persons, whether black or coloured: it was an assertion of arrival at a position of power and control over others. We hear the evidence of this in the case of an elderly house slave who accosted a young white store keeper with the boast and abuse: "Me have fe me [my] *house,* for me *ground* [provision plot], for me *nigger* [slave]; where for you house, you ground, you nigger?"[29] And what, in the specific case of Archibald, was the correlation between these two opposing conditions of existence – slave and exploiter?

His first identifiable master was John Monteath of Scotland. The details of John's maternal parentage are ambiguous and sketchy. What seems most important is the connection between the Monteaths and the Douglases, most clearly established in the union of Archibald Walter Monteath, John's paternal grandfather, and Jean Douglas, daughter of James Campbell Douglas. Between the late twelfth and late fifteenth centuries

> the house of Douglas rose to a degree of power scarcely inferior to that of royalty itself, and as an old historian remarks, it became a saying that "nae man was safe in the country, unless he were either a Douglas or a Douglas man". . . . The greatness of the family, indeed, attained to such a pitch that it matched eleven times with the royal house of Scotland, and once, under the Angus branch, with that of England.[30]

The value of the connection between the Monteaths and Douglases was further enhanced by the good relationship between Archibald Walter's son, Walter I, and his sister-in-law, Margaret Douglas. As dowager of Archibald, Duke of Douglas, Margaret nominated Walter I as one of her executors and trustees, in much the same way that her husband the Duke had earlier nominated "Walter Monteath of Kipp the Elder" as his cautioner or guarantor to his will and also as one of the witnesses to the will.[31] The dowager's healthy financial standing allowed her to be a benefactress, and her testamentary request that thereafter lands purchased by her legatees in Scotland should be called Douglas Support or Mains Support of Scotland serves as one of several signs of her sense of history and heritage. Both Mains and Support or Succoth were already Douglas family estates. These status orientations were to be maintained in the tenor of the testamentary instructions left by her great-nephew, Major Archibald Douglas Monteath. These instructions were intended to magnify as well as yoke both the lineages of Monteath and Douglas.

In his will dated 9 May 1838, Archibald Douglas Monteath instructs his brother, James Monteath, to dedicate the hefty £25,000 residue of his estate to "the purchase of lands in Scotland in the County of Lanarkshire of the greatest . . . extent of surface, and holding of the Crown, and when purchased to be forever after called and styled the Lands and Estate of Menteth". He then instructed that "three of the principal farms on the Estate to be called

Menteth should be named Arnmore, Arnbeg and Shannhill".[32] Another £10,000 was to be spent in "the purchase of lands in Perthshire to be called Armore [sic] and to be added to the entail of lands to be called Kepp but at the same time to be held as a separate Estate".[33] The fact that lands to be purchased were to be called Arnmore, after his grandfather's Arnmore in Dumbartonshire, might suggest that the original estate had been lost or sold, most likely in his father's generation, and indeed may have been a casualty of the bankruptcy of Walter I, the merchant.

Like the generous bequests of his great-aunt Margaret, Archibald Douglas Monteath left handsome legacies of £1,000 each for his cousin, Lieutenant Colonel Thomas Monteath, son of the Jamaica merchant Thomas Monteath, for the lieutenant colonel's son, Archibald Douglas Monteath, for each of the lieutenant colonel's daughters,[34] and for Margaretta Monteath, the lieutenant colonel's sister. Another £1,000 was left for Helen, the daughter of his cousin John Campbell Douglas. By another codicil dated 3 November 1840 he willed £1,000 to Douglas Monteath Campbell, son of Archibald Campbell of Blythswood. Prior to this, on 9 January 1839 the major wrote a letter to "[His] Dear James", indicating that he felt reasonably sure that a Douglas estate named Rosehall would be inherited by James himself. He writes:

> As I conceive our succession to the Estate of Rosehall to be certain, it would be adviseable to change the name of Monteath to Douglas in order to enable the same person to hold the Estates of Rosehall and Menteth.
>
> I prefer the name of Monteath as pointing out the source from whence it came. I know our lamented brother Walter would approve of this arrangement and trust you will give it all the aid in your power and believe me to be my dear James your affectionate brother.

These Monteaths, that is, Archibald Douglas, who had inherited from Captain Walter his brother, together with James, had thus by the 1840s comfortably reasserted their gentrified status. So much so that Archibald Douglas could leave tidy annuities for hospitals and infirmaries of Glasgow, and the poor of the parishes where their soon-to-be acquired lands would be located. As Archibald Douglas was unmarried, he willed succession to the Menteth Estate to James and his lawful issue, failing that to his cousin Margaretta and her lawful issue, and in the event of default on these previous conditionalities, then to his cousin Campbell Douglas and his lawful heirs. The properties must have eventually gone to cousins, since James mentions neither wife nor child in his final testament. In fact, General Sir Thomas Monteath Douglas "of Douglas Support, a distinguished Indian officer", inherited Gillbank, "the last portion of [a] once magnificent estate" that

James Monteath had purchased from John Inglis, a Lanark native and London merchant, in 1842.[35]

The extent to which the two brothers were acting in concert over their passion for land, wealth and gentrification is evidenced by the synchrony between the wordings of Archibald Douglas Monteath's 1838–39 will with its codicils, and statements in the 1850 will of James Monteath. The latter takes up the matter of the family name or names by agreeing to the cementing of the houses of Menteth and Douglas. It thus prescribes that "all heirs succeeding to the Estate to be called Menteth should assume the name of Douglas". So he identifies himself at the end of his will as "I James Monteath Douglas", adding the locative ascriptions "of Rosehall and Stonebyres", and also "of Douglas-Support". James had purchased the lands and estate of Stonebyres in Lanark country that had belonged to the Douglases; while he had also bought lands called Kingston previously the property of the Maxwells of Dargavel, also relatives. Was it his acquisition of all, or at least some, of these lands that brought him into conflict with his cousin Robert Douglas whom he had intended as one of his trustees and executors, but whose future services he revoked by 1850?

It would therefore seem that John Monteath, as his father's eldest son, was himself dedicated to an agenda for the rescue and restoration of family lands and an advancement of the family status from landed gentry to aristocrats. Such expectations were consonant with those entertained by other such families. Hamilton illuminates the use of imperial wealth to acquire and improve land in Scotland by the Barclay and Malcolm families, who used Caribbean money as a means of upward social mobility and heightened social standing.[36] John Monteath, however, striving through the period, may not have been fully aware of the difficulty of the career on which he had embarked so late in the 1700s, but he was in fact attempting to achieve ownership of extensive lands and copious slaves at a time when the heyday of Jamaica's plantation supremacy was waning, and when contentions over the morality of slavery had arisen to agitate the religious conscience in Great Britain. These moral issues together with slave insurrections catalysed political debates and decisions, pushing up land values and slave prices in the sugar colonies; at the same time increasing mechanization was slowly providing an alternative to intensive labour enterprises. Further to these external factors, John's early death put paid to his long-term plans, but his modest Jamaica acreages and his embryonic export produce must have made some small contribution to the overall patriarchal strategy of the Monteath sons. Perhaps this contribution was deemed too meagre to be of account, given the achievements and exalted self-perceptions that emerge from the careers of the military, legal and mercantilist brothers. Just as the major had conceived of tablets to the family's memory, their cousin and inheritor, General Sir Thomas, had added the surname Douglas to his original name and in 1865–66 had had a mausoleum prepared for his burial, which was therefore ready when he died on 17 October 1868.[37]

John's omission from the extravagant mausoleum in Glasgow's necropolis seems therefore to indicate that his role in the family's endeavour was reckoned as minimal, compared to contributions made by Walter the army captain, Archibald Douglass Monteath the army major, and James Monteath the merchant, lawyer and administrator. His omission is glaring, seeing that John had passed away in 1815, whereas his brother Walter had pre-deceased him in 1799. We are therefore left to surmise that John had disappointed his brothers in some way. Was rancour caused by his establishment of a coloured family, who, through his position as first son and heir, might have made claims on the Glasgow relatives after John's death and thus have become a nuisance? Were John's brothers annoyed that he had catered so handsomely for the coloured ex-slave Nancy and her son, James, and her other children as well, benefits that could have added to the Scots family's coffers? Was displeasure caused by his untidy wills and codicils considered by his brothers as ill-befitting his first son ranking? Or was it that the precision and clarity of mind and action to be detected in the wills of Captain Walter, Major Archibald Douglas, and even more so in that of James, were the result of character traits lacking in John? If he were given to an unmethodical manner of handling business, such inclinations were not likely to have been corrected or improved by the culture of easy sex and drink that typified plantation culture. Even though Walter and Archibald Douglas had also abandoned the rigidities of Scottish life to make their fortune overseas, the discipline of regimental life might have checked the extent of the degeneration that the unbridled power and indulgences of plantation life encouraged.

Whatever the interpersonal politics involved in the ambitions, pretensions and yearnings for aristocratic title on the part of these Scots landowners-cum-merchants-cum-military expansionists, it is important to appreciate the networks of kinship, inheritance, legal support and financial backing that each of them was able to call upon in his life's enterprise(s). By the converse, Archibald our subject lacked any such cushioning. This deficiency was the bedrock of what constituted slavery: severance from natal family structures and linkages. The shipmate fraternity was an emotionally helpful surrogate, and so too was the fraternity of co-religionists, but these were both social organs of the dispossessed and quite unable to provide the financial capital that the Douglas-Monteath kin could loan or bequeath their own. Nor could the financial pooling of the "pardner" or "susu"[38] mobilize the amount of cash or credit realized in the co-partnerships that built so many Scots factories, inventions and enterprises.

But in other ways, "the slaveholder, as well as the slave, [was] the victim of the slave system".[39] For one, owner and slave alike often had their emotional lives entangled in dysfunctional social and psychological relationships. It was unhealthy for men to have fathered children who then had no benefit of their nurture, yet children who might eventually have received from them some boon that could distinguish them financially from the pack of deprived people. Dr Thomas Ford evidently had several children who, slave property like their mothers, were scattered around several estates, rather than being brought up in one coherent location. John Monteath's attitude to his offspring by women other than Nancy remains a question mark, since his will gives no indication of his provision for them. The parallel families created by Richard Meyler, James Hart and James Daly, to name a few, must have caused the women involved much emotional distress, but the women must have murmured the consolation: "what cannot be changed, must be endured". One means of endurance was to maintain good relations with one's rival concubines. There are several instances where the children of different mothers were baptized together, suggesting some element of collaboration among the female adults. But we lack evidence of how these rival personalities and interests and claims played out on a daily basis, as the women themselves grew older, as their children matured and their needs became more pressing, and as the women themselves sought modest avenues for gentrification.

The success of the sugar-based economy of the mid-eighteenth century meant that for whites Jamaica "was a place in which to make a fortune, not to make a life, and its white population comprised at least two men to every woman".[40] The rigours of the climate, and even worse yet, the unequal sexual competition that black and coloured females posed for white women, kept many metropolitan women in Britain;[41] while the males, having come out to the island to initiate their overseas careers and investments, returned to live off their profits in the suburbs of London or Glasgow. The effect of their absence from Jamaica and, while there, their unbridled access to women of all strata and ethnicities

> meant that, far from the "higher orders" providing a model for a proper bourgeois life, they offered instead a model of disorder, licentious sexuality, illegitimacy, irregularity, with coloured mistresses kept openly, and concubinage a completely accepted form. For the anti-slavery movement, formed in the crucible of the evangelical revival, deeply committed to the notion of the ordered Christian household as prototype of the family in heaven, this was profanity indeed.[42]

The European nuclear family was therefore not a lifestyle of the planters and pen-keepers and their white staff, but rather of the missionaries who exemplified the ideal by their resident family units. An alternative pattern was that which appears to be encountered in Sarah Donaldson who, to our knowledge, mothered six children with three fathers. She was evidently able to secure enough from these alliances to have been able to buy herself land and a house in Savanna-la-Mar, and to have left a will with bequests to her relatives, among them one of her sons who spoke of her as "[his] dear mother".[43] Sarah's daughter, Jesse Monteath, in her turn birthed five children with three different males. Lacking then the restraints of social and organizational codes built up by both African and European societies, the family structures of both cultures went into shock and free fall. But there was a socio-economic, even apart from an affective, rationale to such a structure. Indeed, the bearing of children to serial partners has typified the mating strategies of unemployed and marginally employed women in the twentieth century Caribbean.[44] Now, as then, child support from the various fathers serves as one means of economic survival for the woman – and her children. So, paradoxically, her widening affective relationships, with their increased possibility of pregnancies together with the economic burden they carry, yet broaden her channels of economic support. It is thus for her one of a series of "flexible behavioural patterns and a choice among several potential sources of support". It is illuminating that this was also one of the options of free women of colour in eighteenth-century Jamaica. As this study tangentially shows, these women, like their latter-day black counterparts, battled to survive in a "context of poverty and uncertainty, limited options and little control". As such they "remain[ed] economically vulnerable", with "economic security . . . elusive".[45] Sarah's and Jesse's emotional and economic life stories may or may not have accorded with the options depicted for them in twentieth-century analyses of financially deprived women.[46]

And what of our immediate subject – Archibald Monteath? How close to or how distant from an external view of him was his representation of himself? How did he appear from an angle which was not that of the missionaries? We are privileged to know in some measure that they held him in esteem. Yet, a second- or third-party's view of the subject is constricted by the arenas of activity in which the parties operate, so that Rebecca the wife might have added some narratives and assessments that would either have undercut or substantiated Archibald's projection of himself. What kind of a father was he? And what was it like to have worked under Archibald the estate driver and headman? What was he like with his friends? These are issues touching on "point of view". And speaking of friendships, the narrative's silencing of this topic is highlighted by the fact that we only know superficial aspects of Archibald's personal relationships from secondary sources, mainly the missionaries. The fact that two persons were his shipmates, Rose Brown and the Woodlands recalcitrant, derives from missionary sources; and so too is the information that Richard, later James Monteith, was a fellow Igbo.

In regard to the matter of narrative silencing, we may take the opportunity to comment on the invisibility of women in these texts. One is amazed that the missionaries make almost no mention of Rebecca, Archibald's wife; then they virtually write Rebecca the daughter and her fortunes out of their assessments of Archibald's life and emotions, and erase "the other daughter". They are as guilty of overlooking women as one missionary observed in respect of the African-Jamaican men who rode on their horses and had their wives walking behind or eating in the kitchens after feeding their men at table.[47] Another glaring distortion is the erasure of Nancy Monteath from the story. This could have been done by Archibald himself, who might have felt belittled to have been owned by a woman, and one who had once been herself a slave to boot! Or was it that he was genuinely unaware of Nancy's legal status and rights, surrounded as she must have appeared to him by men of authority: men like her sons who were literate, and in the case of her eldest son, one who had travelled to the Mother Country and met "the Great"![48] In addition, there were around her male overseers, executors, creditors, and business partners like James McGregor. Her deprived background appears to have cheated her of the opportunity to assert her business rights in a manner that was overt to her slaves, but this may not necessarily have meant that she was not a formidable and savvy individual in her own way. As for John Monteath's mother, she is virtually nameless, her identity as wife of Walter I being overshadowed by the élan of his mother's Douglas surnames that one nineteenth-century source confuses Walter I with his father, asserting that Walter I's sons were the children of Jean Douglas, who was in fact their grandmother![49]

With regard to content, we may ask further: what narratives would have emerged if Archibald's story had been more a secular biography rather than a testament of faith? And what details would he have mentioned concerning his life before he took on the Cross of Christianity?

It might be of some interest to pursue here the matter of Aniaso's information regarding his Igbo experience. Anthropological data suggest that by age nine "a Nri boy has taken about six or seven titles which are directed towards transforming him into a social and ritual personality". The last of these, which he takes at about nine, is *ima mmanwu* "knowing the secret of the ritual mask". The *mmanwu* are "spirits of the dead persons of a town" who reappear among the living on certain festival occasions "to entertain, bless, reprimand or curse individuals or groups of the whole society".[50] The

Figure 11.2 *Mmanwu* at Nri town, 1994.

ceremony in question involves a "revelation" occasioned by taking the child to a meeting house of the *mmanwu* or masqueraders.

> The mask comes in dancing and singing and uncovering his "hands", his "feet" and, finally, his "face" and "head". The child recognizes the masked dancer as his relation. He is next shown the whole paraphernalia of the mask. . . . The child is warned of the grave consequences of revealing or talking to any female about the secret. He is reminded that he is a man and the secret is known only to initiated men and a few elderly women. The revealing of the secret of the mask is called *itikpo isi mmanwu* (literally, breaking the skull of the mask). It is a major abomination to break this taboo [51]

The next title, about a year later, is the *ozo ichi,* "the ordeal of having his face marked with elaborate parallel marks made with a knife". Unlike the secret prior ritual, the *ichi* is an external sign – "a mark of royalty". Furthermore, it "confers on the child the rights of a full male citizen of the state and the right to become an emissary of Eze Nri [the king of Nri]". As such, he is entitled to carry "for his master or father the *ofo* staff and the *otonsi* staff"[52] among the principal insignia of the office. Aniaso's leadership career was therefore aborted by his capture, indeed before he could achieve adulthood. We have already suggested that his internalization of the need to assume the responsibilities of adulthood may have been one of the factors impelling him to dare to challenge the unknown, to plumb the secrets of Christian belief

Figure 11.3 Igbo status insignia: *ofo* at left, *otonsi* spears at centre, *ikenga* at right. Odinani Museum, Nri.

and practice, and the technology of hand-shaped signs on paper. This new arena of activity also permitted him myriad opportunities to exercise the arts of public speaking and of the persuasive tongue, gifts highly prized by his natal society.

So had Aniaso undergone the "revelation" of the mask? Perhaps he had not, since it is not mentioned. But if he had, why would he have suppressed this information? Or did he speak of it, and was it expunged by the missionary recorders? Given the missionaries' intransigent objection to jonkunu, did they feel that their subject, Archibald, would forfeit the respect and empathy of his readers if they allowed him to confess such intimate association with the masquerade? Or did Aniaso conceal this association because he felt himself spiritually tainted by the ritual? Yet again, did he conceal this episode because he would have committed an abomination against the taboos of his society, not only by unmasking the spirit, that is, acknowledging that the spirit was emblematized by a human, but also by speaking such knowledge to a woman, Sister Geissler! And in what light, to a missionary audience, would his relatives be seen, if it were to be revealed that his father, or either of his grandfathers, had shrouded himself in the cloth and straw and wood of the mask? Indeed, the strength of non-conformist Protestant churches in Jamaica and their opposition to masking festivals, and to African dancing and music have been so profound that the eventual decline of jonkunu in Jamaica becomes understandable, in contrast to its survival and development in other Caribbean islands by names such as mas', *gumbay, kambule* and carnival.[53]

Another ritual regarding which it would have been useful to know was whether Aniaso had "performed the ceremony of 'coming of age', called *iwo ogodo,* in which the male covers his nakedness with a piece of loin cloth for the first time, around the age of puberty. At that age he is considered ritually accountable for his actions."[54] Reference to this ceremony would have enabled us to calculate his age with more certainty.

Filtered as they are through the purposes and worldview of their original authors and subsequent disseminators, the texts of this autobiography hide secrets about some of the life-events and the psychology of their subject. But what they do allow us and future generations to glimpse is the personhood of the enslaved: vital lives, intelligent thinkers, perceptive social actors and resourceful characters, individuals too often hidden under the anonymity of their generalized disadvantaged condition. Furthermore, it gives us pause to consider that Archibald, despite the fact of his enslavement, assumed a similar role vis-à-vis Christianity to that for which he was intended to be groomed in his natal society, that is, to be arbiter and executor of a positive and idealistic moral order of living that was the kernel philosophy of the Nri people. We have no information as to whether, on his part, this was a conscious rationale for the career he eventually adopted. Was it a fortuitous choice, or was it an outcome of his early conditioning? The synchrony between the moral thrust of his life as an Nri and as a Christian leader invites us to speculate on the extent to which this pre- and post-slavery resemblance in mental outlook, emotional direction and active physical engagement occurred among the dislocated peoples of the transatlantic trade. Where this mirroring relationship between one's life's prospects before and after enslavement was frustrated, we are left to empathize even more keenly with their disabling depth of sorrow and rage of resentment, aspects of apathy and psychological traumas that such disconnection spawned. Archibald's apparent equanimity and charm of disposition on which one of the missionaries remarked may in no small measure have been due to the satisfactions he felt on account of the high stature he was able to achieve morally and spiritually, his comparative material success and the good reputation he won among his peers and in his church and civic communities.

Appendix 1

Experiences of a Former Slave in Jamaica

This text was originally published in *Missions-Blatt aus der Brüdergemeine* 28, no. 5 (1864): 87–102, and no. 6 (1864): 105–15. Translated by Mary Kuck.

——•—••—••——

Often recently, because of the emancipation of the slaves in Suriname, we have spoken about the conditions of slavery in the distant colonies. It will now surely interest our dear readers to hear the experiences of a former West Indian slave, one of our national assistants in Jamaica, in his own words. He dictated these to one of our sisters (Sister Geissler), at her request, since he cannot himself write fluently. We present his story here in free translation without addition or omission. It would be easy to re-word this story into a novel, according to the modern fashion, in which our readers are accustomed to learn only the simple, reliable, historical truth.

The editor knew the dear man very well 25 years ago. He made many a hot ride with him, and heard many of his lectures, many details of which he can still remember word for word. They were lectures in poor English with African accents, but original, thorough, full of examples from experience, full of fire, and of love as well as gravity. He (the editor) also heard many of the life experiences of this dear man from his own mouth and can guarantee that these corroborate exactly with what is told here. Our dear speaker was at that time a tall, stately man with very black skin and thick, wooly hair, genuine flat African facial features, but a very attractive, friendly expression of those features. The late Brother Collis called him "a mass of activity", in order to point out his corpulent figure and at the same time the inexhaustible, restless agility and zealousness of his spirit. This was something that was very unusual among the Negroes, who were generally sluggish, and even though passionate, were still dull and violent and avoided mental exertion. He worked as a helper in the congregation he belonged to, loyal from the bottom of his heart, and was also often to be found in neighbouring congregations; wherever there was a need for help, he was there on the spot. When the big man came riding up on his unsightly nag, young and old rejoiced and welcomed him.

We hear that even though he has aged now, he is still fully active. One could say of him that his old age is like his youth, and in him the word is fulfilled: Those who are planted in the house of the Lord and in the courts of our God become green, and when they age still bloom and are fruitful and fresh (Psalm 92: 14–15). [Translator's Note: In my RSV Bible, verses 13–14: They are planted in the house of the Lord, they flourish in the courts of our God. They still bring forth fruit in old age, they are ever full of sap and green.] His otherwise ironclad good health received a blow a few years ago. He had a companion in misfortune, who as a boy was brought over from Africa with him and sold in the same part of the island. Later, however, after he gained his freedom, he settled in the city of Black River and through fortunate business transactions became a very prosperous Negro. Suddenly he was called into eternity. Both had visited each other often and had been fond of each other for a long time. Both had become important men, but in very different ways. One was rich in earthly goods, the other rich in God. This man took it so to heart that his friend left this world without a confession of his faith in Jesus, whose saving name he had brought near to him so often, that he suffered for quite a long time and aged visibly. However, God restored his spiritual liveliness together with the necessary physical strength for his calling. He was very involved in the great Awakening a few years ago, but not so much as an activist. He rather, as would be expected from his maturity in years and experience, directed, led, and corrected, keeping everything on track. We have good reasons not to mention the name of this dear man, since he is, as I said, still living. We ask our dear readers to grant us this restraint. – (We also beg our brothers in England not to record the story of this dear man in public, current newsletters. We are afraid that it could be dangerous if he saw himself become an object of public conversation. Everyone who is acquainted with the characteristic disposition of the Negro will find this concern justified. Such a religious man should not be led astray in this way. Of this we are convinced, and we also wanted to spare him the temptation.)

I was born in Africa around the year 1799 – of course I cannot be sure of the year. The land of the Ibos is my homeland.[1] My father's name was Durl, my mother was the daughter of a great prince and she was called Dirinejah. My name was Aneaso. I remember for certain that my father did not have more than one wife, but lived with my mother alone. Among four children, I was the only son, and thus my father's favourite. I had to be with him all the time, and even when he went to the field, he always took me along. There the very same provisions were grown that serve to nourish the blacks here in Jamaica: yam, European corn, potatoes, etc. While I was happy to accompany my father when he went out, my sisters hardly ever left the house, as was the custom in the land, and if a male guest came, they hid. Even in our heathen ignorance, we were still aware of a highest Being, as indeed every heathen can conclude from the works of creation. We named this Being Tschukudama [Tr: phonetically: chukudama], which means the one who makes the thunder. We also called on this Being for help when we were sick. In addition, we thought that our whole existence ended with death, and we never thought about the future, least of all about a further life of our souls in another world.

I don't remember our heathen pleasures well enough to tell much about them. Just one has stayed in my memory in any detail: The festival of the tattoos. It went this way. When a number of young people from respected aristocratic families grew up and came into adolescence, a great ceremony was held. An outdoor spot was leveled, cleaned and laid with mats, and a trough with a hole was dug to catch the blood. Now some of the designated men who were practised in this operation stepped up, the dense crowd stood around the clearing, and the young people were laid one after the other on the mats, where the operation was performed. The operation often lasted a long time, perhaps about an hour. The symbols that were cut into the skin were different in the different African tribes. For the Iboes the most painful part of the operation was the cutting of a piece of the skin of the head and forehead which was cut an inch long above the eyes. The loss of blood was great, and it sometimes happened that someone died as a martyr to this process. Never, however, could anyone utter the slightest sound of pain. That would be an ineradicable disgrace and shame for the rest of his life. If the operation was successful, the body was rubbed with blood-clotting medicines, and the adolescent was given something to eat. The poor thing then had to prove his courage and strength to endure by approaching the food boldly and enjoying it. When he recuperated and his wounds healed, he appeared before the society of aristocratic men with triumphant pride. He was greeted with great rejoicing, with dancing and joy, was given gifts and invited to parties. Also, from this point on he was free to court any woman, even the daughter of a prince. As the son of an aristocratic woman, I too should have undergone this tattooing, and I must say that I looked forward to this honour.

At one time a young man often visited us, who said, and we believed him, that he wanted to marry one of my sisters. Without a doubt, however, his treacherous eyes were on me, a boy 10 or 12 years old, growing tall and strong. One day he found me alone with my sisters, because my father had gone out for a longer period of time and had not taken me with him as he usually did. The man spent this opportune time trying to convince me by every possible means to accompany him to a nearby market, whose grandness he described colourfully. I was thoughtless enough, or innocent enough, or foolish enough to be persuaded. We walked a whole day without ever reaching the market. Then we stayed with an acquaintance of my guide to rest and then walked further the next day. I noticed that my guide was asked repeatedly along the way what he planned to do with the boy. Did he want to sell him? He always answered that that was not his intention because I was the son of a great and respected man. I was about to experience only too soon, however, what he was up to. Our destination finally came into view: A trade centre on the seacoast. I was in awe of the throng of people, the number of things for sale, everything I saw there. I didn't dare to move ahead until my guide encouraged me to come closer and watch everything boldly. What attracted me the most and made the greatest impression on me was the view before my eyes of the endless wide sea with its turbulent waves, with the ships that lay at some distance at anchor and the boats that were travelling back and forth and rocking on the water. I had never seen this before. As if drunk from the charm of this completely new drama, I lay down under a big tree and just couldn't watch enough of it.

Then a strange man came up to me and said: Come, my boy, come into my boat and try to pilot it on the water. I drew back and answered: No, that I won't do! However, in that same second the man grabbed me with his strong hand and I was carried by force into the boat. Now it was clear that I had been betrayed by my guide and had been sold as a slave; my guide stood calmly on the shore and watched while I was carried away. I rushed to call to him to ask him at least to greet my father and tell him what had become of me. I screamed and cried, as did the other poor blacks whom I saw in the boat, some already bound and some arriving after me in chains. Meanwhile the boat pushed off from the land. After such an intense and upsetting shock, the unaccustomed movement of the waves put me to sleep. When I woke, we had docked on the side of the ship. I watched the great swimming house with great astonishment; we were brought up on board. Once again I was in awe when I saw the white colour of the captain's face and hands, as well as his shiny black feet without toes – he was wearing highly polished boots!

Otherwise the deck was fairly empty, since it was late evening. On the next morning I was horrified and astonished to see a great crowd of bound, moaning and crying people. There could have been six to seven thousand of them, who came out of various lower rooms whose hatches had been opened so they could get air and be served yam and rum on the deck. They kept me together with several other boys my age up on the deck, and we slept in the captain's quarters. I had soon forgotten my troubles as I ran around and ate and drank. I would have been quite happy had I not been terrified each time I saw the other poor slaves coming up on deck out of their caves once every day. I heard their heart-rending wailing; parents shrieked for their children, others for their homeland and their friends. They wanted neither food nor drink. They were cruelly treated and kept in the most secure custody. It was altogether a heart-rending scene.

Finally we reached Kingston (the capital city of Jamaica). The slaves were gradually unloaded. I looked at the land longingly, but remained on the ship while week after week passed. Then I asked the captain to have me brought on land as well. He answered that I had been designated to stay on board and be his servant. I, however, let him know that I wanted to be on land. If he held me back I would jump overboard at the first opportunity. This declaration worked; on that same afternoon I was disembarked and received on the shore by another white man, who had me brought to his estate in the city with eleven other blacks. The gentleman had bought us for the owner of the plantation Krepp, and we were soon carried there. There on the plantation the others were sent to work in the fields, but I had to serve the manager in his house and was given the name Tobi.

After a year, the master of the plantation himself took me into his house as his servant, and I can say that I was treated well there and was loved as the playmate of his children.[2] When the master later, after about eight years, went on a trip to England, the children, and I with them as their servant, were housed in the seaport Savanna la Mar, where we were also supposed to attend church and school. Admittedly, I had no interest in that, even though the opportunity was offered to me as well. I didn't want to hear anything about learning, and during church services I ran around outside in front of the church and enjoyed myself, as the children of the master usually did as well. Thus we spent three years until the master came back. He took us back to the plantation, but he was sick and died not long afterwards. The plantation now fell into the hands of the oldest son, and he made me – at 20 years of age – a lower administrator, or an overseer. A few years later the plantation Krepp was sold and we moved to Dumbasten, another property of my master, where I was again made overseer.

One day the children of my master were baptized there by a priest of the

Anglican State church in Black River.[3] I was invited to be baptized as well at the same time. It had become the fashion at the time to pay to have slaves baptized. No form of Christian instruction was included, however, and the poor slaves had no idea what the holy act really meant.[4] The priest had offered it to me free as a special favour. When I came the next Sunday to actually ask for the baptism, however, I had to pay a shilling to a different priest, who performed it on me and a few other slaves in the church. I imagined that as a result of the act I would go to a good place when I died. The priest said not a single word about Christ, the Saviour of sinners, whose possession we become through the Holy Sacrament after He has won for us everlasting life and the forgiveness of our sins through His blood. I remained in the greatest ignorance, and, just as before the baptism, lived together with a young woman, having no idea that this was no longer appropriate for me as a Christian.

However, thanks be to God, it was about to change. In 1824 the owner of the neighbouring plantation, Paynstown, came back to Jamaica from England. This Mr Cook was a revivalist, and his wife shared his beliefs.[5] Now one evening as I was passing by his plantation on my way home, I met a servant of the master's house by the name of Christine, who was carrying a jug to a spring to collect fresh drinking water. I struck up a conversation with her and heard that on the next day, Sunday, there would be prayers and singing in Paynstown. The master and mistress always did this and had the servants of the house take part in it, too. I asked, "May strangers also attend?"

"Yes, of course", was the answer. "Mrs Cook has already said she is sorry that no one from the neighbourhood wants to come to prayers; strangers may come, and not just on Sunday, but every day to morning and evening prayers."[6]

This conversation made a particular impression on me. Day and night I could not rid myself of the thought of the prayers in Paynstown. It was as if something were pricking my heart, and finally I decided to go there on Sunday. My fellow slaves, whom I told about this, laughed at me and said I was a fool. They said I wanted to be subservient, that I was intruding in the house of a white man. I stayed with my decision, however, and thought: If they don't want me, a black creature, to be there, then they can chase me away; I probably won't get a severe punishment for it. So when Sunday came, I went at the appointed hour. On the way, however, I was still not just a little afraid. I stopped frequently and thought about what I would say if someone asked me why I came. In any case, I came near and was spotted by a black servant who was standing in the doorway of the big grand house. This man called to me cheerfully. Then I saw Mrs Cook herself step into the doorway. I heard how the servant told her my name and she answered him: "Let him come in. I'm happy that he came." Very shyly I came into the house and waited outside the hall until a little bell announced the beginning of the prayers. This was the first time in my life, even as long as I had been in contact with whites, that I had experienced anything like that. Mr Cook held the prayers. People sang, then he read a little from the Bible, and finally he prayed. I don't remember what he read or what he said in the prayers. I understood little or nothing of it because I still knew nothing of the Saviour. Nevertheless, I will never, never forget this hour. It was one of the deciding hours of my whole life. I felt the presence of the almighty God, my Lord. I was deeply terrified; my limbs trembled. Unable to say a single word, I rushed away afterwards and stayed very quietly at home.

On the next day I met with our sister Elizabeth Dickenson, who at that time was still completely unawakened and lived indifferently. She did have some knowledge of Christian teachings, however, because her parents had visited the Brotherhood Mission Church at the Old Carmel station that was later abandoned.[7] I told her what I had experienced, and she took it in with interest. She accompanied me first on Sundays, and then every evening to Paynstown. After a bit, others joined us on Sundays, and finally we were a little crowd that went to Paynstown to the meeting. One Sunday Mr Cook greeted us with the notice that a missionary had arrived at the nearby plantation Hopeton.[8] He would hold a worship service there. He himself was going there with his family, and he invited us to follow him. We started on the way immediately. In Hopeton the good old Mrs Senior (the mother-in-law of Mr Scott) greeted us with a friendliness that moved me. She said: "It is good that you have come. I am always very happy when I see Negroes that want to love Jesus too. I will lead you now to a doctor for your souls, who will tell you what to do to be saved."

For us all, this man was the unforgettable Brother Ellis. We heard the sermon and then the Brother spoke to us one by one. He wrote down my name. Brother Ellis lived then rather far away at the Mesopotamian Station and from that time on came to Hopeton every eight weeks to hold meetings in Mr Scott's house and to instruct the Negroes. In between, we went to Paynstown.

One Sunday Mrs Cooper asked me if I would like to learn to read. She wanted to teach me. That was very nice for me. Indeed, I brought the scorn and derision of my fellow slaves upon myself with this, because it seemed foolish to them that I wanted to read the white people's book. I didn't let that drive me crazy, though. Rather, I happily took advantage of every opportunity – and how often I have thanked my dear Saviour, and how I still thank him now, that in this way I was so lucky to be able to read His word myself!

In the house of Mr Cooper, the servants also consisted of Christian-minded people. Once the white nanny complained to me that people danced on Sunday in Jamaica, and that living in sin was very commonplace.[9] I was quite struck by this because I was a passionate dancer and was already living with a fourth woman, totally unaware that this was a sin. Every day I saw and was a witness to the fact that the white gentlemen, who were Christians and were far above us in education, lived the same way. I had already acquired a little Christian knowledge: I had memorized the Ten Commandments, and I had taken deep into my heart what I had heard about the love of Jesus, our Saviour, with the sincere desire to love him in return and to follow him. However, "my knowledge and understanding were still shrouded in darkness". I still could not discern clearly and certainly what was right and wrong. I was surrounded by people who were just as ignorant as I or even completely heathen. I did not dare to ask a white man like Mr Cooper; the distance between white and black, master and slave, was still so great at that time that such communication was unthinkable. Brother Ellis lived too far away from us. When he did come once to Hopeton, he was in too much demand for me to be able to speak with him. It was then the Saviour's especially merciful leading that caused Mr Cooper one day to come to me. Just as if he could read my soul, he said in a friendly way that I should not be afraid to ask him about anything that still wasn't clear to me, or that I didn't understand. He wanted to give me information and to teach me. I accepted gratefully, and from that time on he often instructed me. This was a great blessing to my heart and supported me on my way to salvation.

At that same time I made a new discovery in relationship to the observance of Sunday. We slaves had Saturday and Sunday free. That applied to me as well, even though I was no longer a common field worker, but supervised as a sort of manager. Sunday was market day in Black River and other cities. We used to go to the fields on Sundays, I, too, when I came from Paynstown, to tend our own fruits, or to carry these to sell. At one time I was so taken up with getting more for myself that from very early on Sundays I strenuously worked, dug and planted, instead of going to church. Then the thought that this was not right, that it was not according to God's command, came over me with such force I could not resist it. I threw away the pickaxe, knelt down in the hole that I had just dug, and implored, indeed, shouted at the Saviour to make His path and His will known to me, to advise and help me and lighten my darkness. Immediately my prayer was heard, and I knew in my heart that my profit-motivated Sunday labours had displeased the Saviour greatly. At the same time I was absolutely convinced that none of the necessities of my life as a poor slave would be denied me if I only strived above all things towards the kingdom of God and his righteousness. This last I said from the bottom of my heart to my Lord and my Saviour. From this time on I have not touched my hoe on Sunday, but have worked all the harder on Saturday in my field. The Saviour, however, has blessed me outwardly above my expectations and my understanding, so that I have never suffered any need.

Now during this time that I began to know Jesus as my Saviour and was in the first fiery love for Him, eagerly confessing Him to others, my master, to whom I had clung from my youth on, really did not like me. He treated me very harshly and strictly and sought opportunities to find fault with my work. When I was not able to work as usual because I was sick, he never missed the chance to add to his invective that all this came from my running to the accursed Paynestown and from the praying. He wouldn't stand this piety in the blacks any longer, and so on. Finally we were forbidden to go to Paynestown after work or on Sundays. There was another reason, however, since my master, who had been so prosperous, had squandered his money and fallen deep into debt. He was afraid that his creditors would catch us slaves and sell us. Now I couldn't attend the gatherings any more. My master's anger hurt me; consequently, I became gradually more lethargic and indifferent. My heart felt cold without the earlier love of Jesus. (Oh, what a great thing the Christian community is!) I had no peace; I was very worried and depressed and just didn't know what to do. During this time the words of one of the missionaries of the Brethren whom I once met were very helpful. He said to me: "When things go badly for you, it is a test. Just pray harder that the light of the sun that is hidden behind the clouds will shine again." It was like that. I turned to the Lord, told him in unceasing prayer of my need, was comforted and thus warmed again to new love. A little at a time I returned to the earlier relationship of the heart with the Saviour, in which superficial need no longer could disturb me.

To my great joy and encouragement, and also as proof that the Lord had not abandoned me, the following circumstance restored my inner peace. The aforementioned Christine, who first showed me the way to the prayers in Paynestown, who thus through the hand of the Lord had been the first instrument of my conversion, and whom out of gratitude I had visited often, became ill. I went as soon as I heard of it and found her suffering so terribly that I thought immediately that her end might be near. But the state of her heart did not seem to be right, and in the silence this bothered me inexpressibly. She seemed to be still caught up in self-righteousness and thus was also without the proper comfort of faith. I sat down near her bed and asked if she were sure of the forgiveness of her sins. She answered, when she did anything bad, she always called upon God for forgiveness; however, she had always tried to do good, etc.

"No," I said, "dear Christine, that is not what I mean. Let me ask it another way: Do you know and are you convinced that we humans would all have to be lost and damned as eternal sinners if God had not sent His Son into the world for our salvation? Can you now take comfort that the blood of the Son of God shed on the cross is a full ransom for the whole world and also for your sins?"

I was given the chance to witness the sins and the grace, when the patient said without prompting: "Yes, so it is. I am also a lost sinful creature, but I trust that the blood of Christ justifies me and God will accept me through the mercy of Christ!"

"What did you say?" I called out, as I moved very close to her bed. "Dear Christine, oh, say that once more. I badly want to hear these words from your mouth again!" She repeated it and I went on, "Oh, dear Christine, please tell me if I can really believe that you want to go into eternity with this belief." She repeated her confession once more, and I knelt down and prayed fervently at her bedside. The expression on her face now showed her inner peace and comfort and was sweet to look upon. The fear was gone; the Lord had returned to her. After some time she sat up straight in bed, her eyes toward heaven. I noticed that her eyes were already blank. Immediately she sank back and died without any pain or struggle. I was shocked that the end came so soon because I had not expected it. Yet my heart was full of praise and thanks and adoration to God that in her last hour I could lead the person who was the instrument of His hand that first put my foot on the path of salvation, to the source of all comfort and peace. Yes, the name of the Lord be praised for that!

Also, when I could get permission, I gradually began to attend the church in Black River again, where I had been baptized. I also wanted to become a communicant and asked the superintending minister about it. He said that I would have to be married in the church to do it. The woman with whom I was living, however, did not share my faith. She hated the gospel, swore at the church, and was angry every time I went. My attempts to convince her otherwise were all in vain, so a church wedding was impossible. I decided, however, to leave her completely, and lived for a considerable while alone. The Lord is my witness that I also was not guilty of any wrongdoing with the opposite sex. The Lord protected me despite all the dangers of the customs of the country, particularly in the relationships in the lives of the slaves. By the grace of the Lord, although I was outwardly bound, I had still become inwardly free. I was so blessed by my Saviour, he was so near to me. I trusted Him with my whole heart. No matter where I went or stood, working or resting, my heart was so full of peace and joy. In Him I had enough; I had my joy in the Lord, and he gave me what my heart desired.

Since I now couldn't remain single because of my circumstances, I proposed marriage to a young person in Paynstown, who I was sure loved the Saviour – I got to know her as the most faithful attendee of the devotions in the manor house – and she said yes. At first my master did not want to hear of it. However, as I brought the matter to the Saviour in prayer, and fervently asked Him to lead everything according to His will, then it happened that my master and his wife thought better of it during a visit to the church in Black River and took back their ban. After that I was actually married in the church there on the 8th of June, 1826. Since it was an especially popular market day, the church was more full than usual. As the wedding ceremony for us and a few other black couples who followed our example went on, the white spectators broke out in laughter. In loud voices they made fun of us, that now black people were so pretentious as to consider themselves equal to whites. The agitation was so great by the end that the pastor could barely restore the peace of the holy place, even with the most serious words. His rebuke did work, however, and the wedding ceremony could be carried out. Now I had in my Rebecca a legitimately married lifelong companion, and was very happy about that.

The year 1827 finally brought us the great joy of seeing a missionary stay among us. It was the same Brother Scholefield[10] who had visited us earlier from Mesopotamia. Now he came to Hopeton, where the Scott family furnished an apartment for him until the new station on their property, New Carmel, was built. I cannot express in words how happy I and another converted slave in our area were that we had a pastor of our own for our own well-being, and that we were to have a church building in which we could gather undisturbed. Brother Scholefield gave the first sermon on Good Friday on the text: I do not pretend among you that I know anything but Jesus the Crucified. It made a deep impression on all those present. And as we prayed the Easter litany on the morning of the first Easter celebration at the open area at the new station, we were completely taken. Yes, the Saviour who was crucified for us and rose was there with us, not visible, but tangibly near our hearts. Now after a few months I was taken in as a member of the congregation. The number of members at that time was twelve persons. Many others came with us to church, however, at our dear own Carmel, and the number of those who wanted to become members grew from week to week in an amazing way.

This was a blessed time for me, a time of refreshment, after which, according to the will of God, a painful test was to follow. I became ill with gout and in the end became so incapacitated that I could move neither head nor foot and had to be fed like a little child. My master had me cared for well and called white doctors himself for their advice, but all was in vain. No one believed that I would ever recover. I withered into a shadow. The faithful Mrs Cooper took an interest in me, too, and did many good deeds for me. Then, after I had lain in this state for more than half a year, a coloured man appeared with an offer to help me. He had me drink tea from a plant that grew in the country. This was so sharp and biting that my whole mouth hurt from it. However, the painful first effects gradually could be seen, and by continued use of the substance, to the astonishment of all, I actually finally regained the use of my arms and legs completely. My master then sent me to the sea, where I had to bathe twice a day in order to regain my earlier strength. By God's blessing this goal was reached.

But it was not just my body that was supposed to recuperate; the Lord healed my soul as well. My heart burned with love for Him, my gracious and merciful Saviour, who had drawn me, a poor lost sinner, to him out of pure grace and mercy. This love received new power and strength in that I became a communicant in Carmel. Since shortly after that I was appointed to the office of national assistant, from that time on I had many opportunities to tell others what the Lord had done for me, and to point them to the same Saviour. With this goal I attended the evening lessons after work finished on the plantations here and there. I was readily received when I brought out the Bible and read to the people and spoke to their hearts. In Woodlands these meetings were forbidden by the administrator and the participants punished. They didn't let themselves be frightened away, however; I know of only one man who stayed away because of this, while he made untruthful excuses to us. Unfortunately, I have to say that this same person is still a lost sheep who neither knows nor loves Jesus.

A meeting that I held on the plantation Hampstadt, where my wife was from, made a lasting impression on my mind at this time. After I had read from the Holy Scriptures and was speaking about how we are redeemed not by gold or silver, but rather with the costly blood of Christ, the blessed certainty came to me that I too was a child of God and Jesus' possession. The feeling that the presence of the Saviour was in the midst of us who were gathered in His name came over me with such power and force that it was as if I were enchanted; my mouth overflowed with what filled my heart. Even if my poor words were just a weak expression of it, my listeners still felt the power of the holy truths that I told them in such a way that one could see in most of them the emotion and the moving of their hearts. Each one went home from this meeting quietly moved. A few pressed my hand hard, and one said: "Brother, the Lord restored you out of love for us; we need to be strengthened in faith."

In 1832, in the northern part of our island, in the area of Montego Bay, a rebellion broke out. The slaves refused to work and moved through the countryside with fire and sword. The fear was great. I first heard about it from my master, who told me about it in great agitation, and at first didn't want to believe it. My master was able to convince himself soon, however, that he had nothing to fear. We went to work peacefully and in an emergency would have protected our masters. It was the same way in Hopeton and on the other plantations where the mission work already had firm roots among the people. Nevertheless, military troops saturated our area as well, and on Sundays a post was set at the church in Carmel to watch over us. Because short shrift was made of the disturbance and also many innocent people along with the guilty ones suffered, it was natural that many of us greatly feared the red jackets.[II]

Later came the announcement of the pending emancipation; a period of preparation was supposed to precede it, of six years for field workers and four years for house servants. When Brother Scholefield read the announcement to us in church, the long period of preparation was hard for many, for the longing for freedom was very great. However, we were all still happy and thankful, as we all had reason to be. As concerned work, the conditions of slavery were quite bearable and orderly, and no one could forbid Sunday church attendance any longer. Now whole throngs, even sick and elderly who had to drag themselves there, came to church from the plantations whose hard and cruel masters had until then kept them away by strict bans and hard physical punishment. Now and then one would try to put obstacles in the way because of enmity toward the gospel, but the power of these men had been broken. The church in Carmel was more full every successive Sunday, and often there was so little space for the people that outside the church there was preaching in three different places at the same time in the shade of the trees. Then our dear preacher, Brother Scholefield, usually asked me to preach, together with Brother Hamilton. At that time poor Brother Hamilton seemed to be very moved, but later he became an unbeliever again.

On one plantation, a depraved overseer had earlier derived disgraceful pleasure in tempting young people of both sexes to do sinful things with each other. Now they refused, after they had been taught better things in the church. The overseer became furious with me because I visited there often and held meetings. Before the attorney or inspector of the plantation, who lived in Savanna la Mar, he accused me of keeping the people up until 12 midnight so that they were unable to work the next day, and other things. Thus I was summoned to this attorney, but went confidently and convinced that the Saviour would stand by me. So it was. I answered all the questions quietly and truthfully, and at the end the attorney said to me: "All right, I now believe that you do no harm. As a matter of fact, I'd like you to visit my plantation, if the people would like it." A week later he himself gathered the people together on his plantation and asked them. When they all requested heartily that I come to them, in front of everyone he ceremoniously gave me permission and pardoned me. Thus the Lord helped me marvelously, but he did more than that.

Not long afterwards the true owner of this and several other plantations came back from England to our island. His return was celebrated in the usual way by all the slaves he owned: That is, they were allowed to gather in the evenings in front of the great house. Rum was distributed and then they danced and spent the whole night until bright morning in drunkenness and festivity, with much sinful and disgraceful heathen behaviour. Now when this master came to the abovementioned plantation and let the people know that they could come and drink and dance, he was completely amazed at the answer he received: "Master, we are no longer heathens. We have become Christians, and we don't enjoy drinking rum and dancing, but we will pray for you."

"Fine," said the master. "Then come up here and pray for me!" The people did so very simply. They sang some blessings for the master who had returned, and then the assistant, Brother Pinnok, read a chapter from the Bible and spoke a few words to express the joy of everyone at the arrival of the master. Finally the whole crowd knelt down for the prayer that Brother Pinnok gave, and – what did the master and the overseer do? They bent their knees and prayed as well. Then everyone went back to their cottages quietly and peacefully, as they had come.

When I visited the plantation the next day, I was ordered to come into the great house. When I arrived, the owner, the overseer and a few other white men were together in the hall. I was asked to come in; they even asked me to sit on one of the chairs. "Why do you keep my Negroes from dancing?" the owner asked.

"My master," I answered, "I don't do that. The word of God forbids them the earlier heathen festivities."

"That's nonsense!" called one of the others, a certain Dr Gilpin, "the Bible tells how David danced, and that Solomon kept no less than 300 wives."

The gentlemen laughed, I kept still, and so the owner continued: "Show me the places in the Bible that you believe you are referring to."

"Now," I said, "Dear sir, for one thing I don't place much value on the Old Testament although I would have something to say regarding the leadership of King David and his son Solomon. For we live in the era of the New Covenant and the question is what we can learn from the gospel of our Saviour Jesus Christ. If you, dear sir, commanded one of your slaves to do something, and he refused and wanted to do something else, because he referred to what had been the custom on the plantation during your father's time, would you allow him to do it?"

"No," answered the master. "I would have him whipped."

"Thus, then," I said, "the gospel of the New Testament has to be the guideline for our life. I mean the teachings of Christ, the son of God, who died for us and rose and now sits at the right hand of God and leads the regiment that the Father has given power over all flesh, by which he makes everyone blessed who believes in him. And what does this teaching say to us? Look right here at this place I have open right here, Galatians 5, v. 16–22: 'But I say,' writes Paul there, 'walk by the Spirit, and do not gratify the desires of the flesh. For the desires of the flesh are against the Spirit, and the desires of the Spirit are against the flesh; for these are opposed to each other, to prevent you from doing what you would. But if you are led by the Spirit you are not under the law. Now the works of the flesh are plain; immorality, impurity, licentiousness, idolatry, sorcery, enmity, strife, jealously, anger, selfishness, dissension, party spirit, envy, drunkenness, carousing and the like. I warn you, as I warned you before, that those who do such things shall not inherit the kingdom of God. But the fruits of the Spirit are love, joy, peace, patience, kindness, goodness, faithfulness, gentleness, self-control; against such there is no law. And those who belong to Christ Jesus have crucified the flesh with its passions and desires.' " The conversation had now taken a serious turn.

When the master of the plantation stood up after a time, he gave me his hand and said: "There is nothing wrong with that. You may go ahead and teach on my plantation. As a matter of fact, I would like it."

The wagon had come by then, the men got in, and the master put out his hand to me once more and said, "Just come as often as you can and want to."

This event opened the doors not just to this plantation, but to many. I was now, so to speak, recognized and was publicly confirmed in my position as visitor to plantations. I just did not have time, because I was very bound up in my work. Once, in Black River, I visited Mr Dodridge, who was the highest magistrate in our district. He had always proven to be a warm friend of the mission, and was also warm towards me. I told him what I related above and said that I now greatly desired to buy my freedom. Up to this point he had always advised me against this because he believed that I would be viewed with more suspicion as a free man and would be even more hindered from holding meetings. But with these new developments, he no longer objected and advised me not to let my value be set by the courts. They would set such a high price that I would not be able to pay it. Rather, I should go to my master and try to arrange a price privately with him. I went to him immediately and presented my request. He was not really pleased, and tried everything he could to dissuade me. He reminded me that in three years, when Emancipation came, I would be free without paying anything, etc. My longing to be free was, however, so great that I persisted. On the next day my master brought me his decision himself.

"I have discussed your request with my family and thought it over. We have loved you from the time you were small, and it is true that you have given us immense service on this plantation and have kept the people in order, especially during the rebellion. Therefore we want no more than £30 for each of the remaining three years. That means £90 (450 Talers) altogether."

The figure shocked me. It exceeded my expectations by far. I did not dare to say anything, though, so I was silent. On the next morning my master came again and said: "We calculated it again, and you can be free for £50." I paid then everything I had saved, and after some time brought the rest. For that sum my letter of freedom was drawn up. Oh, how my heart beat, full of praise and thanks to God, when I finally received the longed-for certificate of freedom! This day has always remained a holiday for celebration for me. It was 1 June 1837.

The first thing I did as a free man was to put on my Sunday clothes and ride to Mount Carmel, where our preacher and pastor Brother Collis now was. Everyone was amazed to see me on a weekday that was also a workday, but I shouted loudly from far away: "Rejoice with me! I am free, thanks be to God!" Brother Collis and all the others in Carmel shared my joy and praised the Lord, the giver of all good things, with me.

After this time I was offered opportunities to manage several plantations and other similar things, but that was not what I wanted because my effectiveness in working for the kingdom of God just could not connect with these. However, I was very happy when Brother Zorn from the mission asked me to dedicate my time and energy fully to service as a national assistant, with the annual support of £12 for myself and my family.[12] I bought a little piece of land and a small house in Rose Hall, in which I have lived since then with my wife and our only daughter, who was given to us by the Lord after eleven years of marriage. An older daughter from an earlier woman married one of our schoolteachers. It is my deepest desire that both learn to love Jesus more and more as their Saviour and as our highest good and follow Him in faith to the end!

Unexpectedly rapidly, already in April 1838, Emancipation came about, and all the slaves received complete civil freedom. That was a magnificent change in all circumstances, and I rejoiced in my heart to see everyone who had been under the same yoke as I was now released. Many of my earlier fellow slaves were very thankful, not just for this or that good that I had done for them as overseer, but also that I had never allowed them, for example, to take anything that belonged to the master, even though this was a common practice during slavery, and considered to be permitted. It was not hard for them, as free people, to be honest and keep their hands away from possessions of others. Others who continued in the usual unfaithfulness and theft caused a lot of trouble in their areas and found themselves punished. – Thank the Lord that we are free! The yoke of slavery was in many ways a barrier to the conversion of the poor Negroes. In many ways it made growth difficult, as well as the recognition and following of Jesus! Oh, however, I hope all of us, my black brothers and sisters and I, to whom this great gift of freedom has been given, not only will hear the Word of Life, but also will take it to heart, repent and believe. I hope we will prove our faith through deeds, so that on that great day when we must account for whether or not we have made the most of the pound of grace we were entrusted, our tribesmen still living in the shadow of darkness and death in heathen Africa will not witness against us! And now for the end of my story:

What grace, what mercy, that the Lord brought me, a poor African, born a heathen, an ignorant, despised slave, to his light! That even I may take his word as having been said to me: I have loved you forever and ever, out of pure goodness and mercy I have drawn you to me! That I may see myself as his dearly bought possession, that in faith through grace I have been reborn to a living hope in eternal life! That he deems me worthy to help spread the Gospel in his service! That I may dedicate my whole life to this occupation in which I already feel so blessed, to win souls for his kingdom! These are all matters about which I cannot say enough; words fail me.

I am heartily thankful to all my dear missionaries, who have shown me so much goodness and love. When I visit them individually here and there, or when I see them together at their conferences, they say to me, "Brother, when are you coming to see me again? Why don't you go here or there? There is work to do. They need help." Then I feel so humble and ashamed, and so happy in my service! The Lord who found me in my blood said to me: You shall live, for you believe that even the least and the most unworthy are not too lowly to receive my mercy. Now he will keep me in his grace and faith until the end of my life. Christ's blood and righteousness are my jewelry and clothes of honour; in these I want to stand before God when I enter heaven.

With sadness I look across from our land here, where we now have the Word of God living among us in such abundance, and also enjoy so many of the good deeds of God in our external lives as free people, to the land of my birth, heathen, dark Africa! Oh, that the light of the Gospel may soon brighten it!

Notes

1. In West Africa, belonging to Nigritien (Nigeria?), known for its slave trade, as was the land of the Mandingos on the Gambia River as well. The Ibos were formerly known in Jamaica, more than the Congolese, Mandingos, and others, for their peacefulness and industry, but also for their modest intelligence, apparent in their difficulty in speaking English. The example in this story shows, however, that there could also be intelligent people among them. (By now the noticeable differences among the different African tribes have long since disappeared.)

2. It was partly this preferential treatment that accounts for his pleasant appearance and his cheerful, clever personality. Otherwise, slavery at that time, in Jamaica as well, was harsh. On many plantations that were in the hands of non-Christian owners, or in the absence of the owners were managed by officers of the same sort, the required amount of work could barely be accomplished. The punishments were cruel, for example, the terrible treadmills, useful instruments of torture that took many lives.

3. This was also a seaport on the south coast of the island, like Savanna-la-Mar.

4. The baptism of slaves was allowed by an act of Parliament and was done for money at the request of the aristocracy. One did not feel obliged, however, to impart an arduous religious instruction to the despised blacks.

5. Most planters of that time lived together with black or coloured mistresses without the benefit of marriage and were completely un-Christian and unchurched.

6. The clergy of the High Church did no mission work itself among the heathen black slaves, but certainly did nothing to hinder the Christian efforts of private revivalists to spread the kingdom of God among the slaves who were living in their wretched ignorance. This noble freedom was useful for the salvation of many poor slaves, who were brought to Christian faith and won for the Lord by unconventional means. They became active members of the State church itself, or of another denomination.

7. In 1823, after all the sisters there died of poor health that resulted from the swampy, low location, the Old Carmel station was abandoned. In its place Fairfield on the Mayday Mountains was established in the Manchester District, a few days' trip from the setting of this story in the St Elizabeth District. The Mesopotamia Station, not far from the coast in the south, and New Eden, at the foot of the mountains going through the Manchester District, lay somewhat nearer. In 1827 New Carmel was established in the area of Hopeton, near to Paynstown. In this earlier time the expansion of the mission of the Brothers in all directions was hindered by the conditions of slavery.

8. The very rich and aristocratic Scott family resided on this plantation, a white Christian family who facilitated the mission work of the Brothers in this area and donated the land for the establishment of the New Carmel Station in their neighbourhood. Later they became less prosperous, but to this day they remain very closely bound to the mission and through their faithful confession in word and deed are a blessing to their area.

9. It was called at that time: Jamaica fashion, living after the fashion in Jamaica.

10. Brother Scholefield, a conscientious missionary, especially gifted in revival, activating, and gathering people, less prone to order and leading. Later he also established the Bethany station and managed it himself with great success until he returned to England because of illness and died still in the best years of his life.

11. In many places on the island war courts were set up. Those who were suspected of being agitators or participants were brought in, interrogated briefly, and if found guilty, shot immediately. It is certain that some completely innocent members of our congregations, who had dared out of ignorance to leave their plantations, were caught, or also were denounced by those who were hostile to the church. Even a few national assistants were executed. Our brother Pfeiffer, missionary in New Eden, was picked up by soldiers and brought before the war court in Mandeville. A white man who had allowed unspeakable cruelties against the Negroes while overseeing a neighbouring plantation in order to gain more for himself through their work, and to whom Brother Pfeiffer occasionally had been a hindrance in this cruelty, bribed a couple of Negroes to swear that Brother Pfeiffer had instigated rebellion in a sermon. Brother Pfeiffer was in harsh imprisonment for about two weeks, during which executions followed one after the other, and only through the marvelous help of God did he escape death. One of the perjurers was himself accused and shot shortly afterwards; the other lived several more years, but went about as if he had been banned and finally, we hope, died peacefully. In the northern part of the island, in the area surrounding Montego Bay, where the rebellion first broke out against the big sugar plantations there, the churches, not of the blacks, but of the whites, were destroyed due to the harsh treatment of the slaves. The Baptist missionaries who were active there (who, however, involved themselves in political affairs really more than was seemly for their occupation) barely escaped their hands by fleeing.

12. John Collis, a very gifted speaker, whose affability and unusual wit and good cheer made him especially loved by the slaves, died in New Carmel in 1838 after a short, very busy period of service. Jacob Zorn died in Fairfield on 27 May 1843 at forty years of age, worn out by the excessive amount of work. He was the generally highly esteemed president of the Mission Conference, serving as preacher at the same time as representative in external affairs. Because of his gift not just to activate, but also to organize and to lead, he was the major tool in the hand of the Lord during the upturn of our mission work in Jamaica at the time.

Appendix 2

Archibald John Monteith

Native Helper and Assistant in the
Jamaica Mission at New Carmel

This text was originally published in *Transactions of the Moravian Historical Society* 21, part 1 (1966): 29–51.

Editorial Note

When the Rev. Joseph Horsfield Kummer served New Carmel, Jamaica, he became well-acquainted with Archibald Monteith, a former slave who was then a prominent Helper in the Moravian Church on that island. The account of Monteith's life printed on the following pages is reproduced from a manuscript booklet in the Archives of the Moravian Church in Bethlehem, Pennsylvania. Dated 1853, the account is written in Kummer's own hand.[1] As was the case in previous printings, Archibald Monteith's story will be allowed to speak for itself. Only a few notes will be added for the reader's convenience . . .

– Vernon H. Nelson, Editor

Archibald Monteeth,[2] a Helper in the Congregation at New Carmal, Jamaica,[3] and a member of that church, often called on us, and during my official stay at that station during *1853* and part of *1854*, I had many interesting and edifying conversations with him. He gave me at various times *this account*, or *fragments* of account of his life.—He was also a *General Helper* for all our stations in the island, and at stated times, say once or twice a year made visits, to see and speak with the people, both in Churches and at their houses. He also frequently *assisted* me in the *very large New Carmel* Congregation by keeping the 2nd Meeting on Sunday, and *always* had something to say, to the point, in Monthly Missionary Prayer Meetings. I considered him a *remarkable* man. An *eminent* subject of *divine grace;* very humble; full of confidence in the Lord Jesus; believing with all his heart the glorious gospel, and delighting to make it known to his fellowmen. I was always much impressed by listening to his prayers & addresses.—

J.H. Kummer.[4]

I was born, as far as I can remember, taking into account the time when I left my native land, in the year 1799. I was born in Africa, and belong to the nation or tribe called Eboe's.[5] My fathers name was ———.[6] My mother was called Dirinejah; her father was a prince, and the daughter was named after the father. My name was Aneaso. Although my native land is a heathen land, and though my father was a heathen, and polygamy is generally prevalent, I can distinctly remember, that my father only lived with the above mentioned Dirinejah, with whom he had 4 children, three daughters, and myself was the only son. As an only Son I was the favorite of my father with whom I generally labored in the field and provision ground, the yield of which is very much the same as here in Jamaica; yams, potatoes, Indian Corn etc. etc. My sisters seldom went out of the house, but kept themselves within, according to the custom of the land; and especially if any one of the male sex came to see us; they would closely conceal themselves.

The God or Being in whose existence every heathen believes, because the works of creation declare this, was called Tschuku, or Tschuku-damma. He makes the thunder and lightning etc. etc. We only prayed to him when we were sick, so that he should speedily make us well. Did we recover and get well again, then there was an end of prayer. When death came, then everything ceased to be, at least so we thought, and as is customary among the heathen, we did not trouble ourselves about futurity. As to what is called "pleasures", I did not know much, for I was too young: Still, the festival of Tatooing, is best remembered by me, for, as the Son of a Prince's daughter, I was soon to attain unto that honour, in view of which I very much rejoiced, but you know, my minister, that it was never performed upon me, for I left my native country before it could be done. I know however how it is done and have witnessed the process young as I was. The process is as follows.

When a number of young people, of distinguished parents, have attained the proper age, the men who perform the tatooing are sent for; then a large place is cleared and cleansed, a mat is laid down, and a hole dug, to catch the blood. Then one after the other lays down on the mat, in order to have the operation performed, whilst a numerous company stand in a circle around the place. The operation takes from half an hour, to an hour, to have it performed. Each tribe has its own special sign; that of the Eboe tribe is one of the most difficult and painful, as the skin is so loosened from the head, that after the healing has taken place the skin hangs over the eyes for a considerable space. Although the operation is very painful and the loss of blood so great that those standing around can see and hear the blood running, the suffering subject, for the sake of his honour must not make the slightest noise, or give any token of feeling. When the cutting is accomplished, the wounds were rubbed with powder and salt, and to the one tatooed was given a piece of yam or corn cake, which he must eat, and apparently enjoy, as though he felt no pain. After some time, when the wounds have been healed, and the lad comes for the first time into company, there is great rejoicing and festivity. He is highly honoured; receives many presents, and can obtain any rich woman whom he desires, for his wife. The operation, however often ends in death. If the one so wounded and martyred, does not remain steadfast, and unflinchingly goes through the whole process, but becomes weakened, or cries, or shows any feeling,—he will be derided and ridiculed as long as he lives. As painful as this process is, yet, for the sake of the honour, the most desire it and rejoice to have it performed.

When I was about 10 years old, a young man came frequently to see us; he wished to have my sister for his wife. One day he asked me to go with him to the market place. Knowing nothing about the distance to the place, I, at once complied, without saying any thing to my father, who no doubt would not have given his consent. After we had walked for a whole day, we came to an acquaintance of the young man, and here we remained several days. Then we all went together to the market which we soon reached. Here I saw a great many things I had never seen before, and which greatly astonished me; but most of all was I pleased with the great water, the ocean. Then my companion and guide said, "Go nearer to the water, then you can see every thing better." I did so, and leaning on a Kenepp tree, looked around, and was filled with astonishment to see the boats floating on the water, and most of all to see the great water itself. A man said to me; "Come into my boat, and try how you like the sailing about." I said, "No, that I will not do." Then he suddenly came upon me took me up, and carried me to his boat, and put me in.—Now I immediately knew that I would be made a slave, for I remembered that during the whole day I had frequently heard, when my guide was asked;—"What are you going to do with boy; Sell him?["] say in reply; "Oh no; he is a great man's son!" But still when the right man came along, he sold me, and I could do nothing but call to him; "tell my father where I am, and salute him" I was frightened and wept a little, but soon comforted myself, because I was fond of sailing in the boat. The other slaves screamed loud, and would neither eat nor drink. I however soon fell asleep. When I awoke I saw a large ship before me. I was not a little astonished to see such a beautiful house floating on the water; and when I was put on board nothing surprised me more, than to see the Captain with white face and hands, and with shining black feet without toes; (he wore boots) On the ship, there was scarcely any one else to be seen, as it was towards evening, and getting dark; hence I was not a little surprised the next morning, when various holes were opened to see 600 or 700[7] slaves brought up on deck, to whom yams were given for food, and rum for drink. Myself and 11 other boys were taken by the Captain into the cabin. We were happy; skipped about, eat and drank, and yet I felt very sorry when I saw the other slaves come up from the hold of the ship daily, into the air, and heard their heartrending cries of anguish; fathers & mothers longing for their homes and children, and often would neither eat nor drink, and were so strictly watched and held in such rigid confinement.—

We reached Kingston, Jamaica safely, and here the sale of the slaves began. We lay in the harbour about six weeks; as yet I had never got on shore, which I wished very much to see. I then said to the Captain; "Let me go on shore!" he answered, "No, you shall remain with me and be my servant!" I answered, "No! that I do not wish, I want to go on shore, if you will not let me go, I will jump overboard." In the afternoon the Captain consented, and immediately as I reached shore, a gentleman came and bought me, together with 11 other slaves, for our future master and drove us all into his yard. After 8 days, our new master, Mr Monteeth, to whom the Estate Kepp, which is near to New Carmel, belonged, sent for us. Having reached that place, we had one weeks rest given us; then the others went to the field-work, and me the manager of the Estate took as his servant in the house, and called me Tobi. In the course of a year Mr Monteeth took me as servant in his house, and I cannot but say, he always treated me the same as a father; Yes, minister, the Lord be praised, I had no cruel master like some other slaves. After 8 years my master went to England, and sent me with other children to Savannah La Mar to attend school. I however saw no use of learning or going to school & church, and I never heard, from those who had charge of us, a word about God, or about what was done in Church. I learned nothing; but we jumped, and danced and romped, and did pretty much as we pleased.—

After 3 years Mr Monteeth returned. We then went back to the Kepp. Not long after, however, my master died, and I then belonged to his son, and he made me "overseer." When I was in my *20th* year I lived with a young woman; I did not know that it was wrong and sinful. After some years, the Kepp was sold, and we moved to Dunbarken, where I became the head manager for Mr Monteeth's large property. Here one day Mr Monteeth's children were baptised, by the Parish Minister of the Church of England. On this occasion the minister said to me; "Come Tobi, in 8 days I will baptise you, gratis." This minister however did not return, but another one came, and I was obliged to pay him 8/ (8 shillings) for the service. He baptised me, and named me Archibald John Monteeth. He also baptised many others at the same time; all done in the Church at Black River, without saying one word to us, as to why we were baptised, and what it meant; this no one told us. It had become customary to baptise, and we negroes thought, that if we are baptised, then when we died, we would come into a beautiful place. That there is a Saviour who died for us, and that we are to love and serve him; of this we heard nothing.

In the year 1824, the gentleman to whom Paynestown Estate belonged, Mr Coke,[8] returned from England. Soon after this, late one Saturday evening as I was returning from Lennox to Dunbarton, I met a woman coming from the spring (well) from where she was fetching water for Mr Coke. I asked her, why she came so late to the well? She answered: "You see, tomorrow is Sunday, and then there is singing and prayer in the morning!" I said; "Is that so! I would like to know whether they would allow strangers to listen!" The woman said; "Oh yes! I heard Missus say, she wondered why no one from the Cottage came to the meeting which Mr Coke keeps every morning especially for these people." This answer went through me as though something had pierced my heart. I went home, thought the whole night about it, and concluded to go on Sunday to Paynestown. I told it to my companions, and invited them to go along; but they called me a fool, to think that I would go to white people whom I did not know; and they tried to persuade me not to go. I had however great uneasyness and felt restless the whole week, and when Sunday came, I dressed myself, said nothing to any one, and went, thinking to myself, they can do no more than to turn me off and send me back. When I drew near to Paynestown I thought; "What shall I say, if they ask me, why I came?" Still I fared better than I had thought. As soon as I stepped into the large garden that surrounds the house, the herdsman, who stood near the house, saw me, and called to his Missus; "Mrs Coke, here comes Archie Monteeth, to say goodmorning." Mr Coke answered from within the house "That is good, I am glad to see him." I waited a short time near the entrance; then a bell was rung, and we went in to morning prayer; I, for the *first* time in my life. Mr Coke opened the Bible, and read. What he read I do not know, also, understood but little, for I knew of no Saviour, no salvation, no grace; nothing! but nevertheless, I shall *never, never*! forget that hour! What I *felt* I cannot express. I felt such a power, as of a chill seizing my whole body. I could say nothing, but went home and told the others, what I had heard and felt. "Good", said they, "next Sunday we all go with you."

On Monday I met Sister Elizabeth Dickenson on the street. (an aged Helper Sister of Carmel Congregation whom I also knew well. J.H.K.) Her parents had belonged to the Congregation at Old Carmel, but at that time she was not yet awakened, had however heard from her parents something about Jesus. I told her that I had been to Paynestown to prayers, and how I felt to hear God's word. She went the next day, and felt the same as I did; and after that we went every evening to Paynestown, where Mr Coke had evening prayer.

Every Sunday a goodly number from our plantation, and also from other plantations accompanied me to Paynestown. I asked the people to go along, and many a one came. At this time there was no minister in the neighborhood, but Mr Coke was a good religious man, and always read prayers in his family, and he allowed any one to be present, and was glad to see the people come.

On one Sunday Mr Coke requested us to go to Hopeton[9] with him; a minister was to keep a meeting there that day; we all followed Mr Coke. Having reached Hopeton, good old Mrs Senior came to me and said; "Now, Archie Monteeth, I rejoice to see in you a negro who loves Jesus, and because you love Him, I also love you, and will lead you to an instructor, and physician for your soul." She then lead me to Br Ellis,[10] who spoke very kindly and affectionately to me, and put down my name as a Candidate. From this time forth we attended the meetings of the Brethren which were held every 8 weeks at Hopeton by Br Ellis who came from Mesopotamia. Mrs Cooper[11] a pious white lady who also always went to Hopeton, asked me one day whether I could read, and on my answering, No! she offered to teach me to read. Although I had to bear with much mockery on this account, namely, that I wished to read the white peoples book, all this did not confuse me, and disturb or hinder me from going for instruction to Mrs Cooper as often as possible; and Oh, how often have I already thanked my Saviour that I can read his word for myself.

One Sunday Mrs Coke asked me, "Archie, who is the woman who always comes with you to prayers?" I said, "That is Elizabeth Dickenson." Upon this she called Elizabeth to follow her, while I, at the same time remained below, in company with the white nurse, who in the course of conversation said; "The people here in Jamaica are so wild; never keep Sunday, but dance and carry on the whole day." I asked her; "Is it a sin to dance?" and was not a little frightened when she said. "Yes!" for I was passionately fond of dancing. She also spoke of bad living, namely, that some men were living with several women. This also struck my conscience, for I was living with 4 women, without thinking it was sin to do so. In Africa this was done, and here in Jamaica we saw many white men, who were called gentlemen, and seemed to be respected, do the same. Although I had heard God's commandments and my heart went out after Jesus Christ, the blessed Saviour, and I wished to follow him, yet you must remember, minister we were in great darkness and ignorance. There was much that I did not properly understand, and I had no clearness to distinguish between what was right and wrong. The difference or contrast between Master and slave, between white and black, was so great, that I did not venture to ask. I was timid and backward to do so. I was so much the more thankful, when soon after this conversation with the nurse, Mr Coke called upon me to come to him, and ask him, if there was any thing I did not understand. Many such opportunities I afterwards made use of, and gained much blessing for my heart, and especially by this means, by the blessing of the Lord, I gained much selfknowledge.

The whole time since I had become acquainted with Jesus my Saviour, and was in my first love to him, Mr Monteeth my master, was very hard towards me. If I was sick, or if every thing on the plantation did not go according to his wish, he said, "This comes from your walking to Paynestown to prayer!" he could not bear to think that I should become pious, and as his riches seemed to dwindle down more and more & grow less and less, and he had many debts, it came so far last that we were no more allowed to go out of the place in the evenings, as it would have been easy for the creditors to catch us up, and sell us. The keeping away from the meetings of the awakened made my heart cold; I did not any more feel the love and warmth in my heart as before, but this did distress me. I complained of my distress to a dear Christian friend, who once came on the plantation. He said; "Archie, you are now placed in the school; you are tried; pray fervently that the Saviour may let the Sun, which is behind the clouds to you, shine forth again." And so I found it; through persevering prayer, my Saviour granted me deliverance from this cold state, and my heart felt again as it had before.

The following circumstance was very remarkable to me soon after I passed through this spiritual dryness. The woman before mentioned, whose name was Christina, and who at first showed me the way to Paynestown, lived near that place. Being the first person through whom I was incited to seek the gospel salvation, I always since that time had a particular affection for her, and visited her every Sunday. One Sunday I came to see her as usual, and found her very sick. I asked; "Christina, do you pray? and what do you pray?" She answered, "I pray, *if* I have done sin, Jesus forgive me." I told her, "You must not say, *if* I have sinned. You *have* sinned, we all sin and are the cause of the death of Jesus, and so also *you*; say rather, Lord Jesus have mercy upon me and forgive my sins." I moved nearer to her bed, and said, "say this after me Christina." She said it; "Lord Jesus etc. etc.["] "Oh, say it again"! she did so, but had hardly finished the last word, when she sank back, and expired! Her soul was gone!—

I thanked my Lord that I could still in the last hour show the soul the way, who first showed me the way to the place where I could hear about and learn to know Jesus!

In those times Saturday and Sunday was given us to work for ourselves. Sunday was also market day. When there was no Church here, there was some service every 8 weeks at Paynestown or at Hopeton, and always morning prayer, at other times on these Sundays we worked in the field in our grounds. When I was once busily occupied on a Sunday digging holes to plant my yams, the thought suddenly came into mind! "How is this; a commandment of God says; Remember the Sabbath day to keep it holy etc. etc. and how do you keep that commandment, missing the morning prayer, and doing work you might do on Saturday?" While I was thinking over this, and reflecting, I felt the presence of God so powerfully, that I threw down my hoe, and seemed to be necessitated and could not do otherwise than fall down on my knees in the hole I had dug, and earnestly prayed my Saviour, to let me find his way and will, and begged him to counsel and help me! He heard me. I arose with a feeling and strong conviction that my laboring on Sunday was displeasing to him, for the Sabbath was given to be kept holy, and he gave me the firm assurance, that if I would follow him, he would supply my needs, and provide for me that I should never want. And this the faithful Saviour has done until this day. I never again from that day to this touched my hoe on Sunday, but rose up very early on Saturdays and labored diligently, and this the Lord has blessed much more than when I labored on Sunday. Oh, its wonderful how I have been prospered! In every thing that concerns temporal things too. Why only think! I now own 15 acres of good land right around my house, that is more than any other negro in this whole neighbourhood. and all good land, and brings forth wonderfully! I have been richly rewarded!

On one occasion when I attended the religious service at Hopeton, Mrs Cooper asked me, whether I did not wish to become a Communicant, (we then had no church here at Carmel, and persons were confirmed at Black River in the Parish Church) and she advised me to go to the Superintendent of the Parish Church at Black River. This I did. However he asked me, *how* I lived, and said, I must be lawfully married, he did not allow any one to come to the Communion, who was living with a woman without being thus married. I would gladly have complied with this, but the person with whom I lived in one house, hated the gospel and scolded as often as I went to the meeting. I prayed a long time that the Lord would change her heart, but her hour was not yet come. I could not persuade her to go with me to the

Church, and as I had a desire for the Communion I parted entirely from her, and lived half a year alone, and can testify before God, that in that time I did not think of nor follow after sinful desires and inclinations. I was at that time so happy in my Saviour; he was so near to me, whether I walked, or labored, or rested, just as though he were at my side. I could speak and pray to him so confidentially.

In Paynestown I had seen a young person who loved the Saviour and visited the meetings regularly. Her name was Rebecca Hart, and I thought she would be a good and suitable wife for me. I made this known to my mistress Mrs Monteeth, but she dissuaded me from marrying any one except a person from the same Estate as myself. This I could not do, and so gave up the idea for some time, but endeavoured to persuade other believers, who were living together as man and wife, to be married in the church. For example Elizabeth Dickenson and her husband. When my Master & Mistress heard their bans published in the Black River church, God changed their minds, and they allowed me to be married; and this took place. On Sunday the *8th* of January 1826 we were married in Black River. As it was also market day, the church was quite filled with people, the most of whom laughed at us, and mocked us, that we, black people would thus be married. The minister saw this and spoke to them so earnestly and sharply; set before them their own sinful way of living so forcibly, that at once the greatest silence prevailed. After we were married we attached ourselves to the church at Black River, and so remained, until 1827 when it was concluded to build a Brethren's Church here, and which became the New Carmel church. Until the house was erected and finished, our new minister Brother Scholefield[12] lived at Hopeton. Oh! how we rejoiced now to have our own minister. The first sermon of Br Scholefield was preached on Good Friday, and was from the text 1 Cor:2,2. "For I determined not to know any thing among you, save Jesus Christ and him crucified."

It made a deep impression on us all, and this was increased, when on Easter morning, the Easter morning Litany was prayed, on the open place before Hopeton house. We were all quite overcome. It was as if we could see before us, the Saviour who also died for us, and for us rose again. We felt his presence very sensibly.

On the first Sunday after the New Carmal house was finished, I, together with some others was received as a Candidate. This took place in the hall of the house, and 8 weeks later, I was received as a Congregation Member. We now visited our dear Carmel every Sunday; Br Scholefield preached and conducted service in the hall. At that time there were 12 Congregation Members.

Soon however the faithful Saviour deemed it good, in this time of spiritual refreshing, to visit me with severe trial and affliction. He laid me upon a sick bed, on which I suffered and lingered for 10 months. Rheumatism had so seized upon me, that I was quite contracted and crippled, so that I could neither move, nor use either hands or feet, and had to be fed like a little child. No one thought it possible that I could recover. All counsel, advise, and means of various kinds seemed useless, though I had the best nursing and attention from my Master and Mistress and Mrs Cooper. All seemed unavailing, until at last a coloured man gave me something to drink; a tea prepared from a bush that grows here. That made my mouth so sore, that I felt very bad, but when the mouth got better, I also felt better otherwise, and was able to walk, and again received the use of my limbs. The Lord be praised for his blessing!

As soon as I got better I was confirmed[13] at Carmel, and appointed and accepted as a Native Assistant or Helper. For the perfect strengthening of my body and limbs, Mr Monteeth advised me to go and bathe daily in the sea; to this also the Lord added his blessing, and I became well and strong. But not only did I become healthy in my body; the Lord also did good to my soul. My heart burned with love to the Saviour, who redeemed me the Chief of sinners by his precious blood, and delivered me from darkness and the power of the devil. And this blessedness I sincerely and earnestly wish may be given to all other people. Whenever I could, I made known to them my Saviour as the friend of sinners. For instance, I once spoke with a man about Christian marriage.—a third person was listening, and he was persuaded to come to Carmel the next Sunday, where the proclamation of the gospel he heard, made such an impression on him, that he and his wife immediately had their names entered as Candidates, & asked me to come to Petersvale to keep meetings; this I did, and the consequence was, that on the next Sunday, all from there came to New Carmel and many soon became Congregation Members.

I also often went to Woodlands, to invite the people there to come to church; kept meetings and read the Bible, which they liked very much. But the manager soon forbad this to be done in future. Still, the desire to hear of Jesus was so great, that only few allowed themselves to be kept from the meetings by the threatenings of the manager. Among them was one man, who always excused himself for staying away, by lying, and to this day, that man is a poor wandering sheep who does not know nor love Jesus.

In Hampstead also, the home of my wife, I often held meetings. And there the first one I held after my severe sickness, remained especially impressed upon me. The house was crammed full of people. I first read the Bible, then I spoke, and while speaking, there came over me such a feeling of the presence of our crucified Saviour, and I felt so powerfully that I was not redeemed with silver or gold, but with the precious blood of Jesus Christ, that it caused me to rise up (for I was seated while I kept the meeting) and my mouth overflowed with that which I felt in my heart. What I felt and experienced in *that* meeting, I cannot express. It appeared to me, that *so near* before my spiritual eyes, and before my heart, I had never yet felt my Saviour, my Jesus, and I thought I could understand something of what Paul said, when he was caught up into the third heaven. All present were deeply moved, and all went home so quietly and silently, that they showed what they felt. One brother pressed my hand with deep emotion and said; "Brother Archie, the Lord has not raised you up from your sick bed for nothing, you shall help to strengthen others."

In the year 1832, one morning Mr Monteeth told me that the slaves around Montego Bay at the North side, were revolting, and setting fire to properties, in order to become free. I could hardly believe it, but alas! it was too true. Very soon sentinel posts were placed in various localities, and on Sundays there were often 50 soldiers to be seen at New Carmel, who were placed there to observe how the people would behave; whether they would take part in the rebellion etc. etc. Many negroes allowed themselves to be frightened from coming to Church, yet, as regards the most of them, so great was their hunger to hear the word of God, that the fear of man, and the red coated soldiers could not keep them away from Church. This state of affairs, however, did not last long, as the magistrate saw that this whole district kept quiet and orderly and the soldiers were ordered away.[14]

Soon after this, the preparation time for freedom began, that is, children under 6 years were free. House servants were to work 4 years, and field laborers 6 years, and then full freedom was to take place. This arrangement Br Scholefield read to us in the Church; but it did not excite general joy, for the people did not suppose that freedom was so far distant.

In many respects however we had cause enough for thankfulness. Many who formerly were hindered by hard treatment of their masters, from going to church, could now go unhindered, and to many who had grown cold and unconcerned and indifferent freedom gave a new impulse to attend the house of God. Even the old and weak, who were excused from hard field labor, came now to church from miles around Carmel, and although angry managers told them "if you can go to Carmel to church, you can also work," and again employed them in the field; yet even this did not keep them from Church. Carmel church filled up more and more, the number was so great that outside of the church, under 3 separate trees, meetings were held by Br Laslie[15] and Hamilton[15] and myself. As often as my time allowed I visited among the people, read to them the Bible, and kept meetings. I knew nothing more blessed than to show poor sinners to Jesus, and the faithful

Saviour let it become true in me poor sinner, that He was strong in the weak; he often so evidently blessed my visiting among the people, that in eternity I shall not be able to thank him enough.

Just now a very remarkable circumstance comes to my mind, which verifies what I have just said.

I often visited the places now belonging to the New Hope district; and here the people were particularly hungry to hear of Jesus Christ. At Mount Edgecomb there was a married overseer, who continually sought to draw the young people into sinful ways and doings; and now, they were not any more willing to do such things, for, as they said, "Archie Monteeth had told them, and read to them out of the Bible, that such life is sin, and they would be excluded from the Congregation, if they would not renounce these things." This made the overseer so angry, that he complained to the Inspector of the plantation, that I, as he said, kept the people from 6 to 12 O'clock in the night, and therefore made them unfit for work the next day. The Inspector wished to see me, and I went to him to Savannah La Mar. He asked me, why I kept the people up so late etc. etc. I said "that I don't do; we sing and pray, but at 9 o'clock each goes to rest etc." Then he asked about many things and we had a long conversation; at the end of which he said to me; "Good; Archie Monteeth, I give you full permission, on the 7 Estates over which I am inspector, to teach the people as much as you like. I see you dont do any harm with it." Then he reached out his hand to me and continued, "Upon my word, Monteeth, the more I speak with you, the more I like you." and then he asked all the people on the Estate whether I should continue to teach them, and all begged him; "Yes Massa, let him teach us." Upon this repeated before them all the permission he had already given me.

A short time after, the master of several plantations returned from England. On his other plantations not situated in this locality, the negroes had received and welcomed him with dancing, and noisy demonstrations of joy. I had heard of this, and warned the people in this neighbourhood, not to receive and welcome their master in such a heathenish manner. The Master came with the above mentioned Inspector to this Estate, and was not a little surprized and astonished, to find the people so silent and quiet. He said to the people, "Come up to my house this evening, then you can dance and play." Upon which all answered him. "Massa we are Christians, we will not play and dance before you, but we will pray for you." "Good," said he, "then come and pray for me!" The people did so in all simplicity; went up to the residence, and sang hymns, and then Br Pinnock a Helper, read the Bible, made an address, and kneeled down and prayed. The Master and Inspector also kneeled down with them, and afterwards all went quietly home.—I was present on a neighbouring Estate, in order to hear how the people would behave, and I was filled with thankfulness when I heard that they had remained firm, and kept the promise they had made.

On the next morning I visited the Estate. As soon as the Inspector saw me, he said to the Master; "Mr Weddesburne, see here, this is the man who keeps the people from dancing!" Upon this he called me into his house, and placed a chair for me to be seated. He asked, "Why do you keep the people from dancing?" ["]Mr Weddesburn," said I, "not I, but the Bible forbids it." Dr Gilpin, another gentleman present said; "Did not David and Solomon dance, and had not Solomon 300 wives?" and Mr Weddesburn said, "show me a passage in the Bible where dancing is forbidden? You must tell me why you forbid this!" "That I will sir;" answered I, and said further, "Mr W. you ask me a question, but pray allow me to ask you something first?" He said, "Ask me whatever you wish!" I then said, "Mr W. does not this property belong to you?" "Yes!" said he: "Did not your father give it to you, as your property?" Mr W. said, "Yes, it is all mine." I said, "suppose now you call one of your house-servants or slaves, and tell him, "go and do your work and make it thus and so, just as I tell you!" Now what would you do with him if he would answer; [']No, no, so I will not do it, for so I did not do it for your father![']" Mr W. answered, "Why I would throw him out of the house, and show him that he has to listen to *me,* and not to my father who is dead!" "Good," said I, "now I have you where I want you Mr W." God has given all into the hands of his son who died for us and rose again, and is now seated at the right hand of God, and governs all. *Him,* we have to follow and obey, and therefore pleasure of that kind we must let along, as is written Galatians 5, v. 19, 20.21 "Now the works of the flesh are manifest, which are these; Adultery, fornication, uncleanness, lasciviousness, Idolatry, witchcraft, hatred, variance, emulations, wrath, strife, seditions, heresies, envyings, murders, drunkenness, *revellings* and *such like:* of the which I tell you before, as I have also told you in time past, that they which do such things, shall not inherit the Kingdom of God."—and we must seek after and follow that which is written in V.22 to 24. ["]But the fruit of the Spirit is love, joy, peace, longsuffering, gentleness, goodness, faith, meekness, temperance; against such there is no law. And they that are Christ's have crucified the flesh with its affections & lusts."

When I had said this Mr. W. arose, shook my hand, and permitted and exhorted me to visit and teach on all his plantations as much as I could, or would desire to do. Soon after he got into his carriage, called me, once more shook my hand, and drove off. Through this permission a clear way was opened to me, to have access to a number of Estates. I made known what had taken place to Mr Dodridge, first magistrate in Black River, who was a dear Christian man, and always showed himself as a friend of the Mission, and as *my* friend. He often dissuaded me when I told him that I wished to buy myself free, because he thought, that as a free man, I would sooner be hindered from keeping meetings on the properties, than as a slave. But as I now had permission from most of the owners to visit their plantations without let or hindrance;—I longed to be free, the sooner the better. Mr Dodridge advised me to have myself appraised or taxed by my Master Mr Monteeth, rather than by the law or court; as in the latter case it would come too high for me. The estimate he thought would be too high a payment for me to make.—That same evening I went to Mr Monteeth and made my request known. He tried in every possible way to bring me off from my plan and desire; promised me all possible liberties if I would remain just as hitherto etc. etc.—Still I longed for liberty, and although I knew that in 3 years, apprentice time would be over, and my freedom would come, my spirit still longed for immediate liberty.

The next morning my master came to me in my house, (I was not well) he said to me, "Archie I have spoken with my family about your wish to become free. We have always loved you, and you have been of great service to us; hence we will give you your freedom for £90. Sterling."—I gave no answer. He said further; "You see, your services in one year are of more value to us than £30. that makes in 3 years £90." I was still silent & thoughtful, for I had not expected that he would ask so much, and I was disappointed, and felt grieved! My master went away.—Next morning he came again and said, "Archie we have thought over the matter still further. You shall be free for £50. Hardly had my master left me, when I took £40. that I had ready[,] went to Mr Monteeth and bought my liberty. The remaining £10. I paid soon after. He gave me my free paper, and herewith my slavery had an end. Oh, how full was my heart of thanks and praise that at length I had attained unto the blessing of *Liberty*. This day always remained to me a holy day. It was the *1st day of June 1837*. Soon after I had come from my masters presence, I dressed myself in my Sunday clothes, and rode to Carmel, where Br Collis[16] as our minister lived and labored. All at Carmel were surprised to see me thus on a week day; all the people present looked at me with astonishment, as I stepped near the house; I took off my hat and waved it about my head, and cried out with a loud voice. *THANK GOD! I AM FREE!*—All rejoiced with me but especially my dear minister Brother Collis!

Several remarkable and honourable offers were soon made to me to become overseer on several plantations, but I did not feel inclined to accept any; till Br Collis made me a proposal, to become a Helper for all the Mission Stations, and for my services to receive a salary of £12. a year. I immediately felt in my heart a cheerfulness to accept this and looked upon it as a call coming from my Lord; and since then I have been engaged in this office, visiting from Station to Station among the people as opportunity offers.

My dwelling place I bought in Rosehall, where I still live with my wife and daughter, whom the Lord gave us after 11 years, and I cannot wish *this* daughter, as well as another daughter born in the time of ignorance, and who is married to a teacher of one of our schools, anything better, than that they may learn to know and love and follow the Lord Jesus, as their highest good, more & more, and be preserved unto their end and brought to his everlasting kingdom.

On the *1st* of August 1838 universal and entire freedom was proclaimed.

How often I have sincerely rejoiced, when I have heard from one and another, formerly slaves, whose overseer I myself a slave, was, that they would for ever thank me, that in their state of slavery, I would not allow them to do certain things, which slaves on other places were not hindered from doing, for instance, I would never allow them to take or appropriate any thing that belonged to the Master which many slaves on other plantations were accustomed to do, hence as slaves they were not in the habit of stealing and much less did this enter into their minds, now since they were free. Many slaves brought upon themselves severe punishments by thinking that what was the property of the master, was also theirs. I taught the people very different! Oh! the yoke of slavery! how it oppresses the poor negro in many ways, how difficult in that degraded state to avoid the bad, and to follow only Jesus. Oh, that all my black brethren and sisters, may soon hear the precious word of God, and follow its teachings, and Oh might all, and myself also, make good use of the opportunities we have to hear the precious gospel proclaimed in all its purity, and to take it to heart, and that our great concern and care be, to repent and believe, so that in the great day when we must render an account how we have made use of the precious word of God, our fathers in Africa who are still living in darkness and the shadow of death may not rise up in judgment against us. May we all obey and follow and love him through whose blood shed for us we may obtain eternal salvation.

What I felt, after having from time to time told you some fragments of my life and experience, I cannot express. That the faithful Saviour took me, a poor African negro slave, who was living in ignorance and sin, and taught me to know and love my Redeemer, and to be the means of teaching others also; that by his blessing I have learned to read, and even to write the English language, and done so much for me,—all this makes me so happy, that I cannot describe my feelings. How often I feel deeply abased at the affectionate manner, and the friendliness and esteem with which I am met by my dear ministers. How deeply am I humbled, when at Conferences one after another puts to me the question; "Br Archie can you not soon go to this or that place." Oh how I then feel myself unworthy of all the Lord has done for me, and that he permits me, to tell to others that glorious message which alone makes us blessed for time and for eternity. What the young and now sainted Br North[17] once said to me, when he shook my hand, remains indelibly impressed upon my heart; "Br Archie your office is great, but your responsibility is much greater.["]

If the Lord should ask me like Peter, "Whom do you say that I am?" I can answer with full assurance of faith, "Thou art Christ the Son of the living God." For so my heart has experienced him. In Him I have found the words of eternal Life. The worst of mankind is not too bad for him, that he cannot have mercy. Of this I am a living proof. My only wish and prayer is, that the Lord who bought me a lost and undone sinner, who purchased me with his precious blood and delivered me from the power of Satan, not with silver and gold, but with his holy and precious blood; may more and more gain ascendency in my heart, that I may be and remain his property, until he calls me from this earth.[18]

I can appear before him with nothing but what is expressed in the verse

> The Saviour's blood and righteousness
> My beauty is, my glorious dress,
> Thus well arrayed I need not fear
> When in his presence I appear.

NEW CARMEL, JAMAICA
1853.

Notes

1. The manuscript booklet used as the basis for the account printed here probably is not Kummer's first copy, but a re-copying made by him at some later time. The date 1853 refers to when he secured the information, rather than to the exact date of the booklet. But there is no question that the handwriting is Kummer's; his baptismal entries in the Brooklyn register, for example, substantiate this conclusion. The text printed here, it should, be noted, is as close a facsimile of Kummer's manuscript as could be attained in print. In the interest of historical accuracy the tendency to correct apparent misspellings has been carefully avoided.

2. Most often the name is spelled Monteith. Another variation is Monteath.

3. New Carmel (not Carmal) was founded in 1827 on Hutchison Mure Scott's property in the south-west part of the island. . . .

4. Joseph Horsfield Kummer was born in Bethlehem on June 28, 1820, the son of John Jacob and Maria (Horsfield) Kummer. From 1842 to 1850 he was a missionary in the Danish West Indies. He was called to Jamaica in 1850. In 1854 he left Jamaica and became the minister at Brooklyn, N.Y. He served several Moravian churches in New York and Pennsylvania and for a time entered the Presbyterian ministry. He died at Lancaster, Pa., on April 23, 1897. According to his special request, no memoir was published after his death. See The Moravian, XLII, 257.

5. The Eboe (or Ibo) tribe inhabited the lower Niger River area.

6. The name Durl appears at this point in the German text. Missions-Blatt, 1864, p. 89.

7. According to the German text there were 6000 to 7000 slaves. Missions-Blatt, 1864, p. 92.

8. E.F. Coke, Esq., and his wife assisted the Moravian mission in many ways. In a lengthly [sic] letter from John Scholefield at New Carmel reporting contributions to the new church in 1828, the Cokes are listed as having contributed £20 for the building of the chapel and having subscribed £10 annually for maintenance. Both Mr and Mrs Coke assisted with the Sunday School; Mr Coke even acted as superintendent. Periodical Accounts, XI, 34–36.

9. The owner of Hopeton (and Lennox) was Hutchison Mure Scott, Esq. Periodical Accounts, XXI, 338, 343.

10. The abbreviation Br means Brother, a term used frequently among Moravians to refer to clergy or laymen. John Ellis (1785–1855), a native of England, came to Jamaica in 1824 after several years on Antigua. He returned to Europe temporarily and was consecrated a bishop at Fulneck, England, on December 29, 1836. He then went to Barbados. He died in retirement at Ockbrook, England, 1855. See his memoir in Periodical Accounts, XXXII, 485–493. See also XIV, 103.

11. According to John Scholefield's letter of October 3, 1828, "F. Cooper, Esq. and his lady" contributed £20 for the chapel at New Carmel and £5 annually for maintenance." Periodical Accounts, XI, 35, 36.

12. John Scholefield (–1845) had served the church on St. Kitts before coming to Jamaica in 1827. In 1840 the Scholefields returned to England because of the poor

state of Br. Scholefield's health. He died at Fulneck on December 3, 1845, at the age of 49. Periodical Accounts, XV, 296; XCII, 408; XXX, 251, 252.

13. Although this statement appears confusing, it probably correctly reflects standard Moravian practice at the time. As far as the Moravians were concerned, Monteith's ex opere operato baptism in the Anglican Church would no doubt be considered valid, but no more so than an infant baptism. It would still be necessary for him to express and demonstrate faith in the Saviour before being admitted to Communion. Hence this probationary period before confirmation and admission to Communion.

14. All was not so quiet. Henry Gottlob Pfeiffer, Moravian missionary at New Eden, was accused of encouraging the rebellion, was arrested and imprisoned, and barely escaped death. Eventually he was cleared completely of what proved to be false charges. The account is told in *The Breaking of the Dawn*, by Walter Hark and Augustus Westphal. See also Periodical Accounts, XXXII, 489.

15. These apparently were not missionaries from abroad, because their names do not appear on the list given in *The Breaking of the Dawn*. Allen Hamilton did not come to Jamaica until 1864.

16. John Collis' career as a missionary was cut short later that summer when he became seriously ill and died on August 14. He had come to Jamaica in 1833 and had been at New Carmel for only half a year. He was from Fulneck, England. Periodical Accounts, XII, 388; XIV, 239–241.

17. Presumably Goodwin North, who served in Jamaica from 1843–1846.

18. Some of the expressions in this account are not too far removed from Monteith's own writing style, which can be seen from a letter he sent to Kummer's father, John Jacob Kummer. It is printed verbatim.

Mount Blessed Novbr 29th 1855

Dear Sir

 Your letter dated August 26th 1854 duly comes to hand quite safe and was more than happy to hear from you and that all your family were all well. But my dear Big Master when I see your letter it put me in mind of Jacob and Joseph of old I am sorry I did not answer you before this But I did promise my dear Timothy to send him my likeness but I have not get it as yet which prevented me from writing you But I have now send you these few lines to let you know I am still alive giving you a thousand thanks for your prayer towards me that I may continue in the service of my Saviour it is what I desire and nothing else I never seen you bodily but I have seen your heart By your letter and I do not expect to see you personally but I hope to see you after this life that I believe not of any thing of my own but from that dear Son who left his throne and came down and die for me that whosoever believeth in him should not perish but have eternal life Your dear Son who was much beloved both at Carmel and New hope and wherever he did preach If they had known that I was writing him they would have send multitude of Howdie for him and partner we bear him in mind very much and all his hymn and

Text which he use to Sing especially the 747 Hymn [note in Kummer's hand: American New Edition] Please to pray for me that I may be faithful unto death as the lord think it fit to Remove our Minister from us to go to Brooklyn we hope the lord may bless his labour there among the white as he did among us as the eye of the Servant looketh unto the hand of his master so my eye looketh beyond the cloud of him that setteth on the throne Please to Remember kindly to the Mother of your dear Timothy that your kind lady and her sister Mrs Holland Mother whom we have seen in Jamaica and the old Gentleman who with us here please if you see Mr & Mrs Holland please to remember me to them I do not know if you live near Mrs Zorn if you do give my Kind howdie I Believe we will meet arount the throne of our dear Saviour to worship him and give him thanks for his dying for us poor sinners My family send Kind howdie to you and Misses I have written your beloved son at Brooklin a few lines I would have written you about our Centennial Jubilee but you must be see it in the Periodical account what beautiful meetings we have and I am your sincere servant

Archibald John Monteath

[Note in Kummer's hand:] written by Archie M to my father John Jacob Kummer with Archie's own hand He really taught himself to write

Notes

Chapter 1

1. Only in Antigua did the Emancipation Act come into force in 1834.
2. The best known of these are the diaries of Thomas Thistlewood. See Hall, *In Miserable Slavery*; Burnard, *Mastery, Tyranny, and Desire.*
3. See Carmichael, *Domestic Manners*; Lewis, *Journal.*
4. See Oldendorp, *Caribbean Mission.*
5. See Perkins, *Busha's Mistress.*
6. See *Periodical Accounts Relating to the Missions of the Church of the United Brethren* (hereafter *PA*) 13 for short biographies of several helpers. Kummer included a short biography of another church member, Mask [Marse] Campbell in the same exercise book Ms. containing for the most part the autobiography of Archibald Monteath. Sensbach, *Separate Canaan*, xxii, indicates that dozens of memoirs of black Moravians are stored at the Moravian Archives at Winston-Salem, North Carolina and he reproduces one on pages 309–11 and provides synopses of others on pages 303–7.
7. Zorn, *PA* 14: 299–300, letter to Brother W.W. Essex of Bristol, 9 October 1837.
8. Editor, Monteith, "Memoir", *PA* 25: 433, 1865.
9. Monteith, "Experiences", 267. Monteath's letter to Joseph Kummer's parents, reproduced in Nelson, "Archibald John Monteith", mentions the likelihood that a portrait of himself would be sent to them, but archival searches have so far not turned up any portrait that might have been of Monteath.
10. Monteith, "Experiences", 284n2.
11. Buchner, *PA* 20: 416, 8 July 1852.
12. Nelson, "Archibald John Monteith", 287.
13. Editor, Monteith, "Memoir", *PA* 25: 433.
14. "Retrospect", 358n.
15. Harvey and Brewin, "Autobiographical Sketch", 88.
16. Ibid., 100.
17. A "driver" in plantation parlance was an overseer, or a headman under a main

overseer, whose responsibility it was to supervise the work of others and urge them on to complete their tasks.

18. Smaby, *Moravian Bethlehem,* 133.
19. Quoted in ibid., 21.
20. Ibid., 133.
21. Ibid., 195.
22. Monteith, "Experiences", 267.
23. Ibid.
24. Ibid.
25. Ibid., 268.
26. Monteith, "Erlebnisse".
27. Smaby, *Moravian Bethlehem,* 26, 129.
28. Monteith, "Experiences", 267.
29. Nelson, "Archibald John Monteith", 286.
30. Clemens, "Report of Visits", 161.
31. Editor, Monteith, "Experiences", 267; Editor, Monteith, "Erlebnisse", 87–88.
32. Similar language issues are raised regarding the autobiography of "Andrew the Moor" in Bethlehem, Pennsylvania. See Thorp, *Chattel with a Soul,* 435.
33. The evidence provided by the earliest fragment of Jamaican Creole English in 1740 indicates that it "bears a clear resemblance to Jamaican usage today". D'Costa and Lalla, *Voices in Exile,* 6.
34. See Schweinitz, "Clergy", 185, for a profile of Joseph Kummer.
35. Monteith, "Memoir", *PA* 25 [1865]: 433.
36. Kummer in Nelson "Archibald John Monteith", 287.
37. Monteith, "Memoir", *PA* 25 [1865]: 433.
38. Kummer in Nelson "Archibald John Monteith", 287.
39. In its nineteenth-century sense, "coloured" refers to someone of mixed African and other ethnicity, while "black" suggests that the person's ethnicity is exclusively African.
40. See Moravian Archives (hereafter MA) O–1 Carmel, Diary of New Carmel from February 1837 to December 1869.
41. Costanzo, *Surprizing Narrative,* 115.
42. Price (*First-Time,* 23) points to the contamination of oral narratives as a result of contact with prior inscriptions of personal and communal histories. In this respect, I have found it telling that twentieth-century oral accounts of Monteath's life do not range outside the events recounted in the accessible printed documentation. Craton (*Invisible Man,* 374) remarks on the erasure of the lives of the enslaved in the consciousness of their descendants. This is partly due to the fractured family arrangements and relationships engineered by slavery. Even where this has not been so, the shame of the slave experience has induced in our populations a very shallow historical sense. Some of the mechanisms by which this shame operated are present in Costanzo's *Surprizing Narrative* account of secrecy and repressed information regarding family connections and slave life. Bailey (*African Voices,* 3–22) deals with this silence regarding Caribbean generational history. We may also recall the colonial education's suppression of

the topic of slavery in Lamming, *Castle of My Skin,* 56–57. The distancing of post-slavery generations is further due to fears of agitating social and ethnic conflict by revelations about the past.

43. Collison, "Recreating the World".

Chapter 2

1. There is often a disconnect between the ethnic identity of an African and the ethnic label that was attached to him by Europeans. The given ethnic label was frequently that of the major ethnic or subethnic group with which Europeans traded in the general area of the African coast, or the name of the port from which the individual exited Africa. Over time, these labels became adopted by Africans themselves, as a shorthand, easily understood nomenclature. Some labels also originated in the multiple identities of some persons who lived in multiethnic zones. For one of several discussions of the omnibus nature of African ethnonyms, see Miller, "Central Africa", 28–29, 40–42; da Costa e Silva, "Portraits", 132. See also Warner-Lewis, "Ethnic and Religious Plurality".

2. "[P]honetic and morphological differences among Ìgbo dialects (some of which, some speakers still publicly prefer to call mutually unintelligible languages) have long hindered emergence of a regional standard spoken variety, even after the strong nationalistic motives of the Nigeria–Biafra war (1967–70). Today the mother tongue remains disfavored as a medium for literate pan-Ìgbo meetings, whether outside Nigeria or within." Manfredi, "Philological Perspectives".

3. Ohadike, "Ekumeku Movement", 21.

4. Onwuejeogwu, *Social Anthropology,* 44.

5. Afigbo, "Igbo Cultural Sub-areas", 157.

6. Sandoval, *Instauranda Aethiopum Salute,* 94.

7. Nwokeji, "Atlantic Slave Trade", 16–19.

8. Eze and Manfredi, "Igbo", 2.

9. Nelson, "Archibald John Monteith", 287.

10. In Achebe, *Things Fall Apart,* 21 we read: "His mother and sisters worked hard enough, but they grew women's crops, like coco-yams, beans and cassava. Yam, the king of crops, was a man's crop."

11. The word *edo* is used for this tuber in the anglophone eastern Caribbean.

12. Onwuejeogwu, "The Patterns of Population Movement", 31.

13. Onwuejeogwu, *Social Anthropology,* 51. Ohadike, *Ekumeku Movement,* 28, speaks of cassava as a staple in Western Igboland only as of the twentieth century.

14. Nelson, "Archibald John Monteith", 288.

15. Monteith, "Memoir", *PA* 25, 434.

16. Allsopp, *Caribbean Dictionary,* 36.

17. See Warner-Lewis, *Central Africa,* 315–16 for the Trinidad Yoruba and Trinidad Kongo cooptation of extant African words to name new crops encountered in Trinidad such as cocoa, mango and sugar cane.

18. See Nelson, "Archibald John Monteith", 287.

19. Sidney Emezue, in discussion with the author, Toronto, 1997.

20. Nwokeji, "Atlantic Slave Trade", 1997.

21. Onwuejeogwu, *Igbo Civilization,* 43.

22. C.C. Agbodike, in discussion with the author, Awka, Nigeria, 1994.

23. Like many other West African languages, Igbo is a tonal language, that is, the vocal pitch is what differentiates one syllable or phrase from another with the same vowel or vowel and consonant combination.

24. Sidney Emezue, in discussion with the author, Toronto, 1997.

25. Onwejeogwu, *Social Anthropology,* 17.

26. C.C. Agbodike, in discussion with the author, Awka, Nigeria, 1994.

27. Azubike Uzoka, in discussion with the author, Awka, Nigeria, 1994.

28. Sidney Emezue, in discussion with the author, Toronto, 1997.

29. Chukwudum Uche, personal communication, 2005.

30. Isidore Okpewho, in discussion with the author, Kingston, 1997.

31. Nelson, "Archibald John Monteith", 287.

32. Onwuejeogwu, *Social Anthropology,* 40.

33. Nelson, "Archibald John Monteith", 287.

34. Onwuejeogwu, *Social Anthropology,* 15–16.

35. Ohadike, *Ekumeku Movement,* 22.

36. Onwuejeogwu, *Social Anthropology,* 44–46; Onwuejeogwu, *Igbo Civilization,* 11.

37. Ohadike, *Ekumeku Movement,* 36.

38. Onwuejeogwu, *Igbo Civilization,* 39. *Chukwu* is the supreme deity among the Igbo.

39. Onwuejeogwu, *Social Anthropology,* 44.

40. Hahn-Waanders, *Eze Institution,* 76.

41. Onwuejeogwu, *Social Anthropology,* 48.

42. Monteith, "Memoir", 433.

43. Equiano, *Travels,* 2.

44. Nelson, "Archibald John Monteith", 288.

45. Onwuejeogwu, *Social Anthropology,* 41.

46. Uzochukwu, "Art of Facial Scarification", 40, 41; Ben Akunne, in discussion with the author, Odinani Museum, Nri, Nigeria, 1994.

47. Uzochukwu, "Art of Facial Scarification", 40.

48. Nelson, "Archibald John Monteith", 288.

49. Equiano, *Travels,* 2. On the basis of two documents assigning the birth of Gustavus Vassa to South Carolina, Carretta, *Equiano,* disputes the Igbo identity proposed in the autobiography of Olaudah Equiano. Without pronouncing on this controversy, one cautions against laying incontrovertible trust in data contained in documents such as baptismal records, as shown by several Scottish and Jamaican instances in this present study. Carelessness and negligence on the part of parsons and slave owners, as well as ignorance on the part of those supplying information are among the reasons for discrepancies.

50. Uzochukwu, "Art of Facial Scarification", 40.

51. Monteith, "Memoir", 433.

52. Nelson, "Archibald John Monteith", 288.

53. Monteith, "Memoir", 434.

54. Ibid.

55. Adams, *Remarks,* 129–31.

56. See Nwokeji, "Atlantic Slave Trade", 26; Oriji, "Igboland, Slavery".

57. Dike and Ekejiuba, *Aro of South-Eastern Nigeria,* 250.

58. Harvey and Brewin, "Autobiographical Sketch", 90.

59. Nelson, "Archibald John Monteith", 288.

60. See da Costa e Silva, "Portraits of African Royalty"; Joseph, *History of Trinidad,* 264; and Fraser, *History of Trinidad,* 351, in recounting the role of Daaga in the 1837 mutiny of West India Regiment soldiers in Trinidad, point out that he was a prince, and as such considered a leader.

61. See Adams, *Remarks,* 133–34.

62. Nelson, "Archibald John Monteith", 288.

63. Ibid.

64. Monteith, "Memoir", 434.

65. Wariboko, "New Calabar", 3, 5.

66. Ohadike, *Ekumeku Movement,* 26.

67. Robinson, *Sailor Boy's Experience,* 55.

68. Ibid., 90.

69. Kolapo, "Trading Ports", 108.

70. Ohadike, *Ekumeku Movement,* 28–30; Kolapo, "Trading Ports", 107–12.

71. Monteith, "Memoir", 434.

72. Wariboko, "Ideological and Cultural Issues", 57.

73. Nwokeji, "Atlantic Slave Trade", 24.

74. Monteith, "Memoir", 434.

75. Ibid.

76. Monteith, "Experiences", 270.

77. Nelson, "Archibald John Monteith", 288.

78. Monteith, "Memoir", 434.

79. Nelson, "Archibald John Monteith", 288–89.

80. Ibid., 289.

81. Ibid.

82. Monteith, "Experiences", 270.

83. Aarons, "Story of Archibald Monteith", 77.

84. Harvey and Brewin, "Autobiographical Sketch", 89.

85. Hall, "Memoirs".

86. Behrendt, Eltis and Richardson, "Bights in Comparative Perspective", 3.

87. See Svalesen, *Slave Ship* Fredensborg, 124. Klein, *Middle Passage,* 192, speaks of French ships taking about 113 days to cross from the Gold and Slave Coasts to St Domingue, whereas Klein, *Atlantic Slave Trade,* 130, gives an average of a month for the crossing from Africa to Brazil and two months from West Africa to the Caribbean and North America.

88. Shyllon, *Black Slaves,* 5, 11. Blacks provided a colour contrast in paintings of British aristocratic life by William Hogarth and Joshua Reynolds.

89. In Svalesen, *Slave Ship* Fredensborg, 141, the captain acquired for himself five barrels of sugar in St Croix that he intended to sell at good profit on the ship's

return to Copenhagen. Equiano too traded goods when the ship on which he worked put in to harbour. See Equiano, *Travels,* 78–79, 93.

90. Burnard, "Who Bought Slaves", 69, referencing Davies, *Royal African Company,* 199–200.

Chapter 3

1. Burnard, "To Separate One from Another", 14–15.
2. Svalesen, *Slave Ship* Fredensborg, 137.
3. Burnard and Morgan, "Dynamics", 216: "[Q]uick sales were uncommon, especially in Kingston", the average time taken in the mid-eighteenth century to dispose of all the human cargo being fifty days; see also Svalesen, *Slave Ship* Fredensborg, 126, 139.
4. Burnard and Morgan, "Dynamics", 216.
5. Burnard, "To Separate One from Another", 25; Burnard and Morgan, "Dynamics", 217.
6. Jamaica Archives (hereafter JA), *New Jamaica Almanack, and Register,* 1801, 131.
7. According to the *New Jamaica Almanack, and Register,* 1808, 144, among the current inspectors were James Blair, D. McConnell and G. Gallery. James Blair commented on Falmouth: "From being a very inconsiderable village 20 years ago, it may be now classed among the largest towns in the Island, where there is a great deal of business done, and much more might be done was it a port of entry."
8. Burnard, "To Separate One from Another", 7; Burnard and Morgan, "Dynamics", 209.
9. *Cornwall Chronicle,* 12 and 21 December 1776.
10. *Cornwall Chronicle,* 21 December 1776.
11. *Cornwall Chronicle,* 18 October 1783.
12. *Cornwall Chronicle,* 20 December 1783.
13. *Cornwall Chronicle Supplement,* 7 June 1794.
14. JA, 1B/11/4 22, f. 214, Crop Accounts.
15. Island Record Office (hereafter IRO), Old Deeds 509, f. 204.
16. From an analysis of twenty-five sales between 1752 and 1780, Burnard and Morgan ("Dynamics", 213, 214) show that "nearly half of all slaves were sold in parcels of fifteen slaves or more. Every sale had large purchasers who bought a disproportionate proportion of Africans: twenty-five purchasers bought fifty or more slaves, and thirteen bought more than 100."
17. Craton, *Searching,* 212.
18. Ibid., 212–13.
19. Senior, *Jamaica,* 29.
20. Nelson, "Archibald John Monteith", 289.
21. Monteith, "Experiences", 271.
22. Senior, *Jamaica,* 59.
23. Ibid.
24. Monteith, "Experiences", 274.

25. Ibid., 271.

26. By 1782 David Fyffe was already "late of Jamaica" and back in Scotland. See JA, Manumissions, 1B/11/6, 15, f. 57.

27. IRO, Old Deeds 640, f. 74.

28. National Library of Jamaica (hereafter NLJ), Map Collection.

29. See maps in IRO, Old Deeds, 482, f. 33, and 515, f. 112.

30. Blair, *Sketches,* 295.

31. IRO, Old Deeds 621, f. 143. Kilmarnock lies in the heights to the south of Kep.

32. IRO, Old Deeds 827, f. 47.

33. Nelson, "Archibald John Monteith", 300.

34. IRO, Old Deeds 827, f. 48.

35. Senior, *Jamaica,* 38.

36. IRO, Old Deeds 719, f. 57.

37. IRO, Old Deeds 827, f. 50.

38. Burnard, *Mastery, Tyranny, and Desire,* 48. Thomas Thistlewood's difficulties in being paid by his employers and the poor quality of some white labour are discussed ibid., 47–54.

39. Quoted by Sheridan, "Role of the Scots", 101.

40. Senior, *Jamaica,* 58.

41. Ibid., 60.

42. Ward, *PA* 6: 420, 7 July 1817.

43. Nelson, "Archibald John Monteith", 296.

44. NLJ Ms.729 details "the condemnation and warrant for execution of six slaves issued by a Slave Court held at Lucea, Hanover, July 14, 1824". Sentenced to hang "at the mill yard of Argyle Estate" were Edward Jarrett, John Nesbitt, Dugald Campbell, Philip Davidson Brown, William Moodie and William Wright, the property of John Malcolm (Ingram, *Manuscript Sources,* 104, entry 0596). John Malcolm owned several estates in Hanover: Alexandria, Argyle, Blenheim, Knockalva, New Paradise, New Retrieve, Old Retrieve, Pell River and Retirement. The plantation dynasty of the Malcolms of Poltalloch was headed by Neil Malcolm. During the 1780s the Malcolms "made extensive use of profits from their Jamaican enterprises when improving their Argyll estate". The wealth generated from Jamaica "far outstripped the revenue raised from the land they had held in Scotland for two centuries". Hamilton, *Scotland,* 197, quoting data from Macinnes, "Scottish Gaeldom".

45. Stobwasser, *PA* 9: 137–38.

46. Zorn, *PA* 12: 174, 18 March 1832.

47. Light, *PA* 12: 172, 6 February 1832.

48. Ibid.

49. Zorn, *PA* 12: 174, 18 March 1832.

50. *St Jago de la Vega Gazette,* 78, no. 1, *Postscript.* 31 December 1831–7 January 1832.

51. Shepherd and Reid, "Rebel Voices", 57.

52. Scholefield, *PA* 12: 263, 15 August 1832.

53. Ibid.

54. Ibid., 264.

55. Ibid.

56. Light, *PA* 12: 171, 10 January 1832.

57. For instance, the Baptist missionary at Lucea reports the accusations that "the slaves had perverted passages of scripture which we had read to them, such as 'Fight the good fight of faith', 'If the Son make you free, ye shall be free indeed,' etc.". Abbott, *Narrative,* 10.

58. Bleby, *Death Struggles,* 151. Bleby also points out that on page fifteen of a pamphlet (see Anonymous, *Facts and Documents*) it asserts that "[i]n the parish of Trelawney, one Magistrate, Mr. William Dyer, publishes a newspaper, called 'the Cornwall Courier,' in which he has repeatedly urged that the Missionaries should be tarred and feathered. . . . William Dyer, Editor, and William Dyer, Magistrate, are one and the same person".

59. Light, *PA* 12: 173, 16 March 1832.

60. Light, *PA* 12: 171, 10 January 1832.

61. Bleby, *Death Struggles,* 239–46.

62. Scholefield, *PA* 12: 265, 15 August 1832.

63. Moravian Archives, Bethlehem, Pennsylvania (hereafter MAB), Kummer Collection, Letters to J.G. Kummer (Warden of Nazareth) from Jac. Zorn, 1827–1836: Zorn to J.G. Kummer, 14 April 1832.

64. MA Q–11, Minutes of the Mission Conference, June 1831–December 1833, 8, Conference at New Eden, 7 March 1832.

65. Zorn, "Diary of the Negro Congregation at New Fulneck, for 1832", 21 July 1832, *PA* 13: 17, 1834.

66. MAB, Kummer Collection, Zorn to J.G. Kummer, 14 April 1832.

67. Shepherd and Reid, "Rebel Voices", 57, based on Turner, *Slaves and Missionaries,* 161.

68. Patterson, *Sociology of Slavery,* 273; Shepherd and Reid, "Rebel Voices", 57.

69. IRO, Old Deeds 827, f. 47.

70. Senior, *Jamaica,* 39.

71. JA, 1B/11/4 49 f. 154 and 50 f. 82, Crop Accounts.

72. JA, 1B/11/3 127 f. 12, 13. Inventories.

73. Shepherd, "Alternative Husbandry", 43.

74. Ibid., 42.

75. Ibid., 46.

76. Senior, *Jamaica,* 59.

77. Joyce Buchanan, in discussion with the author, Kilmarnock, 1995.

78. Shepherd, "Alternative Husbandry", 44, 53.

79. Ibid., 45, 46, 49.

80. Ibid., 44, 45, 47.

81. MA, H–5 Fairfield. Minutes of Conference, 28 January 1830–20 April 1831.

82. Shepherd, "Alternative Husbandry", 47, 51.

83. Ibid., 53.

84. Monteith, "Emancipation and Labour", 126.

85. Trouillot, "Coffee Planters", 130.

86. Ibid., 132.

87. Ibid., 134–36.

88. Monteith, "Memoir", 434–35.

89. Monteith, "Experiences", 280–81. The answer in Kummer (see Nelson, "Archibald John Monteith", 298) reads differently: "Why I would throw him out of the house, and show him that he has to listen to *me,* and not to my father who is dead!"

90. See Douglass, *My Bondage,* 41–42; Prince, *History,* 47.

91. Burnard, *Mastery, Tyranny, and Desire,* 198.

92. Monteith, "Experiences", 275.

93. Monteith, "Memoir", 481.

94. Nelson, "Archibald John Monteith", 297.

95. Monteith, "Experiences", 274.

Chapter 4

1. Information regarding his sequence among the siblings is contained in the will of James Monteath, 7 October 1850. Scottish Record Office (hereafter SRO), SC36/51/29. The numeration appended to Walter's name is not to be understood as his official nomenclature, but merely a device by which this author seeks to differentiate between generations.

2. JA, 1B/11/8/6 1, Parish Register, St Elizabeth, Burials of White Persons.

3. New Register House, Edinburgh, Old Parochial Registers of the Church of Scotland (hereafter OPR), County Lanark, Barony Parish, 622/2 FR 592.

4. OPR, County Lanark, Barony Parish, 622/2 FR 605 in respect of Ann; 622/3 FR 653 in respect of Margaret.

5. OPR, County Lanark, Barony Parish, 622/16 FR 1691.

6. A slight doubt lingers regarding the inclusion of George, whose father is listed as Mathew Monteith and the mother as Margaret Barr. But as has been already noted, an error had previously been made over the father's name, and one can detect some resemblance between Barr and Dunbar. Furthermore, the child is identified as child 3, after John and Ann, and the couple are given as resident at Barony.

7. OPR, County Lanark, Barony Parish, 622/3 FR 681 in respect of James; 622/3 FR 701 with regard to Ann.

8. There are records of the baptism of two infants named Archibald Douglas Monteath, both sons of Walter Monteath and Jean Douglas of Kippen. One was baptized on 6 May 1758, registered at OPR, 484/1 FR 154; the other christened on 15 May 1773 also at Kippen, OPR, 484/1 FR 176. Either (a) the elder was the son of Archibald Walter, and later became Ensign, or (b) the younger was the son of Walter I and his wife who, if the record is correct, was also called Jean Douglas. The latter Archibald Douglas could have been the later major.

9. OPR, 484/1 FR 293, Marriages, 1738.

10. Addison, *Matriculation Albums,* entry 1248.

11. Blair, *Sketches,* 295; Burke, *Burke's Genealogical and Heraldic History,* 680.

12. G.E.C., *The Complete Peerage,* entry 439.

13. SRO, CC8.8.123 f. 1.

14. Under the entry Archibald, Duke of Douglas, 1694–1761, www.scottish

documents.com/content/famous scots.asp reads: "Archibald's duchess was Margaret or 'Peggy' Douglas who was renowned for her beauty, intelligence and her sharp wit." She was considered by one writer as "a recognised leader in Scottish society". On the same website, under the entry Margaret Douglas, there is a quotation from *Scots Peerage* 9: 13, which reads that she was "quite a character" and that "she was the last of the nobility to be attended by halbardiers when going about the country".

15. Cf. SRO, CC8.8.144 f. 46.

16. SRO, CC8.8.76. This Colin Douglas owed Robert his brother £6,012 3s. 4d. principal and interest of which £2,830 12s. 4d. was the original loan made on 15 November 1796. Because of this outstanding debt, Robert took out a stop order regarding claims of inheritance likely to be made by Colin's other siblings – Rebeccah, Campbell, together with Jean and Jean's husband, Archibald Walter.

17. IRO, Old Wills 46, f. 58.

18. Information gleaned from a deed made by Jean Douglas Monteath passing power of attorney for her property in Falmouth to another brother, James Monteath, then in Trelawny. Power of attorney had previously rested with Campbell, described as having owned property in St Thomas in the East. See IRO, Old Deeds 396, f. 10.

19. Addison, *Matriculation Albums,* entry 638.

20. Ibid., entry 3642.

21. IRO, Old Wills 51, f. 194.

22. See James Monteath's will. SRO, SC36/51/29.

23. IRO, Copy Register, Hanover, Baptisms, Marriages, Burials 1, f. 51.

24. National Archives of Scotland (hereafter NAS), RD4.237.607.

25. NAS, RD4.218.870. Also in Dobson, *Scots in the West Indies, 1707–1857,* vol. 2, unpublished. Personal communication with author.

26. SRO, Services of Heirs, 1800–29, 3, C22; SRO, CC8.8.135. His will was given in for probate by James Monteath, his nephew, in 1804.

27. Again this numeral is meant to distinguish him from his nephew with the same name.

28. See NAS, RD4.237.607.

29. See Dobson, *Directory of Scottish Settlers in North America* 2: 156.

30. SRO, CC8.8.76, f. 117, testament of David Monteath.

31. NAS, RD4.237.607.

32. Anderson, *Burgesses,* 219.

33. See McLaughlin, *Wills before 1858,* 2.

34. See JA, 1B/11/8/6 21, Register of Burials, St Elizabeth, 1826–70, entry 18 for 1828. She is described as "coloured", and aged "about 30 years". While the Index to the Parish Register, St Elizabeth, Baptisms, Marriages, Burials, 1 lists a Charlotte Monteath who died between the 1816–18 period, this death is not recorded in the Register itself, nor is it in the Copy Register. A clerical error is responsible for this problem, as her name was eventually discovered in the record of burials for 1828.

35. JA, 1B/11/8/6 1, Parish Register, St Elizabeth, Baptisms of Persons Non-White.

36. See IRO, Old Wills 67, f. 102, will of William Howard.

37. JA, 1B/11/6 36, f. 34, f. 35.

38. Ann occurred in the following forms in England: Hannah, Anna, Anne, Nan, Nancy and Nanny. In Scotland, as Hannah, Anne, Nannie and Annot. See Yonge, *History of Christian Names,* 42.

39. JA, 1B/11/8/6 2, Register of Persons Non-White, St Elizabeth.

40. IRO, Copy Register, Westmoreland 1, Baptisms 1806.

41. JA, 1B/11/8/6 2, Baptisms, St Elizabeth.

42. See IRO, Copy Register of Baptisms, St Elizabeth, 3, f. 254, entry 43; f. 460, entry 198; 4 f. 82, entry 481; f. 130, entry 8; f. 217, entry 1; f. 490, entry 55; f. 503, entry 59; f. 508, entry 31. For Archibald John's marriage, see IRO, Copy Register of Baptisms, Marriage and Burials, St Elizabeth, 3, f. 254.

43. JA, 1B/11/8/6 5, Parish Register, St Elizabeth, Baptisms 1826–41.

44. See JA, 1B/11/8/6 17, Copy Register, Westmoreland, 1 f. 182. Baptisms, Marriages, Burials.

45. JA, 1B/11/6 50 f. 175.

46. IRO, Old Deeds 621, f. 143.

47. See IRO, Old Deeds 609, f. 1.

48. See the *New Jamaica Almanac and Register* 1808, 144.

49. See Olyphant Family, "Perthshire Families", 25.

50. IRO, Old Wills 117, f. 47.

51. Senior, *Jamaica,* 23.

52. These details are written up in IRO, Copy Register, Westmoreland, 1, f. 237, obviously as an apologia for the remissions of the Hanover pastor's deficiencies.

53. JA, 1B/11/8/6 1, Parish Register, St Elizabeth, 1707–1826.

54. See JA 1B/11/8/16 10, Burials for Westmoreland, entry 113 for 1846.

55. JA, 1B/11/8/6 2, Parish Register, St Elizabeth, Baptisms.

56. See IRO, Old Wills 112, f. 233, will of James McGregor.

57. JA, Parish Register, Westmoreland 1, f. 159, entry 203. Baptisms 1826–32.

58. IRO, Old Deeds 609, f. 1.

59. See IRO, Old Wills 117, f. 47, will of Thomas Ford. Also recorded in the baptismal data for Isabella, IRO, Copy Register, Westmoreland, 1, f. 237.

60. JA, 1B/11/6 38, f. 24 and 25.

61. JA, 1B/11/6 34, f. 160 and 161.

62. IRO, Old Wills 91, f. 210–12.

63. IRO, Old Deeds 640, f. 74.

64. See Hamilton, *Scotland,* 204–11.

65. Girdwood had been appointed major of the St Elizabeth Regiment on 5 August 1806 and lieutenant colonel on 23 June 1807, the same periods in which John served in the militia.

66. IRO, Old Deeds 640, f. 74.

67. Public Record Office (hereafter PRO), T71/1440, f. 576.

68. NLJ, Map Collection.

69. See Sibley, *Dictionary of Place-Names,* 164. Between 1668 and 1675 this area between Bluefields and Whitehouse in Westmoreland was settled by English planters from Suriname or Dutch Guiana when Suriname was ceded to the

Dutch by the English in exchange for New Amsterdam, later renamed New York. "About 1,200 people came, including servants and slaves. These settlers made a great contribution to the early development of Jamaica, for they had a good knowledge of sugar production and brought their know-how with them." Senior, *Encyclopedia,* 470.

70. IRO, Old Deeds 761, f. 261.

71. Senior, *Jamaica,* 97–100.

72. IRO, Old Deeds 62, f. 143.

73. In JA, 1B/11/8/6 2, Register of Baptisms for the Parish of Saint Elizabeth, 1820–25. One notes that on 25 June 1820 a number of "persons belonging to Rose Hall Pen" are entered.

74. See Nelson, "Archibald John Monteith", 289.

75. See Monteith, "Experiences", 271.

76. IRO, Old Deeds 827, f. 48.

77. IRO, Old Deeds 827, f. 47 and f. 53.

78. Ibid., f. 49.

79. Ibid., f. 48.

80. IRO, Old Deeds 830, f. 197.

81. IRO, Old Deeds 831, f. 34.

82. JA, 1B/11/8/6 3, Parish Register of Marriages of Slaves, St Elizabeth, 1826–34, entry 6.

83. JA, *Jamaica Almanacs* between 1818 and 1832. In an overview of this period of moderate land redistribution in the island, Satchell, *Plots to Plantations,* 27, reveals that "by 1845 it was estimated that there were 19,397 holdings under 10 acres and in 1841 holdings between 10 and 50 acres numbered 7,919".

84. IRO, Old Wills 91, f. 210.

85. JA, 1B/11/3 127, f. 12, Inventories.

86. JA, 1B/11/4 49, f. 154; 50, f. 82, Crop Accounts.

87. He was buried, aged sixty-five, at Mount Lebanon in December 1822. JA, 1B/11/8/6 2, f. 361, Parish Register, St Elizabeth, Burials.

88. IRO, Old Deeds 589, f. 107.

89. Dobson, *Directory of Scottish Settlers* 7: 16. He is described as having settled in Jamaica.

90. Study of the Anglican Registers for St Elizabeth and Westmoreland has not yielded evidence of Girdwood's passing. Perhaps he had died in Scotland or in some other parish in Jamaica. Church of Scotland records for nineteenth-century Jamaica are scant.

91. See IRO, Old Deeds 682, f. 248.

92. The figure is indecipherable, being either £11,025 or £11,065 or £11,075.

93. IRO, Old Deeds 679, f. 130.

94. See JA, 1B/11/7 10, f. 45–48, Return of Slaves, St Elizabeth.

95. See JA, 1/B/11/7 38a, f. 40. The shifting borders of St Elizabeth, out of which Westmoreland was cut in 1703, is responsible for the fact that Kep records are found in 1820 in the Return of Slaves for Westmoreland, rather than as previously in St Elizabeth.

96. JA, 1B/11/6 1, f. 216, Return of Slaves, 1817, Westmoreland.

97. IRO, Copy Register, St Elizabeth, 4, f. 572, entry 46. It is noticeable that a number of white people who encouraged the Moravian missionaries and even attended their services were given Anglican burials. This no doubt reflected the social status of the Anglican Church in the colony, which in the view of the white community made that church a fitting means of paying respects to the departed of a certain social standing. On the other hand, the Moravian Church must have held the status of the church for Africans. In this connection, we note the burial by Anglican rites of Hutchison Mure Scott and his wife, the Millers, the Farquharsons and Mrs Mary Lauderdale Spence of Hopewell in 1847. Another slant to this issue is presented by the funeral arrangements for John Foster who died in 1831. A notice of his death occupies almost an entire page of the St Elizabeth Register of Burials, 21, 1826–70, kept by the Anglican Church, although he was buried according to Moravian rites at one of his properties. His importance is signified by a listing of descriptors: he was "resident at Brick-hill in the Town and County of Bedford . . . Gt. Britain and late resident of the Bogue Estate". The record is first signed by John Ellis, officiating minister at the interment and then countersigned by Thomas P. Williams, rector of St John's Church.

98. IRO, Old Wills 128, f. 86.

99. See JA, 1B/11/8/16 21, Baptisms and Marriages, Westmoreland, 1821–26. George Marcy seems to have been the son of George Marcy by Anne Evans. The child was baptized on 29 March 1778 (JA, 1B/11/8/16 17), which fits with the age given in the registration of his death in 1857 as eighty-six years old.

100. SRO, CC9/7/83, f. 204.

101. IRO, Old Deeds 702, f. 76.

102. IRO, Old Deeds 719, f. 57.

103. See IRO, Old Wills 100, f. 185. His will is dated 27 March 1821. He identified himself as a planter, having a share in Hopeton Plantation along with five slaves. His father was Archibald McGregor of Kilmadock parish in Perthshire, Scotland.

104. Some examples follow: John Vanheelen married Anna Maria Walker in 1775. Anna Maria having died in June 1777, Vanheelen married Elizabeth Vassall, widow, in February 1781. IRO, Copy Register, St Elizabeth 1, f. 298, 300. When Vanheelen died, Elizabeth Vassall remarried to John Salmon in 1796. IRO, Copy Register, St Elizabeth 1, f. 306. John Salmon having died, Elizabeth Vanheelen married John Mabell Cooper in September 1798. And with Elizabeth Vanheelen dead, John Mabell Cooper married the spinster, Catherine Farquharson, in 1799. IRO, Copy Register, St Elizabeth 1, f. 307. Similarly, Joseph Royall married the widow of Robert Dellap in 1768; Francis Cooke married Mary Armstrong, widow of Joseph Armstrong in 1764; Andrew Malcolm married the widow Judith Blake in 1773; and William Witter married the widow Elizabeth Webley in 1782. JA, 1B/11/8/6 1.

105. JA, 1B/11/7 23, 34, Return of Slaves, St Elizabeth.

106. JA, 1B/11/6 68, f. 46.

107. IRO, Old Wills 112, f. 233.

108. See JA, 1B/11/7 23, f. 9, Return of Slaves, 1817.

109. See JA, 1B/11/7 42, Return of Slaves, 1826; 132, f. 119, Return of Slaves, 1832.

110. IRO, Old Deeds 827, f. 48.

Chapter 5

1. Black, *Surnames of Scotland,* 608.

2. See Addison, *Matriculation Albums,* entry 3642, which indicates that Walter Monteath (I) of Kepp and Arnmore, was the eldest son of Walter Monteath of Kepp, Knight in the Parish of Kippen in the County of Perth. The elder Walter is treated at entry 1573.

3. "Conquest" – the adjudication by courts (called "sasines") of "rights to lands and other heritable rights" which the "deceased has acquired by . . . purchase, donation". It "ascends to the immediate elder brother, or uncle" in cases where the deceased "has died without lawful issue, leaving brothers both older and younger than himself, or the issue of such brothers, or two or more uncles . . . or the descendants of such uncles". Bell, *Dictionary and Digest,* 216. The jury members deciding these sasines were empanelled by the sheriff of the county concerned on order of chancery. "The jury returned or 'retoured' their verdict to Chancery who then issued the heir with his 'retour' and the heir could then take possession of his inheritance. . . . [S]ometimes heirs were not served heir to the property for several years after the death of the owner, particularly if they emigrated." Cory, *Scottish Ancestry,* 51.

4. Groome, *Ordnance Gazetteer.* The late-eighteenth-century land rents for Arnmore and Powside amounted to Scottish £355 6s. 8d.; and Kepp brought in £118. By contrast, William Douglas of Castle Douglas collected £882 for Castle Douglas and seven other properties; James Douglas of Mains earned £414 for Mains and another £900 from lands in Renfrewshire and Inchinnan. See Timperley, *Directory of Landownership,* 117, 195, 291, 330.

5. Devine, *Tobacco Lords,* 4, 171.

6. Ibid.

7. Ibid., 16.

8. Ibid., 8.

9. Anderson, *Burgesses,* 35.

10. Devine, *Tobacco Lords,* 35.

11. Walsh, "Slave Life", 174, 179, 180.

12. Devine, *Tobacco Lords,* 79.

13. PRO, T79/26.

14. Devine, *Tobacco Lords,* 65.

15. Ibid., 64.

16. Ibid., 125–26.

17. Ibid., 116.

18. Ibid., 7.

19. Ibid., 156.

20. Ibid., 159.

21. PRO, AO12/109, f. 152.

22. Ibid.

23. PRO, T79/34, Part 2.

24. PRO, T79/44, Box 2.

25. PRO, T78/44, f. 259, 261.

26. PRO, T79/26.

27. PRO, T79/34 Pt. 2, f. 272.

28. IRO, Old Wills 91, f. 210.

29. See Saville, *Bank of Scotland,* 131. This bank was the second successor to the Ship Bank originally capitalized in 1749 by propertied men such as John Grahame of Douglastoun and wealthy merchants with landed connections such as Colin and Robert Dunlop, Allan Dreghorn, Andrew Buchanan, Alexander Houston and William McDowall, the two latter being wealthy West India merchants.

30. PRO, T79/20, f. 48.

31. Mitchell Library Archives (hereafter MLA), Dreghorn Mansion Papers, TD465.27 Items 8, 10, 15.

32. SRO, SC36/48/29, inventory of Archibald Douglas Monteath, entered 9 May 1838.

33. SRO, SC36/51/29, will of James Monteath Douglas, Glasgow Sheriff Court Wills, 47 pages.

34. Donald, *Minute Book,* 8.

35. Ibid.

36. Smith and Mitchell, *Old Country Houses.*

37. SRO, SC36/48/29, inventory of Archibald Douglas Monteath entered 9 May 1838.

38. SRO, SC36/51/29. Will of James Monteath Douglas.

39. Blair, *Sketches,* 295.

40. Dobson, *Original Scots Colonists: Caribbean Supplement,* v–vi.

41. Ibid., vi.

42. Padrón, *Spanish Jamaica,* 215, 223–24.

43. Lalla and D'Costa, *Language in Exile,* 14.

44. Kiergaard, *PA* 16: 46, June 1841.

45. Ellis and Collis, *PA* 13: 68, 1833

46. Stobwasser, *PA* 9: 75, 26 July 1823.

47. Elliott, *PA* 15: 88, 1 June 1844.

48. Dobson, *Directory of Scottish Settlers* 7: 14.

49. Dobson, *Directory of Scottish Settlers* 5: 39, 42.

50. IRO, Old Wills, 46, f. 58, Margaret Douglass's will, 23 December 1775.

51. IRO, Old Deeds 512, f. 69.

52. SRO, CC9/7, Commissariot Record of Glasgow, Register of Testaments, 1547–1800.

53. See Anderson, *Burgesses,* 457.

54. In Hugh Wallace's will of 2 April 1772, he refers to Arthur Connell of Glasgow as his brother-in-law. See IRO, Old Wills 44, f. 12.

55. IRO, Copy Register, St Elizabeth 1, f. 334.

56. IRO, Old Deeds 367, f. 44.

57. *Edinburgh Advertiser.* In Dobson *Directory of Scottish Settlers* 2: 156.

58. SRO, RD4.237.607. See Dobson, *Original Scots Colonists,* 251.

59. IRO, Copy Register, Hanover, Baptisms, Marriages, Burials, 1, f. 61.

60. Ibid., f. 51.

61. See OPR, 484/1 FR 156, for David's baptismal record. For data regarding his death, see the probate of his will, SRO, CC8.8.76, f. 117.

62. The first name on the record is missing. See SRO, CE60.1.7; also Dobson, *Original Scots Colonists,* 251.

63. SRO, RD3.273.11; also Dobson, *Directory of Scottish Settlers* 4: 105.

64. IRO, Copy Register, Hanover, Baptisms, Marriages, Burials, 1, f. 69, f. 87. This source gives Thomas's date of birth as 25 November 1788, which is clearly an error in light of the fact that Amelia had already given birth on 3 November the same year. Unfortunately this clerical error cannot be rectified as the original Parish Register is missing. An army source, however, dates his birth as 1787. See Douglas, "Brief Description".

65. See Douglas, "Brief Description". For mention of Thomas's military involvement, see Kaye, *War in Afghanistan,* 414, 464; Stubbs, *Bengal Artillery,* 57, 61, 68; and Cardew, *Bengal Native Army,* 179.

66. IRO, Copy Register, Hanover, Baptisms, Marriages, Burials, 1, f. 47.

67. Ibid., f. 58, 83.

68. For the purchase of land, see IRO, Old Deeds, 815, f. 49. On 3 May 1837, Sarah Donaldson sold two lots of land in Savanna-la-Mar, numbers 103 and 104 for £400 to her sons John Monteath and James Wilson. For the registration of John's death, see IRO, Copy Register, St Elizabeth, 3, f. 420.

69. Jacob Zorn, *PA* 12: 361, writing on 5 February 1831, explains the term house-keepers" as "the West Indian term for concubines".

70. IRO, Old Wills 120, f. 99.

71. Sarah Donaldson had children with persons other than Thomas Monteath. She was mother to James Wilson, who became a saddler in Hanover; and had Robert Benjamin Downes with John Benjamin Downes. Jesse, Sarah's eldest daughter, was also prolific. She bore John Alexander Neven or Nevins; William James Thompson and Benjamin Thompson (born 1 January 1810); as well as Sarah Donaldson Lee, Benjamin Lee and Thomas Lee. See Jesse's will of 1 March 1818. IRO, Old Wills 95, f. 32.

72. See IRO, Copy Register, Hanover, 1, f. 83; and Old Wills 143, f. 31.

73. IRO, Copy Register, St Elizabeth, 4, f. 51, entry 17.

74. IRO, Old Deeds 258, f. 28.

75. JA, Crop Accounts, 1B/11/4 8, f. 79.

76. JA, Crop Accounts, 1B/11/4 7, f. 170.

77. IRO, Old Deeds 284, f. 54.

78. IRO, Old Deeds 291, f. 98.

79. IRO, Old Deeds 298, f. 162.

80. IRO, Copy Register, Hanover, Baptisms, Marriages, Burials, 1, f. 61.

81. *Cornwall Chronicle, Supplement,* 10 August 1782.

82. IRO, Old Deeds 338, f. 56.

83. Sheridan, "Role of the Scots", 95.

84. *Cornwall Chronicle, Supplement,* 15 September 1781.

85. IRO, Old Deeds 337, f. 161.

86. IRO, Old Deeds 51, f. 128.

87. See Hall, *In Miserable Slavery,* 8–9. Also Institute of Commonwealth Studies Library, London, Simon Taylor Collection, Box H10. Early 1800s letters from Robert (Bontine) Graham to Simon Taylor include several letters of introduction for persons travelling overseas and seeking employment on estates.

88. Hamilton, *Scotland,* 56, 60–61.

89. Olyphant Family, "Perthshire Families", 38.

90. Letter of John Wedderburn referenced in ibid.

91. See IRO, Old Wills 91, f. 97.

92. See IRO, Old Deeds 338, f. 138.

93. JA, 1B/11/8/6, 1.

94. See, for example, JA, 1B/11/4 5, f. 207, when he signs the crop accounts regarding the Golden Grove Plantation.

95. See IRO, Old Wills 67, f. 102, will of William Howard. A recent monograph on Black River reads: "When the town was laid out, grass tracks were used as roads through the properties. When roads were made, gates were built across the roads to prevent animals straying. This necessitated opening and closing of the gates. Watchmen lived at these points. Any hour of night or day, they were on duty to open and close the gates for traffic to pass through. On the West side of the town were the Hodges gates No. 1 and No. 2. On the North side was the Lower Works gate." Barrett, *Reflections,* 6.

96. Thistlewood arrived in Jamaica in 1750 and died there in 1786. In fact, Thistlewood had noted in 1768 that a number of overseers had changed properties, among them a Monteith who "ha[d] left Mr. Stone at Long Pond". Hall, *In Miserable Slavery,* 164. Was this a reference to one of John's uncles? It might have been William, who by 1773 was described as a planter who had forfeited his property on account of debt. Unfortunately, no Monteith name occurs among the signatures to the crop accounts for Long Pond in the time period under investigation.

97. JA, Crop Accounts, 1B/11/4 22, f. 137 for 1797; 23, f. 235 for 1796; 21, f. 159 for 1798; 27, f. 61 for 1800. In 1799 he testifies to the accounts for 1798.

98. JA, Crop Accounts, 1B/11/4 30, f. 164 for 1802 and 32, f. 44 for 1803.

99. IRO, Old Deeds 507, f. 140; Old Deeds 451, f. 147.

100. IRO, Old Deeds 45, f. 24.

101. Biddulph, *The Nineteenth,* 275–80, seems to suggest that this promotion came in 1797, but Army List 1799 gives the date as 25 December 1795. (www.lib.mq.edu.au/digital/seringapatam/19tharmylist.html)

102. Gopal, *Tipu Sultan's Mysore,* 14–28.

103. Biddulph, *The Nineteenth,* 87.

104. Ibid., 77.

105. Thompson, *The Last Siege,* 60.

106. Biddulph, *The Nineteenth*, 99, 101. See also Milne, "Harris Heritage": Major General George Harris who commanded the Madras Army earned one-eighth share of Tipu's coffers, amounting to an estimated £150,000. In 1815 Harris was made baron of Seringapatam and Mysore, and Belmont in Kent. His grandson was made governor of Trinidad in 1846.

107. Callahan, *East India Company*, 223–24.

108. British Library, Oriental and India Office, Microfilm L/AG/34/39/201, f. 73.

109. There is a John Maxwell of Dargavel who is listed with Douglases of Renfrewshire in respect of land tax payments. John Maxwell, the sixth laird of Dargavel, had married Margaret, daughter of John Campbell of Succoth. Burke, *Genealogical and Heraldic History*, 635. The lawyer died in Glasgow, 16 July 1807. Addison, *Matriculation Albums*, entry 1941.

110. IRO, Old Deeds 493, f. 40.

111. IRO, Old Deeds 526, f. 104.

112. IRO, Old Deeds 472, f. 240.

113. IRO, Old Deeds 482, f. 33.

114. Mather and Speitel, *Linguistic Atlas*, 1; 2, map 26.

115. Ibid., 2, map 26.

116. IRO, Old Deeds 401, f. 229.

117. Mather and Speitel, *Linguistic Atlas*, 2, map 26.

118. IRO, Old Deeds 523, f. 151.

119. IRO, Old Deeds 509, f. 204.

120. IRO, Old Deeds 507, f. 140.

121. IRO, Old Deeds 511, f. 148.

122. IRO, Old Deeds 592, f. 259.

123. IRO, Old Deeds, 645, f. 207.

124. JA, 7/40, *New Jamaica Almanack and Register*, 1801, 153; *Royal Register and Jamaica Almanac*, 1813, 188.

125. JA, 7/40, *Jamaica Almanack* 1807, 181; 1808, 177; 1813, 158.

126. Karras, *Sojourners in the Sun*, 65.

127. Roughley, *Jamaica Planter's Guide*, 9.

128. JA, Crop Accounts, 1B/11/4 35, f. 217; 37, f. 181.

129. Olyphant Family, "Perthsire Families", 75.

130. See McCalman, *Horrors of Slavery*, 45–51, where Robert gives his date of birth as around 1762, identifies his father as James Wedderburn, a planter and doctor, and cites his mother as the coloured Rosanna, owned by a Lady Douglas who died about 1766. Her properties passed to James Charles Sholto Douglas. For further on the Wedderburns, see Higman, *Plantation Jamaica*, 154.

131. See Olyphant Family, "Perthshire Families", 45, 62, 92. Also Dobson, *Directory of Scottish Settlers* 7: 105.

132. JA, 21/3 (1344), *Jamaica Almanack*, 1817, 88.

133. JA, Crop Accounts, 1B/11/4 35 f. 216.

134. See IRO, Copy Register, Hanover, Baptisms, Marriages, Burials, 1725–1839, 1, f. 142. A copy of a letter from Glasgow dated 14 February 1797 indicates that David Connell was "late of Jamaica now in Glasgow, merchant".

135. IRO, Old Deeds 593, f. 45.

136. NLJ, Map Collection, St Elizabeth 965, N/16099.

Chapter 6

1. In this text, used collectively, "Africans" and "blacks" refer to continental Africans as well as their diasporic descendants. Reference to continental Africans exclusively is specified by "the Africans". For perceptions of skin colour in the African conceptions of beauty, see Boone, *Radiance from the Waters*, 119–20, 236; Tembo, "Beautiful Women". "Most Mende are dark brown in color, but skin either lighter or darker than the norm has great allure. A copper complexion, described as a point between the usual brown and a fair color, is unusual and very attractive. . . . Very black skin, completely black, is the most desired and adored. In traditional society, a black person automatically was a celebrity." Boone, *Radiance from the Waters*, 119. Boone's observations coincide with data in a Yoruba song collected in Trinidad that speaks to the attraction of either very black skin or amber-coloured skin. See Warner-Lewis, *Yoruba Songs*, 96–97.

2. Mallalieu, *PA* 18: 143, 22 March 1847.

3. Patterson, *Sociology of Slavery*, 61, speaking with the intimacy of "one who has grown up in a multiracial society" acknowledges that "hair difference is what carries the real symbolic potency" rather than skin colour. While there is much truth in this opinion, extreme shades of black, traditionally, and now also, extreme shades of white, can attract negative responses.

4. See Stephens, *Latin American Terminology*.

5. See Renny, *History of Jamaica*, 188; Higman, *Slave Population*, 139; Baranov and Yelvington, "Ethnicity, Race, Class and Nationality", 217. For the explanation of "white by law", see JA, 1B/11/8/6, 1, Baptisms, St Elizabeth, White, entries related to William Allen on 20 May 1810 and Isaac Thomas Allen on 5 July 1812. The rector opined that they were "white by law", being the reputed sons of Mr James Allen by Rebecca Beavers, a freed Mestize.

6. Ellis and Pemsel, *PA* 12: 19, 23 May 1830.

7. See Allen, "Creole".

8. Buchner, *Moravians in Jamaica*, 19–20.

9. Mathurin, "Women in Jamaica", 39–40.

10. Ibid., 42.

11. Ibid., 43, quoting Taylor, *Life and Travels*.

12. Mathurin, "Women in Jamaica", 236; Burnard, *Mastery, Tyranny, and Desire*, 146–52.

13. Mathurin, "Women in Jamaica", 139.

14. "Diary of Bogue Mission", *PA* 6: 67, 23 June 1813.

15. Zorn, *PA* 12: 25, 5 June 1830.

16. Heuman, *Between Black and White*, 14.

17. His will instructed that Elizabeth Green and her children should live on the 50-acre property called Kippens (see IRO, Old Deeds 401, f. 229), while Mary Scott and her daughters should occupy the 127½ acres of Hartshall. This latter property

bordered on Hampstead, which was also owned by James Hart. Hampstead was apparently the consolidation of the 300 acres between New Savanna and Moko Valley bought for £370 from Alexander and Mary Walker in 1786 (see IRO, Old Deeds 351, f. 28) and another 300 acres (on resurvey found to be 191 acres) for £200 from John and Ann Vanheelen in 1797 (IRO, Old Deeds 449, f. 99). The Moravian, George Robbins, described on 6 May 1846 visiting Hampstead, "a property about 4 miles distant, on one of the summits of the neighboring mountains where the air is delightfully cool and bracing. Many remains of former splendor are exhibited here. Half a dozen twelve pounders still frown over the perpendicular sides of the barbacue. But alas! Ichabad! – where is the glory?" After Hart's death in August 1800, Hampstead was acquired by Thomas Smith.

18. IRO, Old Wills 67, f. 96.

19. See Olyphant Family, "Perthshire Families", 48; Heuman, *Between Black and White,* 5–6.

20. Heuman, *Between Black and White,* 4.

21. JA, 1B/11/8/6 1, Baptisms of Children Not White, 17 August 1791 and 3 March 1800. George died, aged sixteen, in 1813, being buried on 27 November at Hartshall. Copy Register, St Elizabeth, 1, f. 348. Thomas died, about eighty years old, in Black River, and was buried on 6 July 1848. Rebecca died, aged seventy-seven, at Black River, and was buried on 27 March 1859. See IRO, Copy Register, St Elizabeth, 4, f. 517, f. 460. Sarah apparently died in 1822 when she made her will. See IRO, Old Wills 119, f. 201.

22. IRO, Old Wills 119, f. 201.

23. IRO, Copy Register, Hanover, Baptisms, Marriages, Burials, 1, f. 47. Jesse's will was made on 1 March 1818. She identified herself as belonging to Hanover, a "free woman of Colour . . . at present sick in Body". See IRO, Old Wills 95, f. 32.

24. IRO, Copy Register, Hanover, Baptisms, Marriages, Burials, 1, f. 58. John Monteath or Monteith became the harbour master of Black River. He was buried on 10 June 1840 when he was "about 60 years" old. See IRO, Copy Register of Baptisms, Marriages, Burials, St Elizabeth, 3, f. 420. On 5 February 1829 John purchased 87 square feet of land "between the street and the sea in Black River Bay" from George Hook Bawn, mariner, Benjamin Capon, gentleman, and Mary Capon, spinster, all of St Elizabeth. See IRO, Old Deeds 762, f. 180. Then on 3 May 1837 John and his brother, James Wilson, bought from their mother for Jamaican £400 two lots of land, numbers 103 and 104, in Savanna-la-Mar. See IRO, Old Deeds, 815, f. 49.

25. In 1816 Rebecca, described as "a free woman of Colour", bought lot 28 in the town of Savanna-la-Mar for Jamaican £350 from the saddler John Mcfarlane or Macfarlane the younger of Westmoreland. See IRO, Old Deeds 662, f. 193. Rebecca's will is dated 6 March 1861. See IRO, Old Wills 132, f. 31. Rebecca was illiterate.

26. IRO, Copy Register, Hanover, Baptisms, Marriages, Burials, 1, f. 83.

27. See IRO, Old Wills 120, f. 99; Old Deeds 815, f. 49.

28. IRO, Copy Register, Hanover, Baptisms, Marriages, Burials, 1, f. 69, f. 87.

29. JA, 1B/11/8/6 1, Parish Register, St Elizabeth, Marriages of Whites, 9 May 1772.

30. JA, IB/II/8/6 1, Parish Register, St Elizabeth, Marriages of Whites, 19 March 1800.

31. See MA A–1 Carmel, Congregation Lists and Baptismal Register, New Eden. See, for example, William Thomson, son of William of Hartshall and Margaret of Prospect Woodlands, 2 August 1829, entry 103; William Price, son of George and Matilda of Paynestown, 11 July 1830, entry 120; Richard Williams, son of William Smith of Hartshall and Sarah of Pleasant Hill, 20 February 1832, entry 180; David Alexander, son of David and Eleanor Monteith of Green Valley, born 4 November 1848, entry 1508.

32. Goveia, "Amelioration and Emancipation", 2.

33. "Slavery as a sociolegal status, completely marginalized and alienated fatherhood, and focused its attention upon motherhood." Beckles, "Freeing Slavery", 206. "Slavery does away with fathers, as it does away with families. Slavery has no use for either fathers or families, and its laws do not recognize their existence in the social arrangements of the plantation. When they *do* exist, they are not the outgrowths of slavery, but are antagonistic to that system." Douglass, *My Bondage and My Freedom,* 51.

34. There are, however, instances where estates kept a log of their slaves and work regimes. See West Indian Reference Library (hereafter WIRL) manuscript holdings: Indentures, Surrenders and Releases pertaining to Deans Valley Plantation, Westmoreland, 1781–1832; Bodleian Library, Oxford University; Barham Family Papers, bookkeepers' annual inventories of slaves on the family's Jamaica estates, 1736–1832.

35. JA, IB/II/8/6 2, Parish Register, St Elizabeth, Baptisms, Not White.

36. Editor, Monteith, "Memoir", 433.

37. Was this on account of the lot system? Decisions in the Moravian Church were made by lot, which was interpreted as "the voice of the Lord. Their standard practice was to place three papers in a tube, one with a favourable message, another with a negative message, and a third that was blank." Dunn, "Two Jamaican Slaves", 197. The two latter draws were negative. This system was used to arrive at admission for candidacy as a church member, then for readiness for baptism and then for admission to Holy Communion. The lot was also used in the selection of mates for missionaries, and among church members in European Moravian communities. See Gollin, *Moravians in Two Worlds,* chap. 3; Smaby, *Moravian Bethlehem,* 23–24.

38. MA, J–Carmel, Adult Male Baptisms, entry 118.

39. MA, O–1 Carmel, List of Persons Departed, 1850.

40. IRO, IB/II/8/6 2, Parish Register, St Elizabeth.

41. MA, C–1 Carmel, Original Register of Marriages, entry 162.

42. MA, J–Carmel, Adult Female Baptisms, entry 399.

43. MA, C–1 Carmel, Original Register of Marriages, New Carmel, entry 36.

44. MA, J–Carmel, Adult Female Baptisms, entry 482.

45. MA, A–Carmel, Baptism Registers, New Eden.

46. JA, IB/II/8/6 2, Parish Register, St Elizabeth, Baptisms.

47. MA, J–Carmel, Baptismal Register, entry 164.

48. JA, IB/II/8/6 3, Parish Register, St Elizabeth, Marriages 1826–34, entry 31.

49. MA, J–Carmel, Adult Female Baptisms, entry 111.

50. MA, C–Carmel 3, entry 38. No date is given, but the entry falls between a marriage on 26 December 1830 and one on 2 January 1831.

51. Buchner, *Moravians in Jamaica,* 120.

52. JA, 1B/11/8/6 3, Parish Register, St Elizabeth, Marriages, 1831–35. See also MA, J–Carmel, Adult Male Baptisms, entry 61.

53. See NLJ, Maps, St Elizabeth 827.

54. MA, J–Carmel, Male Baptisms, entry 61.

55. MA, J–Carmel, Female Baptisms, entry 166.

56. MA, J–Carmel, Baptism Register, entry 41.

57. Elliott, *PA* 15: 481–82, 31 May 1841.

58. JA, 1B/11/8/6 3, Parish Register, St Elizabeth, Marriages, 1826–34.

59. MA, J–Carmel, Female Adult Baptisms, entry 84.

60. MA, O–5 Carmel. For the children's baptismal dates, see O–Carmel, Register of Baptisms at New Carmel from 1824; A–1 Carmel, Congregation Lists and Baptism Register, New Eden. Thomas Hart Monteith was the father of John Ernest Samuel Monteith mentioned in Aarons, "Story of Aneaso", and Hastings and MacLeavy, *Seedtime and Harvest.* He was in turn the father of Kenneth Monteith and Joyce Buchanan whose help in this research has been acknowledged. Robert George fathered Edward Benjamin, the maternal grandfather of Rupert Lewis mentioned in chapter 1. Edna Lawrence, also referred to in that chapter, is a granddaughter of Thomas Hart Monteith by Thomas's son, Josiah Nathaniel.

61. MA, J–Carmel, Adult Male Baptisms, entry 165.

62. According to MA, J–Carmel, Adult Female Baptisms, entry 451, she was resident at Rosehall at the time of her baptism, but C–Carmel, entry 3, links her to Woodlands, an adjacent property where she must have belonged under the slave regime.

63. JA, 1B/11/8/6 2, Parish Register, St Elizabeth.

64. MA, C–3 Carmel, entry 256.

65. MA, J–Carmel, Female Baptisms, entry 151.

66. MA, C–3 Carmel, entry 582.

67. MA, J–Carmel, Baptisms, entry 185.

68. IRO, 1B/11/8/6 2, Parish Register, St Elizabeth.

69. JA, 1B/8/6 3, Parish Register, Baptisms, St Elizabeth, entry 3.

70. MA, A–1 Carmel, Congregation Lists and Baptismal Register, New Eden, entry 64.

71. MA, J–Carmel, entry 23; JA, 1B/11/8/6 3, St Elizabeth: Marriages 1826–1834, entry 15.

72. JA, 1B/11/8/6 3, St Elizabeth: Marriages 1826–1834, entry 15. There is, however, a record of the marriage of Adam Hart and Ann Hart, both of Hampstead Estate, on 2 April 1837. IRO, Copy Register, St Elizabeth, 3, f. 254, entry 37.

73. MA, O–1 Carmel, List of Persons Departed, 1869, 1870.

74. MA, O–1 Carmel, Diary of New Carmel, 27 February 1839.

75. Ibid. In *PA* 14: 82, 12 March 1836, John Collis had commended the "laudable

custom" of blessing a newly erected house "with singing and prayer", a custom which "has almost universally, in this neighbourhood, superseded the heathenish revelries which marked similar occasions in times gone by". On this occasion, it was also customary to "give name to the cottages which they had built for the use of their families". "Retrospect", 31. One notices that the letter from Archibald to Joseph Kummer's parents is headed "Mount Blessed", which may in fact have been the name he gave his home.

76. NLJ, Maps, St Elizabeth 827.

77. JA, Parish Register, St Elizabeth, Baptisms and Marriages, 1826–34, entry 12.

78. Edwards, *The History*, 285.

79. Monteith, "Experiences", 268.

80. Nelson, "Archibald John Monteith", 295.

81. Lichtenthaeler in Harvey and Brewin, "Autobiographical Sketch", 100.

82. Monteith, "Experiences", 272.

83. JA, 1B/11/7 1, f. 221, 1817 Return of Slaves, Westmoreland. As a shorthand, the same age was given to a large quantity of slaves in the estate list.

84. MA, C–3 Carmel, entry 78. J–Carmel, Adult Male Baptisms, entry 20, lists her as belonging to Hopeton, but they were two contiguous properties owned by the same person.

85. MA, J–Carmel, Adult Male Baptisms, entry 11.

86. MA, A–1 Carmel, Congregation Lists and Baptismal Register, New Eden, p. 200, entry 3.

87. MA, A–1 Carmel, Congregation Lists and Baptismal Register, New Eden, entry 44.

88. MA, J–Carmel, Adult Female Baptisms, entry 25. Also see JA, 1B/11/8/6 2, Parish Register, St Elizabeth, Marriages. In this latter record, both parties are identified as the property of Mary Thompson.

89. Elliott, O–1 Carmel, Diary of New Carmel, 3 March 1839.

90. Elliott, *PA* 16: 408, 26 June 1843.

91. Ellis, *PA* 9: 393, 15 September 1825.

92. Elliott, *PA* 16: 409, 26 June 1843.

93. MA, J–Carmel, Adult Female Baptisms, entry 14.

94. MA, O–2 Carmel, Annual Reports of Church and Day Schools, 1870.

95. Monteith, "Experiences", 10.

96. JA, 1B/11/8/6 3, Parish Register, St Elizabeth, Marriages 1826–1834, entry 12.

97. MA, J–Carmel, Adult Female Baptisms, entry 48.

98. MA, O–Carmel, Register of Families, 1859, entry 5.

99. JA, 1B/11/7 1, f. 113, 1817 Return of Slaves, Westmoreland.

100. MA, J–Carmel, Baptism Register, Males, entries 17, 358.

101. MA, C–1 Carmel, Original Register of Marriages, entry 16.

102. MA, O–1 Carmel, List of Persons Departed, 1847.

103. MA, E–2 Carmel, Deaths, entry 12.

104. MA, O–1 Carmel, List of Persons Departed, 1849.

105. See Buchner, *Moravians in Jamaica*, 80; also MA, O–1 Carmel, List of Persons Departed, 1847.

106. JA, 1B/11/8/6 1, Parish Register, St Elizabeth, Baptisms of Persons, Not White.

107. MA, J–Carmel, entry 32; see also JA, 1B/11/8/6 3, Parish Register, St Elizabeth, Marriages 1826–34, entry 14.

108. JA, 1B/11/7 12, f. 118, 1817 Return of Slaves, St Elizabeth, Hampstead.

109. JA, 1B/11/8/6 3, Parish Register, Westmoreland, entry 2; also MA, J–Carmel, Adult Male Baptisms, entry 19.

110. MA, C–3 Carmel, entry 172.

111. Nelson, "Archibald John Monteith", 297.

112. MA, J–Carmel, Adult Male Baptisms, entry 204.

113. MA, C–1 Carmel, Original Register of Marriages, entry 89.

114. MA, C–Carmel, Minutes of Helpers' Conference, 1847.

115. MA, C–1 Carmel, Original Register of Marriages, entry 133.

116. MA, O–Carmel, Register of Families, 1859.

117. MA, O–1 Carmel, List of Persons Departed, 1868.

118. MA, C–3 Carmel, Marriage Register, entry 159.

119. MA, C–3 Carmel, Marriage Register, entry 79.

120. MA, J–Carmel, Adult Female Baptisms, entry 7.

121. MA, O–1 Carmel, Diary of New Carmel.

122. Nelson, "Archibald John Monteith", 296.

123. Monteith, "Experiences", 279.

124. MA, J–Carmel, Adult Female Baptisms, entry 66; C–3 Carmel, Marriage Register, entry 9.

125. IRO, Copy Register, St Elizabeth 4, f. 458.

126. JA, 1B/11/8/6 2, Parish Register, Baptisms, St Elizabeth.

127. MA, J–Carmel, Adult Male Baptisms, entry 68.

128. MA, J–Carmel, Adult Male Baptisms, entry 68; also J–Carmel, Adult Female Baptisms, entry 81.

129. MA, J–Carmel, Adult Male Baptisms, entry 851.

130. MA, X–2 Carmel, Register of Exclusions and Suspensions, entry 985.

Chapter 7

1. See Hunte, "Protestantism and Slavery".

2. Brathwaite, *Creole Society*, 188–89, notes the occurrence of marriages between ethnic groups in St Elizabeth parish at the close of the eighteenth century and beginning of the nineteenth.

3. Zorn, *PA* 12: 27, 24 October 1830.

4. For this aspect of informal, yet sometimes formally sanctioned, evangelization, there is the example of George Lewis, an enslaved African itinerant vendor who made Manchester and St Elizabeth his field of religious operation. See Brathwaite, *Creole Society*, 163; Buchner, *Moravians in Jamaica*, 47–48. There is also the character of Father Williams in Perkins, *Busha's Mistress*, 93–96. Archibald himself clearly operated in this manner as well. After being appointed as a national missionary assistant, "from that time on I had many opportunities to tell others what the Lord had done for me, and to point them to the same Saviour.

With this goal I attended the evening lessons after work finished on the plantations here and there. I was readily received when I brought out the Bible and read to the people and spoke to their hearts. In Woodlands these meetings were forbidden by the administrator and the participants punished." Monteith, "Experiences", 278. Moses Baker, an American ex-slave of the Baptist Mission, was also in some ways an itinerant preacher. The Moravian John Light held Baker in the highest esteem. Light lived five miles distant from the "brown preacher" who, for him, was "a man of the right stamp, a blessed and active servant of our common Lord and Master, notwithstanding old age has almost blinded his eyes, and made his legs to move slowly". At the time of Light's eulogy in 1818, Baker had already spent "thirty years' labour in these parts" during which time he "[had] had to endure much persecution". *PA* 7: 22, 12 April 1818.

5. Hastings and MacLeavy, *Seedtime and Harvest,* 120.
6. Ibid.
7. Becker, *PA* 9: 78, 20 May 1823.
8. Harvey and Brewin, "Autobiographical Sketch", 88.
9. New York Public Library, Manuscript Division, Horsfield-Kummer Family Papers, 1. See Missionary Lecture, "Greenland", 1 December 1867, and Mission Lecture II, Commencement – West Indies, 3 November 1867.
10. Zorn, *PA* 17: 348, 29 March 1843.
11. Zorn, *PA* 15: 479, 22–29 June 1841.
12. North, *PA* 17: 230, 28 February 1845.
13. Zorn, *PA* 16: 344, 346, 5 January 1843.
14. Elliott, *PA* 15: 287, 25 May 1840.
15. Zorn, *PA* 12: 20, 20 May 1830.
16. Hafa, *PA* 7: 156, 29 April 1819.
17. MAB, Kummer Collection, Zorn to Joseph Kummer, 5 September 1831.
18. Buchner, *Moravians in Jamaica,* 160.
19. Ward, *PA* 6: 412, "Diary of Williamsfield, 1816".
20. Timaeus, *PA* 10: 125, 20 September 1826.
21. Zorn, *PA* 12: 361, 15 July 1832, "Diary of New Fulnec for 1831".
22. Timaeus, *PA* 10: 126, 30 September 1826.
23. Ellis, *PA* 10: 262, 27 August 1827.
24. Ellis, *PA* 9: 393, 15 September 1825.
25. Zorn, *PA* 12: 361, 26 September 1832, "Diary of New Fulnec for 1831".
26. Blandford, *PA* 16: 349, 28 February 1843.
27. Sonderman, *PA* 22: 339, December 1857.
28. Holland, *PA* 18: 302, 25 November 1846.
29. Zorn, *PA* 16: 248, 1 September 1842.
30. *PA* 25: 176, June 1864, "Report of the Congregation at Bethany for 1863".
31. Lang, *PA* 6: 365, "Diary of John Lang, Old Carmel, 1816".
32. An African metaphor calqued into English, deriving from the concept that spirit forces ride the personality of the living like a rider controls a horse.
33. Buchner, *PA* 17: 410, 27 December 1842.
34. See Warner-Lewis, *Central Africa,* 190–98.

35. Elliott, *PA* 16: 88, 1 June 1844.

36. Buchner, *PA* 21: 544, 18 October 1855.

37. Elliott, *PA* 15: 250, 11 July 1842. Craton, *Testing the Chains*, 250, quotes Clarke, *Memorials* (no page cited), regarding the "superstition" he found was "mingled with [the] religious exercises" of blacks in Jamaica. "Some of them thought the old men were to dream dreams, and the young men were to see visions. . . . [M]any had wonderful dreams to tell, which they considered as prophetic visions; some excited themselves by fanatical notions, and fell into wild extravagances which they called '*the convince*' in which they had full faith, as much as in Divine Revelation."

38. Sonderman, *PA* 23: 601, 5 October 1860.

39. Clemens, *PA* 23: 591, 4 January 1861.

40. Lang, *PA* 6: 364, "Diary of Old Carmel, 1816".

41. Buchner, *Moravians in Jamaica*, 50. "Convince" is now a term for a marginal religious cult, also called "bongo" and "flenky". See Hogg, *Convince Cult*.

42. MA, O–1 Carmel, Diary of New Carmel.

43. Buchner, *PA* 21: 544, 18 October 1855.

44. "Diary of Bogue Mission", *PA* 6: 67, 1813.

45. MAB, File: Antigua, WI, Zorn's comments on David Bigler, "State of the System of Economics in the West India Islands, 1832–35".

46. Spence, *PA* 18: 107, 4 December 1846; Ward, *PA* 6: 421, 422, 25 August 1817.

47. Stobwasser, *PA* 9: 138, 2 March 1824. See Hall, *In Miserable Slavery*, 185–86.

48. Renny, *History of Jamaica*, 169.

49. Holland, *PA* 18: 302–31, March 1846.

50. Ward, *PA* 6: 420, 1817, "Diary of Williamsfield, St James".

51. Becker, *PA* 8: 73, 1820. 9 April, "Diary of New Eden".

52. MAB File: Antigua, Zorn's Comments on Bigler, "State of the System".

53. Buchner, *PA* 20: 88–89, 7 May 1851. A "digging-match", also called "len'-han'" [lend-hand], and "morning sport", is a system of rotating cooperative manual labour among neighbours and associates. It is a means of clearing and cleaning fields and roadsides, building houses, and so on, and is known as *dokpwe* in Haiti, *gayap* in Trinidad, and "maroon" in Grenada and Carriacou. The classification of this type of activity among "worldly customs" is found in the 1785 Brotherly Agreement about Rules and Orders for the Brethren's Congregation at Hope Settlement in North Carolina. Other "unbecoming" practices included "Horse-racing, Shooting Matches, boxing and fighting . . . Frolicks, such as night Spinning and Cottonpicking, and Cornhuskings at Night, intended for merriment, to which numbers of People of both sexes are invited to meeting". Sensbach, *Separate Canaan*, 127.

54. MA, O–1 Carmel, Diary of New Carmel.

55. Hennig, *PA* 22: 183, 8 January 1857. See also Bilby, "Gumbay".

56. Spence, *PA* 18: 107, 4 December 1846.

57. "Report of the Congregation at Lititz for 1861", *PA* 24: 297, 1862.

58. Becker, *PA* 6: 81, 26 December 1813.

59. Robbins, O–1 Carmel, Diary of New Carmel.

60. On 9 March 1847 William Mallalieu reported that "two white Emigrants have been severely beaten by some of the Negroes at Lenox. It appears the white men were in liquor and quarreling, when a negro passing and knowing one of them told him not to beat the other on which they set upon him and beat him severely. While they were doing so a Negress passing, ran and alarmed the Negroes on the Estate who came out and fearfully retaliated on the two . . . breaking Two or three limbs and leaving them half dead. We cannot discover that any of our Brn are guilty, we are not however without our fears." MA, O–1 Carmel, Diary of New Carmel.

61. Word derived from Efik *mbakara* "white man".

62. A term, perhaps derived from the town name Omoku, applied to Ijaw, Igbo and Ibibio peoples.

63. Blandford, *PA* 17: 23, 11 July 1843.

64. Renkewitz, *PA* 18: 397, 1846.

65. Zorn, *PA* 16: 183, 19 May 1842.

66. Nelson, "Archibald John Monteith", 291.

67. "Diary of New Eden", *PA* 8: 70, 6 February 1820.

68. Nelson, "Archibald John Monteith", 297.

69. MA, H–5 Fairfield, Minutes of Missionaries' Conference, 1830–31, 27 April 1830, 11a.

70. Nelson, "Archibald John Monteith", 297.

71. "Diary of New Eden", *PA* 8: 70, 6 February 1820.

72. "Diary of New Eden", *PA* 8: 69, 20 January 1820.

73. Heath, *PA* 17: 493, 4 May 1845. "Choirs were groups of people of similar age, the same gender, and the same marital status." Smaby, *Moravian Bethlehem*, 10.

74. Elliott, O–1 Carmel, "Diary of New Carmel", 3 January 1843.

75. Moderau, *PA* 26: 450, June 1868.

76. Zorn, *PA* 16: 248, 1 September 1842.

77. Feurig, *PA* 17: 181, July 1844. See also Zorn, *PA* 12: 24. Lewis's *Journal* is noticeably full of narratives of conflict among enslaved people. In Thistlewood's diaries, in addition to the brutality of master to enslaved, male slaves were frequently at loggerheads. See Hall, *In Miserable Slavery.*

78. Buchner, *PA* 21: 544, 18 October 1855.

79. Nelson, "Archibald John Monteith", 291–92.

80. Zorn, *PA* 12: 24, 7 May 1830.

81. Zorn, *PA* 12: 22, 13 April 1830.

82. MAB, Kummer Collection, B.2, Zorn to John Kummer, 23 December 1830.

83. MA, O–1 Carmel, Diary of New Carmel, 21 September 1846.

84. Buchner, *PA* 17: 230, 18 February 1845.

85. The unusual occurrence of white/partial white marriages in these jurisdictions is noted by Brathwaite, *Creole Society*, 188–90.

86. Zorn, *PA* 14: 27 January 1835.

87. Zorn, *PA* 13: 112, "Report of the Congregation of New Fulnec for 1833".

88. Ellis, *PA* 9: 318, 9 March 1825.

89. Hennig, *PA* 22: 183, 8 January 1857.

90. Zorn, *PA* 12: 24, 7 May 1830.

91. Buchner, *PA* 21: 544, 18 October 1855.

92. MA, O–1 Carmel, Diary of New Carmel, 3 July 1842. John eventually died in an unfortunate manner: he was dragged into his own sugar mill on 25 November 1845. See J–Carmel, Male Baptisms, entry 358, Remarks.

93. Ricksecker, *PA* 13: 436–37, 15 December 1835.

94. Winckler, *PA* 27: 331, June 1870.

95. Robbins, *PA* 14: 294–95, 8 March 1838. A lovefeast was "a service of singing, taking a cup of coffee and a biscuit in unison, and giving each other the Kiss of Peace". Smaby, *Moravian Bethlehem*, 17.

96. Becker, *PA* 9: 78, 20 May 1823.

97. Renkewitz, *PA* 22: 21, 25 August 1855.

98. Mallalieu, *PA* 18: 139, 15 February 1847.

99. Becker, *PA* 6: 77, 11 September 1814.

100. Becker, *PA* 6: 75, 7 August 1814. "Coco", the intended reference, is cocoyam or eddoe.

101. Stobwasser, *PA* 9: 133, 28 October 1823.

102. Blandford, *PA* 16: 184, 7 May 1842.

103. Kiergaard, *PA* 17: 228, 27 December 1844.

104. Heath, *PA* 18: 196, 19 August 1846.

105. Ellis, *PA* 9: 317, 9 March 1825.

106. Collis, *PA* 13: 229, 16 September 1834.

107. Blandford, *PA* 16: 184, 7 May 1842. A seraphine was a kind of small reed organ or harmonium.

108. Hoch, *PA* 8: 121, 27 August 1821.

109. Holland, MA, O–1 Carmel, Diary of New Carmel, 21 January 1845.

110. Sonderman, *PA* 23: 608, 22 October 1861.

111. Ward, *PA* 6: 420, 7 July 1817.

112. Becker, *PA* 8: 77, 16 October 1820. Brother Planta was John Collis's grandfather. See *PA* 13: 68, 29 October 1833.

113. Becker, *PA* 8: 77, 16 October 1820.

114. Hennig, *PA* 22: 224, 8 January 1857.

115. MA, O–1 Carmel, Diary of New Carmel, 27–29 May 1846.

116. Scholefield, *PA* 14: 27, 13 March 1834.

117. Zorn, *PA* 12: 459, 4 October 1830.

118. MA, H–7 Fairfield, 2b, Diary of Br. and Sr. Zorn's Stay at Spring Vale, 5 March 1830.

119. The German "Erlebnisse" attributes this act to Mr Cooper.

120. Nelson, "Archibald John Monteith", 291.

121. Buchner, *Moravians in Jamaica*, 80.

122. Ellis, *PA* 10: 34, 5 May 1826.

123. Zorn, *PA* 13: 116, 16 September 1834.

124. Buchner, *Moravians in Jamaica*, 121.

125. Ellis, *PA* 11: 463, 7 January 1831.

126. Clemens, *PA* 23: 386, 8 February 1860.

127. Blandford, *PA* 15: 384, 22 June 1840.

128. Mallalieu, *PA* 18: 143, 22 March 1847.

129. North, *PA* 17: 231, 28 February 1845.

130. Holland, MA, O–1 Carmel, Diary of New Carmel, 16 March 1845.

131. Elliott, *PA* 15: 481, 31 May 1841; Zorn *PA* 14: 27, 15 January 1835. Mr Marcy had bought Kep from the executor for the will of John Monteath.

132. Collis, *PA* 13: 435, 3 December 1835.

133. Elliott, MA, O–1 Carmel, Diary of New Carmel, 23 April 1839.

134. Zorn, *PA* 15: 70, 20 April 1839.

135. Elliott, *PA* 15: 286, 25 May 1840.

136. Zorn, *PA* 15: 70, 20 April 1839.

137. Elliott, MA, O–1 Carmel, Diary of New Carmel, 21 January 1839.

138. MA, O–Carmel 1, School Statistics in Connection with New Carmel, 1 August 1859.

139. Scholefield, *PA* 11: 123, 14 May 1829.

140. Zorn, *PA* 12: 21–22, 2 April 1830.

141. "Report of the Country-Schools in Jamaica, 1851", *PA* 20: 256.

142. Collis, *PA* 14: 435, 3 December 1835.

143. Clemens, *PA* 23: 386, 8 February 1860.

144. Blandford, *PA* 17: 21, 6 May 1843.

145. "Retrospect", 350.

146. Zorn, *PA* 16: 182, 19 May 1842.

147. Mallalieu, *PA* 18: 143, 22 March 1847.

148. Holland, *PA* 18: 302, November 1846; Coleman, *PA* 20: 89, 16 May 1851.

149. Hamilton, *PA* 26: 218, 1867.

150. Pulkrabek, *PA* 26: 8, 1868.

151. Hamilton, *PA* 26: 453, June 1868.

152. "Retrospect", 350.

153. Sonderman, *PA* 22: 338, December 1857.

154. Ibid.

155. Zorn, *PA* 16: 182, 19 May 1842.

156. Plessing, *PA* 22: 291, 5 May 1857.

157. Sonderman, *PA* 26: 220, June 1867.

Chapter 8

1. MAB, Kummer Collection, B.3, letter to Kummer from Zorn, 1827–1836, 14 April 1832.

2. The second and fourth sons of Colonel John Foster, member of the Privy Council in Jamaica. Joseph assumed the name "Barham" when he inherited the Jamaica lands.

3. Hastings and MacLeavy, *Seedtime and Harvest*, 17.

4. MA, Q–7 Fairfield, Diary of Bogue Mission, 179b. Lang's spelling reflects his German pronunciation. Since word-final consonants in German are voiceless, Lang spells "wicket" for "wicked", and voices English voiceless medial consonants, thus "threadened".

5. Lang, MA, Q–7 Fairfield, Diary of Bogue Mission, 27 August 1817.

6. Robert Peart's original name was Muhammad Kaba. For more on him, see Zorn, *PA* 14: 295–97, 26 September 1837. This is reproduced in Buchner, *Moravians in Jamaica,* 50–53. See also Wilks, "Abu Bakr al-Siddiq", 163–66; Addoun and Lovejoy, "Arabic Manuscript" and *Islamic Knowledge*; Warner-Lewis, "Religious Constancy".

7. MA, Q–7 Fairfield, Diary of Bogue Mission, 23 March 1816.

8. Generally spelled "busha". Derived from "overseer" by elision of the initial vowel and replacement of "v" by "b".

9. Zorn, *PA* 14: 297, 26 September 1837.

10. Mason, *Moravian Church,* 104.

11. Cronie, "Liberation", 18.

12. Ibid., 19.

13. Mason, *Moravian Church,* 126.

14. Vaughan, *Parliamentary Register,* xxix, 199–200, quoted in Mason, *Moravian Church,* 134.

15. Vaughan, *Parliamentary Register,* 197–78, quoted ibid., 135.

16. See Hastings and MacLeavy, *Seedtime and Harvest,* 33, for these defensible justifications. And as they ask on p. 36: "What would [the Baptists, staunch opponents of slavery] have done if they had come as early as the Moravians or the Methodists?" The British Baptists arrived in Jamaica in 1814.

17. Moravians referred to the worldwide Moravian organization as "The Unity". See Smaby, *Moravian Bethlehem,* 27.

18. MA, Q–11 Fairfield, Minutes of Mission Conference, 1831–33.

19. Ellis, *PA* 9: 240–41, 12 October 1824.

20. See Burnard, *Mastery, Tyranny, and Desire,* 103–6.

21. See Patterson, *Sociology of Slavery,* 1967, 266–73; Hart, *Slaves Who Abolished Slavery.*

22. MAB, Kummer Collection, B.1, J.G. Kummer – Relatives, School.

23. Costanzo, *Surprizing Narrative,* 48.

24. Fredrickson, "Long Trek", 40.

25. MAB, Kummer Collection, B.3, letters to Kummer from Zorn.

26. Ibid.

27. Ibid.

28. Zorn, *PA* 15: 72, 11 June 1839.

29. MAB, Kummer Collection, B.3, letter to Kummer from Zorn, 21 December 1838. Zorn probably used the dollar sign ($) so as not to confuse his American reader who would not have been familiar with the pound sign (£).

30. Becker, *PA* 8: 262, 18 May 1820.

31. Nelson, "Archibald John Monteith", 297.

32. Hanna, *PA* 26: 214, June 1867.

33. MA, H–5 Fairfield, Minutes of Mission Conference, 1830–31, 12 August 1830, 6a.

34. MA, O–1 Carmel, Diary of New Carmel, 4 June 1846. Interestingly, "black" is one of the underlined adjectives, and the others are negative.

35. Elliott, MA, O–1 Carmel, Diary of New Carmel, 30 June 1846, emphases his.

36. Buchner, *Moravians in Jamaica*, 17.

37. Timaeus, *PA* 10: 126, 30 September 1826.

38. MA, H–2 Fairfield, Diary for 1826, 18c, 20b.

39. Ellis, *PA* 10: 33, May 1826.

40. MA, Q–11 Fairfield, 8b.

41. Hafa, *PA* 7: 157, 6 June 1819.

42. Hafa, *PA* 7: 157–58, 10 May 1819.

43. MA, H–5 Fairfield, Minutes of Mission Conference, 27 April 1830, 4b.

44. MA, Q–11 Fairfield, Conference at New Fulnec, 20 February 1833.

45. MA, Q–11 Fairfield, Minutes of Mission Conference, Fairfield, 7 August 1833. The signal to start and finish work was given by someone blowing a conch shell. The implication here is that "negro time" was the slaves' rest period and therefore they were entitled to spend it as they thought fit.

46. Becker, *PA* 8: 72, 16 March 1820.

47. Buchner, *Moravians in Jamaica*, 63.

48. Ellis, *PA* 10: 81, 31 July 1826.

49. These were the parents of "Hutcheson" Mure Scott's wife. She was their eldest daughter, and was also known as Eliza Witter, since Witter must have been her first husband's surname. Cf. IRO, Old Wills, 129, f. 216. Will of Hutchison Mure Scott, dated 15 May 1856. Was it the same Mrs Witter to whom the following vestry minute refers? – "Ordered that Mrs. Elizabeth Witter be paid forty pounds the value of a negro Slave Joe prosecuted by her and executed according to law agreeable to a certificate exhibited by the Clerk of the Peace". JA, 2/7/1–1, Vestry Minutes, Westmoreland, 1780–81, Meeting of 17 January 1781 at the Courthouse in Savanna-la-Mar.

50. Light, *PA* 9: 322, 7 February 1825.

51. Light, *PA* 9: 248, 10 October 1824.

52. MA, Q–8 Fairfield, Diary of 1828, 31 August 1828.

53. Becker, *PA* 8: 71, 17 February 1820.

54. Ellis, *PA* 9: 392, 15 September 1825.

55. Collis, *PA* 13: 118, 9 June 1834.

56. Renkewitz, *PA* 13: 30 June 1837.

57. Zorn, *PA* 13: 21, 30 March 1830.

58. Light, *PA* 9: 485, 7 February 1825.

59. Robbins, *PA* 14: 294, 1 June 1837.

60. Zorn, *PA* 13: 419, 18 January 1836.

61. Ricksecker, *PA* 13: 230, 7 October 1834.

62. Zorn, *PA* 13: 468, 18 January 1836.

63. Light, *PA* 10: 77, 1 September 1826.

64. Zorn, *PA* 13: 377, 14 July 1835. Probably today's Scott's Bay between Black River and Whitehouse.

65. Collis, *PA* 14: 85, 1836.

66. Ricksecker, *PA* 13: 231, 7 October 1834.

67. Zorn, *PA* 12: 458, 4 October 1830.

68. MA, Q–11 Fairfield, Minutes of Mission Conference, New Fulnec, 20 February 1833.

69. Haman, *PA* 13: 20, 10 May 1833.

70. "Retrospect", 346.

71. Light, *PA* 9: 321, 7 February 1825.

72. Hastings and McLeavy, *Seedtime and Harvest,* 20.

73. Stobwasser, *PA* 9: 133, 28 October 1823.

74. Light, *PA* 9: 484, 7 February 1825.

75. MA, H–2 Fairfield, Diary for 1826.

76. MA, N–4 Fairfield, Address, 4, 9 August 1923.

77. Light, *PA* 9: 484, 7 February 1825.

78. Ellis, *PA* 11: 35–36, 2 August 1828.

79. Zorn, *PA* 13: 117–18, 20 May 1834.

80. Zorn, *PA* 13: 174–75, 15 September 1834; Collis, *PA* 13: 229, 31 December 1834.

81. Zorn, *PA* 12: 340; MA, H–5 Fairfield, Minutes of Mission Conference, 27 April 1830.

82. Zorn, *PA* 11: 460, 4 October 1830.

83. Davies, *PA* 14: 81, 7 October 1836.

84. Ellis, *PA* 12: 364, 26 February 1833.

85. Zorn, *PA* 12: 264, 15 August 1832.

86. Zorn, *PA* 14: 400, 26 June 1838. There was also a Tryall in Hanover. See Curtin, *Tryall.*

87. Zorn, *PA* 14: 469, 18 January 1836. It was Angell who had alerted Stipendiary Magistrate Richard Madden to the presence of Robert Peart, a Mandingo, on Spice Grove Estate. Madden then put Peart (Mahommed Kaba) in contact with Edward Donlan (Abu Bakr al-Siddiq). See Wilks, "Abu Bakr al-Siddiq".

88. Ellis, *PA* 10: 127, 11 October 1826; Mallalieu, *PA* 18: 139, 15 February 1847.

89. Ellis, *PA* 12: 213, 7 July 1832.

90. MAB, Kummer Collection, B.3, letter to Kummer from Zorn, 26 June 1832.

91. Hoch, *PA* 8: 121, 27 August 1821.

92. Scholefield, *PA* 10: 348, 5 February 1828.

93. Becker, *PA* 8: 68, January 1820.

94. MAB, West Indies – Jamaica, Letters 1796–1797: Towle to Ettwein, 2 June 1796.

95. Hoch, *PA* 8: 119, 24 March 1821.

96. Zorn, *PA* 16: 346, 5 January 1843.

97. Stobwasser, *PA* 9: 75, 26 July 1823.

98. Ricksecker, *PA* 17: 438, 24 February 1846.

99. MAB, Kummer Collection, Letters to J.G. Kummer, 1824–45: letter written from Papine Estate to Rev. John Daniel Anders at Bethlehem, Pennsylvania, 2 November 1832.

100. Wullschlaegel, *PA* 18: 349, 15 March 1848.

101. Ibid.

102. MAB, Kummer Collection, Letters to Kummer: letter written from Papine Estate, 2 November 1832.

103. Kiergaard, *PA* 16: 46, June 1841.

104. Stobwasser, *PA* 9: 75, 26 July 1823.

105. Stobwasser, *PA* 9: 136, 13 February 1824.

106. Ward, *PA* 6: 418, 16 June 1817.

107. Stobwasser, *PA* 9: 133, 28 October 1823.

108. Clemens, *PA* 24: 163, 1861.

109. Becker, *PA* 6: 76, August 1813.

110. Becker, *PA* 8: 74, 25 April 1820.

111. Pfeiffer, *PA* 17: 437, 4 April 1846; Herman, *PA* 18: 137, 25 January 1847.

112. Kiergaard, *PA* 17: 229, 27 December 1844.

113. Herman, *PA* 18: 142, 4 March 1847.

114. Zorn, *PA* 12: 24, May 1830.

115. Mallalieu, *PA* 18: 139, 15 February 1847.

116. Ward, *PA* 6: 371, 2 December 1816.

117. Collis, *PA* 13: 119, 9 June 1834.

118. Ellis/Pemsel, *PA* 12: 19, 4–6 April 1830.

119. Ellis, *PA* 10: 81, 31 July 1826.

120. Zorn, *PA* 12: 360, 2 January 1831.

121. MAB, Kummer Collection, B.3, Zorn to J.G. Kummer, 20 December 1828.

122. Holland, *PA* 18: 107–8, 29 October 1845.

123. Stobwasser, *PA* 9: 133, 28 October 1823.

124. Holland, *PA* 18: 108, 29 October 1845.

125. MA, Q–7 Fairfield, Diary of Bogue Mission, 109.

126. Zorn, *PA* 12: 26.

127. Ricksecker, *PA* 13: 318.

128. Light, *PA* 13: 404.

129. Buchner, *PA* 17: 411, 13 March 1843.

130. Elliott, MA, O–1 Carmel, Diary of New Carmel.

131. MA, O–1 Carmel, Diary of New Carmel, 26 March 1843.

132. Elliott, *PA* 22: 20, 6 December 1855.

133. Seiler, "Report of Congregation at Bethabara for 1863", *PA* 25: 175, June 1864.

134. "Report of the Training Institution, at Fairfield for 1863", *PA* 25: 164, June 1864.

135. Seiler, *PA* 26: 214, June 1867.

136. Weiss, "Report from Bethabara for 1864", *PA* 25: 372–73, June 1865.

137. Geissler, *PA* 26: 447, June 1868.

138. Hamilton, *PA* 26: 6, June 1868.

139. Hanna, *PA* 28: 31–32, 29 June 1871.

140. Ward, *PA* 6: 422, 2 September 1817.

141. Robbins, MA, O–1 Carmel, Diary of New Carmel.

142. MA, C–3 Carmel, entry 3, lists a Thomas Collins and Mary Williams, both of Lenox, who married in July 1828. Perhaps Mary had died, and Sarah was Thomas's second wife.

143. Elliott, MA, O–1 Carmel, Diary for New Carmel, May 1842.

144. Hanna, *PA* 28: 31, 31 June 1871.

145. Quoted in Olyphant Family, "Perthshire Families", 74. No source given. The *Annual Register* for 1781 offers a somewhat different sequence of events. A reconstruction of this occurrence by Robinson and Rowe, "The Great Sav Submarine Slide", based on the latter account indicates that "the repeated

pounding by the waves triggered a submarine slide, depositing up to 20 million cubic metres of the shelf edge into the deeper water beyond. This sudden change in the undersea topography caused the earthquake which registered onshore, and also generated a final large tsunami."

146. Light, *PA* 7: 62–63, 26 November 1818.
147. Ibid., 63.
148. Ibid., 62–63.
149. Light, *PA* 10: 129, 1826.
150. Ellis, *PA* 10: 263, 27 August 1827.
151. MA, Elliott, O–1 Carmel, Diary of New Carmel.
152. Ellis, *PA* 10: 424, April 1827.
153. Ward, *PA* 6: 421, 2 September 1817.
154. Light, *PA* 12: 171, 6 February 1832.
155. In MA, O–1 Carmel, List of Persons Departed, November 1852.
156. Lichtenthaeler, "Report of the Congregation of New Carmel for 1863", *PA* 25: 167, 1864.
157. Light, *PA* 7: 22, 14 May 1818.
158. Light, *PA* 7: 154–55, 22 March 1819.
159. Zorn, *PA* 14: 240–41, 22 August 1837.
160. Kiergaard, *PA* 16: 47, 6 August 1841.
161. Renkewitz, *PA* 14: 300, June 1837.
162. Collis, *PA* 13: 118, 9 June 1834.
163. Mallalieu, *PA* 18: 143, 22 March 1847.
164. Zorn, *PA* 12: 265, 8 August 1832.
165. See Bishop, "Runaway Slaves"; Hart, *Slaves Who Abolished Slavery*; Campbell, *Maroons of Jamaica*.
166. Zorn, *PA* 12: 174, 18 March 1832.

Chapter 9

1. Monteith, "Experiences", 276.
2. Elliott, *PA* 16: 482, 31 May 1841.
3. Robbins, *PA* 14: 294, 1 August 1836.
4. Cronie, "Liberation", 19.
5. Kamalu, *Person, Divinity and Nature,* 145.
6. Nelson, "Archibald John Monteith", 287.
7. Nwoga, *Supreme God,* 59–60.
8. Horton entitles his study of Kalabari religion, *The Gods as Guests.* The work is an explanation of how, through mime, masquerade, and possession, the religion "serve[s] to bring the gods into contact with their people" (p. 20), given that the Kalabari comprehend the world as of two parts: "*oju* – the bodily or material, and . . . *teme* – the spiritual or immaterial" (p. 15). Nwoga, *Supreme God* gives a similar title to his book, but does not devote much space to treatment of the "stranger" or "visitor" concept.
9. See Idowu, *Yoruba Religion*; Iwuagwu, "Igbo Traditional Religion"; p'Bitek,

African Religions, chapters 6 and 10; Chukwukere, "Chi in Igbo Religion", 527; Nwoga, *Supreme God.*

10. See Sawyerr, *God,* for treatment of these issues by the Temne, Akan and Yoruba of West Africa.

11. As, for example, Mawu Lisa of the Fon. The Yoruba deity Obatala, "great god", is male in some cosmogonic tales, female in others.

12. Chukwukere, "Chi in Igbo Religion", 526.

13. Ibid., 527n4.

14. Ibid., 528. See also Ekejiuba and Dike, "Change and Persistence".

15. Nelson, "Archibald John Monteith", 287.

16. Chukwukere, "Chi in Igbo Religion", 525, 530.

17. Manfredi, "Ìgbo Initiation", 188n38. See also Green, *Igbo Village Affairs,* Achebe, *Essays;* and Nwoga, *Supreme God.*

18. Manfredi, "Ìgbo Initiation", 177–78.

19. Ibid., 176.

20. Nwala, *Igbo Philosophy,* 28.

21. Nelson, "Archibald John Monteith", 287.

22. Aiyejina, lecture on "The Orisha Tradition in Trinidad", Mico Teachers' College, Kingston, May 2004. In 1966 Octavia Henry, a Yoruba descendant in Trinidad, reproved me for saying that a particular day was "not good" for me to visit her. She advised me that "every God day is a good day".

23. Achebe, *Essays,* 94.

24. Chukwukere, "Chi in Igbo Religion", 525.

25. Nelson, "Archibald John Monteith", 287.

26. Onwuejeogwu, *Igbo Civilization,* 50.

27. Nwala, *Igbo Philosophy,* 83.

28. Nelson, "Archibald John Monteith", 300. Costanzo, "Narrative", 127–28, also comments on this ambivalence.

29. In Achebe, *Arrow of God,* the chief priest, Ezeulu, hears the Christian church bells sounding loudly within his own shrine. In the context of the opposition between himself and his people, the metaphoric coincidence in this scene makes Ezeulu an ally of Christianity seeking to wreak havoc on the people over whom he has spiritual jurisdiction.

30. Compare the sentiments of two elderly Africans reproduced by Zorn in "Report for New Fulnec for May 2, 1833": "Saviour love me and take away my sin, me try to love Him the same. Me poor thing, me come from Guinea [Africa] over salt water; me got no mother, no father, Saviour every thing to me; He love me, He crucified for me. Every way me go, me cry upon Lord Jesus." Another said, "Me thank God, that He bring me from Guinea country to hear the good word." Such sentiments, as expressed to whites, were apparently fairly common, to judge from the literature of the period, but while not rejecting the internalization of these values by blacks, it is important to realize that these opinions were to some extent governed by speaker awareness of the ideas held by the recipients of the discourse. *PA* 13: 112, 2 May. See similar opinions in Carmichael, *Domestic Manners,* 229–33.

31. Phrase borrowed from Father Garth Minott, based on the exposition in Bujo,

African Ethic, 129–31. Since Christians believe that Jesus is God and is alive, and that Christians are in union with God in the present, then after death, they continue this unity of being. See 1 Corinthians 15. In parallel, African anthropology and religion envisage the unity of the secular and the sacred, so that the dead, the ancestors, continue a spiritual existence and are therefore closer to the Divine.

32. JA, 1B/11/8/6 1, Register of Marriages, White Persons, St Elizabeth.
33. Monteith, "Experiences", 272.
34. In contrast to the restrained liturgical approach of the Church of England and the Calvinist idea of the "elect of God", evangelical religion was primarily concerned with a democratic approach to the salvation of souls, achieved through forceful, even emotionally charged, preaching, the holding of prayer-meetings, confessional testimonies, and congregational singing, often in open-air settings and unconsecrated buildings. See Carwardine, *Trans-Atlantic Revivalism,* 4, 86.
35. See JA, 1B/11/7 72, f. 94, Return of Slaves, 1823.
36. JA, 21/3 (1344), *Jamaica Almanack,* 1817, 76.
37. JA, 21/3 (1344), *Jamaica Almanack,* 1832, 105.
38. Monteith, "Experiences", 273.
39. Senior, *Jamaica,* 24.
40. Nelson, "Archibald John Monteith", 292. "Christine" of Monteith, "Experiences", 272, would have sounded like English "Christina".
41. JA, 1B/11/7 23, f. 194, Return of Slaves, 1817.
42. JA, 1B/11/7 84, f. 58, Return of Slaves, 1826.
43. Nelson, "Archibald John Monteith", 292–93.
44. Smaby, *Moravian Bethlehem,* 8–9.
45. See MA, H–2 Fairfield, Diary for 1826, 2 August 1826.
46. MA, J–Carmel, Adult Male Baptisms, entry 24.
47. *Missionary Manual,* 14.
48. Patterson, *Slavery and Social Death,* 99.
49. Nelson, "Archibald John Monteith", 292.
50. MA, Q–7 Fairfield, Diary of Bogue Mission, f. 162, 17 March 1816.
51. Nelson, "Archibald John Monteith", 292.
52. Monteith, "Memoir", 438.
53. Monteith, "Experiences", 275.
54. Ibid., 282.
55. Ibid., 277.
56. Ibid., 278.
57. Ibid., 279.
58. JA, 1B/11/8/6 3, St Elizabeth Parish Register, Marriages.
59. MA, J–Carmel, Adult Female Baptisms, entry 58.
60. JA, 1B/11/8/6 3, St Elizabeth Parish Register, Baptisms.
61. MA, J–Carmel, Adult Female Baptisms, entry 58.
62. Translated as "Hampstadt" in the German version.
63. The St John's Anglican parish church at Black River had been built between 1715 and 1722, but it was destroyed by a hurricane. It is not certain whether the rebuilt

structure was erected on the same site. It seems to have been built in the late 1760s, as "the earliest memorial tablet in the Church is to Henry Gale, Custos of the Parish, who died in 1767". By 1774 Edward Long described it as a "handsome edifice of red brick and recently rebuilt". By 1836 the building was thought too small for the congregation size and "the corner stone of the new building was laid on 18 July 1837". Aarons, *Short History*.

64. Nelson, "Archibald John Monteith", 294.

65. Jamaican idiom implying presumption on the part of the person being criticized.

66. Monteith, "Experiences", 277.

67. MA, A–1 Carmel, Congregation Lists and Baptismal Register, New Eden, entry 382. Elizabeth's husband was Samuel. He belonged to Bog, whereas she was from Hopeton. See entry 348.

68. MA, J–Carmel, Female Adult Baptisms, entry 753.

69. C–1 Carmel, Original Register of Marriages, New Carmel, entry 253. The marriage was witnessed by Archibald Monteath and Caroline Miller, the latter making her mark.

70. MA, J–Carmel, Baptisms of Children, entries 2372 and 2487.

71. MA, C–1 Carmel, Original Register of Marriages, New Carmel, entry 320.

72. MA, C–3 Carmel, Marriage Register, 1827–40, entry 35.

73. Nelson, "Archibald John Monteith", 300.

74. MA, A–1 Carmel, Congregation Lists and Baptismal Register, New Eden, entries 1018 and 1369.

75. MA, J–Carmel, Adult Female Baptisms, entry 610.

76. MA, A–1 Carmel, Congregation Lists and Baptismal Register, Baptisms of Children, entry 1850.

77. MA, J–Carmel, Baptisms of Children, entry 2080.

78. Ibid., entry 2331.

79. Ibid., entry 2479.

80. Ibid., entry 2651.

81. Nelson, "Archibald John Monteith", 295.

82. MA, O–1 Carmel, Diary of New Carmel.

83. Buchner, *PA* 20: 416, 8 July 1852.

84. Nelson, "Archibald John Monteith", 294–95.

85. MA, Reinke, O–1 Carmel, Diary of New Carmel, 10 October 1846.

86. Smaby, *Moravian Bethlehem*, 28.

87. MA, O–1 Carmel, List of Persons Departed, 1852. Her date of decease is given as 26 November.

88. Buchner, *PA* 20: 85, 23 June 1851.

89. Seiler, *PA* 25: 170, "Report of the Congregation of Bethabara for 1863".

90. Lichtenthaeler, *PA* 25: 167, "Report of the Congregation of New Carmel for 1863".

91. Harvey and Brewin, "Autobiographical Sketch", 99–100.

92. Monteith, "Experiences", 268.

93. MA, O–1 Carmel, Diary of New Carmel, List of Persons Departed. Archibald's age is given in this record as sixty-six. This is more or less in keeping with the official church timeline of his birth given in the biography, as 1799.

94. *PA* 25: 376, "Report from New Carmel, June 1865".

95. "Retrospect", 358n.

96. MA, O–1 Carmel, Diary of New Carmel, List of Persons Departed, 1865.

97. MA, Elliott, O–1 Carmel, 1 September 1837.

98. MA, Elliott, O–1 Carmel, Diary of New Carmel, 4 August 1843.

99. MA, Robbins, O–1 Carmel, Diary of New Carmel, 10 April 1846.

100. MA, O–1 Carmel, Diary of New Carmel, 4 October 1846.

101. MA, O–1 Carmel, Diary of New Carmel, 1 August 1846.

102. MA, Holland, O–1 Carmel, Diary of New Carmel, 21 January 1845.

103. MA, Heath, O–1 Carmel, Diary of New Carmel, 7 April 1846; Buchner, *PA* 21: 475, 4 August 1855.

104. MA, Mallalieu, O–1 Carmel, Diary of New Carmel, 9 March 1847.

105. Nelson, "Archibald John Monteith", 297.

106. Ibid., 295.

107. Mallalieu, *PA* 18: 140, 15 February 1847.

108. Buchner, *PA* 16: 409, 27 December 1842.

109. Minutes of Mission Conference, 15 June 1831, quoted in *PA* 25: 177–78, June 1864.

110. A reference to the Queen of Sheba. See 1 Kings 10.

111. MA, O–1 Carmel, Elliott, Diary of New Carmel, 26 June 1843, 409.

112. Nelson, "Archibald John Monteith", 293.

113. "Report of the Country-Schools in Jamaica, 1851", *PA* 20: 256–57.

114. Buchner, *PA* 21: 32–33, 5 October 1853.

115. Collis, *PA* 14: 83, 1836.

116. MA, O–1 Carmel, Robbins, Diary of New Carmel, 25 December 1846.

117. Collis, *PA* 14: 83–84, 25 July 1836.

118. MA, O–1 Carmel, Diary of Carmel Congregation, 8 July 1846.

119. Handler, *Unappropriated People,* 53.

120. Ibid., 36n30.

121. Burnard, *Mastery, Tyranny, and Desire,* 149.

122. See ibid., 149–52.

123. Monteith, "Experiences", 282.

124. Nelson, "Archibald John Monteith", 297.

125. See p. 116 of this text.

126. JA, 21/3 (1344), *Jamaica Almanack,* 1817, 85.

127. See JA, 21/3 (1344), *Jamaica Almanack,* 101.

128. Nelson, "Archibald John Monteith", 298.

129. NLJ, *Jamaica Almanack,* 1838, 84.

130. Nelson, "Archibald John Monteith", 298–99. By 1841, when the post of stipendiary magistrate had been overtaken by the freedom granted to the enslaved in 1838, Zorn referred to a T. Daughtrey as inspector of prisons in Jamaica, and as "our esteemed friend", who rendered hospitality to Brother and Sister Renkewitz while they were in transit at Kingston on their way to their new posting in Tobago. *PA* 16: 182, 19 May 1842. However, if we are to believe the footnote in Harvey and Brewin, "Autobiographical Sketch", 98, these two persons were one and the same, since they refer to the "late John Daughtrey" who had been

stipendiary magistrate and afterwards inspector of prisons. This suggests that the "T" in the printed version of Zorn's communication should really have been "J".

131. Zorn, *PA* 13: 118, 20 May 1834. The whites had expected bloodshed as the response by blacks to their freedom. See MAB, Kummer Collection, B.3, letter to Kummer from Zorn, 7 May 1833: "Most persons dread the event [emancipation] as the commencement of a season of anarchy and bloodshed."

132. Collis, *PA* 14: 86, 1836.

133. Handler, *Unappropriated People*, 36n30.

134. Nelson, "Archibald John Monteith", 299.

135. See, for example, the case of a Muslim by the name of Anna Musa who became known as Benjamin Cochrane. Although freed when his slave ship was seized by a British naval patrol off Tortola, he was then indentured in Jamaica, and having escaped, was then treated as a runaway. Captured, he was re-indentured, sent to Antigua, then Barbados, where he was eventually freed and later returned to Jamaica. See Madden, *Twelvemonth's Residence*, 129–30.

136. Handler, *Unappropriated People*, 59–60.

137. Ibid., 53.

138. Nelson, "Archibald John Monteith", 299.

139. We may compare Archibald's reaction with that of an earlier head driver named Nathaniel, who had professed Christianity since 1814. His end on 23 March 1820 "was hastened by a misunderstanding which arose between him and the overseer, who was displeased because [Nathaniel] did not behave with sufficient severity to the negroes. . . . Being conscious that he had acted with faithfulness in his station, [Nathaniel] felt these reproaches keenly" and by 16 March he had become "very weak, and scarcely able to speak". Becker, *PA* 8: 72.

140. Zorn, *PA* 14: 299, 9 October 1837.

141. Ibid., 299–300.

142. Nelson, "Archibald John Monteith", 299.

143. Zorn, *PA* 13: 240–41, 22 August 1837.

Chapter 10

1. Holland, *PA* 17: 277, 11 April 1845.

2. Muslims were among the slave cohorts brought to the Caribbean. See Lovejoy and Trotman "Community of Believers"; Warner-Lewis, "Religious Constancy".

3. Patterson, *Slavery and Social Death*, 80, drawing on Pitt-Rivers, *Encyclopedia*.

4. Patterson, *Slavery and Social Death*, 78.

5. Lewis, *Journal*, 37.

6. MA, O–1 Carmel, Diary of New Carmel, 9 April 1843.

7. There seem to be some other African names in the slave inventory lists. Might these also have been day-names from other ethnic groups? Craton, *Searching*, 416n14, lists a number of "apparent African names or corruptions thereof . . . in the Worthy Park lists". One such name is Affir, which occurs in Dunn, "Two Jamaican Slaves". The Ewe names are, for females: Ajo/Ajua – Monday; Abla – Tuesday; Aku – Wednesday; Awo – Thursday; Afi/Efua – Friday; Ami – Saturday;

Aa/Amba/Ama – Saturday; Kwasiho – Sunday. For males: Kojo – Monday; Kobla – Tuesday; Koku – Wednesday; Yawo – Thursday; Kofi – Friday; Kwami – Saturday; Kosi/Kwasi – Sunday. See Madubuike, *African Names,* 109.

8. MA, O–1 Carmel, Diary of New Carmel, 9 April 1843. Elliott errs in attributing "Feiba" to Monday. The name here should have been "Juba" or "Ajua".

9. A similar assessment of slave names is found in Dunn, "Two Jamaican Slaves", 190.

10. Zorn, *PA* 12: 361, 6 February 1831.

11. Ellis and Collis, *PA* 13: 67, 29 October 1833.

12. MA, H–5 Fairfield, Minutes of Conference, 28 January 1830–20 April 1831, paragraph 3 ii. There are two estates in the western Manchester area that carried names associated with Islam: Medina and Tombuctoo (Timbuctoo). This suggests that an owner or owners might have been "orientalists", Oriental and Middle Eastern interest being fashionable at the height of the British Empire in the nineteenth century. See Said, *Orientalism,* chap. 2.

13. MA, Q–7 Fairfield, Diary of John Lang, 29 October 1816.

14. Ibid., 20 March 1818.

15. Ibid., 10 June 1817.

16. David Davies had been called to baptize an old woman on the point of death. Next day, when he was informed that the woman had indeed died, the messenger thanked the missionary by saying, "Ah! Massa, you gave her a good passage", meaning, explains Davies, "that I had made a passage for her into heaven. I told him that the outward form of baptism could not save the soul, and explained to him the necessity of a change of heart, before any one could enter the kingdom of Heaven." Davies, *PA* 14: 189, 9 May 1837.

17. Burnard, "Slave Naming Patterns", 342.

18. Collis, *PA* 14: 83, 17 July 1836; Buchner, *Moravians in Jamaica,* 119.

19. Burnard, "Slave Naming Patterns", 343.

20. Buchner, *Moravians in Jamaica,* 119.

21. Heuman, *Between Black and White,* 14.

22. Mathurin, "Women in Jamaica", 152.

23. IRO, Old Deeds, 827, f. 47.

24. Nelson, "Archibald John Monteith", 292.

25. See ibid.

26. Herman, *PA* 18: 142, March 1847.

27. Lewis, *Journal,* 349.

28. Nelson, "Archibald John Monteith", 289.

29. Ibid.

30. JA, 1B/11/8/6 2, Parish Register, St Elizabeth.

31. Nelson, "Archibald John Monteith", 290.

32. Ibid.

33. JA, 1B/11/8/6, 2, Parish Register, St Elizabeth.

34. Turner, *Slaves and Missionaries,* 11; see also Hall, *Civilising Subjects,* 77.

35. Burnard, "Slave Naming Patterns", 343.

36. Patterson, *Slavery and Social Death,* 54.

37. Nelson, "Archibald John Monteith", 290, 291.

38. Ibid., 297.

39. See Sensbach, *Separate Canaan,* 138–43.

40. See Patterson, *Slavery and Social Death,* 62–65.

41. MA, J–Carmel, Adult Male Baptisms, entry 33.

42. MA, J–Carmel, Adult Female Baptisms, entry 29; Adult Male Baptisms, entry 15.

43. JA, Parish Register, St Elizabeth, Marriages, 1829–31.

44. It was customary to bury the baby's "navel string" or umbilical cord and put it in the same hole as a plant seed or seedling. See Dunham, *Katherine Dunham's Journey,* 114.

45. NLJ, Ms. 230, Chapone Yeates to Joseph Manesty, 9 February 1754, in Letter/Account Book, Estate of Mrs Sarah Smith, Rio Grande, Portland, 1753–55. Quoted by Robertson, "Notes and Queries", 40.

46. "Retrospect", 350.

47. Ibid., 25.

48. Mallalieu, *PA* 18: 143, 22 March 1847.

49. Buchner, *Moravians in Jamaica,* 130.

50. Ibid., 130–31.

51. Elliott, *PA* 15: 481, May 31, 1841.

52. Holland, *PA* 18: 108, 29 October 1845.

53. See IRO, Old Deeds, 827, f. 47. Also in NLJ, Maps: St Elizabeth 636 of 1842, the same settlers' names are mentioned in the legend for the diagram.

54. MA, O–1 Carmel, Diary of New Carmel.

55. Ibid.

56. Elliott, O–1 Carmel, Diary of New Carmel, 23 September 1837; 10 February 1838.

57. Buchner, *Moravians in Jamaica,* 157

58. These names occur in JA, A–1 Carmel.

59. Elliott, *PA* 15: 480–81, 31 May 1841.

Chapter 11

1. See King, *Autobiography.*

2. See Strickland, "Ashton Warner's Account".

3. See Prince, *History of Mary Prince.*

4. See Burnard, *Mastery, Tyranny, and Desire,* chapters 6 and 7.

5. Zorn, *PA* 12: 27, 17 December 1830.

6. Becker, *PA* 8: 69, 5 February 1820.

7. Nelson, "Archibald John Monteith", 300.

8. Smaby, *Moravian Bethlehem,* 8.

9. See Warner-Lewis, *Yoruba Songs,* 36, where Yoruba *eru dele* translates "Your slave/devotee has come to your shrine", and page 133 where the "we" of the song identify themselves as *eru Olofa* "the slaves/servants/subjects of the King of Ofa town".

10. Nelson, "Archibald John Monteith", 301.

11. Harvey and Brewin, "Autobiographical Sketch", 99.

12. Monteith, "Experiences", 283.
13. Patterson, *Slavery and Social Death*, 80.
14. Uchendu, *Igbo*, 88.
15. Ibid., 89.
16. Patterson, *Slavery and Social Death*, 99.
17. Ibid., 82–83. For discussion of "the 'slavery'-to kinship continuum", see Kopytoff and Miers, 22–26.
18. McClelland, *Human Motivation*, 229–30. My thanks to Dr Sylvia Lawson for this reference.
19. Patterson, *Slavery and Social Death*, 5.
20. Ibid., 97.
21. *PA* 14: 85, "Diary of New Carmel".
22. Patterson, *Slavery and Social Death*, 12.
23. Craton, *Searching*, 209.
24. Patterson, *Slavery and Social Death*, 78.
25. Quoted from Kamau Brathwaite's poem "Wake" in *Islands* from *The Arrivants* trilogy.
26. See Warner-Lewis, *Central Africa*, 38–39, for the details of this self-perception.
27. "Diary of Gracehill, Antigua, for 1829", *PA* 11: 451.
28. Patterson, *Slavery and Social Death*, 79.
29. Barclay, *Present State of Slavery*, 265–66n.
30. Anderson, *Scottish Nation*, 45.
31. See SRO, CC9/7/64.
32. SRO, CC36/51/18, f. 400.
33. Codicil to Archibald Douglas Monteath's will, dated 31 January 1839.
34. These were apparently Amelia Murray Monteath (named for her grandmother), born in 1834, and Augusta Emmeline Monteath, born two years later. See British Census, 1851, East Indies Extract (http://valmayukuk.tripod.com/1851british/id1.htm).
35. *Annals of Lesmahagow.*
36. See, for example, Monteath Mausoleum. Accessed at www.scottish-walks.co.uk/cuthbert/monteath.html
37. See Hamilton, *Scotland*, 198.
38. See Barrow, "Meetings".
39. Douglass, *My Bondage and My Freedom*, 80.
40. Hall, *Civilising Subjects*, 72.
41. See Bush, "White 'Ladies' ".
42. Hall, *Civilising Subjects*, 72–73.
43. IRO, Old Wills, 120, f. 99, will of John Monteith, 25 August 1840.
44. See Powell, "Caribbean Women".
45. Barrow, "Finding the Support", 167, 169.
46. See Mathurin, "Women in Jamaica"; Beckles, "Freeing Slavery"; Boa, "Free Black and Coloured Women".
47. Buchner, *PA* 21: 544, 18 October 1855.
48. See Lamming, *Castle of My Skin*, 273, where a villager sarcastically uses this term

to refer to the black plantation overseer and his master, the white landowner.

49. See Donald, "James Monteath" in Notices of the Members in *Minute Book of the Board of Green Cloth, 1809–1820*. However, Blair, *Sketches,* 295, indicates that Walter I was a nephew of the Duchess of Douglas.

50. Onwuejeogwu, *Igbo Civilization,* 38, 43.

51. Ibid., 78.

52. Ibid., 81.

53. See Warner-Lewis, *Guinea's Other Suns,* 175–86.

54. Onwuejeogwu, *Igbo Civilization,* 45.

Bibliography

Aarons, John. "The Story of Aneaso, the Son of Durl and Dirinejah". *Jamaican Historical Society Bulletin* 7, nos. 3 and 4 (1977): 53–58.

———. *A Short History of the Church of St. John, the Evangelist, Black River, St. Elizabeth*. Leaflet, n.d.

———. "The Story of Archibald Monteith". *Jamaican Historical Society Bulletin* 7, no. 5 (1978): 73–77.

Abbott, Thomas. *Narrative of Certain Events connected with the Late Disturbances in Jamaica, and the Charges Preferred against the Baptist Missionaries in that Island. Being the Substance of a Letter to the Secretary of the Baptist Missionary Society, dated March 13, 1832*. London: Holdsworth and Ball, 1832.

Achebe, Chinua. *Arrow of God*. London: Heinemann Educational, 1964.

———. *Morning Yet on Creation Day: Essays*. London: Heinemann Educational, 1977 [1975].

———. *Things Fall Apart*. London: Heinemann Educational, 1965 [1958].

Adams, John. *Remarks on the Country Extending from Cape Palmas to the River Congo*. London: Frank Cass, 1966 [1832].

Addison, W. Innes. *The Matriculation Albums of the University of Glasgow from 1728 to 1858*. Glasgow: James Maclehose and Sons, 1913.

Addoun, Yacine Daddi, and Paul Lovejoy. "The Arabic Manuscript of Muhammad Kaba Saghanughu of Jamaica, *c.* 1823". Paper presented at the Second Conference on Caribbean Culture, University of the West Indies, Mona, 2002.

———. *The Transmission of Islamic Knowledge in the Western Sudan: The Jamaican Saghanughu Connection*. www.yorku.ca/nhp/shadd/kitab_salat/index.asp, 2003.

Afigbo, A. "Igbo Cultural Sub-areas: Their Rise and Development". In *Ethnohistorical Studies 1: Groundwork of Igbo History*, edited by A. Afigbo, 144–60. Lagos: Vista, 1992.

Aiyejina, Funso. "The Orisha Tradition in Trinidad". Lecture, Mico Teachers' College, Kingston, 2004.

Allen, Carolyn. "Creole: The Problem of Definition". In *Questioning Creole: Creolisation Discourses in Caribbean Culture*, edited by Verene Shepherd and Glen Richards, 47–63. Kingston: Ian Randle, 2002.

Allen, Walser H. "The Life of Archibald Monteith". B.Divinity thesis, Moravian Theological Seminary, Bethlehem, Pennsylvania, 1920

Allen, William. *Picturesque Views on the River Niger.* London: Thomas Murray, 1840.

Allsopp, Jeannette. *The Caribbean Multilingual Dictionary of Flora, Fauna and Foods in English, French, French Creole and Spanish.* Kingston: Arawak, 2003.

Anderson, James R., ed. *The Burgesses and Guild Brethren of Glasgow, 1573–1750.* Edinburgh: Scottish Record Society, 1925.

Anderson, William. *The Scottish Nation; or the Surnames, Families, Literature, Honours and Biographical History of the People of Scotland.* Vol. 2. Edinburgh: A. Fullarton and Co., 1863.

Annals of Lesmahagow: A Narrative of Events Year by Year of Written Records and Pictures dating from 1179 AD to 1884 AD. Chap. 5. "Landed Estates, Families, and History Connected with Them". 2000. At www.lesmahagow.com/history/annals/CH05/05(s04)002.htm

Anonymous. *Facts and Documents connected with the Late Insurrection in Jamaica, and the Violations of Civil and Religious Liberty Arising out of It.* London: Holdsworth and Ball, 1832.

Army List 1799. *Nineteenth Regiment of (Light) Dragoons.* Accessed July 2006 at www.lib.mq.edu.au/digital/seringapatam/19tharmylist.html

Bailey, Anne. *African Voices of the Atlantic Slave Trade: Beyond the Silence and the Shame.* Boston: Beacon, 2005.

Barclay, Alexander. *A Practical View of the Present State of Slavery in the West Indies.* London: Smith, Elder and Co., 1826.

Baronov, David, and Kevin A. Yelvington. "Ethnicity, Race, Class and Nationality". In *Understanding the Contemporary Caribbean,* edited by Richard S. Hillman and Thomas J. D'Agostino, 209–38. Boulder: Lynne Rienner.

Barrett, H. May. *Reflections on Black River.* Kingston: Jamaica Library Service, 1976.

Barrow, Christine. "Finding the Support: A Study of Strategies for Survival". *Social and Economic Studies* 35, no. 2 (1986): 131–76.

———. "Meetings: A Group Savings Arrangement in Barbados". *African Studies Association of the West Indies Bulletin,* no. 8 (1976): 32–40.

Basden, G.T. *Among the Ibos of Nigeria.* London: Frank Cass, 1966 [1921].

Becker, John. *Periodical Accounts* 6 (1813, 1814); 8 (1820); 9 (1823).

Beckles, Hilary McD. "Freeing Slavery: Gender Paradigms in the Social History of Caribbean Slavery". In *Slavery, Freedom and Gender: The Dynamics of Caribbean Society,* edited by Brian Moore, B.W. Higman, Carl Campbell and Patrick Bryan, 197–231. Kingston: University of the West Indies Press, 2001.

Behrendt, S.D., David Eltis and David Richardson. "The Bights in Comparative Perspective: The Economics of Long-Term Trends in Population Displacement from West and West-Central Africa to the Americas before 1850". Paper presented to the Summer Institute "Identifying Enslaved Africans: The Nigerian Hinterland and the Creation of the African Diaspora". York University, Toronto, 1997.

Bell, William. *Dictionary and Digest of the Law of Scotland, with Short Explanations of the Most Ordinary English Law Terms.* Edinburgh: John Anderson, Bell and Bradfute, 1838.

Biddulph, John. *The Nineteenth and Their Times: Being an Account of the Four Cavalry Regiments in the British Army that Have Borne the Number Nineteen and of the Campaigns in Which They Served.* London: John Murray, 1899.

Bilby, Kenneth. "Gumbay, Myal, and the Great House: New Evidence on the Religious Background of Jonkonnu in Jamaica". *African-Caribbean Institute of Jamaica Research Review* 4 (1999): 47–70.

Bishop, Pat A. "Runaway Slaves in Jamaica, 1740–1807: A Study Based on Newspaper Advertisements Published during that Period for Runaways". MA thesis, University of the West Indies, Mona, 1970.

Black, George Fraser. *The Surnames of Scotland: Their Origin, Meaning and History.* New York: New York Public Library, 1965 [1946].

Blair, George. *Biographic and Descriptive Sketches of Glasgow Necropolis.* Glasgow: M. Ogle and Sons, 1857.

Blandford, William. *Periodical Accounts* 15 (1840); 16 (1842, 1843); 17 (1843).

Bleby, Henry. *Death Struggles of Slavery: Being a Narrative of Facts and Incidents, which Occurred in a British Colony, during the Two Years Immediately Preceding Negro Emancipation.* London: Hamilton, Adams and Co., 1853.

Boa, Shena. "Free Black and Coloured Women in a White Man's Slave Society, Jamaica, 1760–1823". MPhil thesis, University of the West Indies, Mona, 1987.

Boone, Sylvia Ardyn. *Radiance from the Waters: Ideals of Feminine Beauty in Mende Art.* New Haven: Yale University Press, 1986.

Brathwaite, Edward Kamau. *The Arrivants: A New World Trilogy.* London: Oxford University Press, 1973.

———. *The Development of Creole Society in Jamaica, 1770–1820.* Oxford: Clarendon Press, 1971.

Brown, Carolyn A. "Epilogue: Memory as Resistance: Identity and the Contested History of Slavery in Southeastern Nigeria, an Oral History Project". In *Fighting the Slave Trade: West African Strategies,* edited by Sylviane A. Diouf, 219–25. Athens: Ohio University Press, 2003.

Buchanan, Joyce. Personal communication with author. Kilmarnock, Westmoreland. 1995.

Buchner, John H. *The Moravians in Jamaica.* London: Longman, Brown and Co., 1854.

———. *Periodical Accounts* 16 (1842); 17 (1843, 1845); 20 (1851, 1855); 21 (1856).

Bujo, Bénézet. *Foundations of an African Ethic: Beyond the Universal Claims of Western Morality.* Translated by Brian McNeil. Nairobi: Paulines Publications Africa, 2003 [2001].

Burke, John Bernard. *Burke's Genealogical and Heraldic History of the Landed Gentry,* edited by L.G. Pine. London: Burke's Peerage, 1952.

Burnard, Trevor. *Mastery, Tyranny, and Desire: Thomas Thistlewood and His Slaves in the Anglo-Jamaican World.* Kingston: University of the West Indies Press, 2004.

———. " 'To Separate One from Another': The Dynamics of the Slave Market in Mid-Eighteenth Century Jamaica". Paper presented at the conference Black Diasporas in the Western Hemisphere, Humanities Research Centre, Australian National University, Canberra, April 1998.

———. "Slave Naming Patterns: Onomastics and the Taxonomy of Race in

Eighteenth-Century Jamaica". *Journal of Interdisciplinary History* 31, no. 3 (2001): 325–46.

———. "Who Bought Slaves in Early America? Purchasers of Slaves from the Royal African Company in Jamaica, 1674–1708". *Slavery and Abolition* 17, no. 2 (1996): 68–92.

Burnard, Trevor, and Kenneth Morgan. "The Dynamics of the Slave Market and Slave Purchasing Patterns in Jamaica, 1655–1788". *William and Mary Quarterly*, 3rd ser., 58, no. 1 (2001): 205–28.

Bush, Barbara. "White 'Ladies', Coloured 'Favourites' and Black 'Wenches': Some Considerations on Sex, Race and Class Factors in Social Relations in White Creole Society in the British Caribbean". *Slavery and Abolition* 2, no. 3 (1981): 245–62.

Callahan, Raymond. *The East India Company and Army Reform, 1738–1798*. Cambridge: Harvard University Press, 1972.

Campbell, Mavis. *The Maroons of Jamaica, 1655–1796*. Trenton, NJ: Africa World Press, 1990.

Cardew, F.G. *A Sketch of the Services of the Bengal Native Army to the Year 1895*. Calcutta: Office of the Superintendent of the Government Printery, 1903.

Carmichael, A.C. *Domestic Manners and Social Conditions of the White, Coloured, and Negro Populations of the West Indies*. London: Whittaker, Treacher and Co., 1833.

Carretta, Vincent. *Equiano, the African: Biography of a Self Made Man*. Athens: University of Georgia Press, 2005.

Carwardine, Richard. *Trans-Atlantic Revivalism: Popular Evangelicalism in Britain and America, 1790–1865*. Westport, Conn.: Greenwood, 1978.

Chukwukere, I. "Chi in Igbo Religion and Thought: The God in Every Man". *Anthropos: International Review of Ethnology and Linguistics* 78, nos. 3 and 4 (1983): 519–34.

Church Missionary Society. *The Church Missionary Intelligencer* 10. London, 1859.

Clarke, John. *Memorials of Baptist Missionaries in Jamaica, including a Sketch of the Labours of Early Religious Instructors in Jamaica*. London: Yates and Alexander, 1869.

Clemens, August. *Periodical Accounts* 23, 24 (1861).

———. "Report of Visits to Some Missionary Stations in Jamaica". *Periodical Accounts* 24 (1861).

Coleman, John. *Periodical Accounts* 20 (1851).

Collis, John. *Periodical Accounts* 13 (1834, 1835); 14 (1836).

Collison, Gary. "Recreating the World of an Illiterate Fugitive Slave". *Chronicle of Higher Education*, 11 April 1997, A60.

Cory, Kathleen. *Tracing Your Scottish Ancestry*. Edinburgh: Polygon, 1990.

Costanzo, Angelo. "The Narrative of Archibald Monteith, a Jamaican Slave". *Callaloo* 13, no. 1 (1990): 115–30.

———. "A Living Slave Narrative". *Contours* 1, no. 2 (2003): 219–28.

———. *Surprizing Narrative: Olaudah Equiano and the Beginnings of Black Autobiography*. Westport, Conn.: Greenwood, 1987.

Craton, Michael. *Searching for the Invisible Man: Slaves and Plantation Life in Jamaica*. Cambridge: Harvard University Press, 1978.

————. *Testing the Chains: Resistance to Slavery in the British West Indies*. Ithaca: Cornell University Press, 1982.

Cronie, Mildred. "Liberation". Paper presented at the conference Genesis of a Nation, sponsored by University of Guyana and the Guyana Commemoration Commission, Georgetown, Guyana, 29–31 July 1988. Paramaribo: Anton De Com University of Suriname, 1988.

Curtin, Marguerite. *Tryall, Hanover, Jamaica*. Kingston: The author, 2004.

da Costa e Silva, Alberto. "Portraits of African Royalty in Brazil". In *Identity in the Shadow of Slavery*, edited by Paul E. Lovejoy, 129–36. London: Continuum, 2000.

D'Costa, Jean, and Barbara Lalla, eds. *Voices in Exile: Jamaican Texts of the Eighteenth and Nineteenth Centuries*. Tuscaloosa: University of Alabama Press, 1989.

Davidson, Basil. *Africa: History of a Continent*. London: Hamlyn Publishing Group, 1972 [1966].

Davies, David. *Periodical Accounts* 14 (1836, 1837).

Davies, K.G. *The Royal African Company*. London: Longmans Green, 1957.

Devine, Thomas M. *The Tobacco Lords: A Study of Their Activities, c. 1740–90*. Edinburgh: John Donald, 1975.

"Diary of Bogue Mission". *Periodical Accounts* 6 (1813).

"Diary of Gracehill, Antigua". *Periodical Accounts* 11 (1829).

"Diary of New-Carmel". *Periodical Accounts* 14 (1838).

"Diary of New Eden". *Periodical Accounts* 8 (1820).

"Diary of Old Carmel". *Periodical Accounts* 6 (1816).

Dike, K.O., and F.I. Ekejiuba. *The Aro of South-Eastern Nigeria, 1650–1980: A Study of Socio-Economic Formation and Transformation in Nigeria*. Ibadan: University of Ibadan Press, 1990.

Dobson, David. *Directory of Scottish Settlers in North America, 1625–1825*. Vol. 1. Baltimore: Genealogical Publishing Co., 1984.

————. *Directory of Scottish Settlers in North America, 1625–1825*. Vol. 2. Baltimore: Genealogical Publishing Co., 1984.

————. *Directory of Scottish Settlers in North America, 1625–1825*. Vol. 4. Baltimore: Genealogical Publishing Co., 1985.

————. *Directory of Scottish Settlers in North America, 1625–1825*. Vol. 5. Baltimore: Genealogical Publishing Co., 1985.

————. *Directory of Scottish Settlers in North America, 1625–1825*. Vol. 7. Baltimore: Genealogical Publishing Co., 1993.

————. *The Original Scots Colonists of Early America, 1612–1783*. Baltimore: Genealogical Publishing Co., 1989.

————. *The Original Scots Colonists of Early America: Caribbean Supplement, 1611–1707*. Baltimore: Genealogical Publishing Co., 1999.

————. *Scots in the West Indies, 1707–1857*. Vol. 2. Unpublished.

Donald, Colin Dunlop. *Minute Book of the Board of Green Cloth, 1809–1820*. Glasgow: James Maclehouse and Sons, 1891. Accessed July 2006 at http://stirnet.com/HTML/treasures/litgems/bah01.htm

Douglas, General Sir Thomas Monteath. "Brief description". www.jbautographs.com/Military/military.html, entry 3587.

Douglass, Frederick. *My Bondage and My Freedom.* New York: Dover, 1969 [1855].

Dunham, Katherine. *Katherine Dunham's Journey to Accompong.* Westport, Conn.: Negro Universities Press, 1971.

Dunn, Richard. "The Story of Two Jamaican Slaves: Sarah Affir and Robert McAlpine of Mesopotamia Estate". In *West Indies Accounts: Essays on the History of the British Caribbean and the Atlantic Economy in Honour of Richard Sheridan,* edited by Roderick A. McDonald, 188–208. Kingston: The Press, University of the West Indies, 1966.

Edwards, Bryan. *The History, Civil and Commercial, of the British Colonies in the West Indies.* Vol. 2. Philadelphia: James Humphreys, 1806 [1793].

Ekejiuba, F.L., and K.O. Dike. "Change and Persistence in Aro Oral History". *Journal of African Studies* 3, no. 3 (1976).

Elliott, John. *Periodical Accounts* 15 (1840, 1841); 16 (1842, 1843); 17 (1844); 22 (1855).

Ellis, John. *Periodical Accounts* 9 (1824, 1825); 10 (1826, 1827); 11 (1828, 1831); 12 (1832).

Ellis, John, and John Collis. *Periodical Accounts* 13 (1833).

Ellis, John, and George Pemsel. "Report from Congregation at Fairfield for 1830". *Periodical Accounts* 12 (1830).

Equiano, Olaudah. *Equiano's Travels.* Edited by Paul Edwards. London: Heinemann, 1967.

Eze, E., and Victor Manfredi. "Igbo". In *Facts about the World's Major Languages: an Encyclopedia of the World's Major Languages, Past and Present,* edited by J. Garry and C. Rubino, 322–30. New York: H.W. Wilson, 2001.

Feurig, Gustavus. *Periodical Accounts* 17 (1844).

Fraser, Lionel M. *History of Trinidad, 1814 to 1839.* Vol. 2. London: Frank Cass, 1971 [1896].

Fredrickson, George M. "The Long Trek to Freedom". *New York Review of Books* 52, no. 12 (2005): 40–42.

G.E.C. *The Complete Peerage of England, Scotland, Ireland, Great Britain and the United Kingdom, Extant, Extinct or Dormant* 2, new revised edition. Gloucester: Alan Sutton, 1982.

Geissler, August. *Periodical Accounts* 22 (1855); 26 (1868).

———. "Report from Fairfield, 1863". *Periodical Accounts* 25 (1864).

Gollin, Gillian Lindt. *Moravians in Two Worlds: A Study of Changing Communities.* New York: Columbia University Press, 1967.

Gopal, M.H. *Tipu Sultan's Mysore: An Economic Study.* Bombay: Popular Prakashan, 1971.

Goveia, Elsa. "Amelioration and Emancipation in the British Caribbean". Seminar paper, Department of History, University of the West Indies, Mona, Jamaica, 1977.

Green, Margaret. *Igbo Village Affairs.* London: Frank Cass, 1964 [1947].

Groome, Francis H., ed. *Ordnance Gazetteer of Scotland: A Survey of Scottish Topography, Statistical, Biographical, and Historical.* Vol. 1. Edinburgh: Thomas C. Jack. Grange Publishing Works, 1882.

Hafa, John. *Periodical Accounts* 7 (1819).

Hahn-Waanders, Hanny. *Eze Institution in Igboland.* Nimo: Documentation Centre, 1990.

Haley, Alex. *Roots.* New York: Dell, 1977.

Hall, Catherine. *Civilising Subjects: Colony and Metropole in the English Imagination, 1830–1867.* Chicago: University of Chicago Press, 2002.

Hall, Douglas. *In Miserable Slavery: Thomas Thistlewood in Jamaica, 1750–86.* London: Macmillan, 1989.

Hall, Florence. "Memoirs of the Life of Florence Hall". Ms. fragment. The Historical Society of Pennsylvania Library, ca. 1800.

Haman, Adam. *Periodical Accounts* 13 (1833).

Hamilton, Allan. *Periodical Accounts* 26 (1867, 1868).

Hamilton, Douglas J. *Scotland, the Caribbean and the Atlantic World, 1750–1820.* Manchester: Manchester University Press, 2005.

Handler, Jerome S. *The Unappropriated People: Freedmen in the Slave Society of Barbados.* Baltimore: Johns Hopkins University Press, 1974.

Handler, Jerome S., and JoAnn Cody. "Slave Names and Naming in Barbados, 1650–1830". *William and Mary Quarterly,* 3rd ser., 53, no. 4 (1996): 685–728.

Hanna, George. *Periodical Accounts* 26 (1867); 28 (1871).

Hannan, Thomas. *Famous Scottish Houses: The Lowlands.* London: A. and C. Black, 1928.

Hark, Walter, and Augustus Westphal. *The Breaking of the Dawn, or, Moravian Work in Jamaica, 1754–1904.* London: Moravian Mission Agency, 1904.

Hart, Richard. *Slaves Who Abolished Slavery.* Vol. 2. *Blacks in Rebellion.* Kingston: Institute of Social and Economic Research, University of the West Indies, 1985.

Harvey, Thomas, and William Brewin. "Autobiographical Sketch of Archibald Monteith". In *Jamaica in 1866: A Narrative of a Tour through the Island,* 88–100. London: Bennett, 1867.

Hastings, S.U., and B.L. MacLeavy. *Seedtime and Harvest: A Brief History of the Moravian Church in Jamaica, 1754–1979.* Kingston: Moravian Church Corporation, 1979.

Heath, George. *Periodical Accounts* 17 (1845); 18 (1846).

Hennig, Franz. *Periodical Accounts* 22 (1857).

Herman, J.G. *Periodical Accounts* 18 (1847).

Heuman, Gad. *Between Black and White: Race, Politics, and the Free Coloreds in Jamaica, 1792–1865.* Westport, Conn.: Greenwood, 1981.

Higman, Barry. *Plantation Jamaica, 1750–1850: Capital and Control in a Colonial Economy.* Kingston: University of the West Indies Press, 2005.

———. *Slave Population and Economy in Jamaica, 1807–1834.* Cambridge: Cambridge University Press, 1976.

Hoch, Samuel. *Periodical Accounts* 8 (1821).

Hogg, Donald. *The Convince Cult in Jamaica.* New Haven: Department of Anthropology, Yale University, 1960.

Holland, Francis. *Periodical Accounts* 17 (1845); 18 (1846).

Horton, Robin. *The Gods as Guests: An Aspect of Kalabari Religious Life.* Lagos: Nigeria Magazine, 1960.

Hunte, Keith. "Protestantism and Slavery in the British Caribbean". In *Christianity in the Caribbean: Essays on Church History,* edited by Armando Lampe, 86–125. Kingston: University of the West Indies Press, 2001.

Hutton, J.E. *A History of Moravian Missions.* Vol. 2, *The Builders.* London: Moravian Publication Office, 1923.

Idowu, Bolaji. *Olódùmarè: God in Yoruba Religion.* London: Longman, 1962.

Ingram, Kenneth. *Manuscript Sources for the History of the West Indies.* Kingston: University of the West Indies Press, 2000.

Iwuagwu, A.O. "Chukwu: Towards a Definition of Igbo Traditional Religion". *West African Religion* 16, no. 1 (n.d.): 26–34.

Joseph, E.L. *A History of Trinidad.* London: Frank Cass, 1970 [1838].

Kamalu, Chukwunyere. *Person, Divinity and Nature: A Modern View of the Person and the Cosmos in African Thought.* London: Karnak House, 1998.

Karras, Alan L. *Sojourners in the Sun: Scottish Migrants in Jamaica and the Chesapeake, 1740–1800.* Ithaca: Cornell University Press, 1992.

Kaye, John William. *History of the War in Afghanistan.* Vol. 3. London: W.H. Allen and Co., 1878.

Kiergaard, Hans Juergen. *Periodical Accounts* 16 (1841); 17 (1844).

King, Lloyd, ed. *The Autobiography of a Cuban Slave.* St Augustine: University of the West Indies, *c.* 1989.

Klein, Herbert. *The Atlantic Slave Trade.* Cambridge: Cambridge University Press, 1999.
———. *The Middle Passage: Comparative Studies in the Atlantic Slave Trade.* Princeton: Princeton University Press, 1978.

Kolapo, Femi James. "Trading Ports of the Niger-Benue Confluence Area, *c.* 1830–1873". In *Ports of the Slave Trade (Bights of Benin and Biafra),* edited by Robin Law and Silke Stickrodt, 96–121. Occasional Paper No. 6, Centre of Common-wealth Studies, University of Stirling, 1999.

Kopytoff, Igor, and Suzanne Miers. "African 'Slavery' as an Institution of Marginality". In *Slavery in Africa: Historical and Anthropological Perspectives,* edited by Suzanne Miers and Igor Kopytoff, 3–81. Madison: University of Wisconsin Press, 1977.

Kummer, Joseph. "Life-story of Archibald Monteith". Ms. Moravian Archives, Bethlehem, Pennsylvania, 1853.

Lalla, Barbara, and Jean D'Costa. *Language in Exile: Three Hundred Years of Jamaican Creole.* Tuscaloosa: University of Alabama Press, 1990.

Lamming, George. *In the Castle of My Skin.* New York: Collier, 1970 [1953].

Lang, John. *Periodical Accounts* 6 (1816).

Lewis, Matthew. *Journal of a Residence among the Negroes in the West Indies.* London: Murray, 1845 [1834].

Lichtenthaeler, Abraham. *Periodical Accounts* 25 (1864).
———. "Report of the Congregation of New Carmel for 1863". *Periodical Accounts* 25 (1864).

Light, John. *Periodical Accounts* 7 (1818, 1819); 9 (1824, 1825); 10 (1826); 12 (1832, 1833).

Lovejoy, Paul, and David Trotman. "Community of Believers: Trinidad Muslims and the Return to Africa, 1810–1850". In *Slavery on the Frontiers of Islam,* edited by Paul E. Lovejoy. Princeton, NJ: Markus Wiener, 2003.

McCalman, Ian, ed. *The Horrors of Slavery and Other Writings by Robert Wedderburn.* Princeton, NJ: Markus Wiener.

McClelland, David C. *Human Motivation.* New York: Cambridge University Press, 1995 [1987].

McLaughlin, Eve. *Wills before 1858.* Haddenham: Varneys, 2002.

Macinnes, A.I. "Scottish Gaeldom from Clanship to Commercial Landlordism, c. 1600–c. 1850". In *Scottish Power Centres,* edited by S. Foster et al., 174–75, 179. Glasgow: Cruithne, 1999.

Macmillan, Allister, comp. *The West Indies and Bermuda, Illustrated, including the Isthmus of Panama, Historical and Descriptive, Commercial and Industrial Facts, Figures and Resources.* London: W.H. and L. Collingridge, 1912.

Madden, Richard. *A Twelvemonth's Residence in the West Indies, during the Transition from Slavery to Apprenticeship.* Vol. 1. London: James Cochrane and Co., 1835.

Madubuike, Ihechukwu. *A Handbook of African Names.* Washington, DC: Three Continents Press, 1976.

Mallalieu, William. *Periodical Accounts* 18 (1847).

Manfredi, Victor. "Ìgbo". In *Encyclopedia of the World's Major Languages: Past and Present.* Westport, Conn.: Greenwood, 2001.

———. "Ìgbo Initiation: Phallus or Umbilicus?" *Cahiers d'etudes africaines* 145 (1997): 157–211.

———. "Philological Perspectives on the Southeastern Nigerian Diaspora". *Contours: A Journal of the African Diaspora,* forthcoming.

Mason, J.C.S. *The Moravian Church and the Missionary Awakening in England, 1760–1800.* Woodbridge, Suffolk, and Rochester, NY: Boydell, 2001.

Mather, James Y., and H.H. Speitel, eds. *The Linguistic Atlas of Scotland.* Vol. 2. London: Croom Helm, 1977.

Mathurin, Lucille. "A Historical Study of Women in Jamaica from 1655 to 1844". PhD diss., University of the West Indies, 1974.

Miers, Suzanne, and Richard Roberts, eds. *The End of Slavery in Africa.* Madison: University of Wisconsin Press, 1988.

Miller, Joseph C. "Central Africa during the Era of the Slave Trade, c. 1490s–1850". In *Central Africans and Cultural Transformations in the American Diaspora,* edited by Linda Heywood, 21–69. Cambridge: Cambridge University Press, 2002.

Milne, Anthony. "The Harris Heritage". *Sunday Express* (Trinidad). Section 2, 3, 14 April 1996.

Missionary Manual and Directory of the Moravian Church. Bethlehem: Moravian Publication Office, 1880.

Moderau, Fred. *Periodical Accounts* 26 (1868).

Monteith, Archibald. "Archibald Monteith". Translated by Mary Kuck. *Missionsstunden aus der Brüdergemeine* 21 (1997 [1898]).

———. "Erlebnisse eines ehemaligen sclaven in Jamaica", *Missions-Blatt aus der Brüdergemeine* 28, no. 5 (1864): 87–102, and no. 6 (1864): 105–15.

———. "Experiences of a Former Slave in Jamaica". Translated by Mary Kuck. Typescript, 2002. Originally published as "Erlebnisse eines ehemaligen sclaven in Jamaica", *Missions-Blatt aus der Brüdergemeine* 28, no. 5 (1864): 87–102, and no. 6 (1864): 105–15.

————. "Memoir of Br. Archibald Monteith". *Periodical Accounts* 25 (1865): 433–41, 481–85.

Monteith, Kathleen. "Emancipation and Labour on Jamaican Coffee Plantations, 1838–48". *Slavery and Abolition* 21, no. 3 (2000): 125–35.

Moravian Missionary Atlas, containing An Account of the Various Countries in which the Missions of the Moravian Church are Carried on, and of Its Missionary Operations. London: The Moravian Church and Mission Agency, 1908.

Nelson, Vernon H., ed. "Archibald John Monteith: Native Helper and Assistant in the Jamaica Mission at New Carmel". *Transactions of the Moravian Historical Society* 21, no. 1 (1966): 29–52. Republished in *Callaloo* 13, no. 1 (1990): 102–14.

North, Goodwin. *Periodical Accounts* 17 (1845).

Nwala, Uzodinma. *Igbo Philosophy.* Lagos: Literamed, 1985.

Nwoga, Donatus Ibe. *The Supreme God as Stranger in Igbo Religious Thought.* Ahiazu Mbaise: Hawk, 1984.

Nwokeji, G. Ugo. "The Atlantic Slave Trade and Population Density: A Historical Demography of the Biafran Hinterland". Typescript, 1997.

Ohadike, Don C. *The Ekumeku Movement: Western Igbo Resistance to the British Conquest of Nigeria, 1883–1914.* Athens: Ohio University Press, 1991.

Oldendorp, Christian G.A. *A Caribbean Mission: History of the Mission of the Evangelical Brethren on the Caribbean Islands of St. Thomas, St. Croix, and St. John.* Edited by Johann Bossard. Translated by Arnold Highfield and Vladimir Barac. Ann Arbor: Karoma, 1987 [1770].

Olyphant Family. "A Group of Perthshire Families in the West Indies". National Library of Jamaica. Typescript, 1957.

Onwuejeogwu, M. Angulu. *An Igbo Civilization: Nri Kingdom and Hegemony.* London: Ethnographica and Benin: Ethiope Publishing Corporation, 1981.

————. "The Patterns of Population Movement in the Ìgbò Culture Area". *Odinani: Journal of the Odinani Museum, Nri,* no. 2 (1977): 21–37.

————. *The Social Anthropology of Africa: An Introduction.* London: Heinemann, 1975.

Oriji, John N. "Igboland, Slavery, and the Drums of War and Heroism". In *Fighting the Slave Trade: West African Strategies,* edited by Sylviane A. Diouf, 121–31. Athens: Ohio University Press, 2003.

Ortiz, Fernando. *Los negros esclavos.* Habana: Editorial de Ciencias Sociales, 1987 [1916].

Padrón, Francisco Morales. *Spanish Jamaica.* Translated by Patrick Bryan, Michael Gronow and Felix Oviedo Moral. Kingston: Ian Randle, 2003.

Patterson, Orlando. *Slavery and Social Death: A Comparative Study.* Cambridge: Harvard University Press, 1982.

————. *The Sociology of Slavery: An Analysis of the Origins, Development and Structure of Negro Slave Society in Jamaica.* London: Macgibbon and Kee, 1967.

p'Bitek, Okot. *African Religions in Western Scholarship.* Nairobi: East African Literature Bureau, *c.* 1971.

Perkins, Cyrus Francis. *Busha's Mistress or Catherine the Fugitive: A Stirring Romance from the Days of Slavery in Jamaica.* Kingston: Ian Randle, 2003 [1855].

Pfeiffer, Henry. *Periodical Accounts* 17 (1846).

Pitt-Rivers, Julian. "Honor". *Encyclopedia of the Social Sciences.* Vol. 6: 503–11. New York: Macmillan, 1968.

Plessing, Gustavus. *Periodical Accounts* 22 (1857).

Powell, Dorian. "Caribbean Women and Their Response to Familial Experiences". *Social and Economic Studies* 35, no. 2 (1986): 83–130.

Price, Richard. *First-Time: The Historical Vision of an Afro-American People.* Baltimore: Johns Hopkins University Press, 1983.

Prince, Mary. *The History of Mary Prince, a West Indian Slave, Related by Herself.* Edited by Moira Ferguson. Ann Arbor: University of Michigan Press, 1993 [1831].

Pulkrabek, John Paul. *Periodical Accounts* 26 (1868).

Renault, Jean-Michel. *Bons baisers de la Colonie: La Guadeloupe en 1900.* Lyon: Les Créations du Pelican, 1994.

Renkewitz, Julius. *Periodical Accounts* 13 (1837); 14 (1837); 18 (1846); 22 (1855).

Renny, Robert. *An History of Jamaica, with Observations on the Climate, Scenery etc.* London: J. Cawthorn, 1807.

"Report of the Congregation at Lititz for 1861". *Periodical Accounts* 24 (1862).

"Report of the Congregation at Bethany for 1863". *Periodical Accounts* 25 (1864).

"Report of the Country-Schools in Jamaica". *Periodical Accounts* 20 (1851).

"Report of the Training Institution at Fairfield for 1863". *Periodical Accounts* 25 (1864).

"Retrospect on the History of the Mission of the Brethren's Church in Jamaica for the Past Hundred Years". *Periodical Accounts* 21 (1854): 337–60.

Ricksecker, Peter. *Periodical Accounts* 13 (1834, 1835); 17 (1846).

Robbins, George. *Periodical Accounts* 14 (1836, 1837, 1838).

Robertson, Glory. "Notes and Queries: Breaking up a Slave Community". *Jamaica Historical Society Bulletin* 7 (1977): 40.

Robinson, Edward, and Deborah-Ann Rowe. "The Great Sav Submarine Slide". *Gleaner.* 27 September 2005, A5.

Robinson, Samuel. *A Sailor Boy's Experience Aboard a Slave Ship.* Wigtown: G.C. Book Publishers, 1966 [1867].

Roughley, Thomas. *The Jamaica Planter's Guide; or, a System for Planting and Managing a Sugar Estate, or Other Plantations in That Island, and Throughout the British West Indies in General.* London: Longman, Hurst, Rees, Orme and Brown, 1823.

Said, Edward. *Orientalism.* London: Penguin Books, 1978.

Sandoval, Alonso de. *De instauranda Aethiopum salute: el mundo de la esclavitud negra en América.* Bogotá: Biblioteca de la Presidencia de Colombia, 1956 [1627].

Satchell, Veront. *From Plots to Plantations: Land Transactions in Jamaica, 1866–1900.* Kingston: Institute of Social and Economic Research, University of the West Indies, 1990.

Saville, Richard. *Bank of Scotland: A History, 1695–1995.* Edinburgh: Edinburgh University Press, 1996.

Sawyerr, Harry. *God: Ancestor or Creator? Aspects of Traditional Belief in Ghana, Nigeria and Sierra Leone.* London: Longman, 1970.

Scholefield, John. *Periodical Accounts* 10 (1828); 11 (1829); 12 (1832); 14 (1834).

Schweinitz, Edmund de. "The Clergy of the American Province of the Unitas Fratrum". Typescript. Moravian Archives, Bethlehem, Pennsylvania, 1873.

Seiler, John. *Periodical Accounts* 26 (1867).

———. "Report of the Congregation of Bethabara for 1863". *Periodical Accounts* 25 (1864).

Senior, Bernard Martin. *Jamaica, As It Was, As It Is, and As It May Be.* New York: Negro Universities Press, 1969 [1835].

Senior, Olive. *Encyclopedia of Jamaican Heritage.* St Andrew, Jamaica: Twin Guinep, 2003.

Sensbach, Jon F. *Rebecca's Revival: Creating Black Christianity in the Atlantic World.* Cambridge: Harvard University Press, 2005.

———. *A Separate Canaan: The Making of an Afro-Moravian World in North Carolina, 1763–1840.* Chapel Hill: University of North Carolina Press, 1998.

Shepherd, Verene. "Alternative Husbandry: Slaves and Free Labourers on Livestock Farms in Jamaica in the Eighteenth and Nineteenth Centuries". *Slavery and Abolition* 14, no. 1 (1993): 41–66.

Shepherd, Verene, and Ahmed Reid. "Rebel Voices: Testimonies from the 1831–32 Emancipation War in Jamaica". *Jamaica Journal* 27, nos. 2 and 3 (2004): 54–63.

Sheridan, Richard. "The Role of the Scots in the Economy and Society of the West Indies". In *Comparative Perspectives on Slavery in New World Plantations,* edited by Vera Rubin and Arthur Tuden, 94–106. New York: New York Academy of Sciences, 1977.

Shyllon, F.O. *Black Slaves in Britain.* London: Institute of Race Relations and Oxford University Press, 1974.

Sibley, Inez Knibb. *Dictionary of Place-Names in Jamaica.* Kingston: Institute of Jamaica, 1978.

Smaby, Beverly Prior. *The Transformation of Moravian Bethlehem.* Philadelphia: University of Pennsylvania Press, 1988.

Smith, John Guthrie, and John Oswald Mitchell, *The Old Country Houses of the Old Glasgow Gentry.* Glasgow: James MacLehose and Sons, 1878. Accessed July 2006 at http://gdl.cdlr.strath.ac.uk/smihou/smihou062.htm.

Sonderman, Theodore. *Periodical Accounts* 22 (1857); 23 (1860, 1861); 26 (1867).

Spence, James. *Periodical Accounts* 18 (1846).

Stephens, Thomas M. *Dictionary of Latin American Racial and Ethnic Terminology.* Gainesville: University of Florida Press, 1989.

Strickland, S., ed. "Ashton Warner's Account of Slavery". [1831] In *The Evolution of the Negro,* edited by Norman Cameron, 2: 62–85. Georgetown: Argosy Co., 1934.

Stobwasser, Lewis. *Periodical Accounts* 9 (1823, 1824).

Stubbs, Francis W. *History of the Organization, Equipment, and War Services of the Regiment of Bengal Artillery.* Vol. 3. London: W.H. Allen and Co., 1895.

Svalesen, Leif. *The Slave Ship* Fredensborg. Kingston: Ian Randle, 2000.

Taylor, John. "Life and Travels in America". Ms. National Library of Jamaica, 1689.

Tembo, Mwizenge. "Eurocentric Destruction of Indigenous Conceptions: Beautiful Women in African Societies". Unpublished, 2004.

Thompson, Augustus. *Moravian Missions: Twelve Lectures.* New York: Charles Scribner, 1882.

Thompson, Edgar W. *The Last Siege of Seringapatam: An Account of the Final Assault, May 4, 1779.* Mysore: Wesleyan Mission Press, [?1907].

Thorp, Daniel B. "Chattel with a Soul: The Autobiography of a Moravian Slave". *Pennsylvania Magazine of History and Biography* 112, no. 3 (1988): 433–51.

Thurber, Francis. *Coffee: From Plantation to Cup: A Brief History of Coffee Production and Consumption.* New York: American Grocer Publishing Association, 1884 [1881].

Timaeus, George. *Periodical Accounts* 10 (1826).

Timperley, Loretta R., ed. *A Directory of Landownership in Scotland c. 1770.* Edinburgh: Scottish Record Society, 1976.

Trouillot, Michel-Rolph. "Coffee Planters and Coffee Slaves in the Antilles: The Impact of a Secondary Crop". In *Cultivation and Culture: Labor and the Shaping of Slave Life in the Americas,* edited by Ira Berlin and Philip D. Morgan, 124–37, 331–35. Charlottesville: University Press of Virginia, 1993.

Turner, Mary. *Slaves and Missionaries: The Disintegration of Jamaican Slave Society, 1787–1834.* Kingston: University of the West Indies Press, 1998.

Uchendu, Victor. *The Igbo of Southeast Nigeria.* New York: Holt, Rinehart and Winston, 1965.

Uzochukwu, Sam. "The Art of Facial Scarification among the Igbo". *Nigeria Magazine* 55, no. 1 (1987): 39–42.

Vaughan, Benjamin. *The Parliamentary Register.* London, 1792.

Walsh, Lorena. "Slave Life, Slave Society, and Tobacco Production in the Tidewater Chesapeake, 1620–1820". In *Cultivation and Culture: Labor and the Shaping of Slave Life in the Americas,* edited by Ira Berlin and Philip D. Morgan, 170–99. Charlottesville: University Press of Virginia, 1993.

Ward, Thomas. *Periodical Accounts* 6 (1816, 1817).

Wariboko, Waibinte. "Ideological and Cultural Issues in the Implantation of Christianity: The Example of New Calabar, 1865–1900". In *Caribbean Perspectives on African History and Culture,* edited by Richard Goodridge, 54–78. Cave Hill: Department of History and Philosophy, 2003.

———. "New Calabar, British Traders and Consular Roles in Eastern Niger Delta during the Latter Half of the Nineteenth and Early Twentieth Centuries". Paper presented at the Department of History Staff/Postgraduate Seminar, University of the West Indies, Mona, Jamaica, 1995.

Warner-Lewis, Maureen. *Central Africa in the Caribbean: Transcending Time, Transforming Cultures.* Kingston: University of the West Indies Press, 2003.

———. "Ethnic and Religious Plurality among Yoruba Immigrants in Trinidad in the Nineteenth Century". In *Identity in the Shadow of Slavery,* edited by Paul E. Lovejoy, 113–28. London: Continuum, 2000.

———. *Guinea's Other Suns: The African Dynamic in Trinidad Culture.* Dover, Mass.: Majority Press, 1991.

———. "Religious Constancy and Compromise among Nineteenth Century Caribbean-based African Muslims". In *Islam, Slavery and Diaspora,* edited by Paul Lovejoy, Behnaz Mirzai Asl and Ismael Musah Montana. Trenton, NJ: Africa World Press. Forthcoming.

———. *Yoruba Songs of Trinidad.* London: Karnak House, 1994.

Weiss, Emanuel. "Report from Bethabara for 1864". *Periodical Accounts* 25 (1865).

———. "Report for Lititz for 1865". *Periodical Accounts* 26 (1866).

Wilks, Ivor. "Abu Bakr al-Siddiq of Timbuktu". In *Africa Remembered: Narratives by West Africans from the Era of the Slave Trade,* edited by Philip Curtin, 152–69. Madison: University of Wisconsin Press, 1967.

Wilmot, Swithin. "Emancipation in Action: Workers and Wage Conflict in Jamaica, 1838–1840". *Jamaica Journal* 19, no. 3 (1986): 55–62.

Winckler, Theophilus. *Periodical Accounts* 27 (1870).

Wullschlaegel, Henry. *Periodical Accounts* 18 (1848).

Yonge, Charlotte M. *History of Christian Names.* London: Macmillan and Co., 1884.

Zorn, Jacob. *Periodical Accounts* 11, (1830); 12 (1830, 1831, 1832); 13 (1834); 14 (1835, 1836, 1837, 1838); 15 (1841); 16 (1842, 1843); 17 (1843).

Index

DATE DUE